I0140473

Into the Vast Nothingness

The Recapitulation Diaries

Volume 3

January-June 2003

J. E. Ketchel

Riverwalker Press

Copyright ©2014 by J. E. Ketchel. All rights reserved. No part of this book may be used or reproduced in any manner whatsoever without the written permission of the publisher except in the case of brief quotations embodied within a review.

Cover art and design by J. E. Ketchel with Nick Reilingh

Riverwalker Press
PO Box 101
Red Hook, NY 12571
www.riverwalkerpress.com

ISBN: 978-0-9800506-6-0

MEDICAL DISCLAIMER: The information in this book is intended for informational purposes only. It is not meant to diagnose or treat any mental health disorder whatsoever, nor is it intended to replace treatment with a competent mental healthcare provider. Please seek appropriate support and put the book aside if it proves to be too disruptive. Any application of the material presentrd in this book is at the reader's discretion and is his or her sole responsibility. The author and publisher are in no way responsible or liable for misuse of this information.

Table of Contents

Prologue

The Path

I am a synesthete. Generally, I perceive the world through more than one sense, often hearing and seeing simultaneously. Sounds produce shapes and concurrent physical sensations in my body. Smells emanate from words I hear or read, or smells might evoke specific images. I have always been very sensitive, keenly aware of what others are feeling. I also seem to be particularly adept at recalling memories. When I see a photograph from my childhood I remember what I was thinking at the time, who else was there, and what they were saying, even though I may be only a few years old.

When I think of something, or grasp an idea or concept, a cosmic panorama, much like the vast nothingness of outer space, appears before me and what I'm thinking or learning about forms into a unique pictorial. Everything I perceive and have ever perceived exists out there in this vast space, swirling around in visual format ready to be retrieved at a moment's notice. When I think of the number twelve, for instance, it appears in exactly the same place within the number-form pattern that shows up every time I think of numbers. Certain numbers appear far away while others are more prominent than others, the pattern always the same. In fact, weeks, days, and months all have their own unique and separate ribbon-like patterns, all residing in that vast outer space. I always thought everyone experienced the world in the same manner, but I've since learned that my visual perception is a little quirky. I now know that most people do not interpret the world through pictures in outer space!

I relay my experiences with synesthesia only to enable the reader to understand how I experience the world. I'm so used to it that I don't even think about it. Perhaps this is why I became a visual artist and why I am clairvoyant. As a channel, I simply pick from what I'm seeing, all of it swirling in the vastness of space before me.

The word *journey* always evokes a visual image of a path meandering across a vast landscape. From the time I was a young child, even before I could speak, I saw this path and knew it represented this life I now live. It began to the left of my vision and traversed to the right, stretching far into infinity. There was no beginning that I could ever see and every step forward was a mystery, for I had no idea where I was going or why. I was both thrilled and frightened by the sight of this path, as expectant as an explorer about to take off on the dream adventure of a lifetime. I could easily shift my awareness and step off the path, for I was both journeyer and observer. "There I am," I'd note from a spot above the path, "taking a rest beside that stream, waiting for something to happen. There I am now, walking on." Shifting again, I'd return to the path, able to observe the minutest details at my feet. Meandering through this vast landscape—sometimes barren and desolate and other times lush and beautiful—I'd see myself traveling along, sometimes sad, sometimes elated, but always determined.

This envisioned path was as potently real and life affirming as my real life. Singularly focused, it compelled me to keep going. In spite of hardships, in spite of fear and worry, it beckoned me always forward. However, I never understood the meaning of it. Where was it leading me and why? As a child, I knew I would be on this path for a long time. I even knew that sometimes it would be a lonely journey and that at other times there would be traveling companions. Challenges and difficulties would arise, but I was strong enough to handle anything. I was aware of its potential to become a joyous journey, offering many opportunities along the way. I knew I would encounter forks in the path and that decisions would have to be made, often at a moment's notice. I sensed that I had been on such journeys many times before, thus the process of traveling along the path held familiarity within its mystery.

When I was barely out of infancy this path led me into the predator's world, shortly after an ostrich bit me while I was on a visit to the Bronx Zoo with my family. Almost fifty years later, I found myself back in familiar territory, an hour from where I had grown up. I was renting, with my then-husband and our two young children, a farmhouse on ten acres of land, our backyard enclosed by a white wooden fence and a rush of tall pines. In one sense, I had come home, the scent of the air and the landscape so like that of my rural childhood home, and yet far enough away that I could claim it as my own. My path had taken me far and wide, across the continent and into foreign lands, but here I was, back where I'd started. It would soon become clear that it was exactly where I needed to be.

Early one spring day, I walked back to the compost heap in the corner of the yard. Surrounded by open fields, I was just about to empty my bucket of scraps when something caught my eye. Looking up, I saw a coyote standing no more than five feet away on the other side of the fence, an enormous groundhog hanging limply from its mouth. Catching sight of me in the same instant, it dropped the dead animal and our eyes locked. Unable to break the intense scrutiny of the coyote's stare, the world around me dissolved and I was pulled into a different world, a world that was timeless, dark and silent, yet as familiar as the path I'd envisioned since childhood, as familiar as the outer space of my synesthesia. I had the sense that the coyote was assessing whether or not I was a threat, while I silently sent it the message that I would neither harm it nor challenge it for its prey. Finally, the coyote shifted its eyes, breaking the spell, and the ancient silence between us dissolved. The world reappeared and I dared to breathe again.

The coyote, assured that I would not interfere, slowly bent down and picked up the large furry animal at its feet. Tossing and juggling it in its powerful jaws, it slowly turned away. It glanced over its shoulder and gave me one last stare before taking off across the field at a brisk pace. I watched it until it disappeared, amazed at what I had just encountered. For a brief moment, our paths had intersected. We had stood so close, both startled to find the other creature intruding upon our private space, our private world, yet we'd simultaneously experienced a unique sense of calmness, deep and surprisingly unthreatening. The world had suddenly ground to a halt. For a moment, we had lost our worldly costumes. No longer a coyote and a woman, we became nothing more than energy flowing through the universe. Indeed, it was as if I had briefly entered the vastness of my own synesthesia.

What did that encounter signify on a personal level? At the time I was uncertain, but I took it as a positive omen. With my spirit uplifted by the experience, I felt sure it meant something good. For the first time in a long time a lightheartedness filled me and a strangely brilliant light appeared on the path ahead of me. All of a sudden life held possibility. A shaman acquaintance told me it was an unusual occurrence. "Coyote rarely shows itself," he said, "especially rare to see one on a sunny afternoon."

Although the coyote's message evaded me at the time, the buoyancy of the moment remained, and I gradually allowed myself to expect positive change coming my way. Indeed, it soon became clear that it was time to move on. Moving on this time meant recapitulating my childhood. It meant rediscovering the world that the bite of the ostrich had marked me for, the world I had lost all memory of, the secret world of the human sexual predator and its innocent child prey.

Foreshadowing what was to come, I believe the coyote was hinting that I had once been locked in a battle with a predator like itself, and that I would only discover this by reliving the past. I would only free myself from it by staring it down until it held no power over me. I believe the coyote was signaling that I would have to go into a place as darkly mysterious as the silence that drew me into its stare, preparing me for a *conscious* encounter with the predator. In retrospect, I understand that it was telling me to be fearless, to not flinch at what I would see and experience. It was telling me to not back down when I looked the predator in the eyes, and to pay attention to everything I would encounter along the way. It was telling me that my experience would be an energetic encounter like none other. In utter silence, the coyote heralded these things.

At the time, I was only vaguely aware of the strange and intriguing worlds of ancient shamanic practices. Yet, the encounter with this shy and furtive creature, a significant shamanic symbol, struck a deep chord and I could not let it pass as mere coincidence. I had learned a long time ago that everything was meaningful in some way, though I was equally aware that one had to be ready to understand the extraordinary guidance that often comes while one is in the midst of living ordinary life. Or was I just a fool, tricked into thinking I was being offered something by the wily coyote? Only time and hindsight would tell. For just as the coyote had turned and looked back at me, so too would I have to turn back and look at it—and all the other people and things that had at one time intersected my path—if I was to make sense of my life.

Not long after my encounter with the coyote, my path entered the brilliant light I had envisioned, though it immediately pitched into difficult territory as well. The predictable terrain I had traveled along for many years suddenly dipped sharply. Along a serpentine route that steadily wove its way downward through the strangest of worlds, I took a journey like no other, what came to be known to me as a shamanic journey called *recapitulation*. When I use the term *shamanic journey* I do so in the broadest sense, implying an *energetic* journey into worlds that are much like the vastness of my synesthesia. I don't consider myself a shaman, nor do I attach to any shamanic line. All I can say is that when I was in those other worlds they were *real* and I was *really* there, having *real* experiences.

It was clear that I had suffered some haunting trauma as a child, for something had been chasing me my entire life. It was finally revealed as I took that journey into the darkness within myself, along the path that I had always envisioned, its meaning finally made clear. Only in entering the darkness, I discovered, would I ever truly experience the light. I just had to be ready to face what the coyote had hinted at: *the predator lodged inside me.*

The intent of my recapitulation was to heal from my trauma and give life to my true self. For three years I worked constantly on this transformational process. While doing deep inner work with Chuck Ketchel, a psychotherapist specializing in Post-traumatic Stress Disorder and a practitioner of the magical passes of Tensegrity, I kept up and even intensified my own spiritual practices of yoga and meditation. Before long, all my hard work began to yield positive experiential results. I often found myself catapulted into states of non-ordinary reality. I experienced myself as expanded consciousness, interconnected with all of life, beyond reality as we know it. These mystical, transpersonal states became pivotal moments, and so I attempt to convey to the reader that recapitulation is not only a healing model for PTSD, but that it also offers those who seek greater fulfillment beyond the known world a gateway to experiencing the oneness of everything.

My mystical experiences literally changed my view of life. In ecstatic moments true reality was revealed, and I could not deny it. As a result, I began to embrace a whole new self, an Authentic Self whom I always knew existed inside me. I also understood that if I did not fully face the old self and all that held it captive, those enlightening experiences would cease to be meaningful in the long run. The dark side had power and it would not easily give way to the light. It needed to be fully encountered and explored if my life was to be complete and fulfilling. Ultimately, my awakened spirit challenged me to continually transform, to follow my path of heart, the same path I've always been traveling. The mystical experiences I've encountered along that path impact me greatly, those I had during my recapitulation and those I continue to have to this day. Indeed, I have based my life and my life's work upon them.

I warn the reader that this book contains disturbing material, as episodes of sexual abuse are documented, not for any sensational purposes but only as part of the process. It's possible that you may find yourself having memories of your own. Triggers may occur. It is not my intention to cause distress to anyone, so if it becomes too difficult to read, I suggest putting the book aside and letting feelings and emotions pass through you. Keep a journal by your side to make notes of things that arise; write them down and put them aside to refer to later. Such a journey, if it is to be deeply healing, must be taken when one is truly ready. Sometimes we need a seasoned guide to accompany us through the journey. I encourage you to get the help you need.

Into the Vast Nothingness continues where *The Edge of the Abyss* left off, at the beginning of 2003. As the New Year began I had just moved into my own home with my two children, my lovely traveling companions. They had journeyed with me through the pain of divorce, suffering their own deep losses as the stability of the family they had known collapsed. Though afraid and in pain themselves, without complaint they journeyed onward with me, into the still greater unknown. We had been through an exhausting year, but we were ready for new life!

Chapter 1

Undertow

January 1, 2003

We sleep late. One of my brothers comes over later in the day to help move the last few big pieces of furniture in from the garage, all except the washer and dryer, which I'll do another time. The house is beginning to feel like home.

I do the sword form, the shamanic magical pass Chuck taught me, going through the series of movements a few times until I've gotten the flow of it. By the time I'm done, I stand in quiet repose, the frantic, gnawing anxiety and tension that are my usual states transformed into calmer energy. The stillness is addictive—I want more of it. At the same time, I'm aware that I must balance the calmness with alertness, as there is still more recapitulating to do. As I do the form—almost mechanically, without having to think about it now—I also realize that I'm learning to care for myself in a more deeply spiritual way. I'm aware that if I don't heal and learn to love myself then I won't really be able to attend to others as fully as I'd like to either. It's taken me a long time to get my priorities straight, but I now know that by seeking reconnection with my spirit I'll become not only a better mother, but a better person overall.

Though I've worried about the kids through all the recent changes, I know they'll thrive as long as I'm present and attentive, honest and open with them. I've continually assured them that they're safe; that everything will be just fine as we begin this new phase in our lives, as we take this part of our journeys together. But it's also important that they understand that I'm a separate being, as separate from them as they are from me, that we each have our personal journeys to take and, in the long run, our individual lives to fulfill. Though I hold them in my heart and love them deeply, one day they too will take the leap into separate lives of their own. Perhaps having lived through this deeply transformative time with me will be helpful when they face their own times of change.

Now it's late at night. We're all tucked in, safe and secure in our new home, a ferocious ice storm raging outside. Winds howl and freezing rain pelts us from all sides as our little house shakes and rattles. Surely there will be no school tomorrow, but I've already decided to keep the kids home for the day, the stress having been so great over the Christmas break. Although it's good for them to get back into the routine, the three of us need some quiet settling-in time together, devoid of any stress whatsoever.

January 2, 2003

There is school today after all, the violent icy beauty that came in the night giving way as warmer temperatures arrive, but I let the kids stay home, as previously planned. We're all tired, a little grumpy and emotionally drained after the last few months. While they get settled into their new rooms and enjoy the peacefulness of a day without any demands, I keep busy, an attentive and tender mother to us all. With my intent for the day firmly set and lines drawn, no old stuff emerges to interfere.

January 3, 2003

Funnily enough, there's no school today. Another big winter storm is rushing through the area. Thankful for another day of calmness and play, the kids indulge in this unexpected day off while I paint my bedroom a glowingly warm orange. Patches of golden yellow show through the darker glaze, the roughness of the faux plaster walls that I'd done last week adding an ancient softness. I love it! I finally move my futon in from the living room where it's been since I moved in and then retrieve my colorfully painted furniture from the garage. It fits perfectly.

Late in the afternoon, the kids get ready to go to their dad's for the weekend, their first official weekend with him under the new arrangement. Even though it seems as if they've just arrived, it feels important to establish the new routine. When my ex-husband comes by at five to pick them up he leaves the two cats, the last members of the family welcomed into our new home. A little skittish as they encounter the sounds of the new house, they sniff and explore for hours before settling down in their favorite spot, right on top of my bed. After a while, I notice a foul smell and discover that one of them has pooped on the newly tiled floor right by the front door!

As if aware that I am vulnerable alone again, a memory chases me long into the night. In truth, it's been pursuing me all week, constantly pressing against me, asking me to turn to it. Fortunately, I've succeeded in keeping it at bay by concentrating on other things, though I've felt it lurking in the shadows. Sooner or later, I knew I'd have to turn to it, and even while I'm curious I'm not happy that it's come creeping into my new house in this way. I guess it was too much to expect that the move would signal a new approach, that the memories might come in a different form. Definitely wishful thinking, because it sure looks like I won't be afforded much of a respite! I am determined, however, to accept what comes. A sense of crumbling, a sense of imminent collapse accompanies this memory, though perhaps it's signaling a *breakthrough* rather than a *breakdown*.

Even as I face the memories, I'm aware that I need rest now, time for healing and recovery from the shock of all that has been revealed as I've done this recapitulation over the past few years. Even as I continue the process, I know I must shift into a new intent. Healing must become the greater focus now, even as I face the continued onslaughts of the unknown self. Perhaps work won't be so busy for a while, as my work partner and I have been trying to schedule our freelance jobs so I can have some time for rest and rejuvenation. Although she is aware of the crippling intensity of the divorce, she is not aware of my recapitulation work; only Chuck is privy to that. One person knowing my secrets is all I can handle. Sometimes I'm surprised that a man has become the only one I can talk to!

As I write these thoughts, the pending memory more fully invades my body, manifesting in my shoulders and hips, the usual holding places. I just don't feel up to dealing with it now. For the moment, I elect to avoid it. For as long as possible I will stay one step ahead of it. I plan on working long into the night, an old habit to be sure, but one that really works!

January 4, 2003

I dream that I work at an art gallery. As soon as I enter the gallery space I'm aware that I've dreamed of this place before. In the previous dream I'd spent a lot of time painting the walls and getting the place up to snuff. My expectation, at that time, was that it would be kept clean and professional in appearance. Now I walk into the gallery to discover that the space has been left in a shambles. Struggling with great disappointment, I set about cleaning up, feeling deeply resentful. By the time I'm halfway through the clean up, however, I'm aware that I must let my disappointments and resentments go. Other people arrive to help. As we work together, my anger and resentment further dissipate until I'm totally free of them. Once the gallery is back in shape, we walk outside in our winter clothing and step right into beautiful summer weather. Surprised by the sudden shift in temperature, we throw off our heavy coats and scarves and dance on the sidewalk, forming a conga line that goes weaving down the street. I'm in the middle of the line with my hands on the shoulders of a man. A woman holds onto my waist. I'm aware that it's possible to get physically close to people without fear, and that now I really want to—I'm ready.

In contrast to my summery dream ending, I awaken to discover that yet another winter storm has dropped another two feet of snow. Spring is a long way off, I think, as I dress warmly and trudge outside with my trusty shovel. I dig my way to the end of the driveway and stand there staring at the huge wall of snow pushed up by the passing of the town snowplow. Barely able to see over it, I greet a new neighbor from across the street. He comes right over with his snow blower and tells me to move out of the way. Then he very kindly blows the driveway and walkways clear. Very nice!

I leave my shovel by the front door, ready for the next snow emergency, and go back to bed. In spite of my happy dream ending, I'd awoken heavy with depression. I find that I only have enough energy to stay up for short periods. I've felt the shadow of fear in pursuit all week, waiting for me to walk past so it could grab me and drag me into its darkness. I still don't know what it means, except that upon its coattails rides an urgency to acquiesce. It asks me to stop avoiding it, to stop running and let it overpower me.

Instead, as usual, I steel against it. I do, however, give in to my exhaustion and stay in bed for the rest of the day. I get up at five, take a shower, eat something, and go back to bed. I'm not really sleeping; I'm just lost somewhere.

"Recognize that fear is probably your most ingrained and automatic response," Chuck said the other day. As soon as he said this I realized that my recapitulation was multilayered. As I'm constantly being bombarded, in a grand effort by the universe to break me down, I must struggle with my habitual responses to fear. As I'm triggered, my initial reaction is to withdraw, to go into the tunnel of numbness, which, like a good companion, immediately shows up to rescue me. While it offers a viable option, I must remain aware that I'm seeking to free myself of its old comforts. In addition, I'm faced with trying to figure out the deeper underlying truth of just what it is that I'm supposed to recapitulate and learn from each experience. I must also determine how to handle the onslaughts of memory in different ways now. As all of these issues request consideration, I must also contend with some unknown part of myself calling for attention from deep beneath the surface of it all.

January 5, 2003

I dream that I'm working at my studio. An old boyfriend is there, an artist, someone I knew and loved deeply but briefly after I divorced my Swedish husband. He looks the way he did twenty-five years ago. He has come from Sweden to visit and work with me. As we calmly work together, he speaks of spending his whole life searching for love but never finding it, except that he has always loved me. I ask him if he wants to stay with me now. He suggests that maybe we should start over from the beginning and get it right this time. We agree that he'll call me up for a date, and we'll take it very slowly. He picks up the phone in the studio to call me, but can't get a connection. I notice that the studio extension is off the hook. "You can't call out when the extension is off the hook, the lines are all connected in this country," I say, as I remember that in Sweden this was not the case. Even though you may have had multiple phones in the house each one was a dedicated line. "Oh, okay," he says when I remind him of this difference. That alone is enough to shift us into a sober acceptance of the truth, which is that there is a lack of true connection. We know it's time for him to leave. We both accept that there will be no new relationship between us, that it was what it was for the time it was; brief and intense. We kiss as he prepares to go, knowing that we will never touch again. I walk him out of the building and wave goodbye, aware that I will never see him again in this life. As he goes off in one direction, I turn and walk the opposite way, only to discover that I'm carrying a baby boy in my arms.

I walk past a park where a group of young girls are practicing acrobatics, doing flips and cartwheels. Another young girl stands off on the side, leaning against a lamppost, watching, smoking a cigarette with a bored and detached attitude. I note her presence as significant, wondering why she's here, as obviously she isn't part of the acrobatic troupe. The baby and I sit on a stone wall and talk with some of the acrobatic girls. After a while, I get up and walk away with the baby in my arms. Suddenly, the quiet narrow street I've been walking down disappears completely and I find myself smack in the middle of a demolition zone, surrounded by roaring backhoes. Huge machines rip violently into old city buildings as the street fills up with chunks of falling concrete and bricks, trapping us. Clouds of white dust fill the air. I begin to panic, sure that we'll be crushed, the workmen seemingly oblivious to our plight. "I can't get out!" I yell as loudly as I can. "I can't get out!" A man on a gigantic backhoe actually hears me. Looking around from his high perch, he points out a passageway beneath a pile of concrete. It appears to be too narrow a space for us to fit into, but I realize I'll just be able to squeeze through. Extremely grateful, I wave my thanks. With the baby in my arms, I worm my way through the passageway, emerging triumphant on the other side. Covered in chalky white dust, I walk on into a beautiful park, aware that the baby and I have just survived an apocalyptic destruction.

I wake from this night of dreaming fully aware that I can't go back to an old lover, that indeed there really is no longer any connection. I have changed too much. As I go outside and meet the girls doing acrobatics, I'm very self-conscious at first, aware of their carefree attitudes. As a child I found such girls intimidating. As soon as I see the girl with the cigarette, I recognize her as more like my child self, though I did not smoke. I stood always on the sidelines, pretending tough aloofness—represented by the cigarette in the dream—though I was really steeped in fear. The smoking girl represents the reluctant part of myself too; the still fearful and protective part that doesn't want to be confronted by change, although she's aware she must face what comes. This is the part of myself that rolls into a comfortable ball at night and wishes to stay in the numbness of withdrawal.

In the dream, I turn away from the smoking girl, though I'm fully aware of her presence. Instead, I engage the carefree girls who represent an aspect of life that I'm hungry for. I've always wanted to be as free as they are, to have a body that does exactly what I want it to do—a body that responds to the joys of life, is fully accessible, untouched by trauma—and I know the reluctant girl does too; she's just really frightened. The demolition zone appears suddenly, a shift as quick as a shift into memory happens during a recapitulation. I'm immediately fearful as the world falls away, but as soon as I slither through the passageway I'm exhilarated.

I see this dream as a metaphor for this recapitulation, as I undergo the apocalyptic destruction of the old self and the creation of a new self with a brighter future ahead. Similar to the dream of the night before, when I had stepped out of the cold winter gallery into the warmth of a summer day, it signals the veritable light at the end of the tunnel, replete with new energy and new experiences totally devoid of the pain and anguish that now permeate my days and nights. As I survive the crumbling of my own world, both inner and outer, I know that I will more than survive this recapitulation process. With that in mind, I relax into a new kind of calmness, more certain that I will emerge a changed being, as energetically exhilarated as in my dream.

I go out at nine in the morning to run some errands. Upon returning, I eat a little and crawl right back into bed. Totally exhausted, I sleep until one in the afternoon when the kids call, letting me know they're ready to come home from their dad's.

January 6, 2003

I dream that I'm living in a large sprawling house on a hillside. There's construction going on. I'm hanging out with a small group of friends when my ex-husband and his girlfriend drive up. He appears to be showing her around the property, but it's my house and he's not supposed to be here. Even while I think these thoughts, I suddenly feel like a criminal. I'm even ashamed that I have a new house and new friends. I don't want to encounter them, so I slink away and hide until they leave.

Then I dream that I'm living in the same large, sprawling house, a rambling combination of structures—old and new—high on a hillside. This time, however, the house is in Sweden and I am once again married to my first husband, who was Swedish. He was very fond of my youngest brother who died at the age of twenty. In the dream, my brother, who is about nine years old, is heading off to soccer camp. I take him down to the bus stop at the bottom of the hill, making sure he has everything he needs and that he knows which bus to take. He doesn't want me to wait with him, saying that he knows what to do, even though we're living in a foreign country. He tells me he needs to be on his own now. I admire his independent spirit. Although I'm worried about him, I leave him waiting for the bus and walk back up the hill to the house. Once there, I stand at the front door and look down toward the road, far below me, where I have a clear view of my brother. The bus comes and I watch him get on. As the bus drives off, he sticks his head out the window and calls up to me that he left his soccer ball and jacket at the bus stop and could I get them and bring them to him at the soccer camp.

As I receive this information from him, I'm fully aware that I am in two worlds simultaneously, that I am both dreaming and that in waking reality my brother is dead. First, I note that after so long—twenty years since he died—his belongings aren't going to be there, and, secondly, that of course they will still be there, since in my dream he has just left. I am keenly aware that I'm in a dream where anything can happen and be true, but also keenly aware of the passage of time in reality. As I watch the bus drive off with my brother waving goodbye to me through the window, I wave back, thinking that this is the last time I will ever see him. I play this final scene over and over again in my dreaming mind, trying to wrap my head around where he could have possibly gone. "He just got on a bus and was never seen again," I say, over and over again, while at the same time I'm keenly aware that he's still alive somewhere—dead to this world perhaps, but not dead in the reality of other worlds.

I wonder if this dream was sparked by a conversation I had with my daughter last night about my brother dying in a car accident a week after his twentieth birthday. Perhaps in telling her what he was like and what happened to him, I stirred up this dream and a brief moment of reconnection with him.

This dream symbolizes taking a journey into the unknown, like doing this recapitulation, leaving everything behind and going off into the mysterious future, never to be seen in quite the same way again. It's a dream about facing changes, facing death alone—whether real death or the death of an old self, it doesn't matter. It's also about seeing from different perspectives, for in both dreams I am in the same house, but I have different experiences in them, and they exist in different countries, worlds apart.

In the first dream, I am my old fearful and ashamed self, unable to handle my new independence. I just want to hide and not be confronted with the past. In the second dream, I experience the past quite differently, from a layer-like perspective of overlapping time and space. It also reminds me of the dream I had the other night when I said goodbye to my old lover, gaining the clear insight that I would never see him again. In this dream, I'm worried about my brother as a parent worries about a child. In reality he was eleven years younger than I and, indeed, I'd spent a great deal of my childhood mothering him. I ask him many questions in the dream, attempting to cover all the practical details of his going away to camp for a long time, such as: "Do you know where you're going? Do you have money, your lunch, enough clean clothes, etc.?" He tells me he has to do this on his own and, understanding this, I back off. Then, as I stand in the doorway and watch him ride away, I know I will never see him again, that he *is* going someplace that only he can go, a place that no one can accompany him. At the same time, I'm aware that he's out there somewhere—even after all these years—that he's still alive in a sense, journeying somewhere in the universe.

I sit calmly. Breathing deeply, I ponder this dream and the idea of journeying in infinity. *You have to be able to go deeper still, beyond the fear, to whatever is there.* These are famous, oft-repeated, and fear-inducing words from Chuck that come to me as I slowly sink into my inner world. Just the thought, the anticipation of going "deeper still," scares the heck out of me, as previous experiences in doing this recapitulation have proven to be quite frightening. Though I am wracked with fear of the unknown, I must, however, let myself go even deeper, just as my brother did in my dream, and as he did in real life too, taking a journey into the vast unknown of death. If he could do that, I ought to be able to do this.

Sitting with my legs drawn up—a position I've adopted because it's so comfortable, but also because it's proven to be quite good for going into recapitulation—I sink a little deeper. Before I know what's happening I'm vibrating, my heart beating in my ears. I let the vibrations take me even deeper, without thought or fear, simply following the lead of my physical body. Before long I detect vaginal pain and the sensation of being raped by my abuser. There's a furious struggle to block out what's happening to my physical body. All of a sudden, I sense myself drifting away. At every thrust of my abuser raping me I am a balloon being inflated, pushed further and further upward until I am floating high above my bed, though I remain still attached to my body by a thin string. Easily, I travel back and forth along this string. I go into my body where I feel the pain of being raped and then quickly retreat to my floating balloon where the thrusts have no pain. From this vantage point, I'm still aware of my body being violated below me. At the same time that I experience the disturbing violations from the past, I also detect my present self, sitting with my warm hands resting on my knees.

Following my consciousness as it goes back and forth, I feel what's happening to my body in the recapitulation. I then retreat and hover above the violence in a puffy etheric state, far from harm. After a while I go back into my physical body and once again feel the pain of what's happening to it. I'm in a strangely protected state, attached yet detached, having a multilayered experience. Able to go back and forth, I experience several different states simultaneously while also being in total control of the experience. I'm fully aware of what's going on, aware of waiting for the rape to be over, aware of being out-of-body. At the same time, I'm equally aware of my physical body, in tremendous pain, being violently abused.

I come back into my body as the memory dissipates, as the sensations of thrusting stop, having fully discovered that I have the power to remove myself from my physical body! Even though I've had many out-of-body experiences while doing this recapitulation,

I've never quite experienced an OBE with such clarity before. My adult present self not only observed, but also experienced every multilayered aspect of the abuse *in full awareness*, while I simultaneously became an energetic being, totally separate from my physical self. I experienced full consciousness outside of the human body! From this experience, I gain a deeper understanding of the separateness of body and spirit.

Just as in the dream of experiencing my younger brother as two separate energies—alive in my dreamworld, dead in this reality—I experienced myself as two totally different energies as well. Each is independent of the other, while at the same time they are in total synergy. Perhaps this is the message from my brother in last night's dream, that he is indeed having his own experience of full conscious awareness, journeying in new form. I suspect that this is Jeanne Ketchel's experience as well, for I have seen her in her energy body and felt her presence on numerous occasions.

This experience of the self as two separate beings in two different places at once is thrilling! I also understand more fully that this is how I survived the abuse, by fragmenting into different states. Over the past week, leading up to this experience, I suffered through such great thumping anxiety, so much so that I could feel and hear my heart pounding quite loudly. When I first elected to sit with my legs pulled up today, it was to calm myself down, as I find it often helps. As the experience began, I noticed the loud pulsing of my heart again—the wildly beating heart of my frightened child self no doubt—synchronized with the expansion of the balloon self.

I understand something else too, that there is no stopping me now. As much as I may want this recapitulation process to be over, it will never be over. For this journey *is* my life, an endless journey of self-discovery—I get that now. Just as I've always wished for such a life, to live spiritually connected and alive, I realize that my entire life has already been filled with many mystical experiences and fascinating adventures. There is no stopping this amazing recapitulation process once embarked upon, and now there's no stopping me either, for I accept that every step of this recapitulation *is* my life's journey. I am fully engaged in this process, and I understand that the tension, pain, and anxiety are all part of it. As I learn what they mean, as I comprehend and utilize them to aid in my growth and change, I know that they will gradually recede. They will have taught me what I need to know.

And the memories, once they have gone through me and taught me what I need to know, will recede as well, for there will no longer be a need for them either.

I am in awe of this one little body, for it holds so much, so much potential and so much power. The experience of being multifaceted energy has exhausted me for the moment, but it also carries me forward. Eventually, when the only energy left is my own calm energy, I'll be in a better place: transformed, different, and even more aware of how best to use it.

January 7, 2003

I definitely felt better yesterday afternoon, after the OBE, as a new lightness and calmness took over, and I feel more stable today. My usual anxiety, although still present, is less critical, its presence noted but not reacted to. Synchronistically, as I tended to my wounded child self yesterday, flying out of my body, I found an injured cardinal lying in the driveway. His bright red body, like spilled blood, lay grimly stark against the cold white snow—a ghastly sight to behold after recapitulating memories of rape. I called a woman who cares for wounded birds and got some information on what to feed him. The kids and I tucked him into a small animal carrying case with a blanket to keep him warm. We fed him and gave him lots of attention. We covered the cage with a blanket for the night, for warmth and to keep the cats away, though they just couldn't resist keeping him company. Instead of coming to bed with me, as is their usual habit, they sat beside the bird, sniffing and whining all night long.

This morning I found one of the cats asleep on top of the cage, the other tucked in next to it, and the bird still alive. Though very weak, he nonetheless lifted his head and greeted us. We were so happy to greet him in return! I thanked the cats for tending him so well, for keeping him warm through the cold night, then headed off to meet with Chuck.

During a recent session, we had talked about training my dreaming intent, to step back from a dream and not only fix it but also view it from a different perspective. Chuck notes the progress I'm making with this intent, especially as I dreamed of my brother going off to soccer camp. As I realized that my brother had died twenty years ago, I was able to step away from what was happening in the dream. At the same time, I held onto my awareness that I was dreaming and that my brother could energetically still be alive.

"Maintaining awareness of other realities simultaneously in dreaming is good practice for shamanic work," Chuck tells me, pointing out how that recently-achieved awareness held up very nicely as I went out-of-body during the recapitulation that followed the dream.

"I just slipped out of my head," I say. "It actually happened quite easily."

"Fantastic! In fact, you actually want to be out of your head!" Chuck says with a burst of laughter. "Seriously! The head, the rational mind, is too confining and doesn't allow for real spiritual exploration."

He suggests I begin using my awareness to explore and experience in other ways too, taking my work to a new level. I tell him that I'm more readily allowing myself to have spiritual and out-of-body experiences now, that I'm more open to them, and I firmly believe the shamanic movements I've been doing have helped solidify my intentions. The sword fighting magical pass has been working very well, the same way yoga and meditation work, and I intend to keep doing it. I see how changing habitual physical postures really does produce change elsewhere. Simply wanting or desiring change doesn't really change anything, I find. The only thing that leads to real change, I'm discovering, is *action*. Through movement, by releasing myself from old stances, old ideas, and old limitations—by breaking apart the old self and forging a new self—I've truly begun to expand my awareness and experience a deeper, more spiritual self.

Chuck encourages me to lie in a different position at night because the comfortable fetal position is also the memory position, full of pain and sorrow. As soon as I lie down the memories latch on, thus the nighttime clenching—and the longer I remain in that position the worse it gets. I've already noticed that if I change my posture, even just a little bit, then everything shifts. I think the dream with the acrobatic girls was hinting at this, suggesting that I must make a choice, either I learn greater flexibility or I will remain the stiff frightened smoking girl standing off to the side.

If I can continue to do what I did yesterday—go from dream to memory, into deep recapitulation and, finally, separation of spirit from body—then I will not only succeed in releasing the memories in a new way, but also more fully experience my innate spiritual potential in the process. In the long run, I'll also have succeeded in releasing myself from the intense mind-thoughts, the crippling anxiety, and the deep depression that constantly shroud me. If I stay in my head, trying to figure things out, going over the same things—the same worries, the same scenarios, perseverating up the wazoo—nothing gets released. It just remains available for me to tighten up and obsess over again and again. The challenge now is to continue releasing, to get out of my thinking head so I can move on from the barrenness of living under the spell of it. I'd like to be able to tap into whatever is out there for me. After that recent OBE, I can't help but feel certain that there are tremendous adventures just waiting to be explored.

As I leave Chuck's office, I notice that I am once again physically and emotionally drained; I have no energy left after the session. As I drive home, I realize it's not just the recapitulation that has me in this state, it's everything: the exhaustion of the divorce and moving, the worry about being a single parent, along with the stress of making ends meet while still being able to give the kids what they need. The tasks of everyday reality loom dauntingly.

The cardinal was very weak when I left the house. When I return from my session I find him lying dead in the cage. Taking him outside, I bury him in the snow, not far from where I'd found him. Aware of the significance of sacrifice if there is to be new life, I place his bloody beauty into the cold white grave. Gently covering him, I give thanks to the energy of synchronicity and for this unfolding process as I seek my innocence, as pure as the white snow. Perhaps his body will become food for another hungry creature, I think. Then I go inside and crawl back into bed, too weak and exhausted to do anything else. The cats come in and crawl under the covers with me. Tired too from their night's work, they settle at my feet, one on either side, and we stay that way until the kids come home from school.

January 8, 2003

Conscious of the intent to change my sleeping posture, I toss and turn all night and wake up feeling like I didn't sleep at all. In addition, the cats are restless and cranky this morning, as if they didn't sleep either. The old one is crying again, as she has done for the past few days, loudly proclaiming that she doesn't like change! When I couldn't get comfortable last night, I let myself go into the usual fetal curl just to be able to fall asleep. I realized, once again, that even though that position is so full of pain it's also *very* comforting, a constantly noted dichotomy, offering such comfort in the midst of extreme terror. It's such a protective posture, and as of yet I don't have a replacement.

I haven't been doing anything on the house over the past few days, as I'm just too exhausted. All of a sudden I feel so sad too. It came over me yesterday, leaving me feeling like my old cat, wondering where I am. As everything changes, the old familiar stuff doesn't feel right anymore. I don't even know how to fall asleep, or how to deal with the new feelings that I'm awash in. I don't even understand what they're about, as they're feelings I've never had before. Cold, stiff, and protectively wooden for so long, I've saved just a touch of warmth for a few special people and things. At my core, however, I am fire. A small bright flame has been burning forever, waiting for a breath of fresh air to spark it to life, waiting for the melting of the cold outer self. And now that breath of fresh air has arrived, stirring the ashes and the flame, bringing with it the most uncomfortable of symptoms.

I know Chuck would advise me to just let the new feelings come, just as he advises to let the old stuff flow out of me in recapitulation, but these new feelings are so unfamiliar. I shouldn't be afraid, but I am—terrified actually—so much so that I just want to hide under the covers with the cats, just hide until I'm used to it all. I know I need to go to my emotions, that I can't just bypass them as I've done in the past, but there are endless heaps of old shit to sort through before I even get to the underlying emotions. If I don't purge myself pretty soon, I fear I'll continue hauling this heavy load around; and far from being the light and airy out-of-body being I was the other day, I fear I'll never be able to fly. I flew the other day because I needed to, but can I also do it because I want to? Can I do it on demand? That's what I yearn to find out!

It's eleven in the morning and I'm going back to bed. Depressed and groggy, I can't muster enthusiasm for anything— I'm a total zombie—my energy completely depleted. At the same time, I understand that everything is being realized, all that I've wished for is unfolding. My life *is* changing. I *am* reconnecting with my spirit, and I'm learning amazing things in the process, yet I find no place of repose in the chaos of this newly forming life. Relief comes only in going under the covers, hiding until the kids get home; and that's what I elect to do now—crawl into bed. Lying on my back, I restate my intent to change and then drift off to sleep.

I'm aware of constantly turning to new positions, switching from the old fetal pose to stretch out my legs, turning onto my back or front. I sleep lightly and any change, even a slight adjustment, is noted.

January 9, 2003

In a dream, I fight a fierce battle, using a sword, karate kicks, and other fighting moves. I am powerful, quick, and agile. I leap and hang magically suspended in the air, each strike landing perfectly on target. I don't think, I just act, and my body knows exactly what to do.

In another dream, I'm with my daughter in a vast stone castle on a hill, filled with large banquet rooms. There are many wide staircases leading to higher levels. We're helping to prepare for an enormous feast, setting up tables, arranging flowers, preparing food. I'm aware of a tall stone tower adjacent to the castle. After completing preparations for the feast, my daughter and I cross a wide gravel-covered courtyard and enter the tower. As we climb up the winding stone steps, I look out the windows of the tower. I see a maze of paths in the gardens below and realize that I've been here before and that I've walked those mazes too. From the top of the tower we look out upon the vast valley below, upon the ornate gardens sprinkled with numerous mazes and labyrinths, to the snow-covered rolling hills in the distance. I think about jumping out the window. It seems a perfectly logical way to exit the tower. I know I won't get hurt because I'll land in the deep snow far below. But I'm also aware that jumping is a copout, and that I should take the stairs and have the valuable experience of descending the tower by going back the way I've come.

As we climb back down the winding stone steps, I perceive it as "taking the hard way." I'm fully aware, however, that there are many meaningful things that I can only learn by descending in this fashion. Once again in the courtyard, I ask a woman to show us how to get off the property, which is a walled-in private estate. The woman points to an open gate and a pathway that leads into the open valley below. Gazing out over the vast landscape in the direction the woman has pointed, I see a maze that I had once walked. Shaped like the spokes of a wheel, and surrounded by four other interconnecting smaller wheel mazes, fit together like machine cogs, I know that I had spent a lot of time wandering along the paths of that machinelike maze, learning what I had to, unable to extricate myself. Now, as I see it in its wholeness, I'm suddenly struck by the realization that in simply looking from a different perspective—from a distance in this case—I'm afforded the opportunity to see things in a new, clearer way. Now the way out of the maze is easy to see. I understand that this new perspective, similar to the one I'd had from the top of the tower—offering a picture of the entire layout of the land—can be achieved at all times, simply by shifting my point of view.

"Oh yes, I see that I don't have to take the same long and circuitous route I took to get here," I say. "Of course, there's always a more direct way, and it's right in front of my eyes! I just have to see it!"

My daughter wants to climb the tower again and although I'm reluctant to let her go alone, I know I must. I give her safety instructions, telling her not to talk to anyone, and to wave to me through the windows as she climbs up so I'll know where she is at all times. I'm fearful that something bad will happen to her, but at the same time the setting and the tower have an extremely peaceful aura about them. I know I'm being challenged to trust that she will be fine in this environment. And so I stand at the bottom of the tower, asking myself to relax, to stay calm, as I let her go. She does exactly as I've asked, waving to me from the windows of the tower. Pretty soon she's standing beside me again. Then, hand in hand, we set off across the gardens together, taking a new route.

My dreaming self knew exactly what to do in the first dream, as I put up a good fight, moving effortlessly and flawlessly. I do have to say that although I succeeded in changing my position throughout the night, as I had intended, I found I couldn't *fall* asleep in any position but the old one. But after that, the intent took over and I flowed with it, easily shifting into new positions, whether asleep or awake, just as I had done in my fighting dream.

The tower, in the second dream, still holds some fear, much as my recapitulation process does. I'm fully aware that doing this recapitulation—taking the hard way—is really the only way that I will fully achieve freedom and a meaningful life. Though the setting in the dream is very peaceful and offers an enlightening perspective, I experience it the same way I do my life at this point: though I know I'm safe now, I find it hard to relax, even in a calm and beautiful setting. I'm aware that the tower still holds lessons to be learned and that I will be returning to it again. But as I awaken, I'm more intrigued by the progress I'm making, as I am indeed constantly shifting, both my body and my perspective, and going in new directions every day. I'm certain that someday I'll achieve the natural calm I experience in this dream.

As my journey deepens, I gain a better sense of where I've been and where I might be going. The final maze that I see in my dream, the wheel interconnected with four smaller wheels—a mandala—seems to indicate lessons learned in the mechanical living of life and in the confusion of the past, now done with, for though they are familiar to me I know I won't be going back to them. Once places of confusion, depression, and hopelessness, I'm now able to clearly see them as cogs in the wheel of a far greater machine. No longer places of doom and gloom, they are part of an enchanting garden, beautifully laid out, lush and well cared for. In finally lifting my eyes from the ground, I'm able to take in the whole picture of where I've been my entire life—in a most rich and lovely garden! I've learned to view my life with new eyes as I've done this recapitulation, and I'm finally experiencing it freed of the memories, the depression, and my old world perspective. I now see my life as beautiful, in spite of my childhood trials.

The clarity and peace I feel after this dream are exquisite, yet there is still work to do, for the calmness I feel upon awakening is clearly contrasted by an old fear that my innocent self—in the guise of my daughter in the dream—may still be in danger, as I still carry old worries about innocence being unsafe in the outer world. But the far greater sense that I take with me into my day is that I really am living in a beautiful paradise. I just have to wake up to the truth of it. However, it will only be more fully realized and more fully revealed as I encounter what still remains in that tower on the hill.

January 11, 2003

I dream that I'm traveling with my business partner, driving along narrow forest roads to a large rustic lodge in Vermont. We are to attend an art exhibit of our work. I'm surprised to be warmly greeted by my entire extended family; many of whom I haven't seen in years, and who I am amazed even remember me. Aunts, uncles, and cousins come up and shower me with hugs and kisses. I introduce them to my business partner and we all go inside the lodge. Our artwork is displayed throughout the building and a boisterous party is in progress. I have little attachment to what's going on. After a while I leave the party.

It's nighttime as I step out the front door of the lodge and find a horse waiting for me. I climb into the saddle and take off, letting the horse lead, for I have no idea where I am or where I'm going. We gallop along narrow winding roads and enter a snowy forest. The ride is effortless, magical, as the horse and I peacefully glide along. We come to the edge of the forest where the horse suddenly stops. I sit calmly in my saddle and gaze out over fields of snow, stretching in all directions, as far as the eye can see. It's beautiful in the crisp night air. With the dark forest behind me now, all that lies ahead is lit by the bright light of the full moon and the twinkling stars above. The white snow glistens and sparkles pristinely under the night sky. A wide river runs past on the right. As I watch, it gently overflows its banks, flooding the fields of snow. The horse takes me down into a field on the left, away from the flooding river. We gallop in a large circle, going tighter and tighter in toward the center of the circle until we've created a large spiral in the snow. Stopping in the middle of the spiral, I look back and see my business partner coming down the road, also riding a horse. She joins me in the field, stopping at the outer edge of the spiral. She tells me she's leaving, that her family has a cabin in Kentucky and that she'll work there now. I wish her luck and watch her gallop away across the snowy fields, at peace in my solitude, aware that my future is calm and beautiful.

I stay in my dream all day, drawn back to the feeling of freedom I felt upon leaving the party, the calmness of complete detachment. Again and again, throughout the day, I ride the horse through the dark forest. After my enchanting ride, I am totally at peace as I look out over the beautiful starlit snowscape. I replay the meandering river gently overflowing its banks and then riding into the snowy field to make the spiral—my life's journey fully known, my recapitulation done, as I see it. Sitting in the center of the spiral, I am totally at peace. There are intensely good feelings in this dream and I long to stay with them, but I know I have to wake up and live in this reality too. And so, as the day goes on, I work on the sword movement to ground myself, to break the trance of the dream state, lovely as it is.

It's still hard to get up in the mornings, still hard to face everything. At the same time I want this recapitulation process to hurry up and be done so I can really be as calm as I was in that dream. My impulse is to force a recapitulation, but I automatically hear Chuck's voice warning me to slow down and let things happen on their own, as *they* will. I must acquiesce to the process by letting go of all manipulation and control, just as I let the horse lead me in that dream. And then, as if on cue, I notice that my teeth hurt, that I've been unconsciously and incessantly grinding them all day. The sharp pain in my jaw reminds me to be conscious of my body at all times now. I've trained myself to be aware when I'm asleep, to shift when I find myself caught in the fetal position, as I'm aware that it's not conducive to progress. Now my body tells me to remain equally aware while awake too.

January 12, 2003

I recapitulate Slave Girl—a memory that emerged during the first year of my recapitulation. Her arms and legs are tied to stakes and yet she constantly wonders why her ankles and wrists are covered with bruises and blisters. Why are my ankles so ugly? "I am Slave Girl," comes the sobering answer. As I recapitulate, my legs and hips cramp from being tied apart for so long. I hear my abuser's voice too. Coming out of the past and into my bedroom, he paces back and forth, commanding that I watch his special preparations. Once again, just as when I was a child, I hear him ranting and raving like a maniac. He sets everything up, prepares everything for me, for his beautiful slave girl, he tells me, because I'm so special. No one else gets his attention the way Slave Girl does. He prepares me too, opening me up, getting me ready. His maniacal talk changes to incoherent mutterings as spittle appears at the corners of his mouth. Clearly he's getting aroused as he violates me. I too feel his mounting arousal, feel it spreading to me, fueling the whole process, making me want to be hurt by him. I desire everything he's going to do. He makes me feel as disgusting and cruel as he is, an accomplice in this Slave Girl game. I'm aware that the only relief is in the pain he will inflict on me. Having become his desire, *I must be punished.* I must feel as much pain as possible if I am to be released, if Slave Girl is to be freed.

In recapitulating, I relive the belief that I must be punished, for I have sinned along with my abuser. Instinctively, I masturbate, crudely punishing myself, intentionally inflicting pain. As I do, the recapitulation takes me deeper. I suddenly find myself in the barn that my abuser took me to so many times. I'm older, perhaps fifteen or sixteen. I have a developed body. He rapes me. I have sexual arousal and climax. To a certain extent, I have knowledge of what's going on and I hate him for it, but at the same time I'm caught in his game. I become exactly what he wants, his slave girl. I become a part of his fantasy—I *am* his fantasy—and I play the part very well. In return, I punish myself by staying fully present in my physical body. Vindicated by the pain, I am punished for being the bad girl that I am. During the game, my abuser tells me that his beautiful slave girl has done something bad and that he's going to give her what she deserves, and I know I deserve exactly what he does to me, and so I take it as my rightful punishment.

I pull out of the memory, deeply confused and needing to talk to Chuck. But, just like Slave Girl, I feel that I must punish myself further by not calling him, denying myself contact, forcing myself to work it out alone, to just wait until our next meeting. I sense my mature adult self being overshadowed by the confusion of Slave Girl and suddenly I am fifteen again, feeling that I deserve whatever happens to me. I must be punished and so punishment becomes the ultimate goal, as I re-experience the vicious cycle of desire, guilt, and the relief of pain that once freed my tortured teenage self. In backing further out of the memory, and looking from a different angle, I'm able to comprehend how I felt at the time, and how I dealt with it, but now I also see that I was caught in the tangled web of a confused young girl's emerging sexuality. Any real, innocent sexual stirrings were entangled in my abuser's games, obscured by his calculated manipulations, as he took full advantage of my availability to get his own needs met. Even now, the memory has me confused, incorrectly thinking that I need to punish myself, that I am just as bad as he tells Slave Girl she is. Punishment, I see from this perspective, is a kind of reward, for once the punishment is dealt I'm granted freedom, my shackles are undone, and I can return to my other life.

January 13, 2003

I dream that I'm walking down a New York City street when a famous graphic artist, Milton Glaser, falls from a skyscraper and lands with a splat on the sidewalk in front of me. Other people gather around to see what's happening. The impact of his fall has left him lying at the bottom of a deep crater. He's able to lift himself slightly. With arms outstretched, he pleads for help before falling back to the bottom of the crater. An ambulance comes. The paramedics roll him onto a stretcher and take him away. He dies at the hospital. Then I'm sitting on a bus reading a newspaper and come across a report of his death. Immediately, I flash back to the actual fall, watching it happen once again. Then I flash even further back to another dream, when I went to meet him at his house in the country, and suddenly I'm *there*. A funny, energetic guy, he greets me dressed in painter's overalls. We're just heading off to work together when I suddenly flash to another dream I'd had of working for his wife, and suddenly I'm transported to *that dream*.

In that dream, Milton Glaser's wife is an advertising designer. She's given me an assignment to research and place an order for wall-mounted shelves. Part of the assignment is to find a manufacturer and write down order numbers for each of three different styles of shelves. I set out to do this. First I go to France and check into a small hotel. I find myself in a roomful of other women, getting dressed for a formal meeting. All the clothes I try on are either dirty or torn. The women help me find something to wear, but nothing is suitable. Finally, I put on a black skirt with a torn seam and a dirty white blouse. I set out on my assignment with a sheaf of papers under my arm and some addresses in hand.

At the first address, I meet with a woman and follow her to the top of a wide staircase. Once there, I suddenly lose sight of her. Now I'm standing at the top of the stairs in the midst of a group of other women in the same predicament, all suddenly left to their own devices, all feeling equally abandoned and lost. A cleaning woman tells us that everything is locked up and, indeed, all the doors have signs on them saying that they are temporarily out of order. We look into one room where the door has been pulled off its hinges. We see a woman lying asleep on a bed on the left side of the room. On the other side of the room, mattresses are piled high. Children are sandwiched between them, their legs dangling out. I'm worried that they can't breathe, especially because there are grown men napping on top of the mattresses.

"Oh, how cute, all the legs hanging out! Look how they stack them for naptime!" one of the women comments, but I don't think it's so cute. I'm aware that I'm the only one who knows that the adults are smothering the children on purpose. I know that they treat them as sex objects. The men pull them out by their legs, have sex with them, and stick them back under the mattresses, headfirst, so no one can hear them screaming. I know the children are screaming under the mattresses.

All the other women leave to go look for their own children in other areas of the building, but I cannot leave these children to their abusers. Determined that the abusers will not get away with this behavior, I go to a phone in the hallway and call the police. I have to speak Swedish in order to be understood, since I don't speak French. I notice that my Swedish accent, which had been perfect at one time, has deteriorated and I sound very American, but I'm able to get my message across. Later, there's a press conference outside the building and the police announce that a huge child pornography and sex ring had been busted apart by an anonymous tip from a visitor from Los Angeles—me. When people find out that I'm the one who made the call, they thank me profusely.

I wake from this dream in the middle of the night. As if I am one of the children in the dream, I find myself curled into a fetal position, shaking and terrified, totally encased in a sensory memory. "It's okay; it's just a memory," I tell my frightened self. "Relax, relax, everything is okay. It's just a memory." Repeating this soothing mantra, I achieve brief moments of relaxation.

Turning away from the disturbing aspects of the dream, I focus instead on the first part of the dream when my dreaming self was triggered to recall previous dreams. I have no memory of ever having really dreamed these dreams, but that I can dream of other dreams that I've never consciously dreamed is representative of the layered aspect of this recapitulation process. As I've gone deeper into the unknown self, other memories, that I have no conscious recall of, have naturally emerged. This dream must be about going deeper still, into the still unrecapitulated self. As soon as I come to this conclusion my body responds and I'm pulled right back into the terror of somatic pain; my teeth clench tightly and my legs, hips and shoulders cramp. I'm yanked right out of my dreamworld and thrust into painful reality. All I know is that I am empty; there is no one inside me. Like the children stuffed under the mattresses, I wait for salvation.

January 14, 2003

I need to talk to Chuck openly and honestly today about issues that are tying in with the slave girl memory. In the beginning, my inability to fully trust him related to my inability to trust anyone at all. There was a time when he'd ask me, every week practically, "Why can't you trust me? What is holding you back?" Once he even asked me if I thought he was going to abuse me, if that was what I was afraid of. If that was the issue, I needed to know, he said, that he was only interested in evolution. It was at that point that I began to realize that not only had I expected to be abused, but that I perceived that I wouldn't be able to continue our work until I had been. Never promiscuous, having had only a few relationships, sexual intercourse had nonetheless become a gauge for knowing how much of myself to expose to another human being, just how innocent, vulnerable, and revealing I could risk being. I realize I used sex as a baseline by which I would decide to fully trust someone or not, and frankly, I could tell a lot about a person during sexual intercourse. As I read the energy of the partner I was with, many questions were answered, such as: Am I safe with this person? Can I trust him enough to allow him to know the inner me? The inner me is so fearful and frightened all the time, although she constantly looks for recognition and acknowledgment outside. Can I expose the vulnerable and gentle soul inside? In therapy, I'm challenged to totally open up without having the use of that sexual gauge. And so I've been forced to really learn what it means to trust another person, in a totally new and different way—by simply talking.

My adult relationships with men, though companionable and committed in many ways, have not involved much of the inner me, for I can only go as far and as deeply into a relationship as feels safe. Even my relationships with women friends are limited; I always maintain my distance. I constantly worry that my desires and dreams will be received with judgments and criticisms—that I'll be hurt or ridiculed and end up feeling stupid for having expressed myself—and that no innocence will be reciprocally exposed or expressed. I just can't risk the bruising that I know will ensue, so I share little of the inner me with the people I become close to. Indeed, my innocence often does suffer. When met with insensitivity, I've become increasing fearful of exposing my true self. It's clear to me now, however, that I need to have the experiences I have with all the people I've been involved with, for as deep and as long as those relationships last. For a time we *are* meant to journey together.

I realize that this inability to trust that my deepest feelings will be honorably received and tenderly treated goes back not only to my abuser but to my family of origin as well—where no feelings were allowed expression—and so, from all sides I was admonished to be secretive. From an early age I knew that feelings were of no value.

Now, here I am in a little room sitting across from this man, Chuck Ketchel, who pokes at the inner me, asking her to wake up and look at the world in a new way; to talk, to feel, to expose the deepest parts of her innermost self to him. I admit that I didn't know how to gauge him at first, how to feel about him, how to feel about the position I found myself in. Without the gauge of sexual intimacy by which to determine how deep my involvement should be, I was lost. I had to find a new way to navigate, to determine whether or not I would trust or not. I was not going to be allowed to use that old method, so I had to learn what it meant to trust in a completely different manner, by openly and honestly expressing what I was *feeling*. I was challenged to finally do what I had never done before, to fully expose my innocence devoid of any certainty that it would be kindly received and respected. I just had to learn to trust.

As I've revealed myself to Chuck, he has, in turn, revealed that he is *totally trustworthy*. He does what he says he will do. He accepts me on every level, without judgment, ridicule, criticism, or rejection. And I *have* learned to trust him, which is exactly what Jeanne asked of me when she appeared in my bathroom on that most strange and ecstatic night almost a year ago when I was in such pain. She asked me to trust Chuck, and I've learned how to do that. I've allowed myself to open up to another human being. Basically, I've learned that whatever I say—even if it really is something silly and flippant, shot out without deeper contemplation—will be accepted as part of my process, taken seriously as a matter to be discussed. The deeper Chuck asks me to go, the deeper he goes with me, so trust has naturally grown between us as part of this recapitulation process. I now understand how vitally important it is and, as I continue to tiptoe deeper into my past and into my inner world, I understand how Chuck is guiding me to trust myself too. Through this slow and painful recapitulation process I've learned to trust someone with barely a touch passing between us.

As I try to explain all of this to Chuck, he assures me that my feelings are perfectly understandable under the circumstances and that he will continue to be here when I need him. He acknowledges my feelings. He asks that I don't punish myself but that I allow the process to lead, accepting where it takes me as meaningful, offering necessary insights. He assures me that he's fully committed to continuing this recapitulation journey with me.

"Being able to trust me," he says, "has allowed you to go as far as you have, and to go even deeper you need to continue to be able to trust."

Most of the session is spent getting past this critical point, for I have indeed felt stuck. The investigation of the use of this old sexual gauge as a means of deciding how deep a relationship to have, is quite insightful. I realize how strange this confession must sound to Chuck, but I have dared myself to tell him. I feel almost like a child again, kneeling in the confessional, telling my sins to Father Chuck, but that's how much I trust him! Then I let myself be vulnerable and suffer through a new confession. I don't know why I'm so bothered by it, but it's hard for me to tell Chuck that the Paxil, the medication I've been on for months now, has not been doing what I'd hoped it would do: reduce my anxiety. Perhaps I feel I'll disappoint him, for he had hoped it would help and here I am still in the throes of crippling anxiety night and day. Perhaps it's because I must finally acquiesce to the rightness of the suggestion he made a while ago, that the dose might not be high enough, and which I rejected outright.

In any case, I called my doctor the other day and we determined that raising the dosage, even incrementally, might give me the added detachment I seek. And so I tell Chuck that I've increased my dosage, and that I'm learning to trust his intuition. To be fair, I must learn to not be so dismissive myself, so quick to dismiss his sense of things. As I increase the dosage, however, I must once again contend with the fact that I made the decision to introduce a chemical substance into my body, something I find abhorrent, and I'm not happy about taking even more of it. Do I want to blame Chuck for getting me into this? I don't think so, in fact, I feel protective towards him. Yet I barge on and reveal how nauseous I am if I don't eat, that the increased dosage is forcing me to think about eating and the importance of good nutrition. He's very happy to hear that it makes me want to eat more! And so the session ends on a light note after all.

After our meeting, I go home and tumble into bed with my jacket, boots, and gloves still on. I pull the covers over my head and sleep for a few hours. I wake at around noon and drag myself over to the studio to get some work done in preparation for a painting job that will take the rest of the week. Though the old stuff still tugs at me, I experience the atmosphere of the studio as energizing. It's good to be out and about, around people again, and busy. The need to sleep and the desire to be isolated constantly pressure me though, pushing me toward a breaking point, at least that's what it feels like. My work partner makes the comment that she's just waiting for it, telling me that I'm overdoing everything, "as usual."

"Stop volunteering!" she yells when I tell her that I'm considering getting involved in yet another local art event.

"Go home! Take a bath! Get a good book and go to bed and drink tea instead!" she recommends.

January 17, 2003

I wake at four in the morning with my legs locked. It's as if I'm trapped in a vise grip, my nerves compressed, everything from my waist down paralyzed. Suffering through rising panic, I fight off the energy of my abuser. I fight as well to hold myself together, my body locked in a battle of wills. At the same time, I admit to myself that I don't want to keep holding on, and I don't want to keep fighting either. In fact, I desperately want to let go! I assume that this paralysis is just a memory trying to emerge, though I have no images to go on, only the excruciating mounting tension pushing me toward complete and total breakdown, toward disintegration, the most frightening of all my childhood fears. I toss and turn as the intensity of the battle rises and reaches a critical point—until I can't hold back any longer. Suddenly, I shatter. My worst nightmare rips through my body. In powerful jerks and deep spasms I disintegrate. As if I have been struck by lightning my body shakes and rattles for what seems like hours. When it's over, I find myself lying limply on my bed in the darkness before dawn—still in one piece.

Shakily, I get out of bed and do as my work partner suggested the other day. I take a bath, drink tea, and do relaxation exercises, but the tension returns as soon as the kids leave for school. It continues to mount as I sit on the edge of my bed and recall the sensation of my legs going stiff before the shattering began. Once again I find myself paralyzed from the waist down, in a stiff deadlock. Memories of trying to fight off my abuser by clamping my legs tightly shut reemerge, my only thought to keep him out. I stand up to break the memory. As soon as I sit down again, however, I immediately go stiff, back into tense fighting mode. I stay this way, sitting perched on the edge of my bed, until I can't hold on any longer. Angrily, reluctantly, against my wishes, I lose the battle once again. As if pushed down by strong hands, I fall onto my back and, like a glass vase toppling to the floor, shatter into a million shards. In pieces, I spiral down through time and space right into a recapitulation. I reassemble as a child. I am confronted by my abuser. I hear his voice telling me over and over again that I want him; that I wait for him; that I want him to do

34

everything he does to me. But I don't; I didn't. I only wanted him to stop, to go away and leave me alone. I wanted to disappear so he'd never find me. I never wanted him to even touch me. In fact, I hated him.

"No! Stay away, go away, stay away for eternity! Leave me alone!" I yell, and then I kick out, fighting him off with both feet, hating him. I want him dead. I want him punished by a terrible painful death. He's evil and despicable. He hurt me. I never had the life I could have had because of him. I wasn't allowed to be the person I was meant to be. He damaged, tortured and hurt me because of his own needs, which had nothing to do with me. He was sick and perverted, deadly to me, contaminating me like a parasite carrying deadly bacteria until I was consumed by his sickness. He filled me with his poison. I kick and kick and kick!

I thought I needed to be the way he wanted me to be, that I was there for him to play games with. Frightened, I became stiff and unreal in his presence, unable to speak or move. From this frozen state of numbness I hated him. Now I ache, as I have ached for decades, with the tightness in my legs, my neck and shoulders, in my clenched and silent throat. The tightness in my jaw reminds me once again of what he did to me so long ago and how I fought to protect myself. My body does me the favor of remembering and I accept its truth—I have learned to trust it. But this time, I fight back. I unleash all that I have been holding back. I kick and kick and kick until I am exhausted.

January 18, 2003

The pain in my hips remains intense. Even all the kicking I did, although empowering, did nothing to release it. It took until two in the morning to get to sleep last night as I dealt with the ferocity of it. Every time I started to fall asleep I was jolted awake. I got up and did sword movements, followed by gentle yoga and some swings with a big stick into the pillows, all offering only temporary relief. I finally gave up and rolled into my familiar ball. I was aware of making sure to change my position throughout the night, but in the end the only thing that provided any relief was to roll up on my side as tightly as I could. Now the tension spreads from my legs and hips to my entire body as another recapitulation sweeps over me.

I'm lying on the ground in the woods, in a T-position, my legs pressed tightly together. I'm cold, frozen in this position, whimpering, aching up to my neck with the tension of keeping closed up, with the effort of keeping him, my abuser, out of my body. I can turn my head, but everything else is wooden and stiff. He's not done with preparing things yet. He's talking and muttering. I'm determined to keep my legs pressed together so he won't be able to pry them apart. I'll close everything up—my legs, my vagina—and he won't be able to penetrate because I have superhuman powers to hold everything sealed off. I am so concentrated on the task of keeping closed that I am no longer aware of what he's doing. I can only focus on keeping my legs clamped shut, certain that if I can keep them closed I'll be okay. Then he's on me like a monster in a dream, coming out of nowhere. Brutally, painfully, he jerks my legs apart and ties them down so I can't move. He's too strong. I can't stop him. I can't stop him!

With the memory comes relief of a sort. However, the recapitulation ends there, almost as if the rape ended right there, but I know it couldn't have. From what I've learned as I've taken this journey, I probably passed out, dissociated, or blocked the rest of it in some manner.

It feels as if the pain is leeching out through my bones and skin now, from somewhere deep, deep inside, from my organs and tissues, from my heart. All the pain of years and years of abuse and the pain of holding it in and keeping it secret is finally emptying out, coming from the deepest caverns in which it has been stored. Finally flowing out of me, it mixes with the air around me, with the words and cries and thoughts released by others who have suffered the same pain. Such painful vibrations have been circulating the globe for centuries. I envision the universe filled with them— vibrations of pain and vibrations of the joy of release alike—waves of energy flowing for eternity. If we're lucky, we might experience that flow of energy during our lifetimes. We might hear a mysterious voice, catch a glimpse of an image, or a thought not our own. We might be lucky enough to be in the position I find myself in right now, merging with that energy, joining with those eternal others. I let my pain and my anguish slip out into the invisible river of vibration that I sense circulating throughout the world. Free to empty my past, I am invited to bath in this river of redemption.

This is where I am offered cleansing release, as I allow the healing waters of my own innocence to wash through me.

I don't get out of bed all day except for about an hour when I walk around the house and make some tea and toast, trying to bring myself into the present, but it's hopeless. The kids are with their dad for the weekend and so I find myself with nothing to anchor to, except my own intent, and that seems to be set on recapitulation this weekend. Now, at two-thirty in the afternoon, the rest of the memory emerges.

My abuser tears my legs apart. I am split open like a captured animal. Ripped apart and bleeding, he only has to put his large, grown man weight on top of me to pin me down. I come out of the memory and realize that I've had trouble breathing all week. Unable to take a full breath, I've felt smothered. I realize I've been recapitulating the heavy weight of my abuser on my chest, my body preparing me for this moment of fuller recapitulation for days now. I gather that there's more to come regarding this specific memory, as I still feel edgy.

I finally get up, the memory largely acknowledged and accepted. I do what seems most natural and go into fighting mode. I draw my sword. Pointing it at the memory, I ask it to back off for the time being so I can go out and do some errands. "With the kids away and the house to myself, I'm choosing how I spend the rest of my time alone," I tell it, "and you are not invited!" As captivating an exercise as recapitulation is, I don't necessarily want to do it all the time, and so I get a movie to watch, some books from the library, and then hook up the washer and dryer that my nephew moved into the laundry room for me last week and do some laundry. The achiness in my body stays with me all day, as more memories come to clutch at me, asking me to remember them too. I pull out my sword and stave them off, while also acknowledging to myself that I'll only be able to hold them off for so long. After all, permission to engage has already been granted, and so I know my quiet time is limited.

Around eleven at night, as I get into bed to sleep, a memory slips under the covers with me. Knowing I have no power over it, I let it cozy up and whisper its secrets in my ear. My body reacts by clenching, until it can no longer bear the tension, and then suddenly I am shattering again. The fullness of the memory bursts through my flimsy barricades. My legs are wrenched apart and, as if they are splintering into shards, pain sears through my hipbones. OW! OW! OW! I toss and turn, wanting only to be rid of the pain, to finally release it! In the throes of this real phantom pain, I declare to the universe how tired I am of doing this recapitulation, how tired of being in pain. But I also acknowledge that the abuse inflicted on me by my abuser was killing me and that it continues to kill me as long as I hold it inside.

"I don't want to be killed!" I shout. "I don't want to hold it in anymore!"

The shouting tires me and simultaneously deepens the pain, as if my body takes the verbal release as a signal that it's okay to recapitulate more fully. I lie in bed and suffer through the searing pain of splintering hips and legs, my muscles screaming of all that they have held onto for the past fifty years. At about one-thirty, with the pain of the memory driving me crazy, I break my number one rule to never call Chuck at night and reach for the phone next to my bed and somehow dial his number.

"Get out of bed. Break the hold it has over you. Get up and move!" he says.

"Okay," I say, and immediately hang up.

As soon as my feet hit the floor, the memory spontaneously releases its hold, just as Chuck suggested it might. I do the sword form, running through it until I'm exhausted, until it feels like I could even cry. *That* longed for release is, however, still distant, as only strangled croaks emerge from my tightly clenched throat, and not one tiny tear emerges. Eventually, the only release I get is in going outside and gently breathing icy cold night air into my stricken body. Filling me up from the bottom of my feet to the top of my head, the coldness pushes the old stale air of abuse out of my body. Then I curl up in bed, my warm cats at my feet, and beg for painless sleep.

January 19, 2003

I awaken flat on my back, paralyzed again, immobilized up to my chin. Staring at the ceiling, I notice that I'm really pretty

38

calm inside, more interested in figuring out what's happening in my body than anything else. I lie still for a long time, unable to move a muscle, wondering what to do. Finally, I remember the command Chuck had given me in the night and, aware that I've shifted out of paralyzing memories many times before, I roll over and sit up, surprised at how easy it is. I get out of bed immediately; too afraid that if I lie back down the paralysis will return.

The house is very cold. It's Sunday morning, only 10 degrees outside, and there's no heat. I realize I haven't heard the furnace rumbling for a long time. I get no response when I turn the thermostat up. When I press the red restart button the furnace grumbles loudly for a few seconds but fails to light. The fuel tank is full, so it has to be some other issue. I check the fuse box, flip the switch a few times and try restarting again, but to no avail. Anger starts to build. I want to blame someone, but I'm the only one here and it's my house. It's up to me to take care of this, my first challenge living alone as a single homeowner.

I get out the phone book, find the name of the company the previous owners had used to service the furnace and dial their number, but I dial wrong. Instead I get a nice man who comes over immediately and within forty-five minutes I have heat again. The charge is minimal and he gives me advice on how to deal with an exposed fuel tank so the nozzles don't clog up again in extremely cold weather. This unexpected distraction energizes me, at least enough that I feel hungry, and so I return to bed with a cup of tea, some toast, cheese and apple. Though my legs and hips are still painfully stiff and tight, I'm intent on drinking my tea in peace, staying warm under the covers while the furnace chugs away. It'll be a while before the house is warmed up. Aware, however, that I must keep moving or risk going into paralysis again, I get out of bed after a while and set about priming the living room walls.

As I paint, I realize there's no one to blame for my troubles, just as there's no one to blame for the broken furnace on this cold day. It just happened. I took care of the furnace, just as I know I have to take care of my body as it takes me on this recapitulation journey. It's just another thing I have to do, as if an old agreement that I solemnly swore to one day uphold is now being fulfilled. I find that nothing I consciously do really takes away the absolute necessity of fulfilling that agreement. Nothing will deter the next wave of memory for long either. In the end, it's only in acquiescing to the pain and fully recapitulating every aspect of it that relief of any lasting sort will come. By keeping busy I do keep things at bay, for a little while, but that doesn't allow for release, which is really the only solution to the kind of pain I'm experiencing. And so I decide that the only thing to do at this point is to acquiesce. I must let my body have its way with me and tell me what I need to know on this day.

Aware that a hot bath is likely to trigger memories, I prepare for their onslaught by doing some empowerment exercises, by breathing, doing grounding yoga poses, and then the sword form. By the time I step into the hot bath I'm physically warmed up, my muscles less taut, my mind calmer, and my anxiety considerably lessened too. Deeply massaging my hips and thighs, I intend and encourage release. I masturbate too, hoping to trigger an even greater release of tension, but I just end up in pain, my body signaling that an underlying memory is about to emerge.

I lie in the tub for a half hour, incrementally releasing as much tension as I can, letting it leech out into the hot water. As soon as I step out of the tub, intense pain strikes and before I know it I'm huddled on the bathroom floor. Nausea strikes, coming over me like a turbulent ocean wave, and I am dragged by the strong undertow of memory into full recapitulation mode.

My abuser uses a pair of pliers to open me up, sticking them into my vagina, splitting me open. The pain sears into my hips and thighs as I recapitulate and the soreness is real again. I know he hates me, and he hates my family with a vengeance—Fucking New Yorkers! Fucking city people! Before I was even born he hated them. He abuses me because he hates us all. I hear him talking about my family, his anger at the invasion into his rural life and territory palpable. My heart bruises deeply as his cruel words and harsh laughter fall upon my young ears. "Things were different before you came," he says as he spits on the ground. Cold needle-nosed pliers pinch and hurt. Although I'm painfully sore, what pours out of me now is such FRUSTRATION! There's stale old stuff caught in my body and I want it out—like a cancer—I WANT IT OUT! I finally pry myself from the bathroom floor, shaking with cold. When I sit on the toilet to pee, everything stings, just as it did when I was a child.

Night finally comes. Once so welcome, now I wonder how I'll ever get through it. As soon as I lie down my legs cramp. I realize that I'm still recapitulating and so I ask my body to tell me what's happening. Once again I feel my abuser's hands prying my knees apart, trying to force them open while my child self fights with all her might to keep them locked shut. Please, let me sleep!

January 20, 2003

Embraced by pain, I awaken, barely able to move, my legs knotted in a permanent cramp now. I call Chuck and mention everything that's been happening and everything I've been doing in order to precipitate a release: the sword form, hip-opening yoga, targeted breathing. I tell him about bathing in hot water, massaging my legs and masturbating to get some kind of relief. I tell him that I'm drinking herbal decoctions that promote calmness and rest, but nothing is working, the recapitulation continues unabated.

"I just can't gain control over it," I say. "I feel helpless at this point, like a pressure cooker, my lid set to blow at any second."

"We'll do EMDR around it tomorrow," he suggests. "Keep doing what you're doing; at some point a breakthrough will happen."

"Okay, I'll see you tomorrow," I say, and then, out of sheer exhaustion, I fall back into bed and right into deep, dreamless sleep.

I wake up later in the morning in deep depression with so little energy I can barely pull myself up to a sitting position. The kids are still away for this holiday Monday and I have no pressing duties. All I want to do is stay in bed anyway, but rather than sleep again, I decide to meditate the pain away. As I breathe deeply down into my body, I discover that my painful legs have lost their usual form. Fused together into a mermaid's tail they float now, rocked by the strong pulse of the ocean waves. I am bound in scales, highly protected in this inhuman state. There are no openings or slits, no human vagina to be peered into, violated, or abused. The fishtail creeps up to my breasts, encasing me. I am a sexless floating being, lulled by the ocean swells, calm and newly strong. And yet I sense danger. My abuser is nearby! Forcefully, I slap my tail on the cresting sea, sending a mighty wave in his direction, catching him off guard, tipping him out of his boat. Can he swim? I don't think so. I strike him with a single mighty swing of my heavy tail, knocking him unconscious. I decide to finish him off, and so I clamp my tail fins around his neck and fork him to the bottom of the ocean until he drowns. He's on my turf now, and I'm in control. In this ocean of mind, I can commit murder and never have to account for it. We all have a dark side.

I force myself out of bed. I go to the video store and rent *SPLASH* with Darryl Hannah and Tom Hanks, the mermaid-human love story. It takes me out of myself for a few hours and when the kids come home in good moods my own is much lighter as well. Happy to settle back into their new rooms and routines, they nonetheless arrive home with piles of homework still to do. At first I'm angry that they didn't get it done while with their dad, but soon find that their bustling presence offers further distraction from the wearing intensity of the weekend's recapitulations.

By midnight, all is quiet, though I can't sleep, as usual. My legs burn with residual cramping, though not nearly as intensely as before, the mermaid's work quite effective. As I seek sleep, the prospect of finally working through some of this stuff with Chuck in the morning lightens my heart.

January 21, 2003

I'm ready to speed this stuff up, to get it moving through my body. Without a moment's hesitation, I take the EMDR pods from Chuck. Holding them tightly in my hands, I sit stiffly, with clenched body and clenched feelings too. Every time Chuck prompts me to relax I'm able to let down my guard a little bit. As I let go, in incremental release after incremental release, I feel how sore my shoulders, stomach, and hip muscles are from all the clenching I've suffered through over the past few days. Chuck calls the whole thing a "fascinating process," my body clearly holding back what it has habitually held back, with no idea how to do otherwise. I agree that the process is fascinating, and scary at the same time, but it's only through his suggestions to relax that any visible change happens. Without his prompting, I can't imagine there would be any significant breakthrough, as the only recent breakthroughs I've experienced have been the shattering kind, which feel like some kind of seizure. By the end of the session I feel quite limp with relief, my body much emptier than it has felt in a long time. Before I leave, Chuck suggests I strengthen my ego and my physical self in a new way now, by speaking, writing, and meditating on empowering statements. I must ground myself and remain strong as I continue this journey to the end, he says.

I am good. I am strong. I am powerful.

I have no energy to go to the studio and so I decide to take a few more days off to rest and regain strength, to indeed empower myself. I intend to break all my old rules, rules of an old world, such as: I can't possibly stay at home and watch a movie in the middle of the morning in the middle of a workweek, but that's what I do. Afterwards, I take a long hot bath. Then I try to get some sleep. *I am good. I am strong. I am powerful.*

The kids come home happy at the end of the school day and soon settle into doing homework while I prepare dinner. I take them out to karate class and then drop them at play rehearsal. With time on my hands, I pick up my pen. I allow myself to be open, to "see what happens," as Chuck tells me the shamans are fond of saying.

I am good. I am good.

Undertow

Do I believe it yet? Am I good?

With still another few hours to go before I have to pick the kids up, I set to work painting the newly primed living room walls. As I roll out the colors, I allow sadness to emerge from deep within, to crawl out of the old tunnel of self and mix with the paint. In this moment, I can do nothing but this. I *must* allow the sadness of my child self to be painted into the walls. Then, letting more sadness seep out through the tip of my pen, I write again, as Chuck suggested. Though it may not empower me to declare this sadness, it is the bitter truth of where I am at this moment.

I am sad. I am sad.

I go out into the cold night and drive the empty roads to the school. Exhausted, the kids fall asleep quickly tonight. The cats meow, circle around on top of my bed, and finally settle in at my feet. Perhaps they sense the loneliness I feel, the sadness that now dries on the walls, letting me know I'm not alone. A little while ago, I even had a sudden urge to cry, feeling that it could finally burst out of me, that the floodgates could open now, but I didn't know how to lift them and get the flood started. I need another vacant day, so I intend on staying home again tomorrow, soaking up the energy of my new house and the truth of my aloneness, my sadness, my childhood, and my Holocaust-like past. My abuser's fiendish experiments, that he so meticulously planned and performed, were no less calculated than what Hitler's doctors did. I need another day to contemplate my other life as Slave Girl, that long-ago-forgotten other self. Old feelings emerged today, strong feelings that I floated in and out of all day on the ocean of this recapitulation. I felt Slave Girl in every release of pain, in every clenched muscle that I asked to relax, in every word I wrote.

Am I good yet?

January 22, 2003

In a dream, there's a war on; a synagogue and a school building are being destroyed, bombed to smithereens. I watch them disintegrate into a pile of rubble and then I see them rebuilt, like watching a film running backwards, everything viewed in reverse. However, the reconstructed buildings are entirely different from the red brick ones that got blown up. Now glowing and shiny, they're being rebuilt with gold. Golden brick after golden brick is laid down by hand. At the same time that I watch this happening, I can't comprehend that these are actually the same synagogue and school going back up, until a child points it out to me. "It's the synagogue and school! That's what we've been watching and talking about the whole time, dummy!" I am stunned still. But as soon as I understand that the new golden synagogue and school are emerging from the rubble of the old brick ones, I know that the children will be safe now. We take a tour inside and it's like walking into a museum. I see familiar things from the past: toys, games, furniture, etc. Then I see a huge pile of dog shit curled up on the floor. "Oh yeah, dog shit everywhere; there's still that problem," I say, and then I notice that animals have indeed soiled the floors. There is shit literally everywhere, though no one else seems to notice it. I also notice that the building isn't complete yet. There are huge gaps in the walls and ceilings. I'm confronted with this beautiful building, the gorgeous ornate exterior, really extravagant and rich looking, made of gold, yet an inside that is far from complete, the floors covered with animal feces. Even so, in some strange way, there's something immensely satisfying about it.

Then I dream that I'm at my grandparent's house with my elderly aunt and my daughter. "Oh no! Oh no! Oh no!" my aunt suddenly shouts, as she points to a note lying on a table in another room. The three of us climb through a very narrow and difficult passageway to reach the table with the note on it. My daughter arrives first and picks up the note, which reads: POLIO.

I awaken from these dreams, caught in a memory. Nothing I do will release me from it, no sword forms or yoga or breathing in cold outside air. I get the kids up and off to school and then return to bed, drawn by the heaviness of the memory begging to be recapitulated. As soon as I lie down, I go into a full body cramp. I am no longer in my bed. I'm in the hunting cabin where my abuser often took me, locked in a large dog cage. My abuser has taken my clothes and put me in the cage with only a scratchy blanket on the floor. Then he crawls into the cage with me and fucks me like a dog. I don't feel anything. I have no body. I am nothing except a head swirling with fear and sadness, swirling in blank nothingness. Somehow able to reach for the phone, I call Chuck.

"I can't feel anything! I need help!" I say into his answering machine, my voice sounding unfamiliar, cracking, distant and very childlike. "I can't move; I can't get out of bed! Please call me back. Please call me. Please help me! Please, please, please, please, please!"

"I'm stuck in a cage. I can't feel my body, it's disappeared. I don't exist," I say when Chuck returns my call within the hour. "I want to feel something! Tell me what to do and I'll do it. Just tell me what to do!"

"What I want you to do," he says very calmly, "is breathe into your chest—deep breaths! Just breathe and fill yourself with breath. That's it; just breathe slowly and fully into your chest. Now extend it down into your stomach area, until you fill your entire torso. Now into your legs and arms. Do you feel anything?"

"Yes, my legs hurt."

"I know. Breathe, breathe, and breathe."

"I'm going to try and sit up," I say, desperate to be sure I've broken through the somatic memory.

"Okay," Chuck says, pausing, waiting for me to sit up. "How did you do?"

"I'm sitting," I say, greatly relieved.

"Good," he says, sounding relieved as well. "You got caught in the memory, caught in the cage."

"It was easy to escape my body, but much harder to return."

"Well, you learned very quickly how to do that as a child; you learned early how to escape. But none of it exists anymore," Chuck says. "He doesn't exist, the places don't exist, the cage doesn't exist; none of it is here anymore. It only exists in memories, but they are very real to you, and when you get caught

46

that's real too. Even though he can't get you, you can get caught in the memories, because the feelings and the memories are stuck in your body. But just remember, he can't get you."

"Okay, I'll be all right," I say. "Thank you."

He can't get me. He can't get me. He cannot get me, I remind myself. *He cannot get me. He cannot get me.*

I take a long bath and just sit in the tub, lost somewhere between here and there, pondering the experiences I've been having lately. It's like being tossed by the ocean waves. Unable to gain any footing, I am dragged down by the undertow and then spit out upon the shore only to be dragged right back in as each memory emerges. In spite of the dizzying, drowning qualities of this process, however, I feel the stirrings of excitement as I wonder where this recapitulation will go next, though right now I'm so weak. My energy depleted, I feel like I'm just getting over a devastating illness.

The significance of the polio note in my dream has not escaped my awareness, its dire warning encouraging me to prepare myself for more encounters with paralysis as I continue this recapitulation. I picture the golden buildings of my dream and know that the dog shit inside represents memories such as the one I've just recapitulated and the many more that still reside unrecapitulated inside me. My dream was letting me know that I'm doing good work. The rebuilding has begun, the future golden structure is going up, but there's still more to do. A lot of details, big and small, still need attention and release. As I put everything I've learned together, understanding, merging, resolving, and healing from it all—as I reconstruct who I am—I do see the mindblowing quality of this recapitulation process and the golden work I'm doing on myself. As Chuck likes to say, this is powerful stuff!

I'm lost for the rest of the day, wandering around my small house, doing one thing or another, trying to settle down, but in reality the day is lost. Night comes and I already know that tomorrow too is lost.

January 23, 2003

In a dream, I'm with some people who have a two or three-year-old child. I'm fearful for the child and try to keep it in sight as we hike through some woods and as we go rock hopping beside a stream. The child is jumping so unsteadily. I'm afraid it might fall into the water and possibly hit its head. I think the parents are too casual, that they don't see the dangers. I try to enjoy being in the woods, but I'm on heightened alert, constantly drawn to watching the child, ready to grab it. It's as if I already know that something bad is going to happen. I am just about to yell, "don't touch that tree," when out of a dead tree springs a huge spiky ball. It immediately leaps on the child and devours it whole before breaking into a dozen little spiky balls that hurtle in all directions. Like a vicious mob, the spiky balls threaten the rest of us. Now I'm aware that none of us are safe. There is a spiky ball present in every situation, just waiting for someone to brush up against it.

The venue shifts and now I'm on a train and I know that the spiky ball is here too. I want to get off the train before it attacks, as I have no doubt that it will; it's just a matter of time. A man with a guitar is entertaining his children and I warn him to watch after them. I plan on getting off the train at the next stop, even though it's not my stop, because I don't want to witness the devastation. I just can't bare the tension of knowing exactly what will happen. Before we even arrive at the next stop, a child brushes against a spiky ball and is instantly devoured. I notice that this ball is smaller than the original one that devoured the child by the stream. There is total chaos as everyone on the train scatters from the torrent of smaller spiky balls that immediately spring from this child-eating ball. The train finally pulls into the station and I manage to pry the doors open so we can get out. People are screaming, but all I can think about is that you have to be so careful. The spiky ball is everywhere. Don't get too close to anyone or anything because it might be the spiky ball!

The venue shifts again and now I'm walking with a group of people through a dark town, looking into the windows of the houses we pass, watching people going about their lives, unaware of the spiky ball always lurking nearby, ready to gobble their children. We settle into a rundown old mansion. We dig for archeological finds, remnants of the original property owners. We find little alabaster cups and vases, some of which are quite ornate. My find is a simple but elegant, perfectly shaped, alabaster bowl, as thin as eggshell and small enough to hold in my cupped palms. Even while I admire this beautiful little bowl, I am aware that the spiky ball is present somewhere in the mansion. I'm cautious, digging carefully, but I'm aware that others are too casual. I wish I could be like that, free of fear and just having fun, but I can't relax because I'm aware that the spiky ball is just waiting to make its next move. Before long, just as expected, it leaps out of a rotten corner of the mansion when a child walks too close. I hear it being savagely devoured. About the size of a basketball now, the spiky ball doesn't break up this time, but stays in one piece.

Next, I'm in an outdoor market working at a bakery stand, slicing and serving pies, cakes, and bars. My aunt and uncle come along and choose some lemon bars from the goods I'm selling. While I work, I keep glancing at the pecan pie on the left, aware that the spiky ball is inside it. I cut the lemon bars. "Do you want ice cream?" I ask. And then it just slips out and I ask, "And how about some pecan pie?" I'm really surprised that I've suggested this. "Yes," they say, "yes, we would like some pecan pie." Again I can't believe what I'm about to do. "Why am I doing this?" I wonder, as I very carefully cut into the pie. I know the spiky ball is inside this pie, so why am I daring myself the risk of brushing up against it like this? But then, all of a sudden, I realize that I'm an adult and that the spiky ball is now small enough to fit into a slice of pecan pie. I could crush it with my bare hands! But the fear remains as I hand platefuls of desserts to my aunt and uncle and give them two forks. "Enjoy!" I say, but the spiky ball never emerges.

I awaken in the protective fetal position that I slept in all night, my hands clenched tightly under my chin. I realize that this

Undertow

nightlong dream is all about this recapitulation process. It's about the gradual diminishment of my old fears and the power they once held over me, as I gain a new perspective on my life and as I discover why I've operated the way I have. Indeed, I'm an adult throughout the entire dream. Fear, in the form of the spiky ball, diminishes as the dream progresses, just as it's been diminishing during this recapitulation, but I'm always conscious of its power, and how watchful and cautious I must be as a result. Even as it grows tiny I remain fearful. It doesn't really have any power left, as I am no longer a vulnerable child. It can't get me anymore, just like my abuser can't get me. In working intently on letting go of fear, in all its manifestations, I've been taking back my own power. Next time, rather than dream of the power of fear, I must dream instead of my own power, for I am powerful!

I am powerful. I am powerful.

Even though I write and speak this *powerful* mantra I stay in bed again all day. I don't have the energy to face the world. I get up to eat a little, but immediately get right back under the covers. It's frightening thinking about being anywhere else.

While lying in bed my thoughts go to the commitment I'd made to do some artwork for an erotic art show. I wonder if I should withdraw from the show, or go ahead with the full body print I've been thinking of doing. I decide to do the artwork as part of my therapy, as part of this journey of reclaiming and recovering my physical self, my body.

January 24, 2003

I dream that I'm riding on a school bus with people I knew in childhood. The bus gets stuck in snow, as was often the case along the windy back roads in the rural area I grew up in. I watch as rough looking men with thick ropes pull a trainload of cars, also stuck in the snow, along railroad tracks that run parallel to the

50

road. They clear the train lines before they finally come and pull the bus out of the snow too. As we take off, I look out the back window of the bus and see the black tracks left by the bus in the white snow. I see the train riding along its rails, parallel to us as we zoom away, its tracks two black lines as well. My abuser's daughter, also riding the bus, comes looking for me. I try to ignore her. "What's a matter with you? You used to be my friend," she whines. "Why don't you like me anymore?" As soon as she says this, the bus turns into a train. Abruptly, I turn away from her and walk to the front of the train. I intend on getting off at the next stop. No longer interested in looking back, I'm only interested in moving on.

I wake up clenched again, my stomach in a tight knot. It's still the middle of the night, but I am hounded by pain. Oh God, are there still more memories? I wake up four hours later to extreme cold. It's below zero outside and the house is chilly. I get up and crank up the thermostat before getting the kids up for school.

When I meet with Chuck I can't help but whine about the state I'm in, depressed and sad, in the grips of a submerged memory. It pushes against my muscles seeking escape, seeking to make itself known, the pain unbearable.

"I don't even know what it is, but I'm so frightened and all I want to do is stay in bed and hide under the covers," I say. "The memories have become like diseases that invade my body and take over. I'm too tired to fight anymore. I don't want to see anyone, go to work, or do anything. All I want to do is roll up in a ball and stay home in bed, disappearing down that tunnel of self, that old place of childhood safety. It still feels safe. I could stay there for days, weeks even."

"You are powerful! Don't let the memories overpower you. Don't get stuck there," Chuck warns me.

"I am stuck! I can barely get myself up and out of the house to buy groceries. The kids are the only reason I'm still functional. They need me to be their parent; and *that* I can still do, but as soon as they leave the house I go right back to bed."

"Listen to my voice," Chuck says rather sternly. "You have power! Step back and view what comes, but don't stay stuck in it.

Observe. You can do it. It's the past; it's not now. It's just a memory."

I wonder if my dream of last night is asking me to confront my abuser's daughter in some way, whom I have not seen or been in contact with in decades. Perhaps I need to reconcile something with her.

"What would you say to her?" Chuck asks.

"You hurt me and I don't want to associate with you. You make me uncomfortable and I don't like what you do to me," I say, letting my little girl self lead the conversation. "I don't want a relationship with you. I don't want to be connected with you in any way. You are not safe to be around. I feel threatened by you. You did awful things to me. I don't care that you also suffered. Right now I only care that I was hurt. I'm sad and angry, and very unhappy about the things you did to me and taught me. I was very hurt by it all, and I still feel hurt."

"Okay, good," says Chuck. "Is there anything else you'd like to say?"

"Not at the moment, but I feel angry."

"Remember that when you leave here, and a memory comes, you have to find some way to stay grounded in the here and now. You can't risk getting caught and stuck back there again. You need to remind yourself that you are here now, an adult, many decades later, and that it's just a memory."

"I can do that," I say, as an intensely sharp pain suddenly grips me.

"What's happening?" Chuck asks.

"Nothing," I say, hunching against the pain, afraid to mention it.

I hobble out to my car and go home to bed. I stay there for the rest of the day, until the kids get home from school.

January 25, 2003

In a dream, I am trying on new jeans from a rack that stands on the side of a road. Each time I select a pair to try on, I step out into the middle of a busy intersection where two highways meet and put the pants on. Cars come from all four directions. I move out of the way as they pass, then step back into the center of the crossroads again. I repeat this scenario numerous times, selecting a pair of jeans, going into the intersect to try them on, stepping out of the way. Even though I try on many pairs of pants, they are all wrong in some way. After a while I don't care anymore. I don't even move out of the intersection when cars come speeding past. I just stand in the road, unselfconsciously trying on pants, totally ignoring the people driving by.

Once again I wake up in pain, my legs so taut and aching that I can barely get out of bed, the dream note that warned of polio still fresh in my thoughts. I sense that I'm not experiencing a memory, but a deeper sadness and loneliness, hiding like a parasite in my body. And even though I finally slept well last night, I awaken completely exhausted. Fighting off sleep and depression, I drag myself out of bed, drop the kids at their karate class, do the Saturday chores and some food shopping, and then crawl back into bed. I know the kids will be home soon, being dropped off by another parent, but I figure I can get a few minutes of sleep in before they arrive.

My dream stays with me. As I recall what it felt like to finally give up all pretenses, to totally let go of self-consciousness and experience a new kind of freedom, I give myself permission to stay in bed as long as possible because I don't care what anyone thinks. But the truth is that all I want to do is sleep; I can't get enough of it.

January 26, 2003

In the middle of the night I awaken in pain. "It's just a memory. It can't hurt me now. He can't hurt me now," I tell myself, but I can't deny that the pain is real. It's not fake pain, it's REAL PAIN. All my scars are hurting down there, the scars from birthing two children, and other scars I may not even know about. This is the kind of pain that stays around for a long time, until the memory fully emerges, which may happen quickly or take weeks. As I lie in bed, wondering what's happening, the pain fills my entire body. It flows right into my hands and feet, down into my fingers and fingertips. Arching through me like a jolt of electricity, my hands clench into tight fists and my toes curl under. I hear

Chuck's voice telling me that it's okay to relax, to let it go, it can't hurt me anymore. But it does hurt; it hurts until it's done. "Breathe!" I hear Chuck's voice say. "Breathe!" Yes, I need to breathe, even if I feel the heavy weight of my abuser on top of me, even if he's suffocating me, even if I think I'm dying, I must breathe. I must breathe into this memory of imminent death so I can go on living.

Eventually, I fall back to sleep and into a dream. I'm standing at the backdoor of a hairdresser's shop. There are many roads that lead to the shop, but from the backdoor only one is visible, a very long road that comes from across the fields that stretch for miles behind the shop. It's an old farm road, with fencing along both sides and grass down the middle, a quaintly picturesque country road. I see it winding away, far off into the distance. I notice how empty of traffic this old road is; no one uses it, while the other newer roads that lead to the shop are busy with traffic. People come into the shop through the front door, taking the busy modern roads to get here, but I am drawn to stand at the backdoor and ponder this old country road. Every now and then I call into the shop and ask the owner where the bedrooms are. She points out across the fields, but all I can see is an old barn. She tells me that the bedrooms are inside the barn, through one of the doors, but she can never remember which one until she's standing right in front of them. As I gaze off into the distance, I see the outline of the barn and the shapes of the big barn doors, but I just can't believe there are bedrooms inside. I ask the shop owner if she's ever been inside the barn. No, she hasn't. I see that the barn is partially covered with vegetation, overgrown with trees and bushes. Every time I look out toward it the sun is shining and the barn is so hidden that you'd have to know it was there to see it.

I wake up unhappy. The barn in my dream, though in the distance and in such an idyllic setting, looms mysterious and threatening, both in the dream and as I wake up. Although I'm standing in a place of transformation and makeover—at a hairdresser's on a modern busy road with traffic flowing in all directions—I am so drawn to what's in the background. I just cannot take my eyes off the barn at the end of the old farm road. And so I wake up with a sense of dread, knowing that sooner or later, I'll have to go into that barn and find out what's in there. The heaviness of that old barn weighs upon me, so much so that I don't care about anything else, not even doing the artwork that I'd promised for the erotica show. I don't care about going to yoga classes, about running—which I haven't done since I moved—about eating or even showering. I don't care about anything at all. I just want to hide under the covers.

I'm aware, however, that movement alone will get me unstuck, that I must shift away from the dream and its heaviness. I replay Chuck's calming voice telling me what to do: to breathe, to move, to sit up, to get out of bed, to eat, to make my way through the day, to let it go through me. And this is how I get through the day. I constantly replay Chuck's voice reminding me to keep moving so I don't succumb to the paralysis of memory.

By evening I'm almost manic, the unhappiness of the earlier part of the day replaced by a sudden burst of creativity as I set about doing the full body print that I had planned for the art show. While the kids are out with friends, I cover my naked body from shoulders to knees with blue paint. Working quickly, before the paint dries, I lie down and press my wet blue torso onto a canvas that I've painted a beautiful orange. When I stand up I'm surprised at the result, my body slightly distorted. I thought I'd look more real, but there I am, a rather illusory shape, not fully formed yet. While the canvas dries, I shoot some photos of my painted body in a full-length mirror.

"A study of the female figure in blue, neck to knees," I say, clicking away. "Now that clearly looks more real, more feminine, and not bad either!"

The depression dissipates as I work and before long I'm actually feeling pretty happy, fairly contented while engaged in this creative project. All of a sudden, I realize I'm having fun, being somewhat daring. I chuckle over my children seeing the painting and wondering about their crazy mom, asking their friends: "Sooo...what did *your* mom do last night?"

I have a heck of a time getting the dried acrylic paint off, first standing in the shower scrubbing it off with a plastic scrubber and then soaking in the tub, which ends up covered in bright blue flecks. It takes me quite a while to clean up the mess, but by the time I'm done the depression has totally worn off and I'm noticeably exhilarated. The creative process was not only a great distraction, breaking the stagnancy of inertia, but it also gifted me with a new appreciation of my own body. In daring to expose it, I'm ready to finally declare that I exist and that I am clearly female. For the first time in my life I accept that I have a beautiful feminine body and I'm proud of it. Oh yeah, and it belongs to me alone!

January 27, 2003

Monday morning dawns, another snowy day and another two-hour school delay. It enables us all to take it slow. I appreciate the extra morning time, as my night was, as usual, incredibly tense. Aware of my physical body holding back and holding in, I countered it throughout the night by constantly shifting my sleeping position. Sometimes I'd achieve release, but I'd invariably wake a few minutes later to find myself curled back up in a tight ball again, the next round of pain coursing through me. Once again, I'd unfurl, stretch my legs out, and turn over. In an endless loop I slept, woke, shifted and then slept, woke, and shifted again throughout the night. I began to notice how there was pain in the holding and pain in the release as well. Now, as I write these words in the light of day, I feel something beginning to build again in my scars down there, achiness and pain washing through me again, clumps forming in my throat, tension knotting my stomach. I understand now that this is pain formed both from holding in so tightly, as well as pain directly related to a memory in need of release, asking me to let it go, to cry out all that I hold inside. The tension that sets in now and fights against the idea of release is as fierce as the old tension that's been holding the memories back.

I return from shopping barely aware of where I've been and what I've been doing. My body went through the motions of walking up and down the aisles of the grocery store, but I wasn't really in it. I wake up to find myself in this body every day and even as I notice how normal I look and act, I'm also aware that I'm barely present. As I'm putting the groceries away I hear a knock on the door and when I open it my parents are standing there—a surprise visit—come to see the house, they say. I put on a fake smile and invite them in, wishing I wasn't home yet.

My mother is tight and hard, too cheery and bright as she inspects my little house, while my father stares vaguely, saying nothing. I have no living room furniture for them to sit on and so I pull out some kitchen chairs and they perch uncomfortably on them in the empty living room. They've arrived just before the kids get home from school, which I'm thankful for, and luckily I'm up and about rather than just emerging from the grogginess of my cocoon bed. I serve tea and cookies, the kids joining us soon enough. We sit stiffly and chat about mundane topics until they leave.

As soon as they're gone I head straight to my bedroom to meditate while the kids retire to their respective rooms to do homework. Sitting comfortably on my bed, I lean into a fat pillow. A deep in-breath immediately triggers a recapitulation. Instantly, I balloon up and out of my body. From my new vantage point, high above my bed, I sense something happening, not pain per se, but an unwelcome intrusion taking place in my body, which lies far below me. Rhythmic thrusting eventually triggers a fuller memory of my abuser raping me anally. I talk myself through what's happening, hearing Chuck's voice too, coaching me to stay with the physical memory, to capture all of it so I can be done with it. I stay floating up there in balloonland—that part's easy—but I stay connected to what's happening in my body as well. I'm equally aware that it's only a memory and that it isn't happening now. I'm able to maintain a sense of detachment that allows me to study the many layers of the experience, and I'm fully aware that I can come out of the recapitulation whenever I'm ready. I like it up in balloonland; it's peaceful and there's no pain or clenching, though far below me I'm aware that my body is suffering terribly.

Coming back into present awareness, I notice the weight of my body and the old tension long ago deposited in my muscles by events such as the one I've just recapitulated. I feel slightly lighter and somewhat exhilarated by the experience itself, but also keenly aware that residual trauma still remains. I realize that seconds ago, when I was up there floating like a balloon, I could feel the motion of my abuser raping me, though no pain was detected. As in previous out-of-body experiences, I once again sensed my body as an empty vessel, while my conscious awareness safely floated above it and thus no pain was detected. However, there is no doubt that I've been encountering the pain of those rapes every day since they happened. Stuck inside my body, I have borne them in somatic experiences for decades. Most recently apparent are the intense pains that jolt me awake at night, that keep me tossing and turning, that keep me a slave to the fetal sleeping pose.

I now know that it's in *conscious* release that I will finally release the pain encapsulated in the memories, ultimately leading to freedom from this lifelong suffering. This is what Chuck has been teaching me. This is what recapitulation is all about. But I am only fully grasping this as I go through these experiences in full conscious recapitulation. As I finally understand the pain for what it truly is, I'm able to release it from my body and psyche. This release in full awareness leads to blissful freedom, which I have experienced, if only briefly.

As I emerge more fully from this recapitulation, I wonder what else I could possibly need to convince myself that these rapes did happen. Are my memories, somatic pains, and recapitulations not enough? I answer my own question: *Experience is everything!* I must allow myself to fully accept the truth. No matter how barbaric and cruel the abuse was, and no matter how deeply ashamed I am that these things are part of my personal history, the abuse happened! *It happened, it happened, it happened!*

I struggle with the changing view of myself that I must encounter each time I go through another recapitulation, as I repeatedly face how different I actually was from other, more normal girls. Though I don't like thinking of myself as different, I have always felt so awkward and uncomfortable in both my skin and my life circumstances, as if I was born into the wrong century. My lifelong wish to just be normal underscores the truths revealed by this recapitulation, for indeed I have been quite a strange and different kind of being. During memories of being with my abuser as a teenager, I must have said to myself: "This is not normal," but by then it was far too late; I'd already been trapped in his world for years. I couldn't have escaped had I tried. The only thing I could escape from was the truth. Too difficult to face, I did what I could: I *forgot* and then *pretended* to be normal.

I find myself resisting the memories because although they reveal my deepest truths they are likewise stealing so much from me, especially the "normalcy" I worked so hard to create and uphold. In essence, the memories are destroying my known life—

pretend though it was—coercing me into accepting a new reality. It's as if I've been handed photographs of unknown people and places and told that this was my life, while the known pictures that I've carried with me for my entire life are snatched and ripped to shreds. I shatter each time this abrupt shift in reality takes place, as the tattered pieces of my life flutter to the ground. Looking down at the remnants of my past, now lying scattered at my feet, I struggle with the truth that the normal life I strove so desperately to uphold was false, just as the little girl I became was false, conjured out of the deeper need to somehow survive the horrors of the woods and the man she encountered there. While the false little girl lived in one world, playing at normalcy, the real little girl hid in the caverns of the tunnel of self, for all intents and purposes lost and forgotten, her reality too annihilating to uphold. It became imperative for her to remain in hiding, I see that now, but I don't need to do that anymore. I don't need to hide anymore.

I don't need to hide anymore. I don't need to hide anymore. I don't need to hide anymore. I don't need to hide anymore. I don't need to hide anymore. I don't need to hide anymore. I don't need to hide anymore. I don't need to hide anymore. I don't need to hide anymore. I don't need to hide anymore. I don't need to hide anymore.

I write this sentence until I believe it—almost.

As this recapitulation progresses, I realize that I somehow gleaned how shameful and morally wrong the world of my abuser was. Even at a very young age I became aware that I had to keep hidden all that happened there if I wanted to appear as normal as possible. So, in the reality of the normalcy I invented in order to survive, nothing untoward actually happened to the false little girl that I became. *Nothing happened!* False girl has been in control. In fact, she met my parents at the door today and pretended that everything was okay. That's been her role, and I have to admit that her lifelong dedication to the creation of normalcy has gotten me where I am, and so she has every right to protest this sudden emergence of another powerful little girl, bearing a different truth. She is being challenged to give up her façade and accept the truth that indeed something did happen, and that is quite shattering. In addition, neither false girl nor real girl had the wherewithal to face the truth of what was happening to them in my abuser's world and so they colluded, actively protecting each other, maintaining a sense of wholeness by suppressing the truth. If nothing was remembered then *nothing happened*, and thus no one would ever know how evil and sinful I really was, for that was the real truth behind the deceptive actions of my little girl selves, a deep sense of having sinned greatly.

In contemplating the little girl I once was, I am stunned by her powerful ability to stoically withstand all that happened to her, physically and mentally holding up under the most shattering of experiences. While false girl ruled in one sense, real girl ruled in another, for her ability to remain silent reigned supreme. She protected the secrets as fiercely as false girl pretended normalcy. With the deeper secrets concealed, and false girl in control, there was never anything wrong with me. I never admitted to being in any kind of pain. Even under the most dire of circumstances, or when suffering serious injuries—such as breaking a bone, having surgery, or receiving cuts that required stitches—I'd declare that I was fine. No tears were shed; not a crack in the façade was detected. But now I find that there was plenty wrong with me. Now I'm not fine at all.

I understand that I not only need to fully recapture what actually happened to me in the past, but I must remain open, nonjudgmental, and compassionate. I must become a fully loving and emotional being. Although I am discovering the secrets of my past and the two false selves, I must accept that they created a life that was livable, and so I must thank those little girls for all they have done for me. In spite of how false or hidden my real experiences were, the life that emerged out of my trauma enabled me to grow into adulthood, and so it was a real life after all. I was, and am, both of those incredible girls. Their decisions, made under great duress, have kept me alive.

I must also figure out how I'm going to continue dealing with the repercussions of things that happened decades ago—put on hold until now—while remaining totally present and active in my current life. How do I go forward while simultaneously going so far back?

I'm also finding that the recapitulation has a tendency to take over, to zap my energy, and with it go my defenses and my ability to handle it, complicating matters exponentially. It's easy to slip into the past at this point in the process, as I've said to Chuck countless times. I just close my eyes and go there. As soon as I feel the pressure of a memory emerging, I'm gone, tumbling down into the past as if I'm falling headfirst into the churning sea. In no time, I forget that I have any power at all. I forget that I can be an active participant in the process instead of its victim. It doesn't have to overwhelm me, but when I'm exhausted it simply takes over, like last week. I was so lost I couldn't swim out of that undertow of recapitulation without help, while today I went there and kept my head above water. I got through it, though now I'm exhausted again. I can do nothing more than lie on my bed like a beached whale, out of air and energy.

However, I've been more grounded lately overall, sitting on shore with only my feet in the waves, far from where the undertow churns. I'm sleeping better, eating better, and I'm even feeling better too, less depressed, although at times I've been fearful of going too far in the other direction, into mania. When I did the body print the other night my imagination was lit on fire by a surge of creativity. So urgent and all-consuming, it was hard to tell if it was just normal creativity hitting hard after languishing for days in the undertow, or if I had indeed gone mad. They feel almost the same.

January 28, 2003

I dream that I look inside a closet and see a baby standing on a high shelf, a happy little girl in pink pajamas. As I stare at her, she walks right off the edge of the shelf and falls to the floor, landing with a big CLUNK! I don't make a move to save her. I'm so exhausted that I can't even lift my arms to catch her; it's simply too difficult. I have no desire to save her anyway, even though I see that she's going to fall and get hurt. I stare down at her rolling around on the floor, trying to get up, hurt and broken. I notice that she isn't making a sound and yet I just cannot react or feel any compassion for her.

I wake up shaking, upset at my total lack of emotional response. I realize how coldhearted it is to leave her like that, especially after yesterday's determination to be more loving and compassionate, and so I fall back into sleep with the intention of fixing the dream. This time as she rolls off the shelf, I catch her easily, a happy baby in my arms.

Undertow

I'm already edgy at six in the morning, exhausted before the day even begins. It's very cold out, below zero again. I have a great desire to crawl back under the covers, but I have to get up. I have to meet with Chuck and then deliver my artwork for the erotic art show. The large body painting and one of the photos that I've framed are due at the gallery today. I didn't like the look of the body print at first, but now I'm quite fond of it, pleased with the prospect of the new me beginning to emerge, being displayed in a public venue.

I'm depressed when I meet with Chuck, bombarded by so many unfamiliar feelings and emotions, worried they might mean something bad about me.

"Maybe I should stop trying to figure them out, stop judging and just allow them to exist, and be fine with them," I say. "Perhaps that's the lesson for the day."

Even though I say that, I immediately begin to question why I did the body print. It's pretty clear that I need to validate my physical presence. This is part of the process of learning to accept my physical body, reclaiming it as my own. But I must face the question that arises: Is it inflated to put my body on display?

"I do exist in the here and now. I am a woman, and I like my body," I say. "I like it enough to expose it on the walls of a gallery. It's part of discovering who I am. It's part of my journey of growth and transformation, and it's definitely a critical moment in my life. It took a lot of deep inner work to get to the point where I could do this. I had to like myself pretty well. I'm ready now, and so I declare: I exist, I own my body. I like my body!"

After my session with Chuck, I bring the artwork over to the gallery. The curators are excited by the vivid body print and are especially intrigued by the photo, which I'm still unsure about exhibiting. They prompt me to leave it with them, saying they'll hang it next to the canvas.

"If you feel it's right," I say, and then I turn and walk away, my decision made.

I drink a lot of coffee during the day, not sure why I'm doing it, except for the vague notion that I want to keep feeling something, anything. In spite of where I got to with the artwork—

62

boldly feeling like I've finally reclaimed my long lost body self—by the end of the day I'm empty and weak again. My sudden inflation abruptly deflates and all the caffeine in the world can't pump it back up again. I wonder if I'm regressing to an old place where access to my feelings is blocked, and other things as well, the undertow dragging me down into the depths of the smoldering sea again. Why do I still feel so separate from the memories and from my physical self? Why do I feel like the memories hardly happened to me, to the real me? Why can't I totally believe them to be the true story of my life?

January 29, 2003

I wake up clenched again, wondering how I'll ever break the habit, wondering if the memories will always remain in the tissues of my body like polio, or if they'll only break their stranglehold once I've released the stuff that's stored in them. Or am I destined to live with the constant reminder that things were once different?

Though I wake up in pain every day, physically suffering through the intensity of my traumatic past, I've lately enjoyed the process of discovering that I do have a real body that feels nice to be in. In fact, lately I've been experiencing myself as more than just a stiff unfeeling board. I've always hidden myself, both from myself and from the world, my physical body and my private inner self kept tightly sealed off, essentially declared nonexistent. It's as if I've gone through life carrying a sign declaring: "I'm not really here, just ignore me!" In fact, I've always felt so much better when I could blend in or, better yet, disappear completely and go totally unnoticed. To be vague and unseen was my cover, yet also a safe means of being in the world, as invisibility affords protection. At an early age, I learned that to be seen is to be abused. Now, however, as I dismantle the internal and external walls and break through the old taboos—finally facing my child self and all that she's been so protectively holding in—I'm able to face the outer world in a new way too, declaring that I do indeed exist.

"Look at me," I'm saying in the thrill of discovery, "I am something to behold." I saw an appreciation of this new bold self when I brought the artwork to the gallery. I saw how intently the women curators stared at the photo of my naked self. "Wow, you are beautiful!" they declared. Yes, thank you. I am beautiful. I *am* beautiful! And it isn't just a narcissistic declaration, for there is a growing sense that I'm being met and appreciated in a new way, for my honest and genuine manner. In return, I find that I'm not so afraid of life anymore either, nor so subservient, for as I am met in this new way the world grows increasingly less frightening. Doing this body art has propelled me forward. And I'm aware that as I move onward I leave a different kind of footprint behind me now. Pressed firmly into the ground it shows just how real and present I am. This body print is my declaration of existence, as I reclaim and validate myself in a new way, in a new world. "Here I am," I'm saying, for the first time really. "I exist."

January 30, 2003

I dream that I'm visiting a house I grew up in. My children are present, as well as some friends, a married couple with their young daughter. We notice a strange little girl in the laundry room. She's kneeling on a low bench, like a church kneeler, a height of about four inches off the floor. She faces the back door leading out to the deck. She has long dark hair and she's wearing a long garment of dark grey or brown, the quiet, muted colors of a monk's robe. She appears to be praying, kneeling perfectly still. We all speculate about who she might be, dubbing her "the Saint."

I step out of the dream at this point and instinctively understand that she is my spiritual child self, my eternal innocence, and that she is here for a reason, although I'm not quite sure what that might be. After the delivery of this insightful knowledge I return to the dream. The little girl ignores all of us, as if she's deaf and blind, staying in her kneeling position, hands in prayer, with an intense aura of light and purpose surrounding her. I tell the others that we must leave her alone until she's used to us, and that she'll join us when she's ready. Unable to sleep, I wander around the house all through the night, checking on everyone, including the Saint. The husband of the married couple can't get comfortable either and finally ends up going downstairs to the basement room that once belonged to my brother who died. His wife tells me that he's having a hard time settling in because their young daughter is so restless. I go downstairs to check on him too and notice that there are piles of dog poop on the basement floor. When I peek into the little room that was my brother's, I see that the husband has settled comfortably into the mattress that's lying on the floor. I notice that the room is packed up, with boxes piled high, most of the furniture stacked. The husband hears me at the door and asks about the Saint. "Is she okay?" he asks. "She's still kneeling in the laundry room," I say, which seems to satisfy him and he falls back to sleep. Before going back upstairs I clean up the dog poop.

After what seems like a long time, the Saint comes out of the laundry room. She joins us, playing with the kids, accepting a lollipop, and speaking a little. Intermittently, she returns to her kneeling position as if recharging, gathering strength. At the end of the visit she walks off alone towards the woods, heading for the path that leads to my abuser's property. I run after her, telling her that she doesn't have to go there, pleading with her to stay. She has to go, she tells me as she turns away. With her back ramrod straight, she very deliberately walks into the woods. I step out of the dream at this point, and hear this spoken very clearly: *You know she has to go and that she'll survive; she is the embodiment of your own inner strength.* And then I'm back in the dream again, aware that she is a spiritual being of unlimited goodness, that she's strong and extremely brave, that she has some kind of internal protection, and that she can handle anything that comes her way. As I watch her walk so bravely into the woods, I am overwhelmed with love and gratitude, filled with the deepest compassion and affection for her. I completely understand why she has to go back into the woods. She has to confront whatever is before her; it's her journey. I know she's destined for it, but also that she has a spiritual holiness, a saintliness about her that will protect her, no matter where she goes and what she encounters.

I dream a second dream in which I'm riding in a car. After a long trip the car pulls up in front of a large mansion. I get out of the car and knock on the door, but there's no answer. I wait around, sitting in the car, returning over and over again to knock on the door, waiting for someone to respond. Finally, I decide to just boldly enter the house. Once inside, I wander up and down many hallways, trying many doors, looking for something, though I'm not sure what that might be. I look into many empty rooms and eventually end up in a room full of naked men. I'm naked too. The men attack me, but I fight back, taking them on one at a time until I've defeated them all. I'm strong and fierce, indefatigable.

I awaken from these dreams with a deeper sense of my own journey as destined and necessary, leading me along an evolutionary path that goes far beyond this one lifetime. More deeply aware that everything that has happened to me is necessary and appropriate, I recognize the strength and utter calmness of the little Saint as residing deep inside myself, just as the fierceness of the fighter in the second dream resides inside me as well. I am both warrior and spiritual being and I know that these two aspects of myself are being rediscovered, fully accepted, and brought forth into new life.

I head out to a yoga class hoping to get some relief from the tightness and clenching that I constantly battle, intent upon finding a means of annihilating the tension stored in my body. Like the men in my dream, it hides within, ready to jump out and attack without a moment's notice. We do third chakra work, releasing the will power from the solar plexus, releasing the hold on old issues and ideas. How appropriate! Afterwards I hear from Chuck that his father-in-law, Jeanne's father, has died and that we have to postpone our next session. He gives me sound encouragement as I face the next memory.

"Remember, you will get through it," he says. "Whatever the memory is, you will get through it, just like you always do. No matter how difficult it feels when you are in the throes of it, it will end, and you will be all right. Just like all the other times, you will be all right. You will make it through this experience; you will get through it."

"Yes, I will."

The tension returns again a mere few hours after the yoga class. As night approaches, I am once again in a full-body clench, my fingers tender and achy, my legs taut with pain. Each attempt to fall asleep sends me deeper and before long I'm rolling in nail-biting, drooling pain, my crotch on fire. Drifting in and out of sleep, I am constantly awoken by the intensity of new flare-ups, until I'm just a stiffened and charred body, incapable of turning or shifting out of the fiery hell I find myself in.

January 31, 2003

I wake up and immediately go into meditation, seeking distance from the ever-present pain. Floating upward, I find myself in familiar territory—balloonland—where I instantly gain peace. Though my body far below holds the pain, I detect none of it, and for a few blissful moments I hover, aware that I must soon return to my body and face what's waiting for me there. I let myself stay out of harm's way for a little while and then slowly make the transition back.

I am greeted by the usual pain as soon as I reenter my body, though nothing else comes, no images or memories. Again, I return to balloonland, hoping for clarity and the peacefulness of no pain. I notice that my body—left behind—is like a pillow, full of cotton stuffing or something equally dense and unfeeling. I'm aware of its existence, but I have no feeling of ownership or connection to it; it simply is. As long as I stay in balloonland I receive a much-needed respite and so I gladly accept the challenge, though I know I can't stay here forever. I hang on as long as I can, until thoughts intrude. Awareness that I must get the kids up for school pops the balloon and I tumble back down into the body sitting on my bed, right back into the clutches of pain.

As the day progresses, I notice tenderness in the third chakra that received such attention during yesterday's yoga class. Energy continues to stir there, releasing a sore lump from the stale confines of my newly awoken solar plexus. The lump rises slowly all day, gradually making its way higher, until it settles in my throat, a leaden crying lump, heavy with sadness. Crying is probably the one release I desperately need and could benefit from, but the tears will not come and my tight throat will not relinquish its stranglehold. I'm aware that it chokes off access to other feelings as well, for I sense them lingering in the depths of me, waiting their turn. Sitting in meditation offers some soothing and softening, but the tightness remains.

By the end of the day, I notice that I'm generally feeling less depressed and I ascertain that the increased dosage of Paxil must have kicked in. My head feels a lot lighter than normal, though I'm slightly headachy. I'm a little shaky and yawning a lot, which is a little weird, but otherwise I'm okay, though I still have no real appetite. I wait for what comes next.

Chapter 2

My Heart of Darkness

February 1, 2003

I dream that I'm making food for a baby. I put the food into small attractive dishes and heat them, one at a time, in a microwave oven that I've stashed away in a closet. I even prepare a bottle, just in case none of the other food is attractive to the baby. I'm doing this in a closet because the man I live with doesn't care about the baby. He doesn't want to hear about or have anything to do with her. I'm careful to not confront him about this baby, but I'm also electing to ignore his sentiments; I do as I wish. Carrying the baby food, I go outside and across a green field. The baby is in the woods, the dark woods on the far side of the field. I must keep her placated and happy at all times; I don't want her upset or crying. She's dependent, needy, and wants only me to take care of her. Besides, no one else knows what her true needs are.

As I come out of this dream, I realize that the baby is stuck inside me and I can't—or I won't—let her out, even though I'm in tremendous pain from holding her in. My episiotomy scars, from having given birth to my own two children, are achingly sore as I wake up, underscoring the truth of this insight and the weight of this phantom pregnancy. My muscles contract and my body clenches in mock labor at the mere thought of giving birth, but it's a birth that isn't going to happen because I'm not letting the baby out! I'm afraid that if I let her out she'll leave me forever and I won't have anything left inside me to take care of. I'll be an empty carcass, with no purpose or reason to live, as I've spent my entire life caring for this baby inside me. I'm equally afraid that after such a long gestation period she'll be born dead or deformed, or she'll cry incessantly and I won't be able to comfort her. Once she's out, I fear I won't be able to give her what she needs anymore. But on the other hand, when she's born, maybe I'll finally be able to comfort her the way she needs to be comforted. Maybe we can finally get through this recapitulation, understand the past together, and move on. Maybe I can love her better when we aren't hurting so much.

So I guess I do want the baby to be born. The labor has gone on for long enough and it's time to enter the next stage: *the release of the baby*. I'm actually preparing for the baby in my dream, but in spite of all the preparations the baby still lies buried in the dark woods, waiting for me to go get her, to give her new life. Yikes! I just realized that my periods have synchronistically stopped, as if I'm truly pregnant! The clenching contractions and the scar tissue pain of old births strike again as I write these words, underscoring the reality of this deep psychological process.

Intent upon easing my discomfort, I get out of bed. Feeling large and cumbersome, I waddle around the house as if I'm actually at full term, my arms encircling the fullness of my phantom belly. It's still early, too early to call Chuck, though I desperately need to talk. I wait until a decent hour, and when I finally call he answers immediately and suggests that I don't push it, that I don't give birth alone.

"If it happens spontaneously, then okay," he says. "You'll get through it like all the other memories and recapitulation experiences, but better to not push or rush it."

In the evening, I go to the opening of the erotic art show. It's my turn to work the night shift. The place is quiet when I arrive, but quickly fills up. Before I know it, it's packed with a crush of people, male and female, a combination of cross-dressers and costumed partyers mixed in with the normal gallery crowd. I only get through the night because I'm extremely busy; running around making sure everything is running smoothly, putting red tags on sold artwork and processing transactions. I don't have much time to mingle, but I do get lots of compliments from strangers and friends alike as they stare at my body prints.

"Nice body!"

"Nice boobs!"

"You look really great!"

"Thank you!" I say, happily accepting the compliments, appearing slender and thin in my black outfit, my inner pregnancy neatly tucked away.

February 2, 2003

I'm a baker in a dream, selling my wares at an outdoor market. I have no shoes on, though I'm standing outside in deep snow. Although I'd searched for my shoes earlier, I'd finally given up, deciding that "getting there" was more important than having shoes on my feet. I decide that I'll be proud of my bare feet as they've always gotten me where I've needed to go. I discover that my abuser's daughter is in the booth next to mine and that she's selling similar items. I also know that she stole my recipes. My goods sell well, while her sales are slow. We speak briefly. I tell her, quite frankly, that her stuff is bad and that she should do something else, that she just doesn't have the knack for baking. I tell her that I know she's jealous and only doing it to compete. This incites her ire and competitiveness. Later, one of her customers comes to my booth and tries to return a small pie, saying it doesn't look like the other ones I have for sale and she wants to exchange it. "Just by looking at it, I know it's not one of mine," I say. "It was made by the woman in the booth next door. You should return it there."

I was aware during the dream that dreaming is reality and reality is a dream, and also that dreaming has taken on a whole new meaning now. My dreams are increasingly vivid, as real as real life. There is no difference between worlds anymore, the lines have blurred. I am lucid all the time. I dream constantly—awake and asleep—and everything is significant, part of this recapitulation and part of life itself.

It's Sunday morning and I don't want to get up. All I want to do is curl up, go back to sleep and dream a new dream. My bed offers a warm place to disappear into, to nurse my wounds, to hold myself together as best I can. I get up, make coffee and bring it back to bed with me. The cats, not wanting to be disturbed either, are happy to curl up at my feet once again. The room is dark and quiet, conducive to my depressed mood.

I give in to my inertia. I just can't get myself out to take a walk or go to my usual Sunday morning yoga class. I can't muster the energy to do anything requiring being in the world, and with the kids away at their dad's for the weekend I have no duties. So I stay in bed all day, sleeping until five in the evening when I'm jolted awake, caught in the throes of a new memory. Rather than allow it to take over and swamp me with its insidious ugliness, I go to battle against it. I get up! I move!

I get out of bed and do yoga breathing to support my physical body to withstand the waves of recapitulation, and then the shamanic sweeping breath to aid my memory and keep me in balance. Floating on a sea of awareness, I know that eventually I'll have to go deeper still into the inevitable process, allow myself to get dragged into it by the undertow, but for the time being I'll keep things under control, thank you very much!

February 3, 2003

I dream that I'm involved in a survivalist game. I stand on a busy sidewalk in New York City with other contestants. At the signal to begin, we run across busy intersections right in front of traffic, dodging cars, crossing street after street, putting our lives at risk. Sometimes I'm quick, light, and agile. At other times I run in slow-motion, heavy dream-running that is incredibly frustrating. I also can't see very well, my eyesight blurry, though I always succeed in getting where I need to go. Some of the people in the group, however, get crushed by the speeding cars. Those of us whom have survived must now face the next dangerous challenge: crossing railroad tracks without getting struck by the trains zooming by. There are many tracks to cross and many trains to dodge. Once again, some people don't make it. Each time I see someone die, I pause momentarily and empathize deeply, but then I move on, for I know I must not stop; it would mean the death of me too. In the final challenge, we must climb down from the rooftops of tall city buildings, down the outer walls to the streets below. Again, some people die, panicking and plunging to their deaths. I climb down slowly, inching my way along ledges and windowsills, feeling for handholds and footholds between stones and bricks on the faces of the buildings. Intent upon survival, I keep my wits about me. Very patiently and calmly, focusing my attention on where I'm placing my hands and feet, I carefully make my way to the safety of the street below.

I wake to find myself lying flat on my back, my spine a column of steel. I'm fully aware that it represents my solid inner strength, that I can handle anything, even challenges similar to the ones in my dream. If I do let go, even in the metaphorical sense of letting go to life's unfolding—as I am being challenged to do as I undertake this recapitulation—I know I'll be okay because of this strong inner core. In comparison to how I used to think—that I would just melt away into nothingness each time I faced another memory—I now know that I can handle anything, in any world. I also know that I will survive this recapitulation, just as I once survived the abuse. Furthermore, I'm gaining a better sense of who I really am as the recapitulation unfolds. Chuck told me this would happen, that I would regain my own energy and that a new, real self would emerge, a true self. I realize that I'm not just a survivor anymore; I've gone way beyond that now.

Somehow I'm able to shift out of steel spine mode and get the kids up and ready for school. Afterwards, I think about all the things I'll get done, but I'm so cold that I crawl back under the covers...to get warm...for just a few minutes. When I wake up it's two hours later and my room is ablaze in light. I'm fully awake, yet my body lies totally inert, heavy with paralysis. My vision, however, is extremely sharp and vivid, my awareness keen. From an incredibly lucid vantage point, I watch, transfixed, as a detailed retrospective of my life plays out before me in brightly illuminated scenes. As if crystal prisms are spinning in front of my eyes, my room fills with twirling diamond-faceted light, and my entire life flickers before me in shimmering scenes, as real as can be. I recognize every detail of my recapitulated memories, and yet it's as if I'm seeing everything clearly for the very first time.

Spellbound, I watch, as scene after scene overlaps, as years overlap years, as all the events of my life stream before me like a documentary film. The action speeds up at times, as if the movie is on fast forward. At other times, the scenes slow down and the details hang suspended like 3D images, clearly visible for deeper contemplation, everything etched in white light. I have the sense that although I'm watching this movie, I also *am* the movie—I am the producer and the projector—it's all coming from me. But I am not the me I know, not the everyday me, but a totally different being. Totally lacking in physicality, I am consciousness alone! I am a numinous being full of wonder and light, without attachment to anything in reality, without fear or worry. Whenever thoughts go to my body, I sense it lying inert on my bed. I find that I can take deep breaths and pause the action for a few seconds, but I can't totally reenter my body or stop the movie. Any attempts to shut it off are repeatedly rejected. In fact, a simple thought of stopping this most dazzling film immediately pulls me right back in again, and the scenes speed up, as if warning me that I don't really have any control at all. As the movie plays, I know I must experience the whole of it—it's absolutely necessary.

For three hours I tumble around inside this incandescent world, completely alert and awake, yet unable to enter my body, which lies stricken and unmoving on my bed. I'm fully aware that I'm being treated to something mystical, something resplendent and out-of-the-ordinary, and I don't, for a moment, doubt its realness. Without fear, I simply have the experience, taking it for what it is: a full-length movie version of my life thus far lived, vividly played out for my personal enjoyment, viewed with utter clarity and comprehension. By the time this crystal storm is over I'm vibrating. My entire body aches, even the roof of my mouth is sore. It's as if I've been struck by a bolt of lightning, the power of it leaving me trembling and charred. Many aftershocks reverberate through me long after the lightning strike is over, and yet I find that I haven't disintegrated. I'm still in one piece.

Wrapped in the afterglow of this numinous experience, I lie exhausted on my bed for a long time, the residual tremors rippling through my body in small jerks and twitches. As the truth of what I've just so clearly observed sinks in, a deep-seated sadness envelops me. I know, without a doubt, the fuller truth of my past now, having been revealed in its entirety, as clear as day. I am as certain of the abuse as I am that the sun will rise and illuminate the world each day, the same way the crystal light came into my room and illuminated my recapitulated memories.

I review what was so vividly revealed to me until it's time to pick up the kids from their afterschool activities. It's easier to step out of the magic of my sensory experience and into reality than I imagine. However, as I drive off to get the kids, I discover that the real world is ablaze too—vividly etched in the same brilliant white light that had been in my bedroom—and my vision is still crystal clear too, exponentially improved in the past few hours. I remember how annoying and frustrating my dream was last night, my eyesight so fuzzy that it was often difficult to see where I was going, but here I am now, living a totally different dream, granted luminous vision.

February 4, 2003

"I'm in the throes of this recapitulation for better or worse, married to the process," I say to Chuck as I describe my numinous experience. "It's practically taken over my life. The process is constant. I'm dreaming all the time now, seeing so clearly. There's no difference between night and day; everything has merged, the past with the present, waking with dreaming. Dreams are reality. Reality is a dream."

"You're *seeing* energy as it flows in the universe," Chuck says, pointing out that, from a shamanic perspective, I've been experiencing the world as it really is. "You seem to be flowing well with it."

"I had no fear when I was in the throes of the experience," I say, "nor was it frightening to see the world all lit up either—it was magical! But even that magical experience pales in comparison to the intensity of the work I must still do, because I'm so fearful of what I must still encounter as I go back into the woods with my child self. She's really in charge, asking me to follow her deeper into the woods to deal with what remains. That's frightening!"

I'm slightly frustrated that I'm unable to speak of what's happening in my body while I sit with Chuck. I'd arrived at his office quite agitated, but he's so calm and calming that I almost immediately calmed down too. As soon as I leave, however, everything revs back up and I drive away angry that I hadn't been more honest when I had the chance. Sometimes it's so much easier to talk about my dreams and the magical wonders I've experienced during this recapitulation than it is to confront what's really going on inside, or to talk about feelings. And so, what I refused to speak of churns away inside me as the day progresses. I gag on and off. Soreness in the back of my throat persists, as memory sensations that started in the night seek emergence. I try not to focus on what's happening in my body, but I can't help wondering if all the memories will appear now in the same manner as they did yesterday, projected before me, replete with spectacular visual effects.

Part of me is interested in pushing this recapitulation, facing the horror and wonder of it all at once, getting through it as quickly as possible because I want it to be over. I contemplate shutting myself off from the world, going into seclusion and letting the recapitulation take over and spin its vivid tales of wonder like it did yesterday. I keep thinking that if I push it, I can get back to my life faster, my *new* life.

February 5, 2003

I dream that I'm a lonely woman, alone for the first time in a long time. I walk sadly through an empty house that sits in a little courtyard, overcome with exhaustion and feelings of emptiness. Then I'm a new bride. I've just gotten married to a man whose face I can't see. We drive into a small courtyard and get out of our car. The man picks me up to carry me over the threshold of the house we've borrowed for our honeymoon. A lonely woman is standing in the courtyard watching us and I realize that she's me, the woman I was in the earlier part of the dream. Now I'm in two places at once, the happy bride but also this tired, sad, and lonely woman. As the bride, I see the lonely woman watching me and I don't want to hurt her feelings by looking too happy. I want to hurry the ritual of being carried over the threshold so I don't have to be confronted with her loneliness and sadness, which I feel so deeply.

Two aspects of self are simultaneously experiencing and observing each other in this dream, the old self and the new self. I'm aware of the deepest needs and feelings of each of them, the lonely emptiness of the sad woman and the happiness of the new bride. But then, as the bride, I'm also aware that I want everything to be flowing and balanced, because I can't stop this new life from happening and I don't want to either. In fact, I want to hurry the process along just like I wanted to hurry the recapitulation yesterday. I want to be carried over the threshold quickly. I want to be a happy bride, full of enthusiasm for my new life, living without restrictions, but I'm sensitive to the old self. I don't want to dismiss her feelings, which are equally legitimate. Since I'm in two places at once, I'm in a bind. I must decide: Can I allow myself to be happy in this marriage, or do I still owe allegiance to the lonely, sad woman? This is exactly where I am now in this recapitulation process. Can I keep moving forward into new life and allow a little happiness in, while I still have so much to deal with that is devastatingly sad and disturbing? Can I be in two places at once, still the old me emptying out and yet also the new me seeking greater fulfillment? These thoughts alone seem to act as triggers, and before I know it I'm caught in memories again. Feeling like the bride on the threshold, I call Chuck and leave him a message.

"I'm going to push this! I want to finish this stuff and move on. I can't stay here like this, it's taking too long, and I'm tired of it. I can't work or care for my children the way I want to. My own needs are usurping the needs of people around me. I have a busy year ahead of me with several art shows to prepare for, and I have a living to make. I want this finished. I need to push this so I can get on with my life. I'm going to force it and I'm going to force myself to endure it!"

I hang up the phone and immediately go into a vivid recapitulation, as illuminated as the other day's experience was, but this memory is all-encompassing; I am no longer just a projector. Now I am the actor in a true reality series, suffering intense physical pain. Clenching and grinding my teeth, I lie back in bed, where I've been for most of the day. I become a child again. Pressing my legs tightly together, I gag repeatedly. My head throbs, as if about to explode. My abuser's penis is in my mouth, his finger in my ass. I can't breathe. I am smothered.

Eventually the experience releases me. I sit up choking and coughing, unable to catch my breath, in somatic pain—my anus throbbing, my mouth and lips chaffed and sore, the physical memory vividly real. There is no denying what I always knew, that I was on my own from the very beginning. My life was my own nightmare to deal with as best I could. This is what comes to me as the memory blitz ends. I'm not bothered by it again, though my mouth, throat, and anus bother me sporadically with phantom sensations throughout the afternoon, letting me know there's residual memory still to recapitulate.

At the end of the day, with the kids working on homework and the dinner dishes done, I finally take some time to sit and meditate on the memory. Going back into it repeatedly, I do the sweeping breath until the tension, pain, and terror of it completely evaporate.

February 6, 2003

My son, sick with the flu and a 103° temperature, sleeps in today. I get my daughter off to school and contemplate what I woke up thinking about earlier this morning: shame, and the child inside me who continues to carry it around like a heavy boulder. I'm pretty sure the adult self let it go a long time ago, but the child self sneaks into the adult world at times still bearing this heavy burden. She plunks it down in front of me and says: "See! It's still here." I peer at this big boulder of shame that she drags around and immediately experience spontaneous separateness from this child self. With utter clarity I understand that *she* is the one who so tightly rolls into that fetal position every night. Clutching all the pain and shame, she's still very much alive, residing somewhere deep inside me, while I—the adult—have gone on into life. I've grown up and done a lot of adult things, distancing myself from her as much as possible in order to do so. Now, I clearly understand that I went on so I could one day return to this moment, so that I could one day be in the position I'm in right now, intent upon rescuing the child self still inside me and, in so doing, rescue myself.

Until today, I've had such a difficult time seeing and believing myself to actually be more than one being, fearful of what that might mean about me, perhaps that I'm crazier than I thought. But only in acknowledging that I am many beings simultaneously am I able to embrace the crystal clear insight that right now, in this moment, hits me: *fragmentation is a valuable skill!* I've simply not been in a position to fully embrace this insight until now. In fragmentation, my fully present adult self is able to step outside the memories and, from her current perspective, carefully and sensitively guide my child self. I realize that in so doing I'm finally able to reciprocate what my child self once so protectively did. When she fragmented, the memories were repressed, and I was allowed the opportunity to grow up. Now my adult self is using fragmentation to reunite all my lost selves. It's very clear that fragmentation is an important tool with a valid place in the healing process. I see this as an evolving aspect of the recapitulation.

As I continue to hone the use of this skill, I imagine that all of my parts will eventually merge. As my adult self joins forces with my fragmented child selves—my sixteen little girl selves—and grants them each an opportunity to express themselves, they will no longer be alienated parts, separate from the whole. Once each part has told her tale and been fully acknowledged for both her pain and her bravery, another part will link into this healing process; another part will find its way home. Clarity and wholeness will eventually come, as new ideas and new perceptions about life in general, and the past in particular, are accepted and assimilated too. It's really the job of the adult self now to make all this happen, to introduce the guidelines, for only she has the wherewithal and the stamina to take on this final, monumental task. It's what I've been preparing for. She must nurture and prepare each of the fragmented selves now too, make them welcome, as she invites them into the inner circle of the new self. It can't happen without a strong adult presence—a loving, respectful, and compassionate self. That kind of maturity is key to the success of this whole process.

My dream of simultaneously being the sad woman and the happy bride finally makes greater sense. In that dream I was two parts in conflict, as of yet unreconciled, each struggling with their separate trauma-related issues. The fragmented parts must meet each other as I go through memories and dreams, and somehow find a means of reconciliation. I have not yet achieved wholeness, though I see it now more clearly etched as the goal of this journey: *to bring my fragmented selves together*. Sometimes, however, the physical aspects of the memories—unbearable pain and the sense that it's happening right now—make it impossible to be the stable, mature adult self. At such times, all I can do is acquiesce and go where I am taken by the child inside me. I'm aware that I'll return with something of value, even though such journeys taken by the unaccompanied child self may also slow the process. Lately, more often than not, I'm rescued by the memory of Chuck's voice calling to me through the fog of countless EMDR sessions. "It's not now, it's a memory," I hear him saying. "It did happen once a long time ago, but it's not happening now, even though it may feel like it is. It's not happening now."

My job is to take this recapitulation forward to fruition. Am I to live a sad life like the woman in the house of emptiness? Or can she merge with the new me, the happy bride expectantly looking forward to new life? I eagerly await the unfolding of this process and the salvation I expect will come as I do this work, as long as I have the stamina. When I'm exhausted I tend to get stuck;

I become like my child self, rolled around that big boulder of shame. Lately, I've envisioned her residing in my third chakra, nestled below the sternum. When she's in pain, my solar plexus aches and winces along with her, the muscles on either side clench and unclench like labor contractions. Am I going to finally give birth to my own inner child as I suspect? Am I going to set her free? Will I be able to facilitate that birth more quickly now that I've acknowledged our separateness? Will I have to give birth sixteen times, to all of my abused child selves?

I understand that I'm the only one capable of helping this poor child self, so tightly clenched and afraid. I long for the days when I'm no longer held in the grips of her fear, no longer a slave to her memories. I fully get that I must take this journey on my own, that I must be my own anchor, though I look to Chuck to provide an anchor as I encounter other worlds, teaching me what to look for, tethering me in reality as I focus on the work at hand. I'm more aware of my physical body as my vehicle through life too, and that this reality is truly my place to be at this time. I'm reminded again of why I'm doing this: *to find my lost self, to become who I truly am, to become whole.* And so I plant my two feet and keep my eyes focused on the mission—*to heal.* With Chuck's guiding voice, his sound judgment, his encouragement, and the shining light of his shamanic teaching, I intend to get there. "Go on, you can do it!" I hear him saying, a twinkle in his eye. "Keep going! See what happens!"

As a very young child, I decided that my parents had only a small part to play in my life. I clearly established that I would and could handle everything that was expected of me and everything that happened to me. By the time I was three I had already distanced myself from them; I didn't need them. I was capable, self-sufficient, and extremely independent. I never even stopped to consider that it should be any other way. So I don't invite them into this re-birthing process, nor do I intend to invite them into my new life. I further detach energetically from them, as I firmly state: *This is about me, separate from everyone. This is about my inner struggles and my deepest needs to live my own life, and to evolve.* I feel different as I write these words, as I let my parents go, and as I release myself from wondering any more about the role they played in my life. I accept that they are simply the way they are, and that they will continue to choose how they live their own lives.

I'm not responsible for them, though I'm fully responsible for myself and my own life. I'm fully responsible for imparting as much wisdom and knowledge as I can to my own children, with the intent that they too will one day fully engage their own inner processes and take their personal journeys to fulfillment. I wish for them to be eager for life, without fear or worry that they're doing something wrong. There's no wrong way to live life, as I've discovered, though it has taken me a long time to realize this. In the process I've learned that only a deeply personal journey is right for me, the inner journey. If I am to heal and really make my life meaningful, I must remain on my path, the seeker's path. As I take this ever-deepening journey into the workings of the innermost self, this path has proven to be of the utmost importance.

As I energetically let go of my parents, I face that I must one day let go of my own children, even as I expect them to let go of me. It is my greatest wish that I not burden them with my own agenda or my personal issues or needs—nor even my energy, good or bad—but that they might achieve total freedom from me. I wish only to set them free to live to *their* fullest potential. We each have to follow our own paths. And so, I declare that my parents are no longer part of my journey; I detach from them. I'm going it alone now. I do not owe them anything, nor they me; we are separate beings taking our separate journeys. I shed another burden by compassionately letting them go, energetically achieving such relief, considerably lightening my load. As I think about letting everything go in this energetic manner, one aspect at a time, I venture to hope that I'll eventually be free enough to live, love, and enjoy this new life I'm creating.

The ultimate creative act is reinventing the self!

February 7, 2003

I dream that I'm making home repairs, replacing broken faucets, patching walls and getting ready to paint. People are amazed that I can do all these things myself. There's even a hole in a wall that a man warns me against patching. "It can never be completely repaired," he says. If I repair it, I'm told, there will be no breathing air left inside the wall.

I wake up choking on construction dust, the heavy weight of a body smothering me, my dream reality once again intersecting waking reality. I'm aware that I must face everything that arises during this process of deconstruction and reinvention, including every fear. As the man spoke his warning, I immediately felt like I was suffocating. Now however, upon awakening, I see his role as that of a trickster. He inserts a note of doubt, questioning if I really want to renovate so completely, implying that my child self will suffocate and die in the process. But in the true reality of the dream, I'm the one making all the repairs. I'm taking charge of changing, and doing it quite well indeed. He represents an old world, where healing isn't an option, but I'm detaching from that old world more and more each day. There is no going back. As I repair my deepest wounds, my child self *will* heal with me—that I am certain of. I have no intention of leaving her to suffocate behind those old walls. All the walls are coming down!

It's a snowy day and no school. I check on my son—still sick but sleeping soundly, as is his sister—before heading out to meet with Chuck. I drive slowly through the gently falling snow, everything covered in white, brightly etched in light, not unlike my recent numinous experiences. We talk about my fragmented selves and how to utilize them to my advantage as I continue my recapitulation. Watching the snow falling outside the window reminds me of the construction dust in my dream and I tell Chuck about it and the fears that arose regarding my inner child self, the fears of suffocation posed by the man in the dream.

"The child will always be there, but needs to feel safe," he says, "needs to let go of the ball of shame and hurt, and understand that she can let it go and be a happy and safe child within you."

I nod in agreement.

"You've been protecting her, since that was all you could do at the time. Now you also need to realize that with separateness comes the responsibility to parent her, to stop simply protecting, and to work with her to be free, to allow her to have all the innocence, without shame, that every child deserves."

After the session, I enter the silence of the snowstorm. It's darker now, the clouds leaden and low, the snow falling more rapidly. I drive slowly home, once again experiencing a changing reality, a new world as dreamlike and magical as my nighttime dream world. I go back to bed and sleep for an hour and have this dream: I give birth to two smiling baby girls. I love them right away. They make me very happy.

I watch movies with the kids all day, including the original *Wizard of Oz* with Judy Garland, which has a powerful tornado scene at the beginning, causing a shattering of reality as Dorothy enters an alternate universe. I notice that although part of me is present with the kids on the sofa watching the movie, another part of me spontaneously and naturally turns to doing inner work. That part ponders again the needs and burdens carried by the child versus those of the adult self. I am certain that I carry childhood shame, not adult shame in my body and psyche. I don't think the adult has anything left to be ashamed of. Do I think the child does? No, but the *child* thinks she does. She's constantly reminded of all the shameful things that happened to her body, to her psyche, to her soul, all the brainwashing that resulted in her hating herself. That childhood burden has been carried forward into adult life. Now my adult self is learning how to love herself, and her body too, learning to let go of the shame still held onto so tightly by the child self. Convincing the child to let it go, however, is tough. "We don't need the shame; it wasn't our fault," I tell her, knowing I still have to prove to her that we're safe without it.

It wasn't my fault. For the first time in a long time this statement suddenly makes complete sense. I excuse myself from the movie for a few minutes to write this down, boldly stating: *It wasn't my fault. It wasn't my fault. It wasn't my fault. It wasn't my fault. It wasn't my fault. It wasn't my fault. It wasn't my fault. It wasn't my fault. It wasn't my fault. It wasn't my fault. It wasn't my fault. It wasn't my fault. It wasn't my fault. It wasn't my fault. It wasn't my fault. It wasn't my fault!!!*

Then I go back to the movie, the child self and the adult self both having been given what they needed for the time being.

Now it's nighttime and I'm tired, but calm. Not too much happened today; the weather kept us all inside, the recapitulation kept at bay by the presence of my children and my need to parent. I've been slightly lightheaded and shaky all day, as if I'm a confused Dorothy just waking up from her experiences in the tornado, wondering where she's landed. This morning Chuck insinuated that I'm probably not eating "properly," but he also acknowledged the impact of venturing into alternate realities.

"Don't underestimate the power of the experiences you're having," he said in warning. "Stay aware."

February 8, 2003

I wake up in a magical place, in a golden glowing world, bedazzled by rich hues. Light as a feather, I float in an ocean of flaming color and light, my spirit buoyantly happy. I lift my hands to touch the golden light and the magical world suddenly shatters as I drop with a thud onto my bed. What just happened?

I struggle to awaken. Now I see that the sun is shining brightly into my orange room, but for the life of me I still can't figure out if I'm awake or dreaming. Sitting up, I wait for reality to strike. It takes only a moment before my body is stricken with its usual pain and I'm fully back in it, and then I know that the light was a dream and I am aflame only with memory. I communicate with my inner child self, gently telling her that I need her to trust Chuck as we go through this recapitulation, for in spite of that moment of floating golden joy I sense her fear. I tell her that it took me a long time to trust him too, but now I understand how important it really is—*it's essential to the process.*

I get out of bed and force my stiff legs to walk, bringing me right back into everyday reality. I am aware, however, that nothing else in my life is of such great importance as this recapitulation. I can't concentrate on anything else anyway. My old world has shattered, my routine is shot, my focus not on work or business or creating art, but only on healing and becoming whole. Most days now I go back to bed as soon as the kids leave for school and I don't get up until they need me again. I don't eat much, perhaps drink some coffee, eat some toast, an apple or two, drink water throughout the day. I make a little dinner, but even that has been relegated to simple meals, because I don't have the energy to cook or attend to anything except in the most minimal way. I worry that my kids are suffering. Their lives have already been torn apart, and now they don't have a mother, for I am so distant, though I hold their innocence and their own sorrow in my heart. I know this is a very tough time for them too. I do the best I can, pulling myself out of bed and back into the present when they get home at the end of the day, but the depression tugs at me, calling me back under the covers, and as soon as I can, I respond. I let it carry me down into the muffled darkness beneath the warm quilts where the cats curl at my feet and the world disappears.

I spent the day tending to my children. Now it's late, the kids asleep, and I have time to attend to my inner child. Strange and complicated feelings arise, begging for attention, as I bring up the topic of trust. I note her usual cautiousness and wonder if I needed to always be so frightened and alert in order to be certain of where I stood with my abuser, heightened awareness necessary as a means of understanding and gauging the relationship. Perhaps, in the presence of such a madman, only a habitually abused child could be fully aware of the circumstances and what was expected, how to react, and what was needed in order to survive. Only such a badly mistreated child knew what it meant to *trust* an abuser; to trust that a bad situation would remain as expected, and that the abuse would seldom deviate from previous experiences. Only a deeply wounded and abused child knew that she could trust herself to always be safe enough, even in the worst of circumstances, for she knew how to survive. In relearning what it means to trust now, my abused child self must discover that trust, at its root, has a positive connotation, that it's not based in negative circumstances as experienced in the past. I see that it's up to me to impart what I've newly learned about trust to that tightly curled up little abused girl hiding inside me.

"It was not your fault. It was never your fault," I say gently, hoping to alleviate some of her fears and worries. "He was a bad man. You knew that adults had power, but he used his power in an evil way, using your tiny body to act out his sick needs. He was bad, not you. He was evil, not you. You never wanted him to do anything to you, not even to touch you once. He touched you when you were even too young to say no, too young to understand. He used you from such a young age that you were absolutely helpless. You never had a chance. You couldn't even have understood what he was doing. He brainwashed you, telling you that you were a dirty little girl, and he put his finger in your vagina because he was manipulative and bad. He was bad, not you! You were a little baby and he was stealing your innocence from you."

"Now you have another chance to be reborn, allowed to be an innocent child with no interference again. No one will interfere this time. I will let you be free and childish because it's what you need and deserve. We both need you to live that innocent life. You don't deserve what he did to you; you never deserved that. No one does."

"I know he said that you were his slave girl and that you had to do everything he told you to do. But, you see, that was how he kept his power over you, an innocent little girl. And you were so brave! I am so thankful that you were as strong and as brave as you were because I'd never have made it to adulthood if you hadn't been. You saved us; your strength saved us. And, in spite of what he did, you survived! You, a tiny little girl, were able to survive some of the most horrible, painful, and demeaning abuses. You survived! And because you did, I was allowed to get away. I could become an adult, finally understand what happened, finally understand all that you did so I could survive."

"I'm so proud of you. You aren't a slave girl; you're a fierce warrior! You fought back with all the strength of the ancient gods, with all the resources available to you. You were brilliant in battle. As a tiny child, and all the way up through your teenage years, you fought back with all the tools and weapons at your disposal, and you did it with tools that most people don't even know they have. I am so proud of you!"

"I'm at a place in my life where I can now acknowledge what happened and what you did to survive, and I don't feel bad about being proud of you. I don't feel that I'm bragging or tooting my own horn, as my mother always used to warn against. "Oh! You're tooting your own horn!" she'd say, immediately implying that it was bad to feel good about personal strengths and talents. Well, it's time to toot my own horn! It's time for us to say that we survived because of our own skills. We're strong, intelligent, powerful and intuitive, and in the end we won! Not him; he didn't win anything. He never got to our strong and powerful core. He thought he controlled our body, but our body became like a robot, doing what he wanted in order to keep us alive. Our core strength was more powerful than any of his games. In the end, we won every battle and we will continue to win them now as we battle his evil for the last time, as we rid his sickness from our body and mind. His power over us has weakened. It's only the memories that exist now. We will go through them and let them go, let them float off into infinity the same way sound floats off."

"When we release sound it's gone, out of our mouths, floating off on the molecules of air, vibrations released. That's what we're doing with the memories now too, releasing them into vibrations and particles of nothing, into nothing that will ever hurt us again. If we keep them inside us, their power remains, continuing to frighten us, constantly hurting us, reminding us that we are not worthy of life. If we keep everything in, we'll be nothing more than a shriveled up clump of fear; we'll be nurturing a permanent tumor, allowing it to continue to grow inside our body."

"I implore you to open up now and let the pain out, let the pain out in sound, in talk, in crying, in screaming, in utter release. You and I have always been so quiet. We have kept sound in, tucked in with those memories for fifty years. We have to dig a sound tunnel now, open a passageway so the sound and the pain can flow out of us like a river. Let the sounds flow and cleanse us!"

"We can't feel guilty about taking time to heal either. Even the greatest warriors, when injured in battle, needed time to recover and regain their strength so they could go back and fight the good fight again. It's okay to be in need of care. It's okay to feel weak and tired; it just means that it's time to take a rest, time to heal. We're doing this for ourselves, but in the end it's also for everyone we come in contact with, because if we don't have strength and health then we won't be good for anything."

It's midnight as I finish my inner dialogue and I'm in pain again, the floodgates opening, just as I requested.

February 9, 2003

I'm with my two children in a dream. We're in a school building. I sense that there's something to fear and then water suddenly floods the building, rushing down the hallways. We go into a dry classroom, packed with people from my past, including my abuser and his wife. They're standing in front of a large window. Behind them I see that the entire countryside has flooded. I try to ignore them, but they're standing right behind a buffet table full of delicious looking food. The kids and I are hungry and I realize that I'll have to confront this old couple if I'm going to get us some food. They recognize me immediately and while I pour cereal into bowls they tell me that I have beautiful children. Now I'm angry. I decide to be perfectly honest. First, I pull my kids aside. Pointing out my abuser and his wife, I tell them that never, under any circumstances, are they to go into a room with them, especially the man. Then I go up to my abuser and tell him to his face what a despicable person he is. I'm nervous, tense, and in pain, but I tell him that I hate him, that I always hated him. The two of them look at each other and say, "Yup, that's her all right, just like when she was a kid, stubborn as a mule," and then they laugh loudly. I immediately flip into deep frustration and bitter anger that they aren't taking me seriously, that they don't respect me, and that they never had.

Frustration and anger suddenly give way to fear, as I feel myself collapsing, getting sucked right back into a negative old place. Now I'm deeply embarrassed and full of self-hatred, wanting only to shrink out of sight and get away from them. Suddenly, I notice that the water has risen even higher and is now flooding even this dry classroom. With great effort, as if my feet are clamped to the ground, as if fighting against a strong magnetic force, I drag myself away from my abuser and his wife, away from the old feelings as well. I grab my kids and take them out into the hallway where the water isn't as deep. Once there, I stand huddled against a wall, shaking with both exhaustion and relief at having escaped the negative energy of old.

I go from fear to anger to fear again in this dream. When my abuser and his wife scoff at me, haughtily laughing, I feel myself being pulled into their aberrant world, into old self-deprecation and feelings of worthlessness. I freeze like my child self did, unable to make a move to save myself. It's only with great effort that I'm able to drag myself away from them. I'm aware that the flooding waters could drag me down and drown me, just as my abuser and his wife's energy could overpower me. As I huddle against the wall in the hallway, I sense that they still have some power over me. Although I've successfully gotten away, fear remains. I can't help but wonder if the fear will always remain and if the pain will always be present.

I'm beginning to have memories of my abuser's wife being present during some of the abuse, more certain every day that she was involved in some of the experiences that took place in the house. I see my foot in a woman's pubic area, a woman holding onto my foot and masturbating with it. My foot is very small in these memories. Perhaps these are the memories that have been brewing, for something has been stirring in my body, in tension and clenching. Fear arises at this flash of memories. In addition, vaginal pain began last night and remained throughout the night, intense enough to wake me up several times. My hips, shoulders and neck are all painfully cramping as well today, and I have no appetite—I just want to stay in bed. It's Sunday so I don't feel bad about this desire. My son is still sick. I got up to check on him several times in the night, his coughing loud and disturbing. I gave him some more cough syrup a little while ago and now he sleeps quietly, but I'm exhausted.

I write **FEAR** in big black letters, ripping the page. **FEAR-FEAR-FEAR-FEAR-FEAR!!!** And then I fill a page with this additional admonishment, underscoring what I've been working on all week: *It wasn't my fault. It wasn't my fault. It wasn't my fault. It wasn't my fault. It wasn't my fault. It wasn't my fault. It wasn't my fault. It wasn't my fault. It wasn't my fault. It wasn't my fault. It wasn't my fault. It wasn't my fault.*

This is what comes next: *I am a survivor. I am a survivor. I am a survivor. I am a survivor. I am a survivor. I am a survivor. I am a survivor. I am a survivor. I am a survivor. I am a survivor. I am a survivor. I am a survivor. I am a survivor. I am a survivor.*

I accomplish nothing as the day progresses, staying in bed all I can manage. I get up every now and then to check on my son, his fever remaining high, his cough loudly hacking. Now my daughter isn't feeling well. I doze on and off throughout the day, occasionally reading, occasionally sitting with the kids while they watch television and play video games. I challenge myself to hold in the fear, which constantly encroaches, begging for more release. If nothing else, I pour it onto the pages of this journal.

As I contemplate last night's dream again, I'm aware that my abuser and his wife are not really paying attention to what I'm saying in the dream. They laugh and make fun of me, but the table of food is between us and I understand that it's more important to be healthy than to make my abuser and his wife listen to me or apologize. The important thing is to take care of and nurture my children, including my inner child—anything else is futile.

Once again, I acknowledge that everyone has made choices in how to live their lives. My abuser and his wife chose to abuse. My own parents chose to ignore the signs of abuse in their daughter. Kids forget. And yes, I did forget, but that was in order to survive. Now, as I go beyond survival and onto healing, I understand that if I'm going to acknowledge that everyone makes choices and is fully responsible for them, I shouldn't be angry or hate anyone involved. I'm not letting them off the hook, by any means, but I'm leaving them with the full burden of having to deal with the consequences of those decisions—and I heartily believe there are consequences for all involved. In so doing, I'm removing my energy from them so I can use it to take care of myself now. By not wasting my energy on others, or being burdened with continual attachment to others, even in blaming, I'm better able to deal with what happened to me, better able to find my way forward, and better able to heal myself. This is what my dream is guiding me to: *healing*. I must learn to trust myself on these discoveries. I don't want the negative energy of hatred and blame marring my positive work as I take this healing journey.

February 10, 2003

In a dream, I'm up on a ladder, painting a wall. I'm determined to keep working, but someone keeps yelling up at me to take a break. "Finish it later!" they yell. "No, I have to do it now. I'm not stopping until I'm done," I say, even though I'm exhausted.

In another dream, I'm at one of the houses I lived in as a child. There's a large party going on and many relatives have come to stay. I've given up my room so guests can use it. I'm trying to find a place to sleep, trying to find my clothes and personal belongings, rifling through dressers, wandering throughout the house looking for what belongs to me. A little girl needs me. I put her to bed, gently tending to her, but I'm still not quite sure where I'll be sleeping, and so I wander around searching for my place all night long. Everyone else has a place to sleep, it seems, but I have no place here. Eventually, I go outside. Looking up into the night sky, I acknowledge that I'm not really one of the family anymore; I'm just a visitor.

I wake in terrible pain, my legs, hips, and hands hurting with the usual all-night tension. My daughter is sick now and my son is still coughing a lot, though his fever is down. We spend another day curled up together, acquiescing to the process; the discomforts of pain and illness leading us toward our eventual healing.

A memory comes to me and now I'm certain that, yes, my abuser's wife was involved in some aspects of the sexual abuse. As the memory unfolds I'm with my abuser's daughter. We're very young. We're naked, hiding in the closet in her parent's bedroom, told to go there and be as quiet as mice. Someone has come into the house. My abuser and his wife are lying in bed, the covers pulled up to their chins, talking to someone standing in the doorway of their bedroom. I hear a man's voice speaking rather harshly to them. I don't know who it is.

I'm trying to let all the outside attachments go, all the projected, life-draining emotional attachments to others—the anger, the disappointment, the sense of being abandoned by the adults in my life—trying to focus instead on the energy of repairing and revitalizing, of fully healing by turning more deeply inward.

February 11, 2003

I dream that I'm in an underground subway station. I can't figure out uptown from downtown, which direction the trains are going in, or where I want to go either. I go upstairs to the street to get a view of the city, but find it shrouded in dark fog, with nothing to orient myself by. I hear a subway train coming into the station and quickly run back down in an attempt to catch it, but at the last second I decide not to get on. It just doesn't seem like the right train to take. I go back up to the street and begin walking. The streets are empty, but I seem to know where to go now. The sidewalks are wet, as if it's just rained, and the setting sun glows warmly. The colors intensify as I walk, brightening the city with a refreshing vividness after the darkness of the underground subway.

When I meet with Chuck, he thinks I'm in a good place, letting go of blame, anger, and regret, focusing on feminine qualities of healing. Little by little my inner child grows more trusting of him as we talk. When I tell him about the dream of my abuser and his wife, he speaks of my dreaming awareness and how good it was that I had spoken out to them, that I didn't retreat and hide, or refuse to confront them.

"I didn't hold back at all, even though I was shaking in my boots."

"It's also good that you've gotten to a place of detachment," Chuck says, "with the focus now on healing and taking care of the child and the child's needs, rather than on anger or resentment."

We remark on the synchronicity of my own children being sick while I holed up, taking care of them over the weekend, intent on getting into a healthier place myself. As we talk, a new kind of lightness about the old stuff begins to take shape, clarity taking the place of confusion and disbelief, much like the clearing out of the fog in last night's dream. I realize that in gaining detachment, I've achieved a different perspective. It's as if the abuse has been an alien planet, orbiting around me all this time. It's always been there, threatening me with its strangeness, frightening in the same way that the idea of infinity is frightening, the endlessness of it. But now that I've explored the planet of abuse and achieved this new place of detachment, it looks like nothing more threatening than a doughy lump, totally unappetizing, yet totally explored.

"I've finally visualized a place I can put the past," I tell Chuck, as this visualization comes to me. "Out there in outer space!"

I realize that eventually the old stuff will no longer have any fear attached to it, because I'll already know every inch of its terrain. It will remain out there, always a part of me, but I won't need to approach it if I don't want to. If something else related to it emerges, I'll examine it thoroughly and then fling it out to that doughy mass floating in outer space where it will immediately adhere, becoming just another part of the planet of the past. One day it will just be that, the past—balled and pounded, compacted and kneaded, on the outer rim of my awareness—a doughy planet floating in the vast nothingness beyond mind and body, no longer necessary, no longer painful, no longer frightening or alien. That planet belongs to me. I lived it, but I can leave it out there in its orbit, present without attachment. In the end, it will be like Venus or Jupiter, just another planet in the galaxy that is my life.

"You're in a good place now; you've established distance," Chuck says.

"Yeah, and with a visual to finally anchor to, I'm certain I can also finally achieve a new sense of release. I'd been wondering where to put all this stuff. If I won't be storing it in my body anymore, where will I put it? I seem to need a visual; the artist in me wants a form to organize, resolve, and neatly package this stuff in. Just speaking about my abuse doesn't solve this need, it's real and tangible to me, and so its displacement has been a critical issue. I've been wondering all along: What am I going to do with all this stuff?"

I am reminded of Joseph Conrad's *Heart of Darkness*, the journey down the Congo River, and the plundering and destruction of a culture, a metaphor for going into the depths of the human soul, taking the inner journey into the darkest reaches of the self. I've gone there, journeyed into the heart of my own darkness, and I'm coming back into the light now. But where do I put the dark knowledge of my past? I don't want it in my heart; I don't even want it in my head, floating around, reminding me all the time. Far better to put it out there, at a distance, where it can reside in a separate place and not get in the way of my immediate self. In such detachment, it will remain at arm's length, but a million miles away as well—in sight, but out of mind. Being able to detach from my own heart of darkness feels like the next step of the journey, keeping it on the outer rim of my awareness where it won't interfere with the things I must do next, as I continue to move forward into new life. By keeping it in my personal galaxy I even have a certain amount of control over it.

"I feel good," I tell Chuck, as I get ready to leave, "though the unknown memories still loom threateningly. I sense them hovering, ready to drop another bomb on me without a moment's notice—BOOM—and I'll be caught again."

"Call on the artist's creativity. Use it, remember that you have it at your disposal," he reminds me.

Each time something disturbing comes up during the day, I compact it into a nice little lump and fling it as far as I can. It feels good when I do it the first time, and it feels good every time after that, another part of my heart of darkness flung into outer space. Residing among the stars and planets, comets and meteors, is a vaguely human heart-shaped, doughy thing. Like a tumor extracted and microscopically explored, I declare it no longer malignant, simply benign.

February 12, 2003

I dream that I'm trying to climb to the top of an icy hill. At first I try to run up it, but I keep slipping. I calm down and tell myself that I can do it, but that I must take my time. As I look down at the ground I see that there are patches of exposed earth, that the hill isn't completely ice-covered. I begin to climb slowly and carefully, looking for uncovered ground to step on. Certain that I'll make it to the top, I move forward with patience, precision, and faith in myself.

In another dream my hair is turning white. Suddenly, I see that I'm the other me—the me I decided I didn't want to be anymore, the sad old woman of a previous dream—and I start to panic, not wanting to be her again. Then I find that by combing my hair over to the other side I can hide the white. I like myself better then, but at the same time I feel like I'm hiding something, and I wonder why I don't like that part of myself?

Again I dream. I'm with several other people, setting up to make a television commercial. All of a sudden there are detectives on the set asking us if anything has been stolen. I look inside my art box and realize that my camera and my special writing pen are missing. The police find them and return them to me, but the camera is a different brand. Someone suggests that maybe I should tell the police that it's not the same camera as the one that got stolen, but I decide to try it out and see if it's any good. I mention that I have one camera that's good for close-ups, another that's good for mid-range, and perhaps this one will be good for wide angles. Maybe a new wide-angle camera will be a good thing, I reason, providing a new perspective.

In yet another dream, I'm searching for a new house, but nothing seems quite right. One house that I'm shown is on a busy road and it's obvious that it's been recently renovated. "Oh, I've already seen this house," I say as soon as we pull up. "It's too small, and I don't want to live on a busy road." But the real estate agent is adamant that I see the house again now that it's been renovated. It's only then that I realize I already have a house. "I have a home! I don't need to move anymore," I say. "I have a place I love, full of personality and we're happy there." I leave, wondering why I'm still looking for a place to live when I'm exactly where I want to be.

I wake up out of this string of dreams still tired, my head achy, having worked through issues all night long, the process unceasing. All I want to do is go outside, lie flat on my back and let the turbulence inside me seep into the cold ground. I want to feel what it might be like to finally free myself of all the holdings, along with all the strange messages and tips that come to me while I sleep. I yearn for calmness and a quiet mind. But then I notice that I can't breathe, that lying on my back makes me feel like I'm suffocating, like a heavy man is lying on top of me. I try to roll over in bed, but I can't. I start to panic, thinking I'm stuck in a memory again, but then realize that I'm starting to panic because, as Chuck told me yesterday, he'll be away for a week. Oh God, how will I manage without my anchor!

I run through all the distracting things I can do while he's away: stay busy at work, continue painting the house, do artwork for an upcoming show, take care of the kids, cook, clean, watch movies, keep myself occupied. All of this planning is to no avail as panic enters my body, riding in on a jangle of nerves. Before long I'm vibrating. A chattering of crickets fills my head and my newly acquired strength and stability go dim. Suddenly awash in sadness and fear, I'm tossed into the old dark tunnel of self where I meet a rising tide of ancient feelings. Abandonment, loss, and loneliness surround me like old friends. I just want to roll up and hide under the covers with them until Chuck returns. But, just as suddenly as the old tunnel appears, a new realization strikes home: I realize that it's the child self who's panicking. She doesn't think I can take care of her!

"I've protected you all these years," I say, "surely you know I'm here for you. I'm here!"

And then I'm struck by another revelation—I'm sure I've had it before—but now it becomes utterly clear that for most of my life it has been the abused child who has reacted, or not, making the majority of decisions in my life. I sense the child's panic at the thought of Chuck going away and in the same instant I feel my separation from her as almost complete. I am the adult with a head on her shoulders, full of compassion and understanding, and I'm making the decisions now! The child is balled up inside me, totally known, separate now for the first time. Even though I've been visualizing her balled up like a fetus—actually feeling pregnant with the pain and clenching of labor pains—the realization of us being two separate entities, in two vastly different worlds, has never been more apparent than at this very moment.

In this sudden moment of clarity, the adult me takes charge and the frightened child scurries back into her tunnel. I tell her I can handle everything. I'm sure she'll come out again when she realizes that with Chuck gone she'll need me. I think I'll be able to manage her, yet I'm aware of how tricky the situation is, how yesterday the adult me felt pretty good, strong and fearless, capable of separation, of rolling up the past into a lump of clay and hurling it out into space, while today the child pops up, fearful of abandonment. My dreams of last night make more sense now, as my new adult self sought to maintain her position. As each new day dawns, and new challenges arise, the differences between my two selves become more abundantly clear. So, although the child self anticipates abandonment, the adult self feels perfectly capable of handling anything that should arise while Chuck is away. As the adult, I'm also struck by the definite differences between these two aspects of self as they struggle to emerge as two distinctly separate beings. And I see now where the dilemma lies: *resolving the need to both separate and merge at the same time.*

The baby that I'm carrying around—Innocence, I've named her—won't be born until we've totally separated, until the child self has achieved independence and self-assuredness, and until I won't feel like I'm deserting her. When we're finally able to stand apart and go our separate ways without attachment to, or need of, each other, then she'll be a real child and I'll be a real adult. At the same time, the adult self and child self must come together and tell each other their separate stories if I am to achieve wholeness. The clearheaded adult has ideas and energy about how to do this, but the child cries out a fearful warning: "No, No, No! Stay with me. Don't leave me alone, don't go, stay, stay!" And so we curl up under the covers and silently huddle like we always did, and I forget about the recapitulation process along with the faucet that drips, the dryer hose that leaks, the trim that is unpainted, and the sheets that lie unwashed in the laundry basket. I curl up too and back we go, back to where curling up was the answer to our troubles and our misery. In this place of curling, the phantom baby in my belly pokes its tiny razor sharp fingernails through our ball of protection, creating air holes, letting pain escape. Flashes of horrible memories leap up out of that belly too, haunting my awareness, and the phantom baby whimpers and the once clear-brained adult, so intent upon this changing journey, only wants to soothe it back into calmness. And so she forgets where she is, the most important task now to lull the baby back to sleep.

February 13, 2003

In a dream, I present my mother with a journal and give her instructions on how to begin writing in it. Then I'm a child playing a game, running around the outside of a circle of people, all holding hands. Every time I pass a chiropractor I'm given an adjustment. When I've gone around the circle and been adjusted by all the chiropractors, my turn is over, but other people offer to adjust me too, because I'm so hard to adjust. Then I'm an adult again and I see an old boyfriend in the distance. I wonder if he'll recognize me, as I haven't seen him in a long time. I approach him, but then realize that I'm invisible to him, that he can't see me at all because he's so busy preening himself. Then I'm dancing on a conga line that winds around in a figure eight. The rule is that you are not allowed to break the conga line, but someone can pull you out of it. I feel like I'll be stuck dancing on this conga line for eternity, but I keep hoping that someone who knows me will see me and rescue me. No one does, not my mother who I see standing at a distance, looking on with distaste, nor my old boyfriend who is only concerned with himself.

I wake up to another day of the same endless battle that has been going on for days now, struggling to breathe, just trying to keep the panic from rising and somehow stay in control. I remind myself that the child's anxiety is normal, to be expected, as I've allowed her to express herself throughout this recapitulation.

"So, everything is okay," I tell her, remembering that I'm the mature adult, the only one with the ability to yank her off the eternal conga line. I'm the only one who can calm her, adjust her, and offer her some parenting and love.

February 14, 2003

In a dream, I'm on a large bed, lying naked with other people, also naked, as if we're having an orgy. An old boyfriend is trying to have sex with me, but I'm impenetrable, my vagina sealed shut with old scar tissue. I know that everyone watching thinks he's having intercourse with me, but he isn't. I get up, grab my clothes, and look for a bathroom so I can get dressed. I wander through an institutional type building until I find a girl's locker room. I notice feces smeared all over the place, piles of it on the floor, every surface covered. A smudge of feces gets on my cheek as I enter a toilet stall, the door of which doesn't close properly. I begin to remove a shawl that I'd wrapped around myself as I got out of the bed, but become concerned that everyone else in the locker room will see me naked. "It's okay, honey," a woman says to me, as if she can read my embarrassment. "If we looked like you, we wouldn't mind other people seeing us naked. Don't mind us watching." Someone else pipes up and says, "Yeah, if I looked like that I'd be very happy." I relax then and do something very unexpected. I stop hiding myself; I get dressed with everyone watching. Then I go outside to find a taxicab. I'm carrying several shoulder bags and suitcases. I finally get a cab, put all of my bags inside, close the door and walk away, leaving everything behind. Strolling down familiar streets, I pass one of the women who had spoken to me earlier in the locker room. Now she's walking quietly with two children, her head covered by a black shawl. I'm aware that she leads a double life, that she too has secrets, that everyone has secrets. I wander along, with no destination, contented to just walk along the quiet tree-lined streets. Eventually, I return to the building I'd started from to find that all the stuff I'd put into the taxicab is now in the lobby. I want to pay the taxi driver. I see him with his back turned away, as if he's purposely ignoring me, perhaps angry. I approach him and apologize. He makes a sarcastic remark and walks away in a huff. I dig around in my bags and find my wallet. He looks relieved when he sees that I intend to pay him. I give him a big bundle of money and thank him for his kindness. I still have to decide what to do with all of my stuff, but at least it's safely intact.

I get up at eight in the morning wondering what the heck this dream means. Perhaps its about my many phases of self as I go through this recapitulation process, all the shit I've had to deal with, taking ownership of my body, being honest and forthright, doing what's right. It's as if I'm wandering around in my dreams waiting for Chuck to return too. I don't spend a lot of time figuring it out, but it stays with me as I take my son to the dentist to have his teeth cleaned and do some errands. When I get home, I finish painting the living room and then talk to several friends on the phone. I don't let more than a few minutes go by when I'm not doing something.

Like in the dream, I did something unexpected today: for the first time in two months I didn't stay in bed all day. Even though my legs ached and I felt dizzy all day, I've stayed up. It's midnight now, as I finally let myself go to bed.

February 15, 2003

Saturday morning. I wake up late. It's a holiday weekend. The kids are with their dad for a few days. I'd like to just stay in bed because everything is aching, even the tops of my ears, but I have an appointment with some buyers at the studio and then a lunch date. I get up. Walking as stiff as a zombie, I get myself ready for the day, which will be long as it's my turn to work at the artist's gallery tonight.

The buyers purchase a number of small items and take some of my painted furniture on consignment to a gallery on the New Jersey shore. As soon as they leave, I head out to meet my friends for lunch, a couple I haven't seen in a year. I find nothing to talk about and feel a little awkward as I stumble to make light conversation. In the end, I stop trying. I let them do all the talking while I nod agreeably. I notice how distant I am from their talk of the world and its problems, as if I'm not fully present. Back at the studio, I clean for a few hours then stop at the house for a quick bite to eat before heading up to the gallery.

It's a bitterly cold night and no one comes in. I watch as a couple rushes out of the restaurant across the street and jumps into their car as fast as they can. That's the kind of night it is. When I get home I force myself to sit and watch movies until midnight. Scrunched up in pain, I'm aware that it's important that I stay out of bed as long as possible.

February 16, 2003

I wake in excruciating pain, strung tight, as if I'm being pulled apart on some medieval torture wheel. My muscles and limbs, brittle as sticks, are ready to snap. My vagina, like in the dream with my old boyfriend, feels like it's sealed shut with scar tissue. Nothing can get in, nothing can get out, and it aches!

"Perform a C-section, slice me open and let the pain out! Do it without anesthesia so I can scream and scream and scream! Do it, so I can get some of this horrible stuff out of me!"

After two days of being up and out in the world, all I want to do now is hide under the covers, scared and alone. I begin to panic, afraid I won't be able to hold on. But I'm so good at holding on—of course I'll be able to do it! I've kept myself sequestered behind a coat of armor for a lifetime, a covering as thick as glacial ice, as cold as steel, as hard as stone. Its impenetrable surface warns to stay away, keeps the intruders out, but the reality is that now the glacier is beginning to melt. Now, each day, I feel the slow drip, drip, drip of change.

This is my real life now—recapitulation—facing the past and reliving it, every aspect of it, as I crack through the surface of my most solid barriers. In the deepest and most fundamentally visceral and psychological ways I am breaking apart, suffering through a total breakdown of the old self. I don't work anymore. All I do is recapitulate. This *is* my work, just as Jeanne Ketchel once told me it would be, before I even knew what I was getting into. For three years, she told me, I'd be doing this. And here I am, doing it!

February 17, 2003

In a dream, I'm in two places at once, simultaneously sitting on a bus and also on a horse galloping down the road ahead of the bus, surrounded by a herd of wild horses. I'm aware of myself in both places, and each self sees the other self as the action of the dream unfolds. Bears run beside the bus, and I notice that the trees alongside the road are shaped like people, human looking figures that I'm aware are spirits caught in the trunks of the trees. The ground is crawling with boa constrictors. From inside the bus, as well as from my seat high on the horse, I watch them slither and writhe along the ground. Everyone on the bus is afraid of the animals, especially the snakes because they're so fast and dangerous looking. The snakes chase cats and dogs. Moving quickly, they dart out and snatch them unhindered. I'm afraid I'll fall off the horse and be snatched up too.

As I express this fear, I'm simultaneously aware of myself sitting on the bus, also afraid. This self on the bus is on heightened alert, trying to figure out when I'm supposed to get off the bus. Each time the bus slows down I wonder if it's the right stop yet. Eventually, I do get off the bus, but now I'm not alone; I'm with a little girl. Hand in hand we walk to a beach. Now I am both the little girl and my adult self simultaneously. No one will play with my little girl self because of the shame surrounding my past. I, the adult self, think people are being judgmental and mean. The other kids on the beach are not allowed to talk to this little girl self. I'm aware that everyone thinks I'm dirty and dangerous because I've been participating in evil things with an evil man.

I wake at six in the morning, hot and sweaty. Almost immediately, fear strikes and a cold chill grabs hold of me. I shiver uncontrollably. I'm afraid, though of what I'm not sure, perhaps of getting stuck in a physically painful state. I take my thoughts off the idea of fear, try to release it, to breathe it out, but my body, shaking violently, holds onto it. What's going to happen to me? What if I get stuck in a memory and can't get out of it? Chuck isn't around to pull me out. I face my loneliness and know, at the deepest level, that it's what I fear the most.

I realize that my dreams last night were all about fear—the fear of missing my stop on the bus, of falling off a galloping horse, of being attacked by a bear, of being bitten by a snake, of being petrified and unable to move like the spirits caught in the trees— and of being lonely and ignored like the girl on the beach whom nobody will play with. And now, as I wake up, I realize I'm sick. I have the same flu the kids had. I'm groggy and feverish. Chills strike and then I break out in cold sweats. My head and muscles ache. I notice that even as I suffer these onslaughts of illness, I feel totally disconnected from my body. But I guess that's nothing new!

I lie in bed in a stupor, my body enveloped by illness, a sudden shift in focus away from my inner work. Perhaps I'll get a rest from the old stuff, I think, but I soon realize my recapitulation has no patience for illness. It simply takes advantage of the compromised state I'm in to catapult me into a memory, my disconnected body a sure sign that I have no control, for suddenly I am somewhere in the past. My hands are tied over my head. The bottom half of my body lies far away, disconnected, unfeeling, numb. "Don't," I plead, in a tiny, panicky voice. "Don't hurt me, don't hurt me!" I don't feel anything, but I clearly hear the strangled cry of a frightened child, the sound coming from such a great distance away.

February 18, 2003

I struggle to awaken. I am held down, begging that the men in my dream not hurt me. I want to scream, but the scream is so deeply buried only a strangled sound emerges. It's enough, however, to awaken me more fully. Agitated and shaky, I stay huddled in bed, caught in the throes of a memory, the dream so reminiscent of what came over me yesterday as I lay sick in bed, as a brutal memory attempted to make itself known. The only thing I can do is hold it at bay.

I finally get up around three in the afternoon and go outside to shovel the snow that's been falling all day. I hate it at first, as I pour all of my anger and frustration into this task that I've come to hate as the winter has continued to dump weekly snowfalls. Pretty soon, however, I'm in a better mood. Just moving around in the cold air feels good. I do some good flops into the snow banks, jarring my mind and body back into this reality. Lying there in the snow, staring up into the swirl of snowflakes falling on my face, I begin to feel that it's good to be alive. As I stick out my tongue and let the cold flakes melt in my mouth, it becomes clear that I'll turn all of this recapitulation stuff into some kind of book, that I won't keep it out there in that lumpy planet circling in my galaxy, but that something else will come of it, something meaningful. I'm certain that the urge to be creative and to express what I'm going through will eventually emerge in words, though just what shape or form those words will take is a mystery, but I do intend to let the words be spoken. I intend to let them take me where they will.

When the kids come home from their dad's later in the evening I'm in a better mood than I've been in for months. Finally, I see a light at the end of the tunnel.

February 19, 2003

My alarm, in one shrill call to awaken, wipes out the dream I'm having and all the others before it. It was hard to fall asleep last night and I tossed and turned until well past two. Now it's six already and time to get the kids up for school. As I make coffee and prepare breakfast, I ponder the way the memory that has been emerging is working its way through me, my outer icy shell beginning to crack, another layer splintering into tiny shards each time I face the onslaught of it. The shards evaporate in the warm air inside the house, but I'm left chilled and shivering nonetheless.

I go to work for a few hours, for the first time in days. I feel okay for a while, but soon head back home, drawn to lie down and sleep, part of me desperate to hide under the covers and make everything disappear, make the memory that's pushing at me disappear too. That's what I *want* to do—lie under the covers—but I force myself to stay out of bed for most of the day. I keep busy instead. Every time my attention strays from what I'm doing around the house, the memory I've been staving off sneaks up and reveals itself a little bit more, and then fear permeates my body. Strong shudders invade every cell as I strain against it, holding it back, a monster intent upon fully revealing itself. Cracks are beginning to appear, here and there, but I don't intend to look into any of them. Not yet. I know I can't do this memory alone, and so I count down the hours until Chuck gets back, keeping the monster at arm's length, holding the cracked pieces of myself together as best I can.

February 20, 2003

I dream that I tell people that I don't have a body; that my body doesn't exist.

"Yes, you do," they say, "We're looking right at it!"

"No," I insist. "It doesn't belong to me; they took it from me a long time ago."

"How can you not exist?" they ask.

"You'll never understand," I say, "but I don't exist. Everything is gone. They took it, they stole it from me."

I fall back to sleep with my coat and boots still on after driving the kids to school, their arms laden with instruments and projects. I'm awoken by a phone call at nine, the shrill ringing like a hammer striking my head. It's the wrong number, but it keeps me awake.

I'm in so much pain, holding this ferocious memory at bay, this wild animal caged against its will. At least I'm admitting that it needs release. It pushes and begs to be let out, though I constantly refuse its ominous call. Last night, I yelled out loud as I dreamed, a long and strangled release. And now, my abdominal muscles ache with the tension and pain of holding in all the strangled cries that I just can't release in waking life.

I fall asleep again for a few hours in the early afternoon, my body twitching with tension as the memory tries to escape, but I won't let it out, not yet. I steel against it, waiting until I meet with Chuck tomorrow. It will just have to wait until then too.

February 21, 2003

I take Chuck with me into the brewing memory, into the barn where several men await me, but that's as far as he can follow. As a visceral memory unfolds out of my body, I am stolen away for forty-five minutes. I can neither speak nor sit up. I am locked in the fear and pain of my nightmare.

"Come back! Come back!" Chuck calls to me.

I hear his voice, far off in the distance, calling to me from somewhere outside the barn.

"I'm not here, I'm not here," I yell back. "I'm not here!"

"I want you to come back now!" he calls rather sternly, but I'm so far away I can barely hear him.

Ever so tentatively, he touches my hands. Slowly, slowly, I return to his office and the clock that says I have to leave, but I can't. I can't see; I'm not fully back yet. I stumble out to the waiting room and lie down on the stiff little loveseat, my head on a small pillow, to wait until he's done with his next session. With my coat over my shoulders, unable to keep my eyes open, I fall into heavy sleep. I wake up when I hear him calling my name again. It feels like only a few seconds have gone by, but he's ready to see me again. I get up and follow him back into the office.

"I want you to come back now and stay back," he says. "Don't go there. We'll go back together, but don't go there on your own. Keep away! Okay?"

"Yes, yes, yes. I don't want to go there, not alone," I say, and I know it's dangerous, too frightening and lonely, and no one listens to me when I'm there, no one hears me, no one helps me. They only hurt me; the men hurt me.

I have trouble falling asleep at night because I can't breathe. I feel pressure, the black weight of those men on my chest.

February 22, 2003

I wake in pools of blood, tampon and clothes soaked with it, blood running in streaks down my legs as I run to the bathroom. It started yesterday, excessive bleeding, after my meeting with Chuck, after the memory. It's like I'm flushing the past out of me.

I crawl back into bed and discover that I can't lie down because I will suffocate. It took forever to get into a comfortable, breathable sleeping position last night, but I finally fell asleep and slept well. It's eight thirty now and luckily it's Saturday. The kids are still asleep so I prop some pillows behind me and sit up with my journal in my lap. Time to have a heart-to-heart with my little girl self.

I've decided that I'm not going to control her any more, except the minimum that's necessary to stay grounded. She's finally awakening and letting it all out. I want her to tell me, and Chuck, everything we need to know, so we can move on. But we also need to rest, we need a break. I intend to distract us as best I can for the next few days, until we meet with Chuck again, until we are in a safe place where we can take the next step on this journey.

"We'll be alright," I tell her. "We'll be fine. This is a very tough time, but we'll get through it; we're strong. Now we're learning to talk about it and we're learning how to look at it again in a very safe environment. I care about you, and Chuck cares about you too. When it's time for us to go back into the memory, we'll take him along too, so we don't get lost. We can stay grounded and still go there too, but only with him, okay? Not alone—we don't have to go there alone anymore. Someone hears us this time. This time when we call for help, Chuck hears us."

"I'm not going to keep anything back. I'm not going to feel embarrassed or ashamed or disgusted, because none of that's important or helpful. I think we've gotten to a point where the only important thing now is to go through each memory until they no longer freak us out, until the fear is obliterated. Okay? We can do that. We'll do it together, and with Chuck, because he knows what happened to us, what those bad men did to us. He's there to pull us out from under them when it gets too overwhelming, so we can breathe again."

"He's our guide, our fellow traveler, and our witness too. Until we meet with him again, we must remain fully present."

I struggle through the day, trying to stay distracted, feeling pummeled and easily bruised, needing tenderness, needing kind words and caring caresses, needing touch to bring me back to life, back to now. I spend most of the day doing chores around the house and being with my children, talking and hanging out with them, feeding and caring for them, loving them, my whole body aching with such tenderness for them.

As night closes in and I retire to the shadows of my inner self once again, I realize that although I'd never be able to kill another person, I could kill my abuser. Easily and without remorse I could shoot him right between the eyes. In fact, worse than that, I could torture him by not killing him right away. I'd let him linger, allow cruelties to be inflicted upon him by all who've lost their innocence to him, for I am sure there are others like me. His ugly hands left fingerprints and bruises inside and outside our tiny delicate bodies, tracks of slime across out tender skin, like silvery snail paths meandering across virgin leaves in spring. His darkness has left eternal shadows of pain that crisscross in and out of our lives, interrupting our waking and dreaming moments with frightful images and haunting nightmares. And, although we often can't quite place them, those images and nightmares are as familiar to us as our own hands, as familiar as our own inner voices whispering their warnings to: *Beware, beware, beware! This man is evil. Take your knife with you into the woods, and strike him dead, for he deserves it!*

February 23, 2003

I'm suffocating. Unable to breathe, I sense the memory encroaching again, like a round dark shadowy ball, and I hear Chuck's voice firmly telling me, "Don't go there; don't go there!" Part of me thinks I should just let it envelop me, just give in, but I listen to Chuck's voice playing in my head, telling me that it's a bad idea, that I'm better off if I control it now. I hear him telling me to hold on until we meet on Tuesday and I know he's right.

I must pay attention to how this recapitulation has so far led me along this journey of self-discovery and continue to follow its lead. In the beginning, it seemed as if nothing would come through, no clear memories, but then images started coming and then disjointed feelings, and now the two are joining. I know where I am and what I'm feeling when I go into a memory now. Even a few weeks ago I couldn't control the memories. I'd just get lost in the intensity of them, which sometimes lasted for hours or even days. It was too much. Now, I've trained myself to wait until I'm in a safer environment, so I don't have to be alone, and so I don't have to suffer needlessly either.

Throughout the day, intense feelings well up in my third chakra, in the seat of power and self, where I've sensed my child self huddled. I use my willpower to hold everything back, suffering through the pain and soreness of unreleased cries and unshed tears. I await the torrent that I know will someday rise up out of me, spilling out of my gut, up through my heart, and out my throat. But not yet, it's not time yet; there are still two more days to go before I meet with Chuck again.

February 24, 2003

I dream that I'm cleaning my studio. I'm washing the floors with buckets of water, when the outside walls suddenly fall away and I'm standing beside the ocean, gentle waves coming on shore. I bathe my feet in the surf, but then notice the water rising higher, suddenly shifting from calm waves to rough seas. An enormous wave begins to form on the horizon. I run back to my studio, now a house perched overlooking the beach, all the doors and windows flung wide open. I stand on the big deck that surrounds the house and watch the tidal wave roll toward shore. It comes from a great distance, growing bigger and more powerful until it crashes over all the people lying on the beach, immersing everything in its path. "Oh, how frightening it is for those people!" I say, as I watch from the safety of my deck. But then I step outside the dream for a second and say, "Oh, that's the old me, being scared. Those people are enjoying themselves; this is a good wave. This is a cleansing wave, come to wash everything away!" Back in the dream again, the giant tidal wave continues towards me and finally crashes over me too, washing everything away.

Next I dream that I'm at my parent's house. I walk in and discover that not one sign of me exists in their house, no pictures, not one clue that I ever existed. My room is gone, all of my things are gone, my total existence wiped out. I'm confused and angry as I approach my father. He's totally oblivious to the fact that it's even important to me to be recognized as having had a place in the family. I'm indignant. I scream right in his face, but he barely flinches, barely reacts. In the end, he calmly tells me that all my stuff is in the garage. That satisfies me. Then I go out shopping, looking for a new dress. I'm trying to decide what will look right, what will fit this new person I now am.

The waves come crashing to shore, bringing change, bringing recapitulation of the memories, washing away the old world, cleansing my soul. Even my outlook changes in the dream, as I confront my old habitual thoughts of fear and horror, and begin to see the tidal wave as a happy, healing event. I receive its healing waters without fear, just as I'm learning to accept the healing aspects of this recapitulation without fear.

My parent's house, where there is no sign of me, as if the tidal wave came through there as well, represents the truth that I have moved on. I've very methodically distanced myself from my family, actually removed my energy from my parents as I've recapitulated. Although I confront my father in the dream about the absence of any sign of me in their house, I'm simultaneously aware that it's right, as I'm no longer connected to my family in the old way—I have changed too much. The only place my stuff could possibly be is stored away in the garage, stored like all the memories always were, because the real me was never part of the family to begin with. This satisfies me, but, at the same time, truthfully, I probably needed to have that confrontation and outburst of anger with my father as part of this healing journey. And finally, I am changing so much inside. How can I possibly be comfortable in the same clothes I've always worn? This calls for new clothes!

February 25, 2003

I meet with Chuck and we go right into the barn, into the same memory that's been stirring for weeks. The intensity is about the same as last time, though I'm determined that it won't sweep me away as it did then. As I go deeper into the memory, I once again hear Chuck speaking from a distance, reminding me that it's not now, that it's over, it's not happening now. I want it to be over, but I'm caught in all the feelings encapsulated in the memory. I relive it, rolled in a tight ball, my feet tucked under me, my head in my lap, my hands covering my face. I hear Chuck's voice far away, a million miles away, while the voices of the men in the barn and my own voice are louder and clearer. My own panic and pain are much, much louder too, rushing through my ears, drowning out Chuck's voice. As if he senses this, he calls out sharply every now and then, pulling me out of the past, asking me to come back to the present. He reminds me where I am, telling me I must not get stuck back there. But even so, each time I dive back in I go further away, to another place that doesn't extend very far beyond my own skin but is eons from the physical self as well.

So deeply embedded in the memory am I that I experience an imploding, a downward spiraling of energy and self. As the memory progresses, I continue collapsing inwardly, rolling down into an even tighter ball of pain, as my muscles clench against the crushing reality that no one loves me. I am frightened, sad, and lonely, crushed to nothingness by the heartless cruelty of it all.

"Did you get it all?" Chuck asks, pulling me out again.

"I'm not sure. I felt like it was going to be over, but it wasn't. The men came back to me again and again," I say, my voice catching in a half cry, and I jerk back suddenly, my hands in front of my face, as if it's happening all over again. "Don't hurt me, no, no, no!"

"It's okay," says Chuck gently. "And you can cry, it's okay to cry."

I try, but all I can do is choke out a few dry, hacking sobs, animalistic and painful in their expression. I haven't quite been able to let go to that extent. I haven't been able to have a cleansing cry, a real washout like in my dream.

"Don't go there. Shut the door on the barn for a few days," says Chuck. "Keep it closed, just for a while. We'll go back when we have to."

Weakly, I nod in agreement and we end the session.

February 26, 2003

I wake up in pain, my legs stiff again, hurting from the habitual all-night clenching. My jaw hurts too and I'm already counting down the days until I can meet with Chuck again.

"Don't open the door! No! Don't!" I hear him telling me.

"Only a crack? Please? I need to." I lean against the barn door, my hip hurting from pressing so hard to keep it closed.

"No! Don't do it!" I hear him admonishing me. But I need to go in there and find out what they're doing to me. I can't breathe and I feel so helpless and abandoned, my child self almost giving up in this memory because they don't stop, they won't stop; they won't leave me alone. No matter what I say, they don't stop. STOP!!! If I open the door, perhaps all the agony and despair will seep out, though I'm aware that they're seeping out anyway, along the floorboards and between the cracks in the walls, coming to meet me, along with the odors of men's bodies, my own sadness, and my own poor tearless tears. The tears won't come, but I dream of water, of salt water, of crashing cleansing tidal waves, but my own tears won't flow even a drop. It's just a matter of time before it happens. I can cry; I can cry. It's okay to cry.

I go somewhere deep inside for a few minutes, to a place of pain and agony, wanting comfort. I fall asleep for an hour, but wake up still clenched. "Close the door, close the door," I hear Chuck saying, but I keep thinking that the door is full of holes and that I can't stop any of this. The phone rings, as resounding as a whack over the head, jolting me out of my despair. It's Chuck calling, responding to an earlier message I had left him.

"Go away," he tells the memory. "Not now! Not now! Go away! We'll get to you, but not now!"

"But it's unbearable," I say.

"I know it is, but remember when you couldn't feel anything and you wanted to feel? You'd say, why can't I feel anything?"

"Yes."

"And you got through that stage and now you *are* feeling, and you have to go through this stage too to get better. You will get better. No matter how unbearable it is, pull yourself together and get moving. Do something to move away from it. Not now! Not now! Not now!"

"Okay," I say. "Not now! Not now! Not now! Not now!"

And so I get through the day, each day, one day at a time. I go out and get my hair done and enjoy the luxury of someone else washing my hair and making me beautiful. Strong hands massage my scalp, and even though it's a slightly painful experience I let it happen, I accept the pain. Don't stop! Make me feel something, make me look nice and neat and fresh.

"It looks so good on you," the hairdresser says about my new hairstyle, and I walk out feeling refreshed, but the agony pursues me all day long, pushing and nudging, reminding me of the real business at hand, letting me know that the memory is still there. I feel its mounting tension, how it grips me. As each day ends, I rejoice that it's over because it brings me one day closer to working with Chuck, to my next hour of release.

February 27, 2003

I dream that I meet Chuck at his house. Jeanne is with him, looking pale and beautifully serene in a neat skirt and blouse. Bathed in an ethereal glow, she seems almost fragile, and yet very attentive and kind, giving of her energy. She speaks to me and tells me that she knows who I am. She tells me that Chuck cares about me, that I can trust him, and that she herself is very accepting of the deep work that I'm doing with Chuck.

In my dream, Jeanne acknowledged the deep work of this recapitulation. I was delighted to see her and I felt how tenderly supportive she is. Although I went to bed all clenched in a tiny ball last night, trying to comfort myself, I was aware of stretching out all through the night, incrementally releasing the tight clenching, relaxing my muscles. It's as if Jeanne's calming presence brought me physical comfort while I slept and dreamed, my intent to change, even while asleep, stirred to action. As a result, I'm not in my usual pain this morning, though I'm still hurting inside. I can't help but wonder how I'll get through the day.

So how did I get through the day? With pain and memories hammering at me. I'm on shaky ground, fragile and exhausted but still here, still determined to stay in this world, though I just want to be in the comfort of my bed or working with Chuck. Everything else is frightening. Life is frightening.

February 28, 2003

I dream that I'm on an airplane, sitting with a group of Iraqi women. We arrive in New York and then I'm riding in a chauffeur-driven car with two of the women and my child, a girl, making polite conversation while we drive into the city. The women are very intelligent, one a surgeon and the other a lawyer, and we discover that we're the same age. I sense that they like me, while I find them very worldly and generous, sharing their car. We drop my child at school. She doesn't want to go, but the women comment that she'll be fine once I'm out of sight. As we drive around the corner, I watch my little girl make her way through the crowd of children to go sit alone on a bench at the very edge of the schoolyard. She sits down and puts her head in her hands, her back to me as the car rounds the corner. I'm in agony, knowing exactly how she feels: frightened and alone. As we drive away, I glimpse a female teacher noticing her, walking towards her where she sits alone on the bench, and I'm thankful that a kind person will take care of her. The Iraqi women and I continue to converse as we travel through the streets of New York. Finally, I get out of the car in a downtown section of Manhattan. I'm not sure where I am and it's only when I walk into a gallery that I discover that I'm in the SoHo district. I go back outside, but immediately get lost again.

And that's how I feel right now, lost, because I have no place to take this stuff, except to Chuck's. I am destined to wander around with it, being uncomfortable and feeling like I have abandoned my child self, because we can't work on this right now. But then I realize that, as luck would have it, I meet with Chuck today. We have decided that for the foreseeable future it would be wise to meet more often while I go through this intense part of the recapitulation.

As soon as I sit down across from Chuck, we open the barn door and I go inside, into the gloom of the rest of the memory that I've been holding onto for days. I curl up into a ball and stay in my tight place of feeling and holding, wrapped in pain and fear, lost and abandoned. I don't say anything. I just stay there for a long time, taking it all in, overwhelmed with feelings, until I hear Chuck's voice.

"We have to talk about it," he says, "not now, if you can't, but you need to *talk* about what was happening in the barn."

I'm immediately stressed about having to verbalize what I've been experiencing, but I know he's right. I know I'll have to piece together all the hours of work—partially done in Chuck's office and what I did on my own—into a cohesive memory, get the fullness of it, and speak about it. So far I've just gone there in my body memory—in feeling, seeing, and smelling, in many vignettes of sensory exploration and assault—but I still have to bring it all together in total awareness and accept the truth of it.

"Yes, I know," I say. "I'll try to piece it together and talk, but not now. I can't yet."

"That's okay," he says very gently. "But when you're ready to talk, I'll be ready to listen."

Chapter 3

Molting

March 1, 2003

Images appear, revealing themselves bit by bit as I do the sweeping breath. I see the men in the barn and what they did to me. Fear and loneliness embrace me as the memory begins to solidify. I want only to hide my face and body, but I push myself to go further, until I touch upon the solid lumps of shame and pain that lie at my core. Then I pull out of the memory, away from the scenes in the barn, away from the men and the feelings. I slam the door shut and return to breathing normally, facing how difficult this will be to talk about with Chuck. He's right though; the only way I'll get through this recapitulation is to talk about it, but this is what comes to me when I think about talking: *Don't look at me!*

Don't look at me when I tell you what they did to me because I feel dirty and disgusting, and you will hate me. You will find me ugly. I'm ashamed. How can I sit up so straight and proper, with my hands clasped so primly in my lap and tell you all the bad things that happened? How can I say these awful things, even to you, Chuck, who knows everything already, who sees me huddle and shake, who hears my whimpers and cries? Agony fills me like a fever that won't abate, consuming my strength so that I have nothing left inside except the memory that sickens me, until I feel that I am dying. I want only a tiny place to crawl into, a place to curl up and hide this body away in, to house this disgust that fills me. I can't dig the disgust out of me—disgust that takes my energy away, turns it into burning shame and consumes me. *Don't look at me!*

I hold things back all day, trying to forget what's going on, trying to distract myself while I feel so bruised, while shame burns my face. The images come again; the horrors of what those men did to me. I want to cry. Why can't I just cry? Why do I have to be so fucking strong! At the same time, I understand that it's the child who wants to hide and cover her face. She feels dirty, defiled, disgusting. She's ashamed of her body and what it was used for. As the memory comes into greater clarity, I hear the men calling me some name I've never heard before. I hear their voices coming out of the darkness of the past, hear them saying things to each other. "Take it easy, man," someone says. I see their greedy eyes, their lusty, quivery lips. I hear their panting breaths. I am clenched tight, tight, tight, holding my legs together. "Flip her; flip her," they say. "No, no, no, no, don't hurt me, don't hurt me, don't hurt me, don't hurt me, don't hurt me, don't hurt me! Ow! Ow! Ow! Ow!" Hands cover my mouth and I can't breathe. I can't breathe!

Not now! Not now! I pull out of the memory. Too much to bear! Better to sit and write what I've already recapitulated than to keep going back for more. Too much to suffer right now.

"What are you actually feeling so ashamed of?" I ask my child self.

"I'm ashamed of what my body has done to those men," she tells me. "My body made them want to do all those ugly things. It made them act so greedy and lusty. It made them spit and drool and grunt. It made them do those ugly things to me."

"Why do you think you're responsible for their actions and desires? Did they say something that made you think that?"

"Yes. They said: *Girl, you make me want to do this to you. You make me do it. You make me do it.*"

"Do you believe that?"

"When they see me, they want to do those things. They tell me it's my fault. It's my fault that they have to rape and sodomize me. But they disgust me! Their lips are disgusting. I see their upper lips and they are ugly with black stubble, quivering and damp with beads of sweat. *Girl, you make me do it! Dirty girls make me do it,* they say. And then they smell bad and I make them that way too."

I feel punched and kicked as I talk this through with my child self, my ribs and diaphragm bruised and hurting, everything hurting. As the feelings take over, pictures flash again and soon all my emotions and physical injuries are riding along on the waves of flashing pictures, as I sink deeper into the recapitulation and deeper into the shame.

"I understand," Chuck says, when I call him out of desperation. "I've been going through it with you."

"I know; I know you have," I say. "I'm back there again. My throat is tight, my chest is tight, my diaphragm is tight, my hips are tight."

"Breathe simple normal breaths, just normal breathing."

"They made me feel it was my fault. It took the blame off them. If I made them do it, then I was the evil one. I was an evil girl, an evil witch."

"Do you really believe that?"

"I don't know. Right now I sure do."

March 2, 2003

I go to the studio for a few hours in the middle of the day to finish some artwork that I'm preparing for a show that opens next week. I've hardly been out of the house or even out of my bed for the past two months. It's hard being out in the world, and harder still to concentrate on the task at hand. The memory constantly pushes at me as I work, daring me to turn around and face it, but I refuse its call. I have more important things to do today. Luckily, I have the place to myself, my studio partner working a part time job now, and no one stops by or interrupts me. I concentrate on the task I've set myself. Just trying to simply breathe my way normally through the day occupies my attention as well, though inside I'm in incredible pain, deeply bruised and desperately in need of crying, but of course I can't, though my heart is heavy with sadness.

By nighttime I'm highly agitated. The phantom energies that pursued me all day are still behind me, shoving and pushing. I'd like to turn around and yell at them. STOP SHOVING ME! But all I'm able to do is move away from them, keeping one step ahead, keeping everything under control as best I can.

"Tell it to wait, it has to wait," I hear Chuck telling me. "Tell it to go away. Not now! Wait!"

March 3, 2003

I dream that I'm back at my family home. Movers have come to pack everything up. My mother is absent, reachable only by phone. Meanwhile, my father grows increasingly mentally dim, incapable of helping out or making decisions. I'm in charge of everything, the movers, the packing, and especially the kids—my kids, as well as my little brothers and sister. At first, I'm slightly frustrated that my parents aren't dealing with their own move, but then I decide that it's just the way it is and I take full charge. While all of this is going on, a baby is crying loudly. I pick her up and console her, a beautiful baby, but she just cannot stop crying. There's also a little girl who will not be moving with the family because she's becoming an astronaut and will be going into outer space. "I will be looking down on all of you as you move on," she says. The movers empty the house, although I keep thinking, why bother? Why take any of it? There isn't really anything worth taking, except the baby, who lies in my arms, contented now, the crying over. I wonder about my parents. Where are they going? I don't have any answers, though I know I'm instrumental in this process. It's only because I take over that the move happens at all. I'm also happy that the young girl is going off to be an astronaut, and I release her without attachment, knowing that it's what she needs to do. In the end, I accept that all of this change is good.

In another dream, I'm driving down a long narrow dirt road with woods on one side and a steep incline down to a lake on the other. I park my car on the side of the road, deciding that I will just abandon it there, for I am intent on finding a way down to the lake. I'm leaving everything behind and I have no intention of returning.

I wake up alert, the significance of the dreams foremost in my thoughts. In the first dream, I'm clearly in charge, as the authority figures in my life no longer exist. I acknowledge the unavailability of my parents and easily let them go, much as I did as a child. I don't need them or want anything from them. I also see no value in material things. I'm only interested in taking what's important, in this case the baby. I'm also aware that the little astronaut girl—my spiritually evolved child self—is intent on fulfilling her dreams, leaving everything behind, and that it's right for her to do so. My adult self is happy to move on as well, taking only the happy baby, who cried out all that pained her and now lies contented in my arms. I acknowledge that this is the way things should be at times of change; take only what matters, letting everything else go—working through emotions and attachments—in order to move on unencumbered. This sentiment is underscored in the second dream, as I leave everything behind once again, even my car, my main means of transportation. I have no intention of returning to it, to the old way of getting through life. I'm only interested in getting to the lake. Nothing else matters.

I see water as a most vital aspect of life, life-giving and deeply resonant of the spirit self, the vibrational energetic self. Personally it means calmness, peace and tranquility; I have always felt safe and at ease in water. It also means connecting with my spirit again, in the deepest way, for astrologically I am a water sign. It means that maybe I will actually finish this recapitulation. Maybe I too will leave the past behind like the little astronaut girl, finally fly away, without attachment, to bathe in my wholeness, at peace at last.

Once again I work at the studio until I get so restless that I can't stay any longer. I go home, eat some lunch, and then lie down for a while. I fall right into memoryland. I don't know where I go, but suddenly I'm aware that it's time to pick up my daughter who has stayed late after school. I'm extremely dizzy when I stand up. Walking is hard, though sitting and driving are manageable. As soon as I get out of the car back at home again I feel lightheaded and drunk. I wonder if it's the meds, if I'm suddenly having a reaction to the dosage of Paxil I'm taking. I lie down again. Every time I move the room swirls, as if I am indeed very drunk. Thinking that perhaps I need to eat something, I roll out of bed and stumble down the hallway to the kitchen. Later, when I go out to pick up my son at a friend's house, I'm still dizzy, but definitely better. I realize I've hardly eaten anything in the past few days, though I had just eaten lunch before the dizziness started. Chuck may be right though, that I'm not eating "properly." Over the weekend I was in such a bad state that I barely took sustenance.

I feel better while having dinner with the kids, and I notice that the more I eat the better I feel. I realize how difficult it's been to juggle everything lately, not only dealing with the past but trying to get ready for the upcoming art show, especially with the kids being sick. I take care of everyone else and end up ignoring myself, which is dangerous. I also realize that the amount of energy I expend every day is tremendous. Just in dealing with the memories

I'm burning calories like crazy. I almost passed out today and I can't let that happen again.

Before bed I take a bath and massage my painful hips and thighs. Afterwards, I do yoga and some deep breathing and then sit in bed and contemplate the memory that I know I must speak with Chuck about in the morning. To prepare, I do the sweeping breath and let the memory unfold as it has so far been revealed. There is only the barest shadowy outline of three men standing over me in the barn. I hear voices, but little else comes through, except the feelings inside my body, still vital after forty years. Gradually working my way deeper into the feelings, I find myself held down by two of the men, the third lying between my legs. A voice clearly says, "Flip her over." I hear it as clear as day, as if the men are in my room. The next thing I know I'm conscious of lying alone on the floor—whatever happened is over. My abuser comes back with money in his hands. I clearly hear him say that he'll be back in a little while. I am totally encased in my physical body; there is no greater world to consider. Nothing exists beyond my skin. I am only aware of my body lying on the floor, suffocating in a cocoon of horror.

I stop the sweeping breath, fearful that if I stay in the memory I *will* suffocate, but the memory begins to spin of its own accord. Panting male voices speak to me once again. I feel man-breath on my face and man-hands holding me down. As I pull away, suffocating darkness surrounds me. Suddenly the real world is gone. Nothing exists except what is happening in this moment of recapitulation. I am lost in a nightmare. Not a good place to be! With all my might, I push myself up and roll out of bed, landing on all fours, my knees hitting the floor with a loud and painful clunk.

"Wait until I get to Chuck!" I gasp. "Not now, please!"

March 4, 2003

Chuck and I go through the brutal rapes in the barn and this time I tell him as much of what's happening as I can.

"And then you're left alone?" he asks.

"Yes, I feel so lonely, ashamed, disgusted and disgusting."

"Those feelings are all lies."

"I know. If they blamed it on me then it was my problem, not theirs."

"Those men believed they could treat a child that way and not have to feel responsible," Chuck says.

"Yes, I know. A child doesn't have rights. Children are told what to do. We were powerless, slaves to our parents and the adults in our lives. Anything done to us was okay, because adults did it."

Chuck acknowledges that he's fully aware of how difficult it is to go through a recapitulation like this. He gently suggests that there might possibly be more of this memory to come. As soon as he says this, I know he's right, more than right.

"Yes, there is more. I didn't tell you everything," I think to myself, and yet I can't say it out loud, it's too shameful. As I get up to leave, I sense how deeply my body wants to let go and just weep like the crying baby in my dream, but it can't yet. Instead, tight with clenching from head to toe, I say goodbye and bolt out the door. I want nothing more than to go home and climb back into bed, to sleep it away, but I have work to do, and appointments to go to. I have living to do!

March 5, 2003

Suddenly, it dawns on me that the dizziness I've been experiencing is related to the memory in the barn! The way it came on so suddenly the other day was so strange. I had, in fact, eaten lunch shortly before it started and then I was stumbling like a drunk. I was deep in memoryland when I pulled myself out of bed to go pick up my daughter. I suspect that part of me stayed in the memory, thus the dizziness, the feeling that I was not fully present—because I wasn't! Then yesterday the dizziness came on again, a little milder, but I very distinctly felt that I might possibly collapse in a heap. When I asked Chuck about it, he said it's a hard call to make, but that it could possibly be related to the memory. "You never know," he said, and suggested that I watch it for a few days. But the more I think about it, and the more I feel what was happening in my body, then and now, the more I believe that part of me—part of the *present* me—is caught back in the memory in the barn.

I woke early this morning to ice and snow and a two-hour school delay, which I'm sincerely thankful for, but the extra hour in bed does nothing for me because I'm still steeped in memory. There's no relaxation or enjoyment in this gift of a lie-in today. Indeed, part of me *is* still lying back there in the past. As I acknowledge this truth, my hand on the sheet is suddenly touching wood. For a brief moment the sheet is something else and I am someplace else, back there in the barn, back on the hard wooden barn floor. Just as suddenly, I shift back into my bedroom again and feel the sheet beneath my fingers, the smooth cool cotton so different from the rough wood I had felt an instant ago. And now I realize that yes, there's more! Oh God, there's more to recapitulate!

Suddenly, I can barely breathe. My room disappears and I feel the wooden floor of the barn beneath my hand again. I kick and the men hold me down. I yell and they cover my mouth, my chest bursting. Help me, I can't breathe! I'm suffocating! I kick with all my might, breaking away from the hands holding me down. I sit up in bed, so dizzy that I swoon. My question is answered: the dizziness is related to the memory in the barn. I have no doubt about it now!

I feel unsafe as the memory presses on me during the day. Although I stringently resist, I begin to lose the fight. Against my will, I give up. Immediately, the memory leaps on me like a prowling animal. I am its child prey. I am pursued, caught, and held captive. My adult body is barely able to cope with the scenario as it unfolds. I am angry as all hell, but I am no match for the three grown men who hold me down and call me "whore baby." And then I am crucified; like a lamb I am slaughtered.

As I come out of this day of recapitulation—out of these slips into past experiences and into greater clarity—I feel totally worthless, unworthy of even the smallest consideration. I haven't been telling Chuck everything because what does it matter, nothing matters. I come out of these memories certain of that. And yet, if it doesn't matter, why can't I tell him everything? At the same time, I know that I must talk, because this abusive past will never be exorcised from me if I don't. Unless I tell Chuck everything, I will continue to suffer the painful consequences of my silence.

The good part of this day's recapitulation is that now I know that the dizziness is related to the memory in the barn. Dizziness also comes on as I fight against the memories—the more I push at them, the dizzier I get. I understand now that if I don't fully recapitulate, I may have to deal with this dizziness for the rest of my life. I've noticed that every time I push back and say, "No, not now, not now, not now," the dizziness synchronistically comes, retaliating in a counterattack, as if to say, "You have to deal with this!" Whether I'm at home going through a memory or in Chuck's office, I am always slightly disoriented and unsteady—in fact, dizzy. The other day, when I went to pick up my daughter at school, I'd put my foot down, expecting it to land one place, and then watch with curiosity as it landed way off to the side, far from where I thought I was placing it. In one way it was almost comical and really quite curious. "Curiouser and curiouser!" as Alice-in-Wonderland said, but now I realize that I wasn't fully in my body.

Chuck suggested that my abuser probably came back to the barn after the rape to make sure I was all right, but no, he really came back to play his last cruel torment, to assure that I was still under his total dominance. But I didn't tell Chuck that, or that one of the men raped me in the rear end. I didn't tell him that my abuser came back to "kiss it and make it all better," bringing me to orgasm, telling me I liked it, that I was just a slut. I was a slut who enjoyed every minute of it. I didn't tell Chuck any of that! But perhaps I'd better, because just as I write these words another flashback leaps out and crashes over me. Like splintered glass, its shards crackle in the air around me, and I once again feel the sharp pains of the rapes. I pull away as quickly as I can, out of the flash of memory. I get up and move, flicking the shards away, shaking off the pain of the rapes and the hands of the men in the barn.

Other thoughts come to my rescue, the recall of my low self-esteem, my meek and self-deprecating self the most urgent. The only thing I was ever proud of was my artwork, my creative self a strange girl who knew how to do things with such confidence. Talented artist, sweet and pretty, but so quiet; those are the words people once used to describe me. But it was all a cover, as much a protective shell as my inner determination was a protective shell. I did what I had to do, but I was never fully present in the world. I was so lost and afraid, stuck halfway between the invisible terror of the abuse and the life I was attempting to live. Indeed, I was half dizzy and groggy most of the time, just trying to stay on the narrow edge of reality. On the other hand, I do have to admit that this too was a real self, as stoic as the abused self, fully intent upon maintaining a hold on life and reality, slim though it may have been.

These contemplations keep me grounded, but only momentarily. Before long I fall helplessly back into the memory in the barn. The men are prominent: their breathing, their faces, their shaved upper lips that always stand out so distinctly, their sweat and cigarette smells, their hands grabbing me. Though I kick furiously, I am very quickly overpowered. Shoved onto a rough table, my legs jerked open, I am crucified once again, entrapped by evil men who thought it was okay to treat a girl like that. "Slut," they called me, "Slut!"

Suddenly, I'm walking down the hallway in high school. A girl strolls right up to another girl and hisses, loud enough for plenty of others to hear, the word scratching the air: *Sluuuut!*

"How do you know she's a slut?" I hear myself asking.

"Everyone knows," the girl says, but the so-called slut is someone I know to be really nice, much nicer than her tormentor.

As soon as I hear the word, I know the girl is more like me than anyone. She doesn't deserve the label. Underneath we are just nice girls who've had the name tacked onto us. "She's not a slut, she's nice, like me," I say to myself, and I know this is true. She's just like me, though on a deeper level I can't really grasp what that means.

As I pull out of these brief dips into the past, I remember the sadness, the heavy heart, the lonely despair of my childhood. I remember my sense of not belonging anywhere. Where do you go to find safety when you don't even belong in this world? There was no person I could turn to—no adult was fully accessible—and who could have borne to hear such disturbing truths, and besides, I was frightened of adults. In addition, I wasn't even really aware that I had a problem, though a dark mysterious shape lurked always in the shadows of my mind. My only real problem, on a daily basis, was how to look and act as normal as possible.

Will I ever be safe? Will I ever get better? Will I ever be totally, fully healed?

March 6, 2003

I'm on an army base, in a dream, meeting with a soldier, a tall black man with a beautiful baby. I hold the baby while he weeps. He tells me that his wife died of cancer shortly after the baby was born. He wants me to become his wife. I tell him that I'm too old for him, but I promise I'll take care of the baby. Meanwhile, I'm stuck on the army base, waiting for permission to leave. "Why can't I leave? Why do I have to stay here?" I yell at Chuck, who's in charge. It's a very depressing place, low barracks lined up in a desert landscape, the threat of terror all around. I feel exposed, unprotected, and totally frustrated. I sit on a low sofa and talk to Chuck, in his role as commander of the base. I'm restless and uncomfortable, my body heavy and cumbersome; it doesn't feel right no matter what position I'm in. "I want to move on now," I say. "When you're ready," Chuck answers, "but until then you just have to go through it."

The dream shifts and now I'm in a bus, driving through the army base. A woman wants to stop at the commissary to buy chocolate chip cookies. She gets out of the bus and returns with three large cookies. I don't want any, not even a bite when she offers, but then immediately regret my decision. I wish I had taken a cookie. A woman sitting in front of me turns around and urges me to take her cookie, speaking to me as if I'm a child. And suddenly I'm a shy five-year-old girl again. Gratefully, I take the cookie and eat it!

I wake up happy, the five-year-old self having totally enjoyed the cookie, contented with having dared herself to finally take something she really wanted. The adult self recognizes the frustration and depression in the first part of the dream. It's what I deal with each day as I go back into the past, as I face the shadow self and the innocent child inside. At the same time, I want the recapitulation to be over. I'm tired of it, uncomfortable in my old skin, ready to jump ahead now into a new me. But, as physically and mentally frustrating as it is, I know I can't skip any part of this process. Just as Chuck tells me, in the dream, that things will shift when I'm ready, it's the same thing he says in real life too. *When I'm ready.*

All day I shift back and forth, half here and half back in the past, my body as heavy and uncomfortable as it was in my dream. Sometimes I'm even caught in the veils between worlds, in a groggy haze, not seeing or hearing well, in a fog between the darkness and the light, in a dreamlike unreality. I spent much of my childhood in this in-between state; so familiar does it feel that I could very easily step off into the void of it and never return.

When I lie in bed at night, my body below the waist becomes a heavy rock wall. I only discover this when I try to roll over and can't, the dreamlike heaviness now a reality. Every time I want to shift my position in bed, I have to reach down and roll the heavy rocks that make up my hips and legs. I move that rock wall over and over again, one boulder at a time, all night long.

March 7, 2003

I'm in a crowded bar in a dream, painting a mural on the walls of the barroom. I'm angry that others have tampered with my supplies, used my brushes and left the lids off the paint cans, leaving my brushes clogged with dried paint. The colors are all different hues of red, except for one can of white, which is unopened. I'm aware of a sinister man watching me. He sits in a dark corner at the back of the bar, facing the entrance, staring straight at me. As I fuss over the mess, he gets up and comes over to me. "This is my place, my bar," he says, threateningly, as if to warn me not to do anything to upset him. "I'm just cleaning up the paints," I say, "and you should watch out, you might get paint on yourself." He's wearing a clean, crisply starched and ironed white shirt. When he sits down, I notice his sleeve brushes against a blob of red paint lying on the arm of the chair. The paint leaves a stain that looks like he's been shot. "Now he's marked," I tell myself. "The police will be able to identify him as the evil one."

The streak of red on the man's white sleeve is like a smear of blood, the blood of the innocents. Though my paints had been used without my permission, the one can of white paint—my innocence—had yet to be opened, yet to be accessed. In truth, it had not been tampered with. Perhaps my innocence is still pure in reality too.

The sinister man in the dream haunts me. Like my abuser he threatens me if I talk, if I reveal what I know. I carry his threatening heaviness to my session with Chuck, seeking relief, and yet no relief comes. I return from the session utterly exhausted. Falling into bed, I sleep for an hour and a half. All day I feel depressed, spongy, in a dream world, not fully present. By seven in the evening I just want to crawl into bed and say, STOP, STOP, STOP! I want the recapitulations to stop, the dreams to stop, and the world to stop spinning.

"Please give me a break!"

March 8, 2003

In a dream, I fight an abusive man who has forced me to give up my son. Fiercely determined to get him back, I attack, punching and kicking the man as hard as I can. I'm also bleeding heavily, my period flowing. I constantly scoop up the blood as it runs down my legs, unable to keep up with the rush of it. My mother suddenly appears. She tells me I had blood transfusions as a child, that it was a treatment that seemed to work for me. As I listen to her, I wonder what other secrets she hides. Are there more secrets of bloodletting and blood cleansing? During the fight I lose an enormous tooth and part of my jaw, but for some reason my mouth feels so much better after this, and I don't look too bad either. After a fierce fight I get my son back. I am intent upon keeping him safe. I tell him and his sister that I will never give them up, that they are part of my life and that we will always be together. I also acknowledge that my son is growing and physically changing, but I'm also aware that he still needs his mother, that he still needs comfort and love.

For the first time in a long time I awaken in an exhilarated mood, though I can make neither heads nor tales of this dream. I've taken back some of my personal energy, I gather, as well as shed some uncomfortable fixtures—the jawbone and tooth—encumberances that didn't really belong to me to begin with perhaps. And so, feeling contented and powerful, I spend a perfect morning with my daughter. We have "girl day," something we haven't done in a long time, which entails spending money, buying my daughter whatever she wants, within reason of course, which

I'm perfectly happy to do. Later in the day, my energy and confidence still high, I go to the studio for a few hours and make a dress out of orange plastic bags. I have so much fun making it and later dressing up for the opening of a costume show at the artist's gallery that I feel like Cinderella getting dressed for the ball. When I show up at the art opening dressed in my finery, someone actually tells me that I look just like Cinderella and that's how I feel, transformed by this colorful dress. With little resistance or interference from my old shy self, a new part of me emerges and comes out to play.

A local cable news anchor comes to film the event. She interviews me, intrigued by the dress I've made. I am equally fascinated by a playful happy self who emerges and romps gaily around the gallery, totally uninhibited. I couldn't have done any of this a year ago! There are plenty of men attracted to this wispy sprite, though I find it slightly annoying to be so blatantly stared at, as if I'm some sort of salacious wench when I'm simply intent upon enjoying the evening. Freed of my usual closeted and shy self, I just want to have fun with my friends—artists expressing themselves—many others in their own handmade masks and costumes as well.

A tipsy man tries repeatedly to pick me up and I easily brush him off. Another, a complete stranger, invites me to dinner. I keep walking away from him, offering polite excuses, but he stares from across the room—just like the man in my dream at the bar. I run away every time I see him approaching. I feel a little sorry for him. He's kind of bedraggled and sloppy, but there's a decidedly negative and bitter undertone to everything he says that's a real turnoff. I know immediately that I'd never be interested in him, especially after he makes some condescending remarks about my friends, including the grand efforts one man makes to entertain everyone, dressed in drag and singing arias. I feel insulted by this repugnant man, who doesn't seem to understand that we're just having fun and that there's no room in this festive atmosphere for judgment. It's an unusually carefree night, everyone's energy high, and the singing is pretty good too!

As soon as I return home and take my costume off, I shed this playful self. My old self returns immediately. The pain creeps back in and the child inside me tucks into a ball. Curling up, I slip right back into my safe place, into the tunnel, where I am deeply hidden. The Cinderella evening ends as the clock strikes midnight, and I wonder if I'll ever see that lighthearted self again. I recall the beginning of the day and the wonderful time I spent with my daughter, so comfortable and chummy, enjoying her bright and engaging personality, doing totally girly things. Life today was good, I conclude. I pushed everything away and went out into the world and had fun! And certainly Cinderella is a fitting description for the self who briefly emerged.

"Do you like my dress?" she asked gaily, an actress playing a part, simply being her art.

March 9, 2003

My morning trials begin as soon as I awaken at dawn and find myself encapsulated in the usual pain. The ever-present duality of this process once again greets me, underscoring the challenges I face, for although I yearn for freedom from pain I must bear the tension of it if I am to discover its true meaning. Although I am often able to work through the pain during the day, every night it comes back over me like a dark blanket and I become its prisoner once again. As I wake up to the same struggles each morning, getting up and staying up are, for the most part, the biggest battles of each day.

March 10, 2003

I dream that I'm with a little girl, walking down darkened hallways in the building where I have my art studio. We thread our way through a tangle of electric wires that hang down from the walls and ceilings, which have crumbled and collapsed. We climb through a tangled mess of black cables lying like coiled snakes on the floor. When we arrive at the studio my work partner tells me that I have to teach a class at seven that evening. She says that she had forgotten to write it down on the schedule and unfortunately she can't do it herself. "No teaching! I told you, no teaching," I shout, furious at her. "I have the child to take care of and I do not want to teach!" I have a good old tantrum, yelling, stomping, and running around the room like a madwoman. Everyone takes it in stride, as if it's a normal thing I do every day.

The dream shifts and now the little girl and I are walking in New York City, on our way to meet up with my mother for tea at the Plaza Hotel. Everything is done properly there, with lots of protocols to follow. As soon as we enter the hotel lobby, we're given a rundown on how to act. We stand around waiting until we're finally led to the table where my mother sits waiting. She ignores us, as if we're not good enough for her. The little girl takes a box out of her pocket that contains a necklace, earrings, and some folded up paper money. I whisper to her that it isn't a good idea to let people know what you have, that you have to keep your valuables and money hidden. I notice Chuck standing across the room, beckoning to me, but I shake my head, "No, not now." The girl and I wait for my mother to decide what she wants to order; she's in charge. She says that instead of having tea she's going to buy a gift for someone. Abruptly, without another word, she gets up and walks away, leaving us sitting there.

After feeling pretty good this weekend—especially my lively Saturday escapades with my daughter and Cinderella—I'm steeped in the old sadness again. As gloomy feelings and anxiety creep in, I wonder what they signify. I wonder if Chuck's presence in the dream is letting me know it's time to get back to work. I'd asked for a break on Friday night because I felt a total breakdown coming, like I was not going to be able to cope anymore. Everything seemed to be piling up around me, set to collapse, much like the hanging wires and cables that hung from the collapsed walls and ceilings in my dream, difficult to maneuver around. Thankfully, my plea for a break was answered—the forces of the universe did their work and I was granted a reprieve for the weekend. I was even afforded some much-needed release in my dreams, shouting, running and stomping. But the appearance of my mother and Chuck bring me back to the work at hand, and now, as Monday morning arrives, I am steeped in such old feelings. I have no energy to even get out of bed. And so, after I send the kids off to school, I stay in bed until noon. I get up then and eat some lunch. I write out some bills and go back to bed. It's only then that I begin to question what's really going on. Do I really *need* to stay in bed?

I go out in the afternoon to run some errands and the memory in the barn descends upon me like a massive tidal wave just as I'm standing in line at the bank. It crashes upon me with great force, the rush of it nearly knocking me off my feet. Anxiety, like a monster from the deep, rears its ugly head and ushers me into its watery world. I barely notice the teller as I make my deposit. When I drive from the bank to the studio and stop at a stop sign, I try to shift into first gear but only get a loud grinding. What am I doing? My car is an automatic! For a second I am a teenager again, driving the old stick shift VW bug that I drove back then. Jerking the car back into drive, I very carefully proceed down the street. I force myself to stay present, but try as I might I can't shake myself free of the memory's grip.

I climb the stairs to the studio, muffled and dizzy, begging the memory to go away. "Not now, not now, not now!" becomes my mantra. Later, as I head back out to pick up the kids from afterschool activities, I notice how poor my driving still is. I make it to the school and home okay, but as soon as I get there I fall into bed, disoriented and shaky. All the signs are here—beyond a doubt, a memory is on its way. I hope it moves along quicker this time. I need to function; I need to work. As always, however, I face the truth that my life will not evolve if I don't go through the details of all the memories.

"So, okay," I say to the universe. "Thank you! I get it. I had my Cinderella night, but it couldn't last, not while I still have more work to do."

March 11, 2003

When I meet with Chuck, concerns about my experiences with the two men at the costume event are uppermost in my mind.

"What did I do that they latched onto me?" I ask Chuck. "As the night wore on, I kept wondering what I was doing that made them attracted to me. I kept thinking there was something wrong with me. I interpreted their interest as my fault, that I was to blame."

"It's not your fault," he says, suggesting that everything that I encounter during my recapitulation is a test. "You have the ability and the skills to deal with everything that comes along, as it should be dealt with, even men. I think you passed your test!"

"If I can only come out of my distant fog and respond with my own voice, actually speak what I really feel, then I might agree that I've passed," I say. "Instead, I hear that calm inner voice, which is always so right, but fails to utter a word."

After the session, I go to a yoga class and feel pretty good. I go home and sleep for a short while afterwards, and then the buzzing dream state returns and I do battle with it for the rest of the day and into the evening. Though I'm momentarily scared that it's something else—a physical malady, my brain going into spasms for some medically explainable reason, like a cancerous tumor— I'm more aware that it's psychosomatic, a memory seeking emergence. It begins as numbness in the frontal area of my brain, a pounding sensation with no pain. It almost feels as if that part of my brain has gone to sleep and is pulsing with a dream, although I'm fully awake! This is accompanied by the same rushing and muffling sound of the wave crashing over me that I'd experienced at the bank yesterday, along with escalating anxiety and the eerie feeling of a bag being pulled over my head.

At night, I stretch out on the couch and watch TV for about forty-five minutes and the pulsing goes away, but a new sensation takes it place. Now I'm unable to breathe. I jolt up, literally gasping for air. Try as I might, I can't catch my breath. It's only the shrill ringing of the telephone that breaks the spell, my daughter calling to be picked up from play rehearsal.

Late at night, unable to sleep, I lie in bed and ask that the truth be revealed. "What is it now?" I ask my psyche, and my psyche answers with sensations and blurry images. "Is it something I don't know yet, or must I rehash all the gory details of something already revealed?" Almost immediately, the sound of rushing water fills my ears and before I know it I'm swamped by the tidal wave that came over me when I stood on line at the bank. The real world closes down as I'm dragged quickly into the undertow. Shaking, I clutch my covers, trying to hang onto reality, but I can't stop the vibrations. I lose my grip. Before I know it, I'm swept away into blurry dreamscapes.

March 12, 2003

I dream that I'm standing on a city street with a group of people. The weather is bad. A storm is expected. We see a huge wave forming on the distant horizon, heading directly toward us. I'm certain that it's going to destroy everything in its path.

Huddling in a corner where two buildings meet, we're completely surrounded by glass. I'm aware that it's not a very safe place to be. I'm standing next to a woman with a baby girl. I tell her that I'll look for a safer place, because the baby will surely be torn from her arms by the force of the water. "She doesn't love her enough," I say to myself, noticing that the mother isn't holding the baby very tightly. Taking the baby from her, I tell her to follow me. I lead the way into an underground garage that's only open on one side, facing away from the ocean and the coming wave. It even has a sturdy overhead door that can be pulled down. "It'll be much safer in here," I say. "The wave will go over the top of the building."

The baby in my arms begins to cry and I realize that she's not used to being hugged. I give her back to the mother and tell her to hold the baby tightly so she doesn't get washed away. We hunker down and nervously await the onslaught of the tidal wave. Finally, after what feels like an eternity, the enormous wave crashes against the outside of the building. Inside the garage, much as I had expected, we remain safe and dry. Several other people had followed us into the underground room and after the storm we discover that we are the only survivors. Everyone and everything outside of our safe haven has gotten washed away. We wander around the now-desolate landscape, scavenging for things we might need.

A selfish young woman doesn't fit in well with the group. She leaves the safety of the parking garage to build herself a shed nearby. She comes back to us begging, sure that we are hiding food from her because we don't like her, but in fact we have none. Angry, she searches through our things and discovers some food we've put aside for the baby. She demands that we give it to her. Appalled that she would steal from a baby, I confront her. I tell her to leave, that she isn't welcome in our place. I follow her outside, intending to talk some sense into her. I sit down on a boulder near her shed and put my foot down on something that I think is moss, but suddenly realize that it's a man's genitals, someone who has drowned in the tidal wave. Suddenly, a huge snake with a fat grey head and bulging yellow eyes latches onto my foot. In tremendous pain, I scream to the young woman to get help, that I'm already going numb. "I'm being poisoned!" I yell. Looking very scared, and forgetting her own problems, the young woman immediately jumps up and calls for help. Just as I sense that I'm about to pass out, the screaming wakes me up.

I notice immediately that my head is perfectly clear, with no fogginess or numbness, no pulsing or pounding, as if the snakebite has cleared the problem. With a new sense of clarity, I lie in bed and think about what was happening in my head as the front half of my brain went numb last night, dragging me into that tidal wave dream, the same way my body goes numb as a memory approaches. I wonder if memories are stored in part of the frontal lobe and if that's where dreams emerge from as well. It makes perfect sense to me that recapitulation would awaken or stir a part of the brain that has been inaccessible, activating it to release its secrets, in waking as well as dreaming states.

I remember that I was able to distract the memory last night by sitting and watching TV for a while. As I became absorbed in a show the numbness and anxiety went away and when I drove out to get my daughter I was fine. Later, while reading in bed, I wondered if it would come back, but it didn't, not until I was lying down. It was only then that the memory washed over me like the tidal wave of my dream, the signal that I was drowsy setting it in motion.

As I shower and get ready for work, I wonder what will transpire during the day, as I'm going to be very busy. I am, however, keenly interested in seeing how this plays out. I'm not really surprised when, almost immediately, before the hour is up, the numbness creeps back in. The buzzing returns, and a slight dizziness comes over me if I turn quickly. The fog of recapitulation appears in front of my eyes and I feel like I could fall right into it.

"Not now!" I plead. "I have to work!"

Before much else happens, I head off to the studio where I'm able to keep "it" away, for the greater part of the morning at least, but as soon as my work partner leaves at eleven the recapitulation starts up again, as if it's been waiting. Like the tidal wave of my dream, it rushes into my head with a whooshing vibration, a cold wave that numbs my brain. I'm so scared that I call Chuck. He suggests that perhaps my memory is manifesting an experience this way, like a dream, like a waking dream.

"Yes," I say, "that's what it feels like, a dream, like I'm entering into a dream. I get groggy, like part of my brain is falling asleep. I shake it awake, splash cold water on my face; the same things I'd do if I were sleepy and trying to stay awake."

"I understand the scariness of it," Chuck says. "Do the sword movements. Keep moving and shifting away from it. That should help."

The fog in my head dissipates as I do the sword form throughout the day. Before long I feel balanced and fully alert. By nighttime my head remains clear and calm.

March 13, 2003

I go to an early morning yoga class and then feel good enough to work at the studio. It's just beginning to snow by the time I get there and soon the schools are closing. The kids call for a ride and so I pick them up and do a little grocery shopping before heading home. The dreamlike buzzing remains in remission, the presence of my children and the energy of our interactions keeping it at bay. The busier I am the better I am, in a place of calmness for long periods of time. As soon as I am no longer physically active and mentally focused, however, the recapitulation returns. As soon as I sit down it drags me into swirling darkness.

"Not now! Go away!" I say sharply, and then I hear the news that Elizabeth Smart is alive. The fifteen-year-old girl—kidnapped from her bed one night nine months ago—is found alive, unbelievably alive. All sorts of people are asking why she didn't speak out, why she didn't ask for help or run away when it appears she had so many chances. Well, I can tell them, she didn't really have a chance. Once traumatized and threatened, she never felt safe enough and she may never feel safe again, at least not for a long, long time. Look at me, fifty years old, and I haven't felt safe my whole life.

Before bed, I notice that the snow has stopped. I hope it warms up enough to melt away so I don't have to shovel in the morning. Just as I climb into bed, I hear a loud creak, as if a door has just opened. Suddenly I'm falling. The world, with its snow and shoveling duties disappears in a flash, as I sense myself tumbling into darkness. Agony and fear fill me as I fall through time and space. Suddenly, I land. I sense that I'm in a moving car, the hum of the motor vibrating beneath my cheek. I'm a scared little child. And then I flash back out again to find myself just about ready to lie down for the night, back in my bedroom, decades later.

March 14, 2003

Once again, I dream of a baby. I ask some friends to help me with her. My hairdresser sets up a crib in her salon and tells me I can bring the baby there any time. The customers will love it, and the baby too, she tells me. "She'll be right here in the room with everyone," she says. I notice that the crib has crooked legs; it doesn't look safe. "Don't worry," she says, "I'll fix it. Everything will be okay." I'm very apprehensive about leaving the baby there, but I make arrangements to bring her the next day anyway.

Then I dream that I'm with a young girl at an amusement park. She wants to go on some wild rides. We get onto a roller coaster that seems very dangerous as there are no seat belts or safety bars. During the ride I'm in constant fear of falling. I hate it, but the girl is nonplussed. "It's not wild enough," she says afterwards, while I try to explain that it wasn't safe. She selects a huge Ferris wheel to ride next, with seats as wide as bleachers. Once again, to my horror, there are no safety mechanisms, nothing to hold us in—we're just sitting on huge swinging bleachers. Gripping the edge of the seat in fear, clinging for dear life, I can't wait for the ride to be over. Again the girl is disappointed. "Too tame," she says, nonchalantly, while I am just relieved to have survived.

I wake with intense leg and hip pain after all the clinging I did in my dreams, constantly fearful, first of leaving the baby in the hands of others and then of falling off the precarious rides. I wonder if my psyche is preparing me for what's to come, as I enter uncharted territory, letting me know that the baby will be safe but that the process into the unknown is always going to feel uncertain at first. The little girl seems to be preparing in her own way, challenging herself to ride the most frightening of rides without batting an eye, while I'm simply afraid. These two dreams seem to reflect both the fears that rule me and my hesitance at taking the next step—but I can't just let go of my fears! And of course I'd like complete assurance that everything will be safe before I take the next step, though I know that's impossible. Uncertainty is par for the course. In fact, it's part of what makes the journey so exciting. The truth revealed by the dream, however, is that although the rides are flimsy and even unsafe, we survive them just fine. And I have to admit, as I've taken this recapitulation journey everything has worked out just fine in the end. I guess I just have to trust that!

As I head out to meet with Chuck, I think about how my fears have kept me so isolated. Fear of just about everything kept me locked inside the tunnel of self and that's what I'm escaping now. From a shamanic perspective, as Chuck has explained, old energy will not let go very easily, so it makes sense that my fears will come out and fight for their right to exist, for they have ruled. If I am to fully heal, however, I must take the initiative to break from old attachments. In other words, if the old energy will not let go of me then I must let go of it. While I drive, I contemplate how my lifelong mental, physical, and emotional fears and attachments have controlled me at the deepest levels. I begin to see everything more clearly, most strikingly how I have clung to a false sense of security my entire life.

The fear seems to have been eavesdropping on my private thoughts because I arrive at Chuck's office cloaked in it! To top it off, I've unknowingly driven right into the buzzing numbness of that tidal wave that keeps appearing in both dream and reality. As soon as I sit down I notice how very far away I am, the air thick and murky. I strain to hear Chuck's voice. It's as if we're sitting at the bottom of the ocean, trying to talk under water. I'm able to nod, making it clear that I'm ready to plow ahead. Putting the EMDR headphones on, I hope the bilateral sounds will clear not only my head but the viscous air as well. I sit hunched over, waiting for some kind of signal, wondering where this process will go next, hoping for a physical release. My body shakes and clenches and the need to cry rises repeatedly, but so muffled is my perception that I am at a loss for words to express it. In addition, I feel as if I'm still on those crazy carnival rides of my dream, clinging for dear life. I cannot let go. I cannot release anything—not one muscle, not one fear, not one thought, not one sound.

"I feel like such a sinner," I finally say, the only words that come through my clenched teeth as I struggle to swim up out of the deep. "I know I'm not a sinner. The sins are my abuser's sins, not mine. I'm not bad. I'm a good person. I deserve good things. He took all of that from me. He took everything from me and left me mauled and half-drowned. That's how I feel right now."

Chuck gently suggests that perhaps the chakra work I've been doing in one of my yoga classes is stirring up too much too quickly, that it may not be a good idea right now, and I know he's right. It's speeding up what I'm not quite getting on my own. The message of my dream becomes more clear now. I see that the little girl is pushing to do what I am clearly not ready for, and not yet comfortable with. It's not time to push ahead; it's time to conserve.

"Do the sword movements; continue strengthening your defenses with that," he suggests.

"I will," I promise, for it's already proven to be most helpful in calming the rising tides of memory, fear, and numbness.

However, for the rest of the day, and in spite of my best intentions, I'm constantly pulled into the tidal wave, into the murkiness of the memory that never clarifies. I sense it nearby, circling like a shark. I do the sword movement every chance I get, cutting and slicing into the impenetrable darkness that surrounds me, trying to ward off its sneaky approach.

The kids go off to their dad's for the weekend and without them to care for I must find other ways to get through the night. I watch two movies that I can't concentrate on and end up fast-forwarding them to the end, watching the action unfold at high speed. The memory synchronously seeks emergence. Egged on by my attempts to defuse it, it fights back, pulsing in my frontal lobe, as fast as the speedily flipping film scenes. It doesn't stop when I turn off the movies and go to bed either, but continues flickering long into the night.

March 15, 2003

I'm with a teenage girl in a dream. Both of us have made it onto Olympic swimming teams. We're waiting to be called to register. I know she's nervous, so I go to check on her. On the way, I pass by my own room. I open the door and I peak inside to see that there is only a rug and two comfortable black chairs, like at Chuck's office. I close the door again, thinking that I'll come back later. I find the teenage girl in the communal bathroom. She tells me that some other girls had warned her that you could see everyone using the toilets, that there is no privacy. She flushes one of the toilets while we talk, slightly embarrassed that someone else had failed to do so. We notice that the sides of the toilet stalls are indeed positioned so high that you can see all the toilets lined up in a row. There is absolutely no privacy. As we talk, the girl worries over why her team has not been called to register yet. She asks if mine has. "Yes, we've registered," I say, telling her to be patient, that her turn will come when it's time, but even so she's extremely nervous and worried, unable to settle down.

I wake up sweaty and in pain, my legs tight with a sense of anticipation, as if I'm the teenage girl in my dream, nervous about being in the Olympics, perhaps a metaphor for this recapitulation, for sometimes it does feel as if I am undergoing rigorous training. The nervousness is partly related to waiting until I meet with Chuck again on Tuesday, until I am once again in the safety and privacy of his office, able to freely register my deepest feelings regarding myself. Until then I intend to stay distracted by keeping busy, as usual.

I go out and run some errands though I continue to feel like the girl in my dream, nervous and unable to settle into calmness. Perhaps, in the telling of my memories, I'm as worried of exposure as she is. In the dream, I acknowledge that I'll return to my room later—set up like Chuck's consulting room—but for the time being I must take care of the nervous girl. This is where I am right now, my dream a continuation of real life, as I must constantly attend to my traumatized child self every day now. I can no longer send her back into the tunnel.

Exhausted after only being in the world for a short time, I crawl back into bed. Taking my child self with me, I sleep all afternoon, the cats tucked in at my feet. I wake up out of deep sleep, heavy and headachy, with just enough time to eat something before heading out to work at the art gallery, my turn to do the night shift. My head thumps and pulses as I drive. I'm aware that I'm perched on the edge of a memory, barely able to keep from tipping over into the abyss of fear. People come into the gallery and I talk as if I'm fine, and while they're present I am fine. As soon as they leave I'm drawn right back to the precipice where I teeter again. I get up every now and then and walk around the gallery, doing a few sword movements, whisking off the energy that seeks to attach. I focus on work too, sketching some new designs, jotting down thoughts for a newsletter I'm commissioned to do, but it's quiet. Not too many people come in, so my attempts at distraction remain futile for the most part.

To pass the time in a more productive manner, I decide to investigate what's happening on a deeper level, without actually acquiescing or caving to the inner tension. I sit calmly centered, confident that I can guide and anchor myself. Fully intent upon staying present, I welcome what comes. Almost immediately, I sense that I'm being reintroduced to memories that have already been evaluated, already gone over so many times, and so I let them come once again. As soon as I give the okay, familiar flashbacks appear, and yet my reaction now is not one of fear but one of wonder. I'm astonished that they are identical to their initial appearances, all the details intact. They'd be different if they weren't real, I intuit, if I were somehow inventing them as I've gone along. But no, every detail is acutely the same, every memory etched exactly as it had originally flashed before me. I'm also aware, in the split second that a flashback lights up the darkness, that there is no time to invent anything; there is barely time to hold onto consciousness, barely time to hold onto awareness of present place and adult self. And so I wonder if this process tonight is urging me to accept just how real the memories are.

"Do you still doubt us?" they seem to be asking. "But see, nothing has changed, and nothing will change because these are true scenes from your life; your truths revealed. Do you believe us now?"

Do I believe? Yes, I BELIEVE! I BELIEVE! I BELIEVE!

Chuck and I have both felt the presence of something or someone conducting this recapitulation. It's eerily apparent that no matter what arises in the unfolding of this process, there is a sense of everything fitting together. We both remarked on this yesterday, the same thought going through our heads simultaneously. In some way, my dreams always show me where to go next—deeper truths revealed while my conscious self is out of the way—while the memories come in such a way as to suggest that everything is orchestrated. And I sense that whatever or whomever is helping me is worried about my energy. I sense that it wants me to be safe and that it's deeply caring, that it wants me to arrive at a place of total healing. I wonder if it's Jeanne Ketchel. Although Chuck and I both admitted to sensing another presence, I still was not able to mention her to Chuck yesterday. I feel that I must keep her a secret. It just hasn't felt right to bring her up, though I've often wondered if she hasn't appeared to Chuck as well. We didn't go there yesterday. We simply noted our mutual sense of continuity and guidance from beyond this world.

"Who are you and why are you helping me? Is it you, Jeanne? Are you still helping me?" I ask, for I have no doubt that I am being guided, nor do I harbor any real doubt about the truth of everything that happened to me as a child.

"Whatever you have to do," I pray, "please do it, so I can be rid of the last shreds of doubt, so I can move on."

And then I admit, to myself and to her, that I've felt stuck, not knowing how to move forward, not knowing how to fully believe what happened to me in my childhood. I've been having trouble finding where the memories fit into the life I remember. I've been having the hardest time fathoming that the abuse was even possible, but it's so clear now that everything about it has been stored in my body, waiting my entire life to reveal itself to me. That's what those flashbacks are, revelations of truth!

I am more aware now, as everything about my personal story changes, that everything else is set to change too. I've lost huge hunks of my life, my known self now shattered to pieces. It's a bit overwhelming having to reconstruct a life with all this new information. Well-known memories are gone and new unfamiliar ones are taking their places, and yet it often doesn't seem that this is actually me and my life that I'm excavating. I often stop in astonishment and ask myself: *Who am I?*

March 16, 2003

I dream that I'm staying at a hotel. I keep running into a man who wants me to go to his room with him, pestering me quite a bit. I try to frighten him off by doing the sword movement, jabbing and sweeping my sword at him, but to no avail; he just won't give up! There's a woman with me and although I know her as "my protector," I instantly recognize her as Jeanne Ketchel. She follows behind me at all times, her presence large in essence, energetically warm, and extremely loving. She sees that I'm having trouble getting rid of the pesky man. She hands me a large jar with a screw top. I hold it against my chest and open it in front of the pesky man and then watch in astonishment as long black snakes come slithering out of it. They scurry down my body and along the hotel corridor. My protector hands me another jar and many more after that. I open each one of them, releasing the snakes in the same manner. I'm not afraid of the snakes; I intuitively know them and understand why they're here. I also know that I won't "be done" until I've emptied every jar of snakes.

The pesky man freaks out at the sight of the snakes, especially at how casually I react to one very long snake that slithers into my coat sleeve. As I gently shake it out, the pesky man takes off running, frightened of the snakes and of me now too. As I watch him disappear down the hallway, the snakes scurrying after him, I take off my coat, shake out the last of the snakes, and see that I have no clothes on underneath. Unselfconsciously, I put my coat back on and walk outside. My protector, Jeanne, stays with me, guiding me through crowds of people as I push my way along busy streets. I'm on my way to meet with Chuck; I know he's waiting for me and I don't want to be late.

I finally discover Chuck sitting at a small round table in a crowded café. As I sit down next to him, I'm aware that he too is only wearing an overcoat. I tell him about the snakes, about their color and size, and how I wasn't afraid of them at all. Jeanne, standing on the other side of the table, hands Chuck a book of poetry, asking him to read aloud. With her back to the bustling café, she creates a quiet energetic bubble around us. I listen as Chuck reads, our heads close together. I feel totally calm. Even though we are both naked underneath our coats, I know I am safe.

I feel the presence of Jeanne again, my protector, more fully returned to me in this dream. Although I'd dreamed of her a few weeks ago, for the most part she's been absent for a long time, months in fact. I have sensed her, however, guiding me from a distance. It feels as if she's here to stay in a new way now. I'm aware that she's been leading me through dreams and reality lately, and last night she enveloped me as I slept. She answered my prayers for help and guidance, and I felt myself literally falling into her arms, her warm embrace and her protective aura wrapping around me as soon as I got into bed. I lay there safe and sound until I fell asleep. And then she accompanied me through my dreams, protecting and guiding me, until the end when she brought me to Chuck, who said he'd been worried about me. "It's okay now," I told him in the dream. "Jeanne's back."

Although Jeanne has been energetically present in my life and my dreams—a major influence in this recapitulation process—I still struggle with knowing if it's right to reference her when I speak with Chuck, unsure of what her presence truly means. I have no idea how he might react. I have simply told him that I dream about her, that she speaks to me in my dreams—if it feels right to say even that much. More often than not, I simply refer to her in our conversations as "my guide." Although she's been present in so many ways over the past two years, I don't quite know how, or if, I'll ever be able to tell Chuck that his dead wife slept with her arms around me last night!

This signifies a definite return after eight or nine months of almost complete silence on Jeanne's part. I sense that she took great care to set me up to work closely with Chuck and then took off for some unknown reason. I wondered if I would ever see or feel her presence again. Last month she appeared in a dream and told me she was well aware of the deep work I've been doing with Chuck and that she wholeheartedly approves of it, but last night's appearance had a totally different quality about it. Not only did she guide me through a dream, but I felt her presence in my bed as well. I'm absolutely amazed to find that she's come back in this new way. I wonder what it all means!

With my energy bolstered by my dream, I get out of bed and take a long hike. Freed of the recapitulation process while I walk, I'm able to relax and enjoy being outside, but as I return to the spot where I'd parked my car everything starts to rev up again. The sense of urgency to recapitulate returns and the dreamlike wave of buzzing numbness descends upon me as I drive home. As soon as I get into the house I crawl back into bed with my jacket, gloves, and muddy boots still on. As I pull the covers up, I have the very clear perception that I'm being led every step of the way through this process, just as Chuck and I had discussed the other day. And even though he often suggests that I should hold off on recapitulating until I'm with him, I know I'm safe. I have other resources to rely on; his one-time partner now supporting and guiding this process as well. And both Chuck and Jeanne have taught me that if I can let myself go with what comes, the anguish and fear will diminish and the tension will diffuse. In addition, I'm aware, in spite of how deeply into the past and into myself I've already gone, that I must go deeper still. And so, I intend to stay anchored in this world as I venture into the shadows of my deepest self, fully aware that I must keep going back into the past if I am to gain the freedom I seek. I hear Chuck's voice kindly granting me permission to go ahead with the recapitulation, while cautioning me to stay grounded: *It's not now! It's not now! It's not now!*

I pull the covers over my head and sink deeper into the murky past, Chuck's anchoring mantra echoing around me. Once again the tidal wave overtakes me and then I hear nothing, only the sucking sound of the waves taking me from the reality of my bed. I flounder like a swimmer caught in the churning undertow. I am no match for this force of nature. I am dragged down deeper still. I disappear into the dimness at the bottom of the ocean where shadowy figures reside, and where strange things happen in the swirling, impenetrable darkness that surrounds me. Nothing is clear, nothing makes sense, yet everything about the experience appears totally familiar.

After what seems like hours in the underworld, I'm able to swim up out of the deep. I slowly sit up and pry myself out of bed. I change my clothes, eat some food, and put the movie channel on. I sit and watch movies as they scroll past, not really seeing or hearing, as if I'm still underwater, but the distraction is helpful, almost calming.

The judging self feels like I've wasted a perfectly beautiful weekend, but the recapitulating self realizes that I have to keep going down into this shadowy underworld—even if I don't always re-emerge with clarity—so I can eventually have a new and different life. Some day soon it will all be clear, the dark mysteries revealed, I'm sure of that. And maybe sometime in the future I won't feel those horrid mens' fingers digging into my hips and thighs every time I turn over in bed. Maybe sometime in the future I won't hear the loud breathing of those men, or hear their voices, or smell their sour breath. The memories have been so deeply buried that it's taken me this long just to access them. Even discovering that they exist is amazing to me, as is understanding that *this* is the stuff that has made me the person I am today. Yet, I must accept that this underworld stuff is what lies at my core, and so it's imperative that I continue facing it.

The kids come home from the weekend with their dad, with homework still to complete and restlessness matching my own. Eventually we're all settled down, lights out, in our beds for the night. Suddenly I startle awake. I'm aware that I've dozed off. Slightly disoriented, not sure of what's happening, I find myself back in my girlhood bedroom. I sit up in bed, surprised to see the pale yellow walls, the furniture I had as a girl, the double closet doors, everything lit with a strange glow. The room shimmers and switches back to now, to my orange-painted walls and my bookshelf on the opposite wall, but even that is shimmery and unreal, lit by some strange light. My perception shifts again and now I'm back in the room I had when I was a child. And now I'm a child again too, a thin, fragile shell of an adolescent peeking out from under the covers, seeking connection with all my familiar belongings, but I'm too distant—in the fog between worlds—and I find nothing to attach to, for nothing matters. Suddenly, there's a noise at the door and my mother rushes in, my father close behind. In anger she hits me while I lie huddled in my bed, her ferocity bringing me to fuller alertness. "How could you? How could you? How could you?" she yells as each strike lands. "Take it easy, take it easy!" my father says. And then the scene shifts. I'm back in my orange bedroom, back in my adult body, certain that this scenario referred to the discovery that I was pregnant at the age of twelve.

The scene before me takes a long time to return to normal. The two worlds shimmer, blending together for a while longer, until the strange light dims, until the air gradually clears and my present reality appears solidly before me, my room in darkness once again.

March 17, 2003

I dream that I'm a child again. My abuser attacks me. I try to fight him off, but I can't. In the end he rapes me. When I return home no one even notices that I've been gone. No one seems to have missed me. No one asks where I've been, though they expect me to do whatever they ask of me, to immediately attend to my younger siblings, to fetch and clean, to be available. Then I'm my adult self, talking to my brother who died. I'm aware that he's my parent's guardian, that he watches over them, and that he's protecting them from me. He warns me not to cause them any sadness. "Don't devastate them anymore; they already have more than they can handle," he says bluntly. "Okay," I say, knowing that he's referring to his own death and how devastating that was for them. I decide I'll help them out too, in my own practical way. I notice that there's an overall lack of basic communication between them, and virtually no planning for the future; they live day to day. I decide I'll help them learn how to communicate better and to plan pragmatically, but before long I see the futility of this idea, as they simply grunt and turn away when I speak, and so I back off. Next we're in my parent's car, which my father is driving. I'm sitting in the back seat, aware that it isn't a good idea; I should be driving instead. We'd argued about this earlier, but he'd insisted and my mother simply went along, as per the usual course of events. Suddenly, he passes out. Now my mother reacts, screaming and hitting him over the head, while I attempt to steer the car from the backseat. "What a bad idea this all is!" I mutter to myself, as I guide us safely to the side of the road.

I wake up crippled with old pain. Needing to get away from the dream, I immediately drag myself out of bed. Walking like Frankenstein, I lurch out to the kitchen to make some coffee, desperate to shake off the depressing weight of my parents. I realize I'm no longer in that old place with them. I'm no longer a kid in the back seat, just along for the ride, though I awaken feeling like I did when I was a kid, depressed, knowing that I'm caught in someone else's world and that I just have to bide my time until I can move on. I must give myself credit for all the hard work I've been doing to release myself from them and the power they once held over me. The fact that I do take action in the dream—first fighting my abuser and then taking over the steering of the vehicle—reflects my changing self.

I recall the shift in perception I'd experienced last night as I'd dozed off—my parents invading my space in more ways than one—and so I acquiesce to the truth of who they have elected to be and the futility of expecting them to change. In addition, the fact that I dreamed of being raped, right after I had that shimmery experience, supports the truth of what has been revealed during this recapitulation. But the beginning of the dream points out another truth as well, which is that no one really seemed to look at me very closely. As the big sister in a family of seven children it was more important that I support my parents, that I be available to help them out. This was pointed out in the dream as I returned from the rape. Their only concern was that I do what they asked of me. Indeed, that was my reality as a child; I was at their beck and call. Far more seriously, as the dream also points out, was the fact that no one ever seemed to notice I was being abused, and if they suspected it, they made the decision not to address it. Just as the dream suggests, this is how they operated. More often than not they just went along, as my mother did in the dream; life bowled them over and they let it. When my mother got angry at my father for passing out, she reacted the same way she reacted to me in my shimmery experience—and as she normally did to life's vicissitudes—hitting and screaming. There was either silence or there was explosion on her part; no emotions between those two extremes existed. No discussions or concerns were raised, no attempts at deeper understanding; there was only quick anger, judgment, criticism, condescension and accusation. But I wonder, how did they think I got pregnant?

As these truths sink in, part of me just wants to collapse back into bed, the heavy weight of my past too much to bear. I don't feel like facing the world today. I only want to stay under the covers and hide out with my pain. I'm ready to just keel over into deeper depression when I hear Chuck's grounding mantra, pulling me back to reality: *It's not now! It's not now! It's not now!*

"Okay, I can do this," I say; to Chuck as much as to myself. "I don't want to be like my parents. I can take what life brings me and learn from it, so I can change. I'm in charge of my life and I can take care of myself."

And with that I head to the shower, aware that I must stay focused on changing my own life, taking my own journey. Each step is vitally important. As I get into the shower, I remind myself of my commitment to this recapitulation. As the hot water rains down upon me, I scrub away all the energetic remnants of my parents and my abuser, what might still be clinging to me, from my dreamworld, this world, and all other worlds that I have been in during this lifetime.

The kids go to school and I head over to the studio. I'm determined to get an early start, but I can't sustain my intent. I make it up the stairs and unlock the door, then turn around and drive back home again, my energy suddenly depleted. I climb right back into bed, depressed and exhausted. It's like I'm running on an endless treadmill, stressed and worn out by the unrelenting intensity of the pace. It doesn't matter that it's a beautiful day, warm and pleasant, I just lie in bed cowering. As agitation builds, I wonder if more stuff is coming, the sound of the tidal wave pounding nearby. *It's not now! It's not now! It's not now!* I'm afraid. I'm afraid. I'm afraid. *It's not now!* I feel helpless and humiliated. I'm full of anger and disgust! *It's not now!*

Frightened, I pull away. I get up, make some coffee and go outside with the cats; the first time they've been outdoors since we moved in. I straighten up the garage and bring in the last boxes that need to be unpacked. I'm able to keep myself going, as difficult as it is, though I have to go back inside and lie down often, as clenching pain periodically overpowers me. Each time this occurs, I only lie down for a little while, just long enough to release the pain. Then I force myself to get up again, go back outside, and keep moving. By the time the kids get home from school I've worked through something, though I'm not sure what.

It's now ten at night and I can't sleep, the caffeine from the coffee I'd had earlier in the day still ticking away. But I don't care, because tomorrow is Tuesday, the day I meet with Chuck.

While I lie in bed waiting for sleep, the disorienting memory of being in my childhood room spontaneously replays. Just as it did last night, my dark room shimmers and changes. Once again the past comes so close that I hear my parents arguing in their room, which is right next to mine. Then my mother angrily bursts in, hitting me, screaming at me and it becomes perfectly clear that this memory does refer to the pregnancy I had when I was twelve. My father pulls her off me; he only wants to know who the guy was. "Who did it? Who did it?" he yells, while my mother weeps into her hands. "How could you? How could you do this to us?" is all she can say, neither of them showing even a hint of compassion. Then, just as had happened last night, my room slowly shimmers back into the present.

I sit up, turn on my light, and grab my journal. Before I lose the connection to her, I turn to my twelve-year-old self, that young girl teetering on the edge of the precipice, about to fall into the ever-present abyss, the same one that constantly looms before me now. With pen in hand, I let myself go deeper into her memory. It's June, after school is out for the year. I'm soon to turn thirteen. Deeply depressed, I lie on my bed a lot, just staring into space. I feel so cold. It's a rainy summer and I wear a heavy, white Irish-knit cardigan all the time. It belongs to my mother. Apparently my parents have decided that I need something to do, that I need both a break from my family duties and something for myself alone, because they surprise me by signing me up for art lessons. They even hire a babysitter to take care of my younger siblings, normally my job. I've already painted several watercolor scenes and gotten some recognition in the local papers and amongst a local art group. Far more important, however, is that this is the summer that I discover not only a passion, but a means of escape. Art becomes a meditative center of calmness and creativity. As soon as I pick up my paints and brushes, the calm eye at the center of the storm immediately appears and I am safely ensconced in another world, without ever having to leave the house.

A hint of some new memory comes as I bid my young self goodnight. I push it away. It can wait. After all, we're working on this together now, all three of us—Chuck, Jeanne, and I. At last I can acknowledge the truth of this new partnership. I believe in it, and once I'm able to trust it more fully—on all levels—perhaps this recapitulation will move more quickly. As I close my journal and put down my pen, I pray for calming sleep.

March 18, 2003

Finally, this long-awaited Tuesday has arrived, my meeting with Chuck! I tell him about the dream with the snakes, but once again I don't mention Jeanne. I'm not ready to broach the subject with him. It's all I can do to accept her for myself and just the thought that my connection with Jeanne might hold some deeper meaning for him is too much to bear. I don't want to be intimately involved with him in anyway, or have to be sensitive to his feelings while in the midst of this deeply personal work. I don't really want to know anything about him. I need him to be neutral, to be detached and yet fully attentive while we work on my process. This work is all that matters.

I notice his face brightening as I try to explain, as best I can, the experiences I had in my bedroom over the past few nights, the blending of past and present, recapitulation and reality. He smiles and then turns ruminant, reminding me of the deeper importance and significance of dreams.

"Dreams both instruct and work in tandem with the recapitulation process," he says. "They must be taken seriously."

"Have no doubt about that," I say, "I do take them very seriously!"

I had automatically assigned the snakes in my dream a negative connotation, as I saw them as suggestive of the poison left inside me by my abuser and his cohorts, which I successfully released in the dream. Chuck, however, reminds me that snakes symbolize not only poisoning or numbing energy, but also medicine, in the form of healing venom. This insight allows me to see the dream in a totally new light, as a positive, healing dream. As if a light bulb has gone off, I suddenly realize that the dream was really all about reclaiming my personal power. In fact, I felt quite strong and happy in the dream, as well as utterly calm as I handled the snakes. Indeed, there was nothing frightening or negative about them. In this state of personal power I was guided to the café, a place of utter calmness and safety.

Chuck recommends that I use my dreams as safe places when anxiety hits. Instead of getting swept up by anxiety and fear, I can go into the comforting arms of my protector. I can take up my jars of snakes and feel my own calming power, my inner knowing of how right everything is. Then we get talking about something else and I forget that I have memories pressing on me, and by the time we're almost done I realize there's no time left to introduce them. I had so looked forward to doing EMDR and I end up a little disappointed that it doesn't happen, but I decide it's okay because I got such clarity from the dream analysis.

Later in the day, the anxiety creeps back in, along with the disappointment that it will have to wait until our next meeting. To combat the rising tide of feelings, I spend some quiet time going back into the café dream, just as Chuck had suggested I do. The calm presence of Jeanne surrounds me immediately as I reenter the dream and once again sit down next to Chuck at the little table. As I listen to the sound of his voice, I concentrate on trying to see the title of the book and to hear the exact words. With Jeanne, my protector, watching over me from the other side of the table, her aura warm and comforting, I bask in the absence of tension, as if I am sitting in the calm eye of a storm. As I come out of this dreamy state, I remember how effective the idea of a safe place really is. I had used it in the very beginning of this recapitulation, the first helpful tool Chuck taught me. In my imagination, I'd go to the field high on the mountaintop, the place of freedom and safety that I had once gone to as a teenager, a place of escape in the midst of a stress-filled life that I could not fully penetrate, until now.

I intend to sink into the aura of my protector whenever I need to. I trust that she'll be available in waking and dreaming states alike. Thank you, Jeanne! And whomever else may be helping, because I sense that someone else has been guiding and protecting me for a long time now. When I was a little girl I prayed to my guardian angel, the one I learned I had but never saw or felt, though I realize now must have been quite active, because, in spite of everything, I was somehow able to survive.

March 19, 2003

I dream that I'm hired by a company to write a daily newsletter. The boss sits me down, describes the layout, and tells me to finish by a certain time each day. No other information is given. I don't even know what the company does. I sit at a desk in a crowded room. I start to write something, then immediately edit it. The boss keeps coming by to see what I've written, nagging me about the deadline. I type something else, then delete it. I write again, delete again; write again and delete again. The boss yells at me. "There's a deadline, damn it!" I decide to quit, but before I do, I loudly and firmly tell the boss off—right to his face. All the other office workers stand up, cheering and clapping! I read a letter I've written to the company management. "No wonder you are doing so badly," I read. "It's time to get rid of the stupid guys at the top and let real people take over." I wake up, hearing Jeanne speaking these words of encouragement: *"Yes, it's time to get rid of the bad guys, quit the old ways of doing things, and go for the new. Find a way to follow your heart. Go where you need to go, not where the old dictator tells you. Take a stand!"*

Even with such words of encouragement resounding in my ears, I wake up in the same tight clench that dominates every morning. One day I'd like to wake up in a totally relaxed and refreshed state, but today is not that day. Instead, I am raw and frustrated, as if my wounds have grown exponentially deeper and more difficult to heal. Can I really get beyond this point and take the advice I so clearly hear?

My urge is to stay in bed and keep working on this important task, but I can't. I'd like to sit quietly in meditation, listening to Chuck reading poetry too, but my car is being looked at and I really do have to write a newsletter today. So I drag myself out of bed, away from the dream and my desire for quiet. However, I soon begin to notice how physically uncomfortable, how leaden and cumbersome I am, how my clothes don't fit right, as if I've put everything on backwards. My body doesn't feel right either. I can't walk right, as if my shoes are on the wrong feet, and I can't breathe right, as if my lungs have shrunken to small heavy balloons that simply will not inflate. It's as if I've woken up in someone else's body and it just doesn't fit!

Later in the day, giving myself a break from the intensity of the day's projects at the studio, I sit and meditate. I go back into the dream at the little café and sit down next to Chuck. I pull my imaginary overcoat around me, as Jeanne—the protector with her bright white aura—hands him a book and says, "Read to her, Chuck. This is what she needs in order to heal." The sound of Chuck's voice, steady and calming, leaves me feeling completely safe, cozily isolated within the calming white aura, while the bustle of life in the café goes on around us. Again, I try to discern the words that Chuck is speaking, wondering if they're important, but I realize they aren't. It's the healing process that's important, and knowing that I'm safe, that a safe place does exist, a gift from my dreamworld working "in tandem," as Chuck said, with this recapitulation.

While Chuck reads, I glance at my naked body beneath my overcoat and see that my flesh is sliced open. An enormous gaping wound, from which live snakes are dangling, travels the length of my torso, from my heart to my pubic bone! I jolt out of the meditation, startled at the sight, wondering what it means. Why are the snakes there? Are they healing me or are they sucking the life out of me? I'm not sure. My immediate reaction, however, is to get rid of them. I'm aware that snakes don't hear the same way we do, that they will need to sense movement if they are to depart, and yet I'm afraid to move for fear they'll clamp down even harder. This is a key moment in my healing process, and so I take it seriously. I must somehow produce nonthreatening sound vibration.

I glance down again, thinking how absurd this is, that it isn't possible, I'm only meditating! But once again I see the big gaping wound, still there, still painful, the snakes still attached. I recall the dream of the tyrannical boss and how I tricked him by letting the management know that the company was failing because the department head sucked. I realize that the dream is about making a change, about getting away from my abuser's domineering presence in my life by boldly speaking out and changing the things that don't work for me, by quitting many an old way of doing things. Jeanne's voice, which I so clearly heard upon waking, reverberates deeply now, as I decide to follow its advice. I clearly understand that these snakes as related to my abuse and the long term repercussions of being energetically attached to things that are not of my own choosing, not the path of my own heart. This wound and these snakes are related to an old world, the old dictators and the foreign installations that have ruled me, my abuser and all else that I seek to free myself from. I am determined to get rid of the snakes and close up the wound.

Once again, I return to meditation. I sit in the café next to Chuck and listen as he reads. I lean my head against his shoulder, allowing the vibration of his voice to flow through me. Soon the snakes begin to feel it too. They feel a shift, a change, a warning tremor that something is happening. I open my overcoat and face the white light, the aura of my protector. "I can do this," I think. "I can remove the snakes." As I turn toward the light, the slight movement—like a zipper unzipping—forces the snakes to lose their grip. One by one, they begin dropping off, slithering along the floor. Chuck and I aren't at all frightened by them, their power gone. As I turn more fully toward the white light I notice how good and healing it feels, like warm sunlight. Chuck continues reading. As the vibrations of his voice course through me, the remaining snakes let go, slipping down my legs. I watch them scurrying off in all directions, unnoticed by the other café patrons. Chuck and I smile at that—the image of all those snakes skittering past all those people and what it implies—all that is in our midst that we are totally unaware of. The white light of the aura heals the wound in my torso. Jeanne tells Chuck that I've healed on the outside, and now I'm ready to heal on the inside too.

No more snakes, no more getting stuck, I promise myself. Only healing light, gentleness, humor, trust, and love now, because yes, I do feel loved.

March 20, 2003

I dream that I'm on the way to a cabin in the mountains, to join up with some other people. My car keeps stalling and conking out and I have to have it jumpstarted several times. A man stops to help at one point. After he's gotten my car going I start to pull away but accidentally bump into his car. He yells at me. Then his car needs starting and I have to give him a jumpstart. He's very nervous that I'll bump his car again. He has a large goiter under his chin, which I think is very strange, and I begin to notice how stiffly he holds himself and how stiffly he moves. His eyes seem glazed over and it suddenly dawns on me that he's an alien. We can't get his car restarted so he travels with me to the cabin to call for assistance. The alien stays outside while I go into the cabin, ostensibly to get him a telephone, but I get caught up in the chaos inside. The cabin is overrun with children. A man and woman—the only adults and supposedly in charge—are engaging in sexual flirtation, oblivious to the chaos. I try to figure out how to get them out of the house so the children don't have to watch them. They make an excuse to go into town together, to get provisions, but I know they're going somewhere to have sex.

As soon as the couple leaves, the alien enters the cabin, followed by a whole army of aliens, hundreds of them with stiff walks and goiters too. There's no doubt in my mind that they have come to take us with them. I realize that the broken car was just a ruse, and now I want the man and woman back, just to have more people to help me protect the children. After sending the children to the back of the house, where I know they'll be safe, I confront the aliens, telling them to leave. I also tell them they won't get the children and they won't get me anymore, either. I'm too strong for them now; I'm not the same person I once was. "I know who you are," I say, as they line up, facing me like a fighting brigade.

As I watch, their faces turn dark with anger and their red goiters puff up. Boldly, I jump into the stance of the sword movement and whip out my sword, but this time a real sword appears in my hand. Without a moment's hesitation, I swing it over my head and cut through the line of puffed up goiters with one swift stroke. As the sword cuts into the aliens, I'm somewhat surprised to hear them let out loud huffs of air as they collapse and fall to the floor like withered balloons. All that's left of them are their empty skins and their horrible dark faces, lying crumpled in a row, like ugly rubber masks. As each row of aliens advances, I dart toward them. Swinging my sword over my head, I bring it down with the agility of a master, advancing and slicing into row upon row. Without hesitation, I kill them all, until the floor is littered with hundreds of dead aliens. "We're all safe now," I say, with a big sigh of relief, as I put my sword away.

Next, I dream that I'm in the café with Chuck and Jeanne again, with the snakes chewing at my bloody wound. Dark droplets of blood run down my legs to the floor. I keep thinking that if only I could move a bit maybe I'd be able to shake them off. I ask Chuck if he thinks this will work. I perseverate, wondering if maybe the light of the Aura will be too bright for the snakes. Maybe they won't be able to stand it and they'll easily let go, so I won't have to do a thing. Then I wonder if the brightness of the light will just cause them to bite down harder. "It's not now," says Chuck, intruding into my obsessive thoughts, "they can't hurt you." Bingo! Of course it's not now! And when I look again, I see that the snakes aren't alive at all; they are now just empty, molted skins. It suddenly dawns on me that the actual snakes left a long time ago, shedding their old skins as they crawled away. I also notice that the wound is healing nicely now, leaving a long red scar. Just as I'm about to pick off the first of the dried snakeskins, I wake up with the most wonderful energy coursing through me!

These two dreams complement the meditation that I did yesterday. The aliens are so like the snakes, with their reptilian goiters and empty skins, but I'm totally without fear as I attack and conquer them. There is absolutely no hesitation on my part. I have trained with that sword for so long, in dreams and in reality—doing the movements numerous times a day—that I simply do what has become so natural. The dream reveals just how important a part of me that sword has become, as it magically appeared, as real as could be.

When I tell the aliens that I know who they are now, I'm declaring that I will no longer be controlled by the past, for they represent my memories and fears, which have controlled and dominated me for so long, in so many ways. They also represent the foreign installation, all that has been implanted in my psyche as I've lived my life in this world, all that I have learned and attached to, all that has kept me from truly living life on my own terms. The second dream goes one step further, reminding me that the snakes—energetic attachments, in all their myriad forms—no longer have any power over me. This dream points out that the memories, as I work through them, become mere molting skins devoid of energy as well. The dream points out the ultimate goal of recapitulation: *to get to a place where the memories no longer have any power.* They will be only molted carcasses in the end, with no energetic charge, nothing to be concerned about.

Of course, I know that all of this is just in my dreams, but even so, my body is in shock, as if it's just gone through a serious operation. There is definite tenderness along the imaginary scar. Sore muscles wrap around my rib cage, and the tight clench of my abdomen reminds me that I've suffered from a lifelong affliction: *I have held onto what has harmed me.* Like the snakes, I have clamped down and held on for dear life. I have, in my ignorance, held myself back from fully living. I have been a prisoner of my own psychological makeup, shackled by my own restraints, by my fears and my need to maintain a sense of safety; a death sentence if ever there was one. It's time to complete the healing process and let everything go, so I can really live! This is my main task right now: *to fully heal.*

Yesterday was a day of transition—when I just didn't feel right in my own skin, when even my most comfortable clothing didn't fit right—and today I'm in a new place. Now I understand that I was shedding my old skin, just as the snakes shed their skins, and the aliens shed their costumes, leaving behind only empty reminders of who they once were. That's what I'm doing too—I'm molting, shedding the old self as I recapitulate, leaving only ghosts of my old self behind.

March 21, 2003

I meet with Chuck. We do EMDR around my dreams. As soon as I go back into the café in my imagination and peek inside my overcoat, I see live snakes hanging from the tight red scar. I'm frightened of what it might mean that I still have them there. I wonder what happened to the dried snakeskins of my dream. Try as I might, I just can't pluck them off without being disgusted, without cringing and clenching. In spite of my good intentions to heal quickly, I'm still holding so much in, still fearful of getting hurt. Even in my imagination I just can't touch the snakes. After several attempts to grab their heads and pluck them off, I finally decide that if they were something less horrible, I might be able to handle them better.

"For some reason, I just can't touch them, but if I imagine them as black rubber hoses that I can detach—like battery hoses—I think I can get rid of them. I know I don't need them. I don't need to be hooked up to anything because I have my own power source, my own inner battery," I explain to Chuck, and in my imagination, I proceed to pull off the hoses, and cap over the battery, my inner power source restored to it's original state.

"Have you ever seen *The Matrix*?" Chuck asks, a look of astonishment on his face as I tell him what I'm doing.

"No, I've never heard of it."

"That's exactly a scene in the film!" he says. "As you are describing this to me, you are blowing my mind. You have to go and rent that film immediately!"

So I do. I get the film and watch it with my son, who loves it. In fact, he's been begging his dad to let him watch it, he tells me. He too can't believe I've never heard of it. I personally relate to the adventures of Neo as if he is going through a process much like recapitulation. I fully understand his initial reluctance, not wanting to face the inevitable challenge, but he can't stop the process, just as there is no stopping the process of recapitulation once embarked upon. As the world, as he knows it, falls away and he begins to accept a new reality, his past becomes like a dream, his new reality the only thing that matters. His battles are much like my fighting dreams, so impeccably well-trained is he. The whole movie is more than mindblowing, especially the scene that Chuck had mentioned. Astonished, I watch Neo unplug himself from the power source of the matrix, the black snakelike hoses attached to his naked torso replicating exactly the black snakes attached to my own torso.

I felt really good today, happy and full of energy for the first time in months. I stayed at the studio all day until it was time to pick up the kids. Now, at bedtime, I'm only slightly burdened by the usual stuff. I hope this good energy lasts!

March 22, 2003

I'm having a conversation with myself in a dream about whether or not the dream has merits, if I'm being shown or taught something important. "Oh, this dream isn't significant," I say. "I'm dreaming like this because I just saw *The Matrix*, even though this isn't at all like *The Matrix*." Then Jeanne speaks. *"No, but your dream is influenced by it. And remember, you always think dreams have no significance while you're dreaming them,"* she says. *"It's only when you wake up that you suddenly understand them, so you can't really say this doesn't have significance, because you aren't awake yet. Wait until you wake up, and then you'll understand what's going on."*

My daughter crawling into bed and cuddling up next to me wakes me up and I immediately lose the larger thread of the dream and what it might be that I'm supposed to understand. I snuggle in with her for the rest of the night. We sleep late and I wake up with little insight into the dream. The old stuff returns, however, and all I want to do is stay in bed all day and work on my recapitulation, but it's Saturday and there are errands to run and places to drop the kids, and I can hear Chuck saying, "don't work on it so hard." And so, even though I want to investigate my feelings on a deeper level, I get up and set my intent to keep busy instead.

As the day goes on, I find that it's easier than it's been in a long time to stay on task. Whenever I get pulled to lie down and roll into a ball, I turn my thoughts to Jeanne instead. I feel how good it is to sink into her energetic embrace, full of unconditional love, and how easy it is to trust that love. At the same time, the old self declares that I don't deserve to be loved, that I'm not worthy. As I lie in the imaginary arms of my protector, the old self challenges the feelings of goodness, happiness, and contentment that I'm experiencing. She doesn't trust the situation, doesn't trust love at all. She even suggests that there must be something wrong with me because, as she points out, *I'm still so afraid most of the time*. At the same time, I'm so drawn to being loved in this unconditional manner.

"It's not allowed," the old self says. "Feeling loved is not allowed. It will ruin everything! It isn't right!" But to me it feels more right than anything I've ever felt, and so I wonder why I still feel so guilty about everything. Am I afraid of rejection? Do I think I can't experience love, even in this ethereal fashion, because of a belief that I am unlovable?

"You don't deserve this!" the old voice rants. "You must remain alert and cautious; there are snakes hiding everywhere!"

If I allow something good to happen then I'll be punished for my enjoyment of it and in return some evil thing will happen, for that has indeed been the pattern in my life. If I allow myself to accept a kindness then I must also expect some reproach as well, for something will be expected of me in return. Something is always expected in return, like the black snakes come to latch on and suck the life out of me. I know this is ancient fear, due to the abuse, and the way my abuser enticed me with friendliness and then turned on me in order to enact his evil deeds.

Chuck and I have talked about the need to let go of fear in order to stop the cycle of fear constantly feeding off new fears, everything spinning out of control as a result. Somehow I must comprehend that fear, represented by the snakes, no longer controls me and that I actually have the power to stop it; not in the old way, not by hiding or taking the blue pill, but by taking the red pill and allowing myself to change. I realize I already took the red pill quite a long time ago. Now I need to finish the quest for freedom, freedom from *all* fears.

The urge to lie down and curl into a ball comes and goes all day, teasing me, enticing me to succumb, but it's not until eleven at night that I finally allow myself to crawl under the covers.

March 23, 2003

I dream the same dream that I dreamed last night, the one I disputed the significance of, the one that got interrupted when my daughter crawled into bed with me. In the dream, I am a "shifter." At a second's notice I can change from one world to the next, shifting back and forth, here in the present, then in an instant in another world. It's an acquired ability that I've learned and as a result I've earned the title *Shifter*.

I wake up full of confusion, fighting to assert my true self. When I look in the mirror, I don't recognize myself. My eyes are puffy, my face white and unrecognizable. It's as if I haven't fully shifted out of my dream state, that even though I've earned the title *Shifter*, I'm not really good at it yet. It's like I'm caught in a strange place, half in and half out of my old skin. The old skin wants me back. I feel it pulling me to return to its comforts, but they don't feel so comfortable anymore. I'm in agony and I want to call Chuck. I need his help, his expertise, but I hesitate to reach out. Why? Do I feel unworthy? Do I feel unsafe? Am I afraid?

I'm not afraid of him, but I feel that I don't deserve such help, that I deserve only what I have, that I'm being punished for past sins—still bound by the tenets of Catholicism. I need to repent, to beg for forgiveness. To be told that it's not my fault, to feel that I can be loved simply because love exists—that it's a fact of life—is unbelievable to me. I feel that I need to beg, pray, and earn it, that nothing comes simply because I need it. How will I ever feel worthy of it? How do I dig out from under those deeply embedded Catholic rules so that I can truly live? How do I live totally freed of all the old beliefs and the old skin, the old self? I know that I must shed the old self and the old beliefs like the snakeskins in my dreams—shed them and discard them because they are no longer helpful. Yet, the beliefs that were stuffed into me as a child are so enmeshed with what happened to me. The idea that I was being punished for something still sits in me, lying there like a snake, coiled and ready to strike. Why else would that man, my abuser, have done those things to me?

I see the significance of *The Matrix* again as I seek to break free of the matrix I live in: *the view of the world as it has been presented to me throughout my life.* Of course, it's real, but equally unreal as well. Chuck has explained to me countless times that the shamans see the world like this matrix too. I now understand what

I'm trying to do! I'm fighting for my life, for my independence, for my creative self, for my dignity and freedom to live my life as a spiritual being. I'm fighting for greater access to my innate abilities, recapturing my free will to choose, to think, to decide how I wish to interpret the world. I'm reclaiming my Aura—my connection to my own spirit—and all else that is available to me as a spiritual being; free and clear of guilt and allegiance to any belief system or set of parameters. I'm restoring my spirit to its rightful place as my own guide. I am freeing myself to fully live.

I don't have to suffer. I don't have to be punished. I don't have to earn love. No one does. Love is available to everyone, *even me*. Love doesn't have a name on it, it's not personal; it's simply a fact of life, like breath, like the energy that flows through the universe. Like the air we all breathe, love flows through the universe too. I just have to be open to it if I am to tap into it and experience it. As I write this, my legs tighten, holding back and clenching, as my old self protests this moment of breakthrough, as I begin to let go of the old world, as I let go of old beliefs and old ideas that just don't hold up any longer. To spite the old world and the old self that says I don't deserve anything, I declare to the heavens: *I deserve! I deserve all kinds of things, including love because it's available for everyone, including me! I don't deserve because I'm special or because I've had a bad childhood. I'm nothing, except I'm here on this earth learning how to live, and I know love exists for the experience of it. So, yes, I deserve love. Dammit! I deserve love!*

I take the breakthrough of the morning's insight seriously. I struggle every minute throughout the day, however, to shed myself of my old skin and fully inhabit my new skin. Every time I feel the need to call Chuck, I do something to take my mind off the needs of the old self. Why? Am I punishing myself, simply for having feelings, for needing someone's help? Do I think I don't deserve it? Do I think I shouldn't have anything good in my life, even attention? I realize how important it is to ask these questions as I break out of the old world. I'm not used to having someone care about me. I'm not used to believing that it's okay to care about myself either, or that it's even okay to say that I need someone to care about me. I decided a long time ago that I would go it alone. There was no one in my life that I could trust except myself and, in the end, there was no one else who could be counted on. Am I worried that I can't count on Chuck? Is that why I don't reach out?

I don't think so. I've learned to trust him, but as I continue to face the shattering of the matrix that I live in, I must also face myself and allow myself to believe in that trust, as purely as I believe in love as a universal force. I'm learning how to let go of so much old stuff so I can enjoy the bounty of what the universe so freely offers. Chuck is the only person in the world that I trust at the moment, besides Jeanne, my Aura and protector from another world. I'm the uncertain one here, still afraid of rejection. Yes, I admit it. I'm afraid that if I tell him everything it will be too much, that he won't be able to handle it and he will turn away. I fear that he'll reject me if I present him with the horrors that lie inside me, the snakes of fear still slumbering, unattractive and unappealing, I believe, to even the staunchest of allies.

My body goes numb, fighting me, as feelings of badness and that I am undeserving rise again. Just bury me in a grave full of shards of glass, leave me to toss and turn and bleed in mud and dampness, my orifices stuffed with sticks and mud. I am evil, for I have partaken in evil, and so I deserve to live in eternal hell, to be punished for even wanting a little bit of something for myself. I'm selfish; I deserve nothing!

At the same time that I write such awful thoughts, I acknowledge that I've been on such a tremendous journey, and I'm so ready for that journey to continue. So it's time to let the old fears and the old self go. It's time to shed the old skin! I think Chuck knows that I trust him, so what am I so afraid of?

March 24, 2003

In a dream, I live in an apartment in New York City. I have a roommate. We're preparing for a feast when I notice that our apartment opens into other apartments. There's no privacy. People have to walk through our place to get in and out of the building, so there's foot traffic at all hours. Cats have wandered into the apartment as well. They want to be warm and cozy inside, loved and cared for, and so they refuse to go outside anymore. Suddenly, we detect a thief in our apartment. We tackle him. "What do you want?" we ask. "Food," he says, pointing to all the food we've prepared.

In another dream, I'm caught in a gigantic storm drain, an open canal with steeply sloping walls impossible to scale. The choppy black water flows rapidly. I swim against the current, desperately trying to avoid being sucked into the tunnel behind me, which I know is clogged with snakes and sticks. Huge black tires hit the water, coming toward me at great speed. I fear being crushed to death. Though I quickly dodge the tires, my only real option is to go with the current, right into the tunnel. My only chance of survival is to go into the black water and clear away all that is clogging the drain. Only then will everything, including myself, flow freely. And so I acquiesce. I stop swimming and let myself get carried away. Just as I'm pulled under the churning water and swept into the blackness of the tunnel I wake with a start, my heart pounding in my chest.

In the first dream, I'm in a new apartment preparing for a feast. There's no privacy, people and cats come through at all hours, including the guy who wants to rob me of the sustenance of life. At the same time, perhaps he's telling me that I'm really hungry for this new life, so why don't I just take it like he attempts to do. Is he really stealing, or is he just taking what's available—the obvious abundance of food, like the abundance of universal love that I finally grasped yesterday? What am I waiting for anyway?

The second dream seems to indicate that something still blocks the flow of this new life that I'm so eager for, yet am also reluctant to fully embrace. In the end, I know I have to stop fighting and face what's still clogging up the tunnel, blocking the flow of my recapitulation. The tires represent my fears, but they have a function as well, for they send me deeper, asking me to go back into the tunnel of self, for only in going into the tunnel will the remaining issues that hold me back be resolved. It's only through clearing the tunnel that life will flow smoothly, and it's the only way that fuller access to that universal energy—that I'm so convinced exists—will be granted. It's interesting that the tunnel is both the problem and the solution. At the same time, I must also deal with all the snakes that are present in my dreams and imaginings, representing both my challenges and my dilemmas.

They are my fears and my healing; just like the tunnel, the problem and the solution both.

Often when I meet with Chuck, Jeanne's energy is present in the room, her aura bringing the warmth of trust and love to my sessions, but the old beliefs argue, whispering in my ear, telling me that I don't deserve any of it, that I am not worthy, and that to receive something that I don't deserve is a sin. Life should be full of giving and sacrifice, the old Catholic belief system says, not full of desire. "You should not want anything for yourself. You should punish yourself for being so greedy, by cutting yourself off from Chuck," the old voices say, still so intensely strong and real as they whisper their well-worn platitudes. Once again the polarity of my predicament presents itself, as my work with Chuck offers both a place to fully encounter and experience the problems—on every level—as well as a method of resolving and transcending them. He offers what I need, yet I punish myself for that need, fighting against the current, when what I need to do is go with the flow, right into his office, into the tunnel of healing and resolution. As this becomes clear, I finally allow myself to accept his role.

To honor him, I get up and do the sword movement and cut through this impasse. Why do I feel so bad all the time? I cut through that thought. Why do I have to punish myself? I slice through that one too. I turn and face the next foe. Why do I feel that I don't deserve anything? Again, I swipe my sword through the idea. Why can't I say what I really feel? Cut! Cut! Cut!

March 25, 2003

I dream that I'm walking home on a dark night, climbing through abandoned buildings, empty bombed-out structures of brick and rubble. I know the way; it's very familiar. I come to a ladder descending into the darkness below, like a fire escape. I'm just about to climb down when I notice a group of men in the darkness at the foot of the ladder. They look like pirates, outlaws, or a gang of thugs. I'm really quiet, but the men see me anyway. They grab me, tape my hands and legs to the ladder and take turns raping me. One man rapes me with a sword and then cuts my clothes into shreds—Cut! Cut! Cut!—until they hang off me like rags. Afterwards, they threaten that if I tell anyone they will hunt me down and kill me.

The dream shifts and I'm with a little dark-haired girl. We're in my art studio where I'm working on a very ornate stained glass sculpture. It's in the shape of a chevron, a shield, with two loopy flower shapes that wrap around the top of it like two fragile arms of glass. I sit in my ragged clothes from the previous dream and work at polishing the rough edges of the glass shield. It crumbles as I work and little shards of glass fall to the floor. I tell the little girl to be careful, but she keeps touching the shield and stepping on the glass. A gallery owner comes in and wants to buy it for his gallery, but I tell him it isn't done yet. We decide that he'll buy it and take it with him now, but bring it back another time for me to finish. He gives me ten dollars for it. As we pack it for transport to the gallery, the little girl says she wants to touch it one last time. As she touches it the flower arms break off. By the time we've gotten it to the gallery it has sustained even more damage.

Again, I mention to the gallery owner that I don't want to sell the shield in this condition, that I'm not happy with it, and that I won't sign it or claim it as my work. He insists that he likes it broken and he asks me to just soften the sharp edges. He says that he can sell it anyway, since it's so unusual. The little girl cries when she sees the condition the shield is in, but I tell her it isn't her fault, that mostly it got broken during the transport to the gallery. She doesn't believe me. I give her the ten-dollar bill and tell her she can keep it. Then the little girl and I get on a bus to go home. It's nighttime, grey and foggy. We travel along old cobblestoned roads, through ancient towns with narrow streets, all of which are very familiar to me. The girl is still upset about the broken sculpture, so I hold her in my lap during the entire trip, hugging her, trying to make her feel better. We get off the bus on a deserted street in a hamlet near where I grew up, in front of an old general store.

I tell the girl that we'll go inside if the store is open, but first I need to tell her something. I stoop down so that I am at her eye level and tell her that back there, in the previous dream, those men who had tied me up and cut my clothes had raped me, that they hurt me. As I speak, she clenches up and begins to shake uncontrollably. I tell her it wasn't our fault, that they were bad men. She looks terrified. I lead her over to the door of the store and we go inside. "I'm hurt," I keep saying, "I'm hurt, I'm really hurt," but mostly to myself because I don't want to upset her anymore.

Inside the store, I make us a bed to rest on. As we're getting ready to lie down a policeman comes in with a flashlight. I see that it's Chuck, with a look of concern in his eyes. I tell the little girl to lie down, that everything will be okay now. I go over to Chuck. We talk quietly, careful that the little girl not overhear us. I tell him that I've been raped and describe it in detail. He takes out a small pad and writes everything down. He asks me if I've told the little girl. "Good," he says, nodding when I tell him I have. "We need to get the little girl home now," he says. And so I take her home. Her mother gets upset when she sees that her daughter has some small cuts on her hands from the broken glass, insisting that I'll have to pay for the bandages she'll need. I tell her that I've already given her daughter ten dollars and that she herself deserves nothing for her daughter's wounds.

Leaving them, I pull my ragged clothes around me and walk down a road leading into a desert. I walk for a long time, until I come to an adobe house. I sit down on a bench outside the house, lean back against the warm adobe wall and gaze up at the stars above. Chuck comes up to me, lighting his way with the flashlight again. He tells me that everything is going to be alright. "The hardest part is over now. All you have to do now is clean up the glass," he says, telling me that he'll help me with everything else.

I meet with Chuck first thing in the morning, my night of dreaming perfect fodder for determining where I must *consciously* go next in my inner work. My adult dreaming self and my child dreaming self are showing me where they stand in the process and where they are stuck, the blockage in the water tunnel and the deeper issues that I must face made clear in these dreams. It's time to find a way for both of them to accept what happened to me in my childhood, for them to come together in agreement. I begin by working within the parameters of the dream.

"I was raped," I tell my child self as we do EMDR, and she immediately freezes—just as she did in the dream—but I notice that she is also listening intently.

"It's my fault; it's all my fault," she says. "Everything is my fault, from the broken shield to the rape."

"No, the men did it; it was their fault." I say.

It wasn't her fault, nor was it mine, but we end up going back and forth—first it's her fault, then it's mine—in an endless cycle of taking the blame. By the time the session is over, I'm exhausted. I don't want to be two people anymore. I want to be one, just one whole person.

March 26, 2003

I'm tired of being separate and apart, unfeeling and numb. My two selves seem always to be either walking next to each other or standing apart, but never quite walking hand in hand, never quite in agreement. Even as I try to bring them together, I sense myself slowly splintering, falling like the glass shards of my dream sculpture, feeling irreparably broken. My head pulses, signaling the descent into the usual dream buzzing state. I feel like I'm going to pass out!

Suddenly, I'm pulled under a wave. My ears close over, as if a hood is being pulled over my head, and I'm dragged into the undertow. Why do I hate myself so much? I don't want to. I'm actually trying to feel compassion for myself. I'm trying to be strong and safe so the little girl will trust me. I just want to be normal. I don't feel very adult or intelligent or logical right now, just raw anger at myself. I can't hold on. I'm crashing!

"I am so angry with myself for needing you, for needing your help," I tell Chuck when I call him in the evening, long into the anger. "I've been feeling so full of blame all day."

"It's the old stuff pulling you back to the old beliefs and you're not yet at a new place," he says. "You're in the birthing process now. You're hanging by a thread."

His words pull me right out of the undertow, out of the old matrix, right back into my new reality.

March 27, 2003

I am literally stuck in a dream. I want to dream a new dream, but I am unable to wake myself up, unable to move or shift in any way, though I try repeatedly. I acquiesce, knowing that I'm stuck back in an old place, back in the past. It's only then, in accepting that truth, that I'm finally able to shift. The old dream begins to fade as I slowly roll over in bed and right into a new dream. Now I dream that I receive large brown envelopes in the mail. They have urgent warnings written on them, but I haven't shifted far enough out of the old dream to clearly read the writing. Finally, after much struggle, I'm able to completely extricate myself from the first dream. But now the envelopes disappear and I'm back in that general store again, the same one I was in the other night. It's dark again and Chuck comes in with his flashlight looking to see if I'm still there. "You can't stay here," he says. "I know, but I'm waiting for something," I say. The little girl is with me again and she's very frightened.

I turn away from Chuck and right into another dream. Now I'm riding in a bus, traveling along a mountain ridge. Looking over the precipice to my left, I see packages tumbling out of the bus, falling down the steep embankment. I know they're mine, the same large brown envelopes that I'd received in the earlier dream, which I didn't have a chance to open. I get off the bus in an attempt to catch them, but it's impossible. I see my name written on them, all addressed to me, sent from places in my past, from Sweden, New Mexico, New York City, and other places I've lived. "Stop!" I yell. "I haven't opened them! I'm not sure I'm done with them!" I turn to see that it's the little girl who's been throwing them out of the bus. "You don't need them. See? Gone! They're gone!" she says, but I'm still afraid I've missed something important. At the same time, I tell myself to just let them go, that I don't need them anymore, but I still feel quite desperate, like I'm going to go tumbling over the precipice too.

Then I shift into another dream. I'm at my grandparent's house, an old crumbling estate now. Two of my uncles are going around in the dark making repairs, to "keep the wild animals locked up," they say. I stand at the small attic window in the peak of the roof and look down onto the circular drive below. There are no cars. I sense that everyone is gone—dead or moved out—and the house is empty. Only the wild animals are left. I stand in the window and experience a sense of bottomless emptiness, as if I have indeed tumbled from the precipice, into the vast nothingness of the abyss.

I can't go on. I'm exhausted, ready to break down. These are the thoughts that come to me as I awaken. It's like I've fallen down for the final time and I just don't have the energy to get up. Even my fears have left me, at least for the moment. Chuck, telling me in my dream that I can't stay in the darkness, offers a warning that I have to take the next step. I can't stay in the old dream. I have to accept what happened and move on now. Even though I'm exhausted, I have to keep going. It really is time for a new dream.

In the first dream, Chuck offers me the clear message that it's time to move on, and in the second dream the little girl delivers the same message. She shows me how much work I've already done, everything neatly packaged and labeled, filed away. I have to face the truth of what she's telling me; the past doesn't really matter now, it's only the new dream and the new self that matter. It's what we've been working on, shedding the old skin and learning to live in the new skin. Just as I have asked her to face the truths of the past, she asks me to accept that I have already molted, already shed the old ideas of the self.

In the final dream, there is no family; the familiar world no longer exists. I experience deep emptiness and yet I'm not sad in this dream. Without judgment, I allow myself to feel grief, a sense of total loss—and it's perfectly okay. In fact, it's absolutely necessary, if I am to truly move on without attachment. Only the deeper feelings that lie at the bottom of my being—as represented by the wild animals, I surmise—need to be released now. But the uncles are trying to rein them in, which is what I ordinarily do as well, but I don't think that's productive anymore. In fact, my true animal nature must be fully expressed and assimilated if I am to make myself whole. So I see, in this string of dreams, that in my new reality, in my new skin, the past has no place. It doesn't fit, and so it can't go forward with me. I must leave it behind, just like the snakes left their molted skins.

This is a major step in the recapitulation. I don't have to stay attached to the past for any reason. It's really okay to begin moving out of the darkness and into the light now, as Chuck suggested. I'm already transformed, advanced to a new level at this point. I have to accept that, and I do, without inflation or ego, for there is no sense of that here. My ego has been breaking down every step of the way. Only the girls will go forward with me, all my sixteen little-girl selves, because now I know that they don't want to stay in the darkness of the past anymore either. In fact, as the little girl in the dream suggests, they are adamant about that. As Chuck said in my dream the other night, the hardest part is done; now I just have to clean up the shards.

I acquiesce. I will not fight another battle. I give up. Let the wild animals come.

I go to the studio. I feel better as I work. As my creative energy stirs and drapes its protective bubble around me, I grow calm. In the evening, I watch my daughter perform in a theatre production dress rehearsal, my son playing in the orchestra. I'm able to forget what's happening in my life long enough to enjoy the show. My daughter is full of energy and has good stage presence. She appears to be having a lot of fun, but afterwards is tired and too hard on herself. I calm her. "Let it go," I tell her. "Let it go." We lie in my bed together, my arms around her, until she finally winds down and falls asleep.

March 28, 2003

I meet with Chuck. I'm distant, unable to focus, as if my recent transformation hasn't stuck. I'm back in an old place, my ability to shift, as of yet, still imperfect. The only thing I know for sure is that I feel unsafe.

"No place has ever felt safe," I say in a tiny child's voice. "I'm always on alert, my awareness heightened, and at a moment's notice I can petrify, go into frozen girl, unable to move. I prefer watching on the sidelines, not getting too close, because everyone is potentially dangerous."

"You're safe here," Chuck says. "You're safe here."

I talk about being bad, feeling bad, or being perceived as bad. It's always the girl's fault. Girls are the ones who get into trouble, girls are stupid, girls never learn. Girls don't consider the consequences of their actions; girls are to blame for the state we're all in. Well, what about the boys? Boys are involved too, but no one will burden the boys with the same responsibilities.

I rant on about this for a little while and then hunker down in my chair, wanting only to hide, to bury myself, to sleep without worry of attack. In recent dreams, my little girl and I are always moving, looking for safe places. I sense that she's asking me to tend to her feelings, what she hides from me, even in dreaming. She's appeared so strong and determined lately, but underneath she's still a traumatized child. Maybe the process now is that she just needs more time. I wonder if she's still afraid of Chuck. Am I? I don't think so, I feel safer when I'm with him than almost anywhere. But am I resistant? Am I still hiding things too?

By the end of the day, I AM NOT HAPPY! Frustrated and angry, I'm ready to explode! I don't want to yell at the kids, but they too are tired and cranky, and so there is tension in our midst. They hate me to be too emotional. They want a calm and stable mother, but the reality is that I'm exhausted, and I don't feel much like being a mother right now either. I don't even feel like hiding it, which feels too much like the old way, but I must be sensitive to my children. They need a loving, considerate, quiet mommy right now.

I've also been in the tension of a dream state all day. Twice I pulled out into traffic without registering what was going on around me. My head hums with dream vibration, and even though I look, I don't see. I'm scared. I don't want to die yet. I haven't even lived! But I can't clear my head. I can't breathe. I can't seem to wake up out of the dream I'm in.

March 29, 2003

I dream that I'm living in a house beside a river. I have a one-year-old baby girl. I look out a window and see her walking through a sunny field. Suddenly a car speeds towards her, an old 1950s Buick, careening through the field. It drives right over her. Just at that moment, I realize that I'm the baby too; I become her. For a split second, I am in two places at once, being run over, but also watching what is happening. Then I become the adult me again. I'm back at the window watching the scene as the car comes around, again and again, and drives over the baby. She's so small that it barely touches her and she remains standing the whole time. I don't want to acknowledge that the child in the field is my daughter, though I clearly recognize her. When I see that her head is gashed open and bleeding, I'm devastated. I run outside, steeped in remorse, castigating myself for letting her go into the field alone. How could I let her wander off, a tiny baby?

Aside from the gashes on her head she appears to be okay. She doesn't have much hair yet, but her hair will eventually cover any scars. I swoop her into my arms and take her into the house. She's not even crying. Telling her I'll clean her cuts, I fill the kitchen sink with warm soapy water and begin washing her. Suddenly we hear a tremendous roar of engines. "Oh, here comes that car again," I say to my daughter. "I'll show you what it was that hurt you." I pick her up and carry her to the window, but I see that it's not the old car at all. This time it's a huge airplane, a jumbo jet with its engines at full throttle, heading straight down into the river that flows beyond the field where the car had recently driven. It's nighttime now and, as I watch, the plane hits the water and sinks. "Atrocities," I say, "a planeload of atrocities."

I'm aware that the plane is full of people sitting petrified in their seats. I am also aware of their experience as being dreamlike. "A planeload of atrocities is crashing and disappearing without a trace," I say. And as the plane goes down, I become every person in the dream. I am myself, watching the plane go down from where I stand at my window holding my baby, while I am simultaneously every passenger on that plane, sitting in every seat. I am also the flight attendant calming everyone, telling them that it's just like a dream, to just relax. "We'll all go through it together. It's not the end," I say in my role as flight attendant. "It's just part of the journey. It will be a new beginning." We are petrified, but as I speak we go into a dreamlike state. And by the time the plane hits the river bed and lodges deeply in the muddy river bottom, we are very relaxed. "When it's over, we'll be at a new beginning," I say. "Let it happen." We experience our demise, but from a muffled dream state, everything happening in slow motion. Then I am once again myself alone, holding the baby, watching the scene outside my window.

I feel responsible for the plane crash, full of such deep remorse that I could not stop what just happened, but I am also petrified. I cannot even call for help. At the same time, I'm aware that it's a hopeless situation, that everyone has died on the plane. I'm equally alert to the fact that I'm experiencing several different perspectives simultaneously. While I'm the observer looking on I feel deep remorse, but when I'm the baby in the field and the passengers and flight attendant on the plane I accept the situations I'm in. "Let it happen, it will be over, we'll go on from here, it's not the end; it's a beginning," I say to everyone, aware that it's the observer self who makes judgments and calls it a planeload of "atrocities," while everyone else accepts their fate.

"A plane has just crashed into the river!" I finally blurt out. From my spot at the window I can see, however, that there is no sign at all that a plane has just gone down or that there are hundreds of people on the bottom of the river, strapped in their seats, drowned. I go outside and see that others are beginning to gather by the river too, that I was not the only one who saw the plane go down. I start walking toward the river too, but I'm uncomfortable in crowds. Abruptly, I turn back toward the house.

I come to a perpendicular ladder and begin climbing, though I'm almost too exhausted to pull myself up. I hear a voice coming over a loudspeaker, announcing that the river approach to the airport is extremely hazardous because of down drafts and that this was bound to happen. The truth has been spoken, not by me, but by someone else, and this is gratifying. I struggle to climb the ladder, dragging my body upward one step at a time while listening to the voice talking about the accident. I pause halfway up and look back, but still don't see any sign of the plane in the river. I know I saw the plane go down; it's down there with all those people! And then I remember my baby and the gashes on her head, and I wake up.

I awaken heavy with exhaustion, as if I'm still climbing up that ladder, so drained and leaden I can barely move. "Get up!" I command, and I force myself to get out of bed, the only way to break the heavy inertia of the dream state. Fearful that I could fall back into the dream state at any moment, I plan my day with the same forceful intent. I eat a good breakfast, take a walk, and go to work. I remind myself that I must continue to place my trust in Chuck, that no matter what I feel about myself, no matter how bad or disgusting I feel, I must not be afraid of him. I must continue speaking about the atrocities of my own life, because it's clear: that planeload of atrocities is all about me. "Trust him, don't be afraid," I tell myself. "Trust him, don't be afraid."

The day is busy, with numerous projects to work on and visitors at the studio during the day, so I'm not alone much. In the evening, with the kids at their dad's for the weekend and no one else to consider, I stretch out on the sofa and watch a movie. I'm able to focus and stay present. Lying in the bathtub afterwards, I recall the dream of the baby self and the planeload of "atrocities." I see how the dream spans a lifetime of abuse, from defilement of innocence in the light of day, to deeply buried traumas, submerged in the psyche, hidden by the darkness of the night. The child and the adult are both bearers of the abuse.

During an encounter with my abuser I wanted only to get through the ordeal, to survive it and walk away from the atrocities. It was afterwards that I would feel disgust, when I'd look down at my body, when I had to put my pants back on. It was then that I knew the plane had gone down, that I would not walk away from the crash a whole person; that, in fact, part of me had to be buried at the bottom of the river if I was to survive. Once again, I hear my abuser yelling at me to get away from him because I make him sick, the things I do make him sick, the filthy, disgusting things I do. And so, I buried those sick and disgusting things about myself, and they've stayed in the dark muck at the bottom of the river of memory—until now.

As I head to bed, I have the distinct sense that something has been pulling me toward this moment for a very long time. My own spirit has brought me here, to this point along my path, to taking this recapitulation journey, to dreaming the dreams I'm dreaming and remembering the memories I'm remembering. I'm certain that all of this was set up a very long time ago.

March 30, 2003

I dream that I'm at a resort, painting a large mural on the walls of a spacious dining room. I'm working right next to a very large bed. There's a little girl sitting on the bed, quietly watching me. Her vagina is hurting. I know this, and I also know that no one else knows why, or how to help her. I absorb her pain. I take her pain into my own vagina, a searing, burning, unbearable pain that I suck up inside me and then paint out onto the canvas. It's the only way to get rid of the pain, by telling my story and painting it, even if I am the only one who can truly understand it.

Next, I dream that I'm watching a film about a little girl who only has one arm. My son is with me. The girl is the subject of a study being conducted by psychologists regarding how people who have suffered trauma fare in life. In the film, I see that the girl has a phantom arm. She's *pretending* she has two arms. She doesn't know that one is missing. She ignores its absence and just gets on with her life. She plays soccer in the film. I ask my son if he remembers her, for we did once know this little girl. "Oh yes," he says, "but I don't remember that she only had one arm, just that she was wild and fun, kind of crazy, so alive!"

I wake up during the night experiencing the same pain that I took into my vagina during the first dream. I let it go through me, just as I did in the dream. In the morning, in a half dreamy state, I float, my body emptied of pain and everything else too. I detach so completely that getting back may be difficult. I sense that part of me needs to stay in this place of no pain, where I don't feel anything. I know this is what's been happening when I drive too, as I enter the numbness of a dissociative state. For the most part, there's no in-between place anymore. As I go through this stage of the recapitulation, I'm either in pain or I'm numb.

I'm aware, however, that I have to get back to reality! I try talking myself back, but I find no place to settle. It's as if I'm the one-armed little girl in my dream: half of me real and the other half phantom. The reality I once knew and lived in no longer exists. I'm living in two separate worlds, yanked back and forth by my arms, one attached to the real girl, the other attached to the pretend girl.

Staying in bed isn't a good idea so I get up and head right over to the studio, aware that I must pay attention to my dreams. My dream suggests that I paint my reality, both the historical reality as it's been revealed through my process of recapitulation and the new one as it develops, as I simultaneously step into a totally new world. The only thing that comes out of my paintbrush, as if my phantom arm is in control, is this phrase: *It wasn't my fault.* And so I paint these words, over and over again, hundreds of times, onto a large sheet of watercolor paper, until I'm wiped out, until I'm exhausted, until the energy of the dream state has left me. But even then, another part of me knows I must keep writing it.

It wasn't my fault. It wasn't my fault. It wasn't my fault. It wasn't my fault. It wasn't my fault. It wasn't my fault. It wasn't

my fault. It wasn't my fault. It wasn't my fault. It wasn't my fault.
It wasn't my fault. It wasn't my fault. It wasn't my fault.

March 31, 2003

I dream that a fearsome storm is approaching, a violent hurricane. As the storm approaches, I stand in my detached garage talking quietly with Chuck. We watch from the open doorway as heavy rains come, bringing ravaging winds that destroy the house. Boards fly off, windows break, leaving gaping holes. The rain pours in. Cracks form where the sections of the house are joined, the whole thing appearing ready to collapse. Chuck notices that I'm uncomfortable with the intensity of the storm, increasingly upset at the deterioration of the house, especially the damage suffered by the old trees in the backyard. "It's all right," he says.

"Yes, I know. The trees are too old and need to come down anyway," I say. "And the house is scheduled for renovations, ready to become elegant again." I ask him if the kids are okay and he tells me they're fine. We stand inside the protection of the garage, watching in awe, as powerful gusts blow down the last of the enormous trees. The whole world shakes as they fall. The hurricane eventually passes by. We venture out to survey the damage. The house is a wreck and all the trees lie in a heap. Stripped of leaves and bark, they look like white dinosaur bones, skeletal remains of long ago life.

As I look over the ruins, I wonder where the kids and I will live while the house is being renovated, but then I see that the garage has been fixed up. I walk back into it and see that it's now a very cute and cozy cottage. I notice that some plants that I had put into the garage to protect them from the storm are growing beautifully. I'm safe, all is good, and now new growth, new building and flourishing life can take place. I'm happy that I don't have to go anywhere. I'm right where I need to be.

Upon awakening, I am flooded with warm feelings. Out of destruction comes new life. New feelings of love for myself flow through me too, as I realize I have just witnessed the final molting.

Chapter 4

The Key

April 1, 2003

I meet a prostitute in a dream. Gaily dressed in a short skirt and red stockings, a tightly-fitted fur jacket and pointy high heels, she tells me she lost three pieces of handmade jewelry, Celtic knots that she wore pinned to her coat. They had been gifts from a special man, she says, and they were very important to her. She asks me to help her find them. We go into some woods and walk along a narrow pathway lined with tall wispy trees and a rich undergrowth of plants and flowers. After walking only a short distance we bump into the man who had given her the three knots, a wizard. Enormously tall and imposing, wearing long dark robes and a soft pointy hat, he stands in the pathway and tells her to look for the knots at this very spot, right where we're standing. He bends down from his great height, parts the tall grass alongside the path with his huge hands, and points out two of the knots. One has the word *Forgiveness* stitched into it, the other *Love*. The third one is a mystery, for although we search for a long time even the wizard can't find it.

Eventually, the woman, the wizard, and I walk back along the narrow pathway. Suddenly the woman, who is in the lead, begins jumping up and down, yelling loudly. "I win! I win! I've fucked more men than anyone in the whole world!" Clowning and laughing, she staggers in front of us and then suddenly falls to the ground. I run and put my arms around her, knowing exactly how she feels and why. Her defenses shatter and she begins to cry. At that moment, a man in a long dark overcoat appears in front of us. He pulls out a gun and shoots the woman and then the wizard. They both fall to the ground. The wizard, seeing that the woman is dead, jumps up and pulls out his own gun. As he fires shots at the man in the dark overcoat, I throw myself to the ground beside the dead woman, bullets flying over my head. "*To get away, change position*," I hear Jeanne saying, and as I begin turning, I wake up. "*Just keep turning*," she continues. "*It will be okay*," and even though I clearly hear these words so reassuredly spoken, I wake up feeling that something is missing. "Forgiveness and love," I think. "They are very meaningful words, but what could the third word possibly be? Indeed, it remains a mystery!"

"Your dreams are mythical and biblical, in the washing away of everything; in tidal waves, floods, hurricanes, and then in the rebuilding of devastated lands," Chuck says when we meet. "Plants are growing now, flourishing and being nurtured. You're being given meaningful symbols in your dreams, leading you to connection with your own feelings."

"I asked for it," I say. "I asked that the wild animals be unleashed, and I also declared that I was giving up, that I knew I couldn't stop this process and that it would just have to wash over me like a tidal wave. And look what's happening, the waves are coming!"

"That's how intent works," says Chuck, laughing. "Watch what you ask for!"

"Actually, I've felt such relief in a lot of the dreams, as I really am acquiescing and releasing something while I sleep. I wake up feeling happier," I say. "In last night's dream I felt such empathy for the prostitute. I knew she was good underneath it all, that she needed a protective shield to keep herself together, because if you've been badly battered, or had to live a life like that, you do what you have to do to protect yourself. You find a shell; you need a shell. I saw her shell as being loud and carefree—cracking jokes about herself—while underneath I knew she was in great pain. I knew exactly what she was doing when she burst out laughing and making fun of herself. I didn't judge her, but felt such compassion for her because I'm the same way, but my shell is silence, the brittle shell of silence."

"I'd like to feel what it's like to go into that shell," Chuck says.

I watch him slowly tuck into a ball, the same way I roll down and put my head into my lap at every session. He hunches his shoulders, clamps his knees and ankles together and, with his fists held against his chest, rolls forward until his head is on his knees, the top of his head vulnerably exposed. He looks so small and helpless. I'm immediately grateful, so touched that he wants to so fully experience my shell state. As I watch him sink into the pain and sadness, into the loneliness that I experience when I go into that favorite position, I become an observer, just as I was in my dream. From a distance, I vicariously experience the painfulness of my inner reality, much as I experienced it with the woman in my dream. Chuck speaks from this tightly rolled up place, his voice muffled, saying he's feeling tense, that he's not able to breathe, that he's sad and full of fear.

"The pose is lonely and suffocating," he says, and I want to rush over to him, the way I rushed to hug the woman in the dream. I want to let him know I understand what he's feeling and that it's okay—that everything will be okay—as Jeanne told me in my dream. And then I watch as he takes a deep breath and breaks out of the shell, as he slowly unfolds and sits up, looking slightly startled to be sitting in his own office.

"The way out is to breathe," he says, taking another deep breath.

We roll into the pose together, each folding down into our laps. As soon as I'm there, tucked into my old place of silence, I feel the suffocating tension of it, more aware of it now that it's been pointed out. A deep breath unfurls me, propelling me up and out of the clenching pose.

"It feels so good to breathe!" I say.

My intent to change solidifies as we do this exercise over and over again and by the time the session is over I no longer want to lie in that suffocating old pose. I'd much rather fully breathe now, open up, move, and even plant something—it's spring after all! Like a tiny seed buried in the warm spring ground, I'm ready to break through my hard outer shell. It's time to shoot out new roots and send my energy in new directions. These are my intentions now. Chuck gives me homework to support this breakthrough. I am to write before bed and at times of stress throughout the day, specifically getting down on paper what I'm *feeling*, allowing for a natural shift to take place now. Already an avid journaler, I know that writing won't be that challenging, but accessing and describing what I'm actually feeling might be!

"Don't agonize too much. Set up a basis to process and work by. Establish it and know it's there, and then you'll naturally fall into it. Be aware of what you feel, write it down, and then let it go," he says. In addition, he suggests that I avoid yoga exercises that reinforce the old stuff—postures and positions that trigger flashbacks—and instead do stomach breathing and chest opening poses. He also suggests that I concentrate on changing positions, at all times, even in dreaming. He suggests that if I can avoid the fetal pose, I may also avoid the sadness and fear affiliated with it.

"How do you feel?" Chuck asks, as I prepare to leave.

"I'm okay," I say, automatically, and leave it at that, but actually I have quite a bit more energy than usual.

I spend the rest of the day with my daughter, who isn't feeling well. I keep moving and active. Aware of not indulging the needs of the old self, I putter around the house, fixing things up. As soon as old feelings arise, rather than lying down in the old pose and sulking, I get out this journal, take pen in hand and write until the need passes. It helps, even if I just scribble the same words over and over again.

It was not my fault. It was not my fault. It was not my fault. It was not my fault. It was not my fault. It was not my fault. It was not my fault. It was not my fault. It was not my fault. It was not my fault. It was not my fault. It was not my fault. It was not my fault. It was not my fault. It was not my fault. It was not my fault. It was not my fault. It was not my fault!

I do notice that I'm calmer as I practice breathing deeply, and as I write out the pain rather than roll and clench into it. My intention is to break the old habits, once and for all, even though I still yearn for the quiet comfort of the fetal pose. It's funny how that sad little place offers such safety, or the illusion of safety, for the truth is that fear is just a thin shell's breadth away. Like the big bad wolf, it comes knocking at my door and every time I hear the knock I am drawn to answer.

In the evening, I listen to public radio while preparing dinner, something I haven't been able to do in months as I've been unable to concentrate on anything for very long. I've also avoided adding unnecessary sensory experiences to my already overladen nervous system. I've had enough going on inside! As I prepare for bed, I notice that I wasn't so lost in my own world today, nor did I feel the tug of the old stuff as often, though the horrors still chill me to the depths of my soul. Here is my prep work before I go off to dreaming:

> *It was not my fault! It was not my fault! It was not my fault! It was not my fault! It was not my fault! It was not my fault! It was not my fault! It was not my fault! It was not my fault! It was not my fault! It was not my fault! It was not my fault! It was not my fault! It was not my fault! It was not my fault! It was not my fault! It was not my fault!*

April 2, 2003

I perch on top of a stone wall in a dream, talking to a man sitting beside me. I perceive of him as the "Voice of Reason." I feel just like Alice-in-Wonderland talking to the caterpillar. "I'm looking for my lost child," I tell him. "Have you seen her?" She has not passed by his wall, he says, and so I ask for advice instead. He tells me that I must be ready to "take the leap." Later, I stand on the edge of a large spinning merry-go-round, telling myself to jump off. I hesitate. "Just do it, or you'll miss your chance!" I command, but I just cannot "take the leap."

I sleep lightly, tossing and turning as I dream. Over and over again I command myself to take the leap, to shift out of the pain that constantly plagues me. I find myself on my back and uncomfortable, so I turn onto my side and curl up in the old pose. "It's okay," I tell myself as the night goes on, but at the same time I feel like I'm giving in, so I shift again. I notice that each time I shift, the pain immediately releases. My dream commands are finally working, as I become a *Shifter* once again, shifting and rolling out of the pain all night long. Indeed, I feel like I'm spinning on a merry-go-round!

In the end it becomes impossible to get any real sleep. Toward morning, I allow myself to roll onto my side, into the old fetal pose. "Just so I can get some solid rest," I tell my dreaming self, but by then I'm so practiced at shifting that I'm able to do it even in deeper sleep. When I wake up, I find myself on my back, and I know I've shifted while in the throes of a few hours of real sleep.

In yoga class, I notice that some of the yoga poses that used to trigger flashbacks—table pose, on all fours, for instance, reminiscent of the Doggie game—don't carry the same intense feelings of disgust anymore, and no flashbacks occur. This is progress, the traumatic triggers finally desensitizing as I go deeper into this recapitulation. Through repeatedly visiting the memories, I am less inclined to experience certain poses as frightening or demoralizing, as I once did.

After yoga and before heading home to spend the day with my daughter, who's still not feeling well, I meet with my work partner at the studio. She comes in and announces that she's going back to school full time. I'm shocked to hear this, especially as I've been working so hard to market our business. I'm reminded of the dream I had in January when she told me she was leaving to work in Kentucky, perhaps a premonition of this moment.

We will continue sharing the studio and gallery space, we decide, but take our work in separate directions. I see this as an opportunity to work at my own pace, to bring my energy back to myself, focusing my priorities, with more time for writing and illustration work. By evening, however, worry and anxiety creep back in, as the news of this sudden change in plans sinks in. "Write about it," I hear Chuck saying, "and then let it go."

I take my worry to bed with me, but as I shift restlessly throughout the night, Jeanne comes to my rescue. "*Let it go*," she whispers in my ear. "*Just let it go. It's alright, everything is alright.*"

April 3, 2003

I wake up with a start. I've overslept! Jumping out of bed, I shake my son awake, practically pushing him out of bed. We're so behind schedule that in the end I have to drive him to school and write a tardy note. Afterwards, I settle in to be available to my daughter on her final day of rest and recuperation.

I suffer abdominal pain and vaginal rawness as the day goes on. Feelings of sadness and loneliness smother me. I'm aware that this excruciating pain is related to my recapitulation process, but at the same time I must acknowledge that what's happening in my outer world—my work partner's decision to go back to school—has struck a sore spot. And so I admit that I'm somewhat hurt and disappointed by her sudden announcement; no hint that it was coming, as nothing had been mentioned or discussed. The old childhood belief that I don't matter rears its ugly head, as well as the dislike of surprises. I sense, however, another truth emerging: I really want and need to work alone, for I am a lone wolf, a solitary being. The vulnerable child inside me, however, takes advantage of my bruised feelings to lead me back into old memories and old pain, demanding that I pay attention to her pain instead of my own disappointment. I sense she's angry, and with good cause, because I've noticed that I'm still holding onto a tiny thread of hope that the abuse didn't happen, that nothing happened to me as a child, though too many things tell me it did.

"IT HAPPENED!" my child self tells me once again, and she shows me so many details to underscore her point. Leading me down memory lane, she touches each tiny button on the pink dress I wore to my high school graduation, the same dress I wore to my abuser's daughter's party, the last time he raped me. She leads me again through that memory—a memory that I recapitulated over a year ago—taking me back into the orchard. "Stop," she says. "Look. Take another step. Stop and look. Slower, that's it, nice and slow. Turn. Now look! Look closely! See? Fingers are poking, prying, prodding, stinging. You were raped. Remember!"

I remember. I remember. I believe. I believe. Yes, I believe. YES, YES, YES! It was not my fault. It was not my fault!

April 4, 2003

I dream that I'm at an airport. Suddenly my father appears next to me, ghostly and pale. "How did you get here, and where's the car?" I ask him. "The keys, just here to give you the keys to everything," he answers, handing me his car keys. "Did Mom come with you?" I ask. "No, she's at home," he says. "There's a book she wants to read; besides, she doesn't matter." And in that instant, I know that they each gave what they could—not much—but there it is. Accept it for what it is, I tell myself. I leave the airport and get on a subway train full of injured people. They lie on stretchers in the wide aisles of the subway cars, attended to by nurses, their limbs rolled in white bandages. Intravenous drips hang from the ceilings and there's blood everywhere. I walk the entire length of the subway train looking for a seat, each car packed with injured, the floors covered in blood. In the last car I finally find a place to sit, crammed in next to some old men. "Things have changed," they complain. "It didn't used to be like this."

I get off the subway train and walk home to a huge stone castle on a vast estate. I put my sixteen little girls to bed for the night in a room at the top of a tower. I'm really worried that if they aren't quiet something bad will happen, and so I tell them to go right to sleep. I go downstairs to the swimming pool in the yard below where a party is in progress. People are swimming, splashing around and making a lot of noise. I ask them to quiet down because the little girls in the tower need to sleep. I need to sleep as well, I say. They all look at me as if I'm nuts, except one woman who glances up at the tower and says that she used to be up there, and she knows how sound travels. She then asks me if I've seen her necklace or did I think it could have been stolen? I can't imagine that anyone would steal it. "It's just lost," I say. "You'll find it soon enough." I tell her about the time I lost an earring in the grass and how I found it again. "I just looked down, and there it was. It had been there the whole time, just waiting for me to find it," I say. I see my brothers standing together, talking about doing some renovations at the estate, including moving a grape arbor to a better spot so it can get some sunlight.

I go back into the tower and find the girls still awake, unable to sleep because of the noisy party. A phone starts ringing and I can't hear anything else, just the phone ringing and ringing, drowning out even the sounds below. A woman I knew when I was young comes into the tower. She gives me a warm hug and tells me that I'm beautiful. "Remember, you are beautiful, inside and out. I always knew it," she says.

These dreams are reminiscent of the process I've gone through as I've taken this recapitulation journey, starting in an airport—a place of departure—where my father gives me the "keys to everything." The keys, the memories, have unlocked the truth of my past. It's as if he's saying, "These keys, really do belong to you; they are your truths." I also gain clear insight into my parental situation, and easily let them go, as it's implied that they don't really matter in the grander scheme of things. With the keys firmly in hand I can move on.

I go down into the depths of the psyche, into the subway car. Here, much like going into the tunnel of self, I'm challenged to withstand the pain of what happened, to face the truth of the abuse and relive my deepest woundings. Things really aren't what they used to be, as the men in the last car imply, for as I've journeyed back into my past I've changed. In reliving the memories and facing the truth, things will never be the same. But the subway train is also a hospital, a place of healing—and healing *is* taking place. I was struck by the fact that the trains were still running on schedule, still barreling ahead, on track and on time. The trains represent the energy of life moving ever forward, much like the recapitulation process, which certainly has taken on a momentum of its own. There is no stopping it, and it's running right on schedule too, always taking me where I need to go next.

I finally arrive at an ancient estate, a place where plans are being made to renovate and where my inner children await me, safely locked away in a tower. I have a sense in the dream that my little girls are still waiting for me to reach resolution. I put them out of harm's way, though they hear and are aware of everything going on. Am I afraid they can't handle the truth of the abuse? There are also inklings of treasures waiting to be discovered. Like in the dream with the prostitute, lost jewels are being searched for. There is a sense of renovation and hope for a good outcome in this dream, as my brothers seek to move the grape arbor so it will get more life-giving sunlight. The woman who approaches me and tells me I'm beautiful seems intent on boosting my self-esteem. She speaks so genuinely to me in the dream that I wake up feeling that she's right, I am beautiful, inside and out. Finally, Jeanne was with me once again, guiding me through the night, prompting me over and over again, telling me to keep shifting. "*Yes, it hurts,*" she said. "*Turn over so it goes away.*"

My father arriving with his keys reminds me of the dream I'd had a few weeks ago when he'd insisted on driving but then passed out. Back then I was still in the throes of detaching from my parent's world, still the child relegated to sitting in the back seat. They still had power to a certain extent, though it was quickly waning, as I was diligently working on detachment from them and their world. Now I'm in charge, more independent, driving my own vehicle, so to speak, navigating life on my own terms. Perhaps my unconscious is letting me know that I've done a good job of detaching from the foreign installation of parental influence.

I meet with Chuck. It soon becomes apparent that I must once again recapitulate the memory at the graduation party, the one my child self presented me with yesterday—for it still frightens me. This time, however, Chuck suggests that I recapitulate from a different physical position. Rather than roll into a tight ball, as I normally do, he suggests that I go through it sitting straight up.

"Your experience may be different," he says.

I put the bilateral EMDR headphones on and slip easily into the memory. Although my automatic impulse is to roll into a ball, I force myself to sit upright. I see a dance floor and hear music playing from a record player set up in the yard. Most of the guests are my abuser's daughter's relatives and there are only a few people my age. Two people go out onto the dance floor, a brother and sister whom I know from school. They try to entice me to join them, but I can't dance. I'm stiff, barely able to walk or breathe, so dancing is impossible. They prod me again to join them, but I won't. Squirming uncomfortably in my chair in Chuck's office, I want nothing more than to slip away from the party—and from my body. I feel myself shutting down, barely able to breathe. Though the party has just begun, I wonder how I might leave without anyone noticing. My abuser looks at me and signals me to follow him. I'm immediately relieved that I won't have to dance. As we walk toward the orchard, he tells me that he wants to show me something.

"Remember what happens with the bees?" he says when we pass by a row of new white hives glistening in the sun. "Yes, I remember," I say, and then I see a tall ladder going up into the branches of an apple tree. I stand frozen, my body and the world shutting down, disappearing. I am already far down inside the tunnel of self as my abuser unbuttons all the tiny pearly buttons and takes off my dress and underwear. I watch him lay them over a large apple crate under the tree. "I know you're going to like this," he says. Like an infant, I am unable to do a thing to save myself. The memory comes easily as I follow his commands to walk up the ladder and out onto a branch of the apple tree.

"You're going to like this," he says, as I jump down into his arms. "You like this," he says, and I see my hands flailing in front of me, unable to find something to grab onto as he rapes me. "Get dressed," he commands when he's done. Nothing happens when I return to the party; no one seems to have noticed my absence. All is as it was before, but I feel as if I've stepped through a time warp, and for a moment I'm not certain where I am. "Get a plate, get food, sit and eat," I tell myself. "Just pretend. Just pretend everything is okay." I sit down with my plate of food at the far end of a long row of chairs in the shade. Running my fingers over the pearly buttons, I make sure they're buttoned tightly. I'm aware that someone sits down next to me, but I'm too stiff to turn my head to see who it is, and besides, I don't want to see who it is.

As the memory unfolds in stark detail, I remember that when I had worn the pale pink dress to the graduation ceremony, I'd unzipped my graduation gown afterwards to discover that all the tiny pearl buttons had come undone. It wasn't noticeable beneath the zipped up gown, but when I went to take it off in the hallway afterwards I was shocked to see my breasts and belly exposed. Pulling the dress together and turning away, I buttoned up quickly, hoping no one had noticed. Now, as I recapitulate, I'm aware of its significance preceding the rape, perhaps a warning that I was not going to be able to keep those buttons fastened. I was never able to wear the dress again. It hung in my closet, a beautiful dress, but every time I thought about wearing it some shadow of fear crossed my mind. I knew the buttons were not reliable; they did not stay closed.

Chuck's hunch was right—I'm not experiencing the recapitulation of this memory in the old way. By sitting upright, I'm able to speak during the entire experience, when normally I'd be so overwhelmed that talking would be impossible. I'm not as frozen as usual, either. Instead, I've become a keen observer. It proves to be a most effective process. Every time I feel like collapsing into a ball, Chuck intuitively senses where I am and reminds me of the intent set at the beginning of the session.

"Stay with it, don't curl up, no curling, stay sitting up," he commands, sternly but supportively.

As I recount what happened so many years ago, I realize more clearly how important it is to talk, to release in words, as well as physically. With Chuck listening, I am no longer alone. He is my witness. Like a reporter on assignment, I relate to him all that is happening, as it happens. I even become aware that at some point I go out-of-body, as part of me watches the rape from above, and then I become *that* observer, relating the experience from an aerial perspective. As I recapitulate, I find that I relive the *entire* experience from two separate perspectives. I am both keen observer, watching from above—from out-of-body—while also viscerally experiencing what is happening in my teenage body on the ground below. Easily, I go back and forth. In addition, my present adult body becomes a vital factor in this enlightening process, offering the vessel through which my fragmented teenage self fully recapitulates. Through maintaining awareness of all parts of self, I garner the complete experience; all parts expressed and all parts reunited in the process.

I'm surprised at the clarity of details that emerge as I speak from the vantage point of my joined self: the hot sunny day, the clear blue sky, the bees buzzing, the grass prickling, my abuser's voice incessantly directing, urging, bossing, convincing me over and over again that I like it, that I like everything he does. I let him do whatever he wants, he says, because I like it. The truth is that I hated it. He hurt me. That's the real truth. He hurt me.

"He lied," I tell Chuck. "I hated it! I hated it! I hated it!"

"I'm afraid of everything and I absolutely despise myself, but now I more fully understand that these are direct results of the abuse. And I understand something else now too," I say, gaining even greater clarity. "I need to love myself before I'll be ready to accept anyone else's love," because this is what flashes through me as the session ends.

"Don't curl up! Don't go back to bed and pull up the covers! No, no, no! Don't you curl up!" Chuck tells me.

"Don't worry, I won't," I say, as I get up to leave, somewhat giddy and yet strangely elated as well.

I acknowledge to myself how difficult it can be to return to the real world after one of those brilliantly clear recapitulations, but I do it, knowing that the fragments of this memory are finally reunited, fully resolved, assimilated. The intent set in the morning's session, to address this process differently, reverberates throughout the day. Every time I feel like curling up, I sit up straight, take out this diary, and write instead, filling pages with the words: *It was not my fault.* I become more certain that it wasn't my fault every time I write. My abuser brainwashed me. He hurt me. I was afraid of him and the bees. It was not my fault. No matter what he said, it was not my fault.

It was not my fault. It was not my fault. It was not my fault. It was not my fault. It was not my fault. It was not my fault. It was not my fault. It was not my fault. It was not my fault. It was not my fault. It was not my fault. It was not my fault. It was not my fault. It was not my fault.

April 5, 2003

I dream of standing at the edge of a golden field, ablaze with sunlight. A little two-story house sits perched in the middle of the field. I'm aware that the house is very old and will soon be demolished. I have come to get my personal belongings out of it. "What a shame," I say to myself as I walk across the field, "such a pretty little house." A bag of birdseed and a wooden easel are among the items I must retrieve from the house. I find my easel and carry it to a little village on the edge of the golden field. I stack it against the wall of a gallery where many other easels are stored. Just as I'm retrieving my bag of birdseed a man shows up in a van, ostensibly to help me move my things. He's convinced, however, that I've taken something that belongs to him and he wants it back. I get into the van to reason with him. I tell him that he's wrong, that I haven't taken anything except what belongs to me. He can go ahead and search, I tell him. He becomes rude and insulting and threatens to drive the van off the edge of a high cliff. He revs the engine loudly and jerks the brakes, stopping just short of the precipice. I feel trapped in the van, but I'm also frozen in my body; I just can't move. After an interminable inner struggle, I'm finally able to force my arm up to open the door. I hop out of the van, telling some friends who've run over to help me that the man's been threatening me. "Don't go with him," they say, and I realize they're right—*just don't go with him.*

Some newspapers have been left for me in the basement of the house in the field. I ask one of my friends, a small woman, to guard the basement door because I'm afraid the threatening man might follow and lock me in. Worried that she isn't big enough to fight him off, I hurry down the stairs. I find the papers in a neat stack and carry them back up. My friend meets me at the top of the stairs and says she's worried about me, but I insist I'm fine. The threatening man meets me outside and tells me that he's searched through the whole house and not found any of his belongings. He then tells me that he bought a new house and he wants to show it to me. Everyone tells me not to get into the van with him again, but I insist that I'll be okay this time, and I pick up my bag of birdseed and my newspapers and follow him.

As I approach his van, I notice how nervous he is and then I realize I don't really want to go with him. I don't *need* to go with him. I'm aware that he's taken so much from me already and I don't want anything to do with him anymore. And then I know that I really will be okay. I glance down at the newspapers I'm carrying and see a huge headline that reads: **IT HAPPENED!** And then I know that everything is different now; I'm at war, and I finally know who the enemy is. I reach into the bag of birdseed and pull out a handful of rice. "Good," I say when I see that it's not birdseed at all. "Rice is good."

It's pretty obvious that the threatening man in the dream is my abuser. He's uncomfortable with what might be left behind in the house—the memories I have of him no doubt—fearful of the power I hold at this point. I had to venture down into the dark basement, into my own inner darkness to find out what happened to me in the past. The news I bring up from the journey into my private underworld is hard to ignore, as the bold headline makes perfectly clear: **IT HAPPENED!**

When my abuser says he wants to show me his new house, he thinks he still has power. For a few moments I waver, on the verge of getting back into the van. Then I see how nervous he is and it triggers memories of my child self, who at some point would realize she'd made the wrong decision. There's no way that I'd go with him again. I easily shift away, for my intent is to do things differently now, to not fall back into old places, but to move into new life. As I dip my hands into the bag of birdseed and see that it's filled with rice, I know I'll be nourished now. I'm immediately aware that I hold my own future in my hands. I'm also aware that my hands are as important as the rice. The past was painful, but my hands—what they can do and what's in them—are fully capable of creating a golden future. I'm completely safe and in charge, and I will be nourished as I go into new life. Everything is in my own hands.

The intent set in the session with Chuck yesterday expands into this tremendous dream. Although it leaves me feeling quite elated and contented with the progress I'm making, I wake up full of self-hatred, experiencing sharp vaginal jabs and a raw chafed feeling between my legs. I'm aware that they are affirmations, signals that the abuse indeed happened, telling me to have no doubt, to please accept the truth that I was abused. I must not fall back into the old bad feelings about myself. I must not doubt and blame myself. I must continue confronting the truth. The headline in my dream is right. **IT HAPPENED!**

The more I think about the dream, the more I realize that it's showing me how to view everything. The easel is good, a connection to my artist self, my creativity. The truth is spelled out in the papers I carry, my recapitulated history. The house in the middle of the golden field, soon to be demolished, represents the last of the old stuff, but as the center of a mandala symbolizes a place of wholeness as well, a result of this recapitulation. The field around it has turned golden, showing the great value of the work I've been doing with Chuck as I've made my way deeper and deeper into my golden self. Going back has been totally necessary, but it's time to move on now, taking forward only what has value. I must not stay in the golden field, beautiful though it is.

I do the sweeping breath, breathing in all the good things I know about myself, breathing out the frozen immobilized self, all the brainwashing, all the misconceptions. It's a struggle to accept that I am good, but in revisioning my life, I discover that I'm really going to be okay.

April 6, 2003

I dream that I'm back in the house in the golden field. I comb through the entire structure, making sure I've taken all that belongs to me, making certain I haven't left anything important behind. I leave it as neat as a pin. Standing in the empty house at the end of the dream, I feel only deep satisfaction and utter calmness.

In spite of how I feel in this dream, I can tell immediately upon awakening that something is wrong. Curling up under the covers only sends me right down into the darkness of the tunnel. There's no way I'm staying in bed, better to be up and about!

Focusing on chores and errands, I create distance between my waking self and the darkness that looms. I just don't feel up to recapitulating today. While walking up and down the aisles of the grocery store, I am inundated by vibrations in my head, the sound of a million bees buzzing. The sensation of a hood being pulled over my face is a sure sign that a memory is on its way, but I refuse it. I push it away, grip my cart, and silently repeat my mantra: GO AWAY! NOT NOW! GO AWAY!

When I get home, I call several friends and talk my way through the muddled confusion that's slowly descending upon me. I'm aware of how imperative it is that I process what comes, but I feel I must be with Chuck to do that. And so, after hanging up the phone for the last time, I do the only thing I can think of to gain some calmness: I conjure up the dream image of Chuck reading poetry to me.

I close my eyes and once again sit with him in quiet repose, surrounded by the Aura, Jeanne's energy. For my efforts, I gain grounding in this world, a peaceful body and quiet mind, as well as unbiased support from my dreaming partners. In calmness, I receive the message that it's time to work on all the negative feelings I carry about myself, especially as I face the loud and blatant truth, the blaring headline in my dream. **IT HAPPENED!**

I write out these discoveries, and the more I write the better I feel. *It did happen,* and I'm being given the evidence, over and over again, both in my dreams and in my physical body. What more do I need to break through the tough shell I constructed around myself so long ago? **IT HAPPENED!**

April 7, 2003

I dream that I'm inside the stone watchtower of an old convent school, similar to the castle tower where I had put my little girls to sleep in a dream several nights ago. Once again, I am protecting a roomful of young girls. From the windows of the tower I have a view of the wide valley below me, through which a long serpentine river flows. Beyond the meandering river lies a vast desert and far beyond that the black silhouette of a tall mountain range is etched against the spreading horizon. I'm up all night, watchful and guarding while everyone else sleeps. In the middle of the night, huge black battleships sail up the river. Silent and threatening, they move into position, their guns facing the tower. I wonder if they are enemies or protectors. I sense that war is imminent.

I'm suddenly aware that I've been locked in this tower my entire life—like a mythical princess—that it's been my fate, and that in spite of my watchfulness, I cannot protect anyone. During the night, men storm into the tower room. I am unable to hinder them. They demand that a certain girl go with them, telling her that she's not allowed to go to school anymore. "Women aren't allowed to go to school; they have to do what the men tell them," they say to all of us. Stunned and deeply saddened, we watch as the chosen girl climbs down from her bunk and silently walks over to the men, accepting her fate. I can do nothing to stop this and I feel so sorry for the girl. I know she won't be able to escape. I also know that it can happen to all of us. But then I remember that war is imminent and that no place is really safe. As the men leave the room, taking the girl with them, I turn back to the window. Once again, I see the black battleships gathered in the river and I know I'm right; war *is* imminent. It's just a matter of time.

This premonition of war has been present for a while now and I wonder just how it will unfold. I'm certain it indicates a final stage in this recapitulation process, as I take control now. I sensed it when I read the proclamation in the newspaper that I found in the house in the golden field. As soon as I read the headline—**IT HAPPENED**—I was aware that I was at war, perhaps in the final battle for the salvation of my fragmented self. In that dream I reacted, while in this dream I am quite passive. This dream seems to confront old beliefs from my childhood, what has shaped and controlled me until now, the solid tower that has dominated both within and without.

What looms so ominously on the horizon is the final confrontation with those old beliefs; the battleships preparing to storm the tower perhaps, come to aid me as I turn to face all that still darkens my life, all that still keeps me captive and locked up— in an ancient tower indeed! As I watch the girl being taken away, I struggle with such self-hatred for being so passive and acquiescent, for just accepting my fate. As that self-hatred flares up, the urge to flee flares up too, the urge to run away from all that I hate about myself. Perhaps the final battle is also about bearing the tension of all that I wish to run from, as I am forced to stay put and face the battles still raging within.

As this final battle wages, I expect the final thread of disbelief will be cut through too, though I also fear that the truth will bring other truths, some harder to accept than others. I fear that all the bad things that I feel about myself will also become true, that like the prostitute in my dream it will be revealed that I'm a slut, unloved, and unlovable. And so, I fear the aftermath of war as much as the brutality of war.

My brain buzzes throughout the day. Flashbacks come in short bursts of light and vibration, piercing reality, their bright camera flashes startling me.

"Why am I here?" I wonder, as I peer into an old outhouse. The musty odor that rises into my nostrils is familiar, as are the frightening black ovals, the two toilet seats yawning wide. I remember that the outhouse was used when the water at my abuser's house ran too low, when the spring in the woods dried up. In spite of my best efforts to leave it alone, the memory does not leave me alone. I constantly turn my back on it during the day, ignoring the flashes, but later in the evening I acquiesce. Intent on discovering what happened in the outhouse, I sit and do the sweeping breath.

A clear memory soon emerges. My abuser tells his daughter and son to leave the outhouse, their faces going blank and pale as he interrupts our play. I watch as they scurry away like little wind-up dolls. "Don't go, don't go! Can't they stay too?" I ask, but to no avail. My abuser doesn't have a lot of time to "open me up." He talks his talk, telling me that I like what he does, as he sits down and pulls me onto his lap. My body clenches tightly. As I sweep my head back and forth, all that was happening then is happening now. The small cobwebby window of the outhouse is before me once again. I see the grain of the weatherworn wooden sill as my abuser squeezes my ribcage with one hand, the other digging between my legs. With his chin pressing hard into the top of my head, I sweep my head back and forth. I keep doing the recapitulation breath. Even though I'm gasping for air, I stay with the memory, intent upon getting to the truth of what happened. Then the fuller picture comes—already bruised and raw, he sodomizes me.

I break out of the memory and out of the outhouse, flooded with self-hatred, the heat of it burning through everything I've accomplished, blinding me, except to the truth that I am hateful. And why shouldn't I hate myself? I can't stand to look at my body. I can't stand the shame and humiliation of who I am.

Once again I am struck by the fact that although I had no memory of the abuse, I always sensed that I was bad. I was far from the pure child of the Virgin Mary that I so desperately wanted to be. I went through Catholic school pretending I was good, trying to figure out how I was going to get through the time between weekly confessions with the terrible burden of black sin I carried always within. Even though I could not specifically relate it to anything in particular, I knew I was a sinner. That sin grew inside me, festering into a weighty cesspool of deep depression. It was this deep depression that alerted me to the truth of myself, that there was something deeply wrong with me, my soul overshadowed by some unknown mortal sin, the worst kind of sin.

As a child, I wanted nothing more than to wake up one morning and find that I was someone else completely, someone good; a pretty little girl with blond curls who did everything perfectly and whom all the nuns loved, for she was light and pure, free of sin, an angel. I've always wished the inner darkness away and I guess I'm still wishing it away. I wished for guardian angels to take me from my bed at night to a place where I would be loved, comforted, and made to feel safe. Why would I give up that dream to embrace the bitter realization that my inner darkness was all too true? In fact, that it was much more sordid and ugly, much worse than I could have imagined! Why would any sane person want to experience such darkness? And yet here I am, fully committed to doing this recapitulation, volitionally facing that darkness every day, as often as I once ran away from it.

My mind is like an ancient cave, full of cobwebs and dust. I peer into its stale musty darkness. Normally there's not enough light to see what's really there, though I detect plenty of vaguely familiar shapes. It's only in the vivid flashbacks that the darkness lights up enough to reveal the stark truth. In the flashes other truths are revealed as well: *that I don't want to believe the abuse happened because it means I must let go of my dreams, and my illusions too.* The truth means I'll have to let go of the pretend self who dreamed the dream that I was really a good girl, a normal girl, and not the way I actually felt. That pretend little girl clung to the innocent belief that my guardian angel was protecting me through all the bad years of my childhood. But now, as I face the truth of the abuse, I must also face the truth of that fantasy, for in reality it *was* an illusion.

The truth is that my guardian angel never protected me from anything and she can't protect me from the memories or the bad feelings about myself now either. I must squarely face that I was abused, that I suffered. Yet I must also face the truth that the illusion also helped me to survive. And so that leads me to wonder if my guardian angel acted on my behalf nonetheless, protecting me by keeping me alive. Did she lead me to Chuck, a meaningful guide in this world, to this recapitulation process and to meeting Jeanne, a new protector from another world?

I want a sign from my old childhood protector, just one sign, that Jeanne, Chuck, and I may understand the truth of it.

April 8, 2003

Last night's dreams aren't clear, except that I seemed to be compartmentalizing everything again. Once again a voice came, guiding me. "*You know what to do and where everything is supposed to go,*" it said. "*That's it, that's the way to do it. Put it away neatly into little houses and leave it there.*"

I don't know who the voice belonged to. It was not my own voice, not Jeanne's voice, yet it was very familiar. Is my old guardian angel, my childhood protector still with me? Stunned by the thought that my plea was actually answered, I get up and go to yoga class, even though I want to spend the whole day in bed, even though I'm very depressed. I work at the studio after the yoga class for a brief amount of time, but can't stand being there, so I go home. I sleep for an hour before picking the kids up after school. Everything feels immensely sad and depressing again. In spite of the thought that I might indeed have a guardian angel beside me, I am too tired to care. I just can't—it takes too much effort.

April 9, 2003

I dream that I'm working in my studio, making little houses out of found objects. A bright blue blouse hangs from a doorknob in the studio; it has white angel wings attached to it. A dog comes in and pees on the blouse, so that it stinks and is utterly ruined. The studio is hot and stuffy, the windows closed up tight. I know it's nice outside and I keep thinking about opening up the windows, but I never do.

After a while, I walk downstairs and go outside. Some musicians are playing in the bell tower of a church across the street. I'm talking on the phone as I walk, trying to find the zip code for Rhode Island, because I have some letters to mail there. Then my mother comes onto the phone, interrupting, demanding that I do things the old way, telling me that she's so disappointed in me. Then I'm walking along a path with the "Queen of Rhode Island." She's dressed like the good witch in the Wizard of Oz, wearing a beautiful white gown and a jeweled tiara. She's carrying a tall golden shepherd's crook. We go back into the rural setting of my childhood, walking through the fields and orchards of my abuse. Many little girls are with us. We find a grape vine with big sweet grapes on it. We find some perfectly fine apples, crisp and delicious, growing on an old bent tree.

At the end of the path, the Queen of Rhode Island tells me she has to leave, that it's time for us to part. Affectionately, we hug. A little sorrowfully, I watch her walk away, going back down the hill that we've just climbed. I stand and gaze after her for a long time as she meanders in and out of sight, her white gown glistening in the sunlight. Later, I see her far away in the valley below, a tiny white figure walking toward the horizon, getting smaller and smaller. Eventually, I turn away and cross a log bridge that the little girls have made. Each log has been ornately carved with words and symbols. The bridge leads across the stream that ran down the mountainside, bordering my abuser's property. The lush summer scene full of fruits and flowers that I have just walked through with the Queen of Rhode Island disappears as I cross the bridge. Now it's cold winter. Standing in deep snow, I stop, hesitant to go any further. My childhood home is on this side of the stream. I see it through the snow-covered cedars and I know that my mother is waiting for me. I'm supposed to be there right now taking pictures of the living room decorated for Christmas. I'm aware that it's expected that I behave like a proper young lady while in her house. As I stand in the deep snow and look toward my childhood home, I know I will never go back there again. I turn away quickly and walk in a new direction. I head straight down the hill, toward the vast valley and the distant horizon where I had last spied the Queen of Rhode Island.

The Queen of Rhode Island—my childhood guardian angel perhaps—appears as a compassionate and loving apparition, taking a final tour with me through the landscape of the past. She points out that there were some sweet fruits to be had there, that it wasn't all bad. Perhaps she's also letting me know that she *was* there all along—she certainly seemed to know the way! I felt sad when she left, but I was aware that she had taken me as far as she could.

The rest of the journey is up to me now; I must decide which direction to take. Do I go back to the cold world of old familial expectations, or do I go in a new direction? As soon as I cross the beautiful bridge, I know I can never go back into the cold world of my childhood. As I stand on the brink of that desolate childhood world, I know that I must choose my own life now. The bridge actually bridges the two worlds of my childhood, my home life and my abuser's world, but it's also a bridge to the future, the bridge of recapitulation. I'm aware that the carvings on the bridge are my memories, my life story, including the truths of the abuse. As my dream indicates, my sixteen little girl selves have been busy documenting this recapitulation journey in their own way.

The recapitulation bridge is leading me someplace new, not back to an old place and old rules of behavior, though I must go back in order to retrieve the truth. Once that is done, however, I must move on! Through the rewriting of my life story I am heading toward total freedom. It's interesting that my abuser's world is depicted in this dream as lush and nourishing, in stark contrast to the rigidity and coldness of my mother's house. I have to admit that it's only in going back into the woods of my abuser that I'm finding what I need to nourish real change and growth. In the riches of my past, I'm discovering myself.

Even as I face the beauty of this dream—the final message being that I must continue my journey into the deeper unknown—a barrage of memories invades my body and mind, depressing my spirit, leaving me limp with fear and fatigue. In desperation, I call Chuck.

"Move your body! Change positions! Don't get stuck!" he says. "Look at what you're being shown and then move on! You can accept it! You *are* strong enough! You *do* believe it! It *is* true! It's true! Acknowledge the pain! Give yourself some compassion! Give yourself some compassion!"

I take his commands to heart. I get out of the house and spend the morning at the studio. It makes it easier that my studio partner is there, though it takes me a long time to get going. I putter around for a while, make coffee, sit on the couch and drink it while deciding what to work on. The pulses zapping my brain are bothersome, the pain in my legs constant. I'm intensely drowsy as well, the depression smothering, the old stuff dragging me down into a dreamy state. In spite of recent progress, I find myself suddenly stranded, having landed in a desolate place where I don't really care about anything at all.

My dreams and dream guides have lately been instructing me in the importance of creating cubbyholes in which to store the pain and the memories. And so, even though I have commissions to work on, the only thing I can focus on is making little wooden boxes, houses for the bitter remnants of my soul searching. As I pour all of my energy into this act of compartmentalization, I watch my hands. As if they don't really belong to me, they select and lay out objects. I watch them arrange and move things, placing them just right.

As my hands work, I return to my dream and feel the loving energy of the Queen of Rhode Island as she embraces me once again. Then I remember the bright blue blouse with the white wings that the dog peed on in the first segment of the dream, and I am more keenly aware that I cannot let the good state I've achieved thus far, and the innocence I've retrieved, be ruined. I must stay positive, and so I intend to keep my guardian angel alive in my thoughts; no need for her to hang up her wings! I will not dismiss or soil the truth of her presence, or forget all that she has done.

The art and act of compartmentalization keeps me focused, present, and aware. Even so, the memories pound back and forth in my head, refusing to be trapped, refusing to be boxed in, and when I head out at the end of the day I find that it's once again hard to drive. By the time I get home, the urge to blank out, to leave this world, is great. A memory pounds, slowly inching open the door of recapitulation, though no details are yet visible.

April 10, 2003

The need to curl up dominated as the memory pounded away through the night, and so although I changed position often while sleeping, I'm also aware that I slipped into the old fetal pose many times.

The memory is ready and willing to present its fullness, but I'm not ready to receive it. I can't do it alone. I'm aware that I have to keep moving if I am to stay one step ahead of it. I notice how queasy my stomach feels, nauseous and weak, with a nagging pain in my side. After getting the kids off to school, I leave a message on Chuck's answering machine. "I'm in agony," I tell him, the simple act of speaking those words a release of sorts. "But don't worry, I'm going to yoga and I'll keep busy, but I'll need to work on this tomorrow. It's pretty disturbing." And then I leave it. I don't go back to bed or to the emerging feelings, though the memory swirls, constantly pulling me toward its dull dreamworld, coming over me with its dark hood when I least expect it. The pain in my side keeps me company, its steady drumbeat pounding through me, heralding what is to come.

The yoga serves its purpose and immediately grounds me. Once at the studio, however, the steadiness slips quickly out from under my feet. Even the detailed decorative techniques and the delicate layering processes required for the pieces I'm working on aren't enough. Struggling to stay present, I face the truth that I'm a deeply disturbed person, so captivated by psychosomatic events that the real world ceases to exist. As the old world and its dreamy veils fall over me, I am dragged away from this reality into its nether world. I actually feel myself, physically and mentally, slipping into the hazy atmosphere of the past. Doubts flare up and questions come in direct counterattack to the blatant truths I'm being shown. Do I truly believe everything that happened? Did I really live such a different life? Can I really believe all that is unfolding before my very eyes? The sharp pain in my side cuts through all doubt, telling me that the agony of the truth and the pain of release must be addressed more fully, in my dreams and in my real life. I will not be whole until I fully accept this changing self and everything that she brings to me.

April 11, 2003

I meet with Chuck first thing in the morning. As I put the EMDR headphones on, he reminds me not to curl up, but to stay sitting up straight and to keep talking as I recapitulate. I nod as I go down into the deeper self, fully intending to face and release the memory that has been causing such agony.

"I'm sixteen or seventeen," I tell Chuck. "I'm in the barn with my abuser. He has tools. I'm lying on my back with my feet up, knees bent. It feels bad. I don't want to be here!"

"Don't hurt me!" I shout, shielding myself with my hands.

"Stay with it," Chuck says, "don't curl up, stay sitting."

"I can't get away. I can't get off my back; I'm held down. His hands are on me, pushing, and he's talking, talking, talking and opening me up, sticking things in me—not good smell, machine oil, garage smell. It makes me gag! I'm going to vomit!" I say, and Chuck quickly hands me the wastebasket.

"I'm mad, disgusted," I say, gagging again. "This is not going in a good direction. He doesn't care about me, will do whatever he wants, whatever he has already planned. Nothing will stop him. He puts all kinds of tools inside me, trying to widen me. It hurts so much! I'm raw and swollen—not a body, just pain. It's not me anymore. I don't feel my body or anything else, just the pain. I don't look; don't want to see what he's doing. I think he's done because he stops, but then he makes me get on his tractor. He gets up on it with me. He forces me to sit on the black knobs, the gearshifts, but I'm not wide enough. He tries to push me down onto the knobs."

"It doesn't work!" I yell at my abuser, then and now. "I don't fit!"

"He says my name," I tell Chuck. "I hear him saying my name, as clear as day. He makes me sit on his penis, pretending he's driving, shifting. He tells me to get down, saying he'll widen me more next time, so I'll fit on the knobs. I'm fighting him too much, he says; next time I won't fight so much. I just want him to go away and leave me alone. Everything hurts; just go away!"

"He's finally gone," I say to Chuck, as I open my eyes and come out of the memory. "He's gone."

"Did you get it all, the whole memory?"

"Yes, and the pain in my side that I've been experiencing all week has finally released, quite easily actually, as I recapitulated from this new perspective, much quicker than when I curl up. Curling up, I realize, just seems to hold the pain in more tightly, gripping me endlessly, like a wheel spinning around and around. In sitting up, the whole experience feels more like a memory and less like it's happening right now."

"Good work!"

All day I'm dizzy. Whenever I turn my head, even slightly, the buzzing starts up and I feel like I could slip right into a dream. It's hard to shut it down. I notice this especially as I'm driving. I have to be so careful.

I had mentioned to Chuck my recent practice of shutting down the left side of my brain when I notice I'm getting too wrapped up in thinking or when fear takes over. I go over to the more Zen-like meditative state of my right brain and just hang out there for a while in empty silence. I was surprised at the interest he showed, almost expecting to be ridiculed for saying I did such a thing. But he got out a book he had on his shelf about just such a technique, saying he was going to make sure to read it.

I successfully practice this new brain switching technique throughout the day, calming my mind so I can get some work done. It becomes an intriguing challenge to see how long I can suspend myself in the mysterious redness of the right side of my brain, for that's the color it is. The left is rather dull in comparison, black and blue, white and gray. At night, I sit and watch a movie, staring at the TV without moving my head for a few hours and it seems to calm it down too. By the time the movie is over my head is slightly sore, with a dull ache right in the frontal lobe, as if my ultimatum has been grudgingly acquiesced to.

My brain and body need a rest now, but my vagina and anus have been hurting all day. I wonder if it's a new memory. Oh God, won't it ever stop?

April 12, 2003

In a dream, I'm caring for a small girl for the day. She's very tiny, only about ten inches tall. She's riding a tricycle along the dirt road near my childhood home. I'm standing far down the road, watching her. I see her get off her tricycle. She calls out to me, but I can't hear her. Suddenly, an enormous dump truck comes roaring up the road behind her and I see devastation before it happens, like a flashback, premonition of disaster to come. I scream at her to get out of the way, but she can't hear me. Totally unaware of what's coming, she's just a tiny speck against the black tread of the approaching tire. Too far away to help, I'm in agony as I watch the enormous tire drive right over her. I feel her pain in my own body. The truck continues down the road, passing right by me. I glance into the cab and see that the driver is totally oblivious to what just happened. From my position, I see the girl's tiny body absolutely flattened into the road like a pancake. Momentarily stepping out of the dream, I wonder how I'll ever explain what just happened. How will I ever tell her mother that I couldn't protect her? As soon as I step back into the dream, however, the tiny girl is alive and well. When her mother comes to pick her up she seems perfectly fine.

Next, I dream that my two children and I are moving into an apartment in New York City with an old boyfriend of mine and his girlfriend. They have a walled-in garden with trees and a path. We're all sitting out there talking. During the entire dream I hold a rolled up newspaper that I'm going to look through for places to rent, an apartment of my own. The girlfriend doesn't like kids, but says mine are different and that it will be okay for us to live there for a while. She asks if I've started looking for a place yet. "I just got here," I tell her, a little defensively, "but yes, I have the newspaper and I'm going to look right away."

I watch as the girlfriend rakes the garden beneath a giant oak tree. Suddenly, a loud crack is heard and a large branch falls and lands at her feet, barely missing her. Unfazed, she calmly moves it out of the way and keeps raking. I, however, take it as a very clear sign that I can't stay, and that devastation of some sort is coming. I get up and go inside to make pizza for everyone. When I open the fridge, I see that it's filled with rolled up newspapers, classified sections, and I know they are for my benefit. My intention is to look through them, but I keep thinking that I just got here. Can't I unpack, eat, and rest? But I hear Jeanne's voice urging me on, saying, *"Don't stop, keep going, this is only a stop along the way to learn something important."*

As soon as I receive this important message, I walk out of the kitchen and right through a set of glass doors into the Metropolitan Museum of Art. There are few visitors. I wander around in the large, empty rooms and end up in a remote area of the museum. Looking for a way out, I see that there are renovations going on all around the outside of the museum and that every exit is blocked. In the end, I realize that in order to get out I will have to retrace my steps; I will have to go back to where I've already been.

I wake up curled in the old fetal pose, with a dull headache in the frontal lobe, feeling cold, tense and thickheaded. As usual, part of me wants to stay curled in the comfort of the familiar, but there really isn't any—only pain and bad memories reside here. Quickly getting up, I put a pot of coffee on and rather than going back to bed, I sit in the living room while it brews.

Contemplating my dreams, I wonder what I'm avoiding in the newspaper. Is there something I don't want to see? This is the second dream I've had lately where a newspaper has carried a personal message. I see the significance of the "classified" sections, the classified top secrets of my childhood abuse waiting for me to fully recapitulate them. When the branch fell out of the tree I knew it was a sign for me to move on. Even Jeanne confirms this, telling me this pause is only temporary.

I realize that the tiny girl who got crushed is my child self, struck down by monstrous energy but always able to get up and go home again. The tiny girl appeared to be hard of hearing, as if my dream was letting me know that innocence does not hear the warnings; it has no context for them. Innocence is pure, totally devoid of any attachment or connotation, so nothing can really harm it. Indeed, I feel this is true, as my own innocence seems quite uncontaminated by all that happened; it's the physical self and the mental self that have sustained harm.

In the dream, as my aware adult self, I worry about having to tell the mother the truth about what happened to the little girl, but the girl handles it just the way my child self once did, she just gets up. She appears to be perfectly normal, as if her innocence had in fact not really been harmed at all. The mother is oblivious to the truth, but I'm not anymore.

I end up in such a maze of confusion at the museum, a fitting metaphor for this recapitulation process. The renovations going on outside are so like the outer changes I myself have been experiencing, but it's in the deep inside work that the real transformation will take place, thus a quick exit is not possible. The only way out is to go back, to retrace where I'd been. Indeed, if I am to totally renovate myself, I must continue to recapitulate. I must first go back and comb through the classifieds, all the inner secrets of self. Only then will I be fully available to construct a new self and a new life.

All day I suffer from dizziness and fogginess. If I focus on something I'm okay, but if I turn too quickly I immediately go into another world where sadness and fear are prevalent. I avoid doing the recapitulation breath because sweeping my head from side to side sends me right over the edge. Besides, I'm more concerned with staying as present and alert as possible right now. And so I practice going into the calm redness of the right side of my brain as often as possible. At other times I hold my head still, not wanting to stir up trouble.

I decide to leave an open journal next to my pillow at night with a pen stuck in it so I can write throughout the night, rather than consolidate my dreams and messages of guidance in the morning. I'm interested in what might transpire, what my unconscious might tell me, as my intention is to train myself to write whether I'm awake or asleep.

April 13, 2003

Once again, I dream that I'm in a stone building high on a mountaintop. Far off on the horizon I see black storm clouds gathering. Spouts descend out of the clouds and touch down, and then ten or twelve fierce tornadoes speed toward the house. I grab the kids and take them to the dark and musty basement then go back upstairs to watch the storm. I see trees lifted out of the ground and rooftops taken off houses in the valley below as the twisters hit. Windows are broken and everything in the storm's path is shattered. I run back downstairs to wait out the storm with the kids. Afterwards, I go out to survey the damage. I don't see any people, just devastation, debris lying everywhere. I return to the basement, the only place that's still intact. I try turning on the lights at the bottom of the stairs, but nothing happens. I fiddle with the wires until I get them working. Once the lights come on, I'm surprised to see that a table is set and eight or ten people are sitting there, including my kids and my mother. My mother acts as if nothing has happened, as if the devastating tornadoes never came through. "No surprise," I tell myself, "that's just how she is."

I offer bread to everyone; it's all I have. Someone else has butter and someone produces a roasted turkey. There's a hole in the basement wall exposing the backyard. After eating, we climb through the broken stone wall into the yard. I ask my mother where my father is. "He'll be here soon," she says gaily, in a high-pitched voice, again acting as if all is normal. I go back inside to find that he has already come. I know this because all the food has been cleared away, including the butter, which I know he has put in the fridge. I like to keep the butter out on the counter, but my parents have always kept it in the fridge and as a result it's always too hard to spread. This brings me to conclude that he's not going to change and that I just have to accept him and my mother the way they are; they will never be different. However, I decide that in my own house I can take the butter out of the fridge if I want to, and so I do. I tell myself not to be angry with them, knowing that they are unaccepting of any new ideas, aware that they are afraid of change, and that they find talk of deeply personal issues confrontational. I'm aware they have created their own world, of which I am no longer a part. In fact, that old world has just been blown apart!

In the morning, I'm surprised to discover that during the night I wrote the following:

MEN! (This is followed by indecipherable scribbling.)

They take away my soul
They *took* away my soul
I am afraid of MEN!

It's Sunday, and the kids are with their dad. It's Spring Break and they'll be with him for most of the week as well. I'll have time alone, time to take care of myself, and I'm thankful for that.

I spend most of the day trying to stay focused, keeping my head facing straight ahead so I don't become dizzy and unbalanced. As soon as the pounding in my head starts up I feel like I'm losing it, like my world will crumble just like the tornado ravaged world of my dream. The dream reminds me of the microburst that occurred several years ago, when I was just beginning to face the ending of my marriage. We really did run to the basement with the kids as falling tree branches crashed into the house and part of the roof got ripped away. It was a very clear sign that something was going to change.

The truth is, my old life has already been destroyed. It will never be the same. Many things have had to end as I've taken this journey. The old is no longer comfortable. I'm intent on doing things my own way now, so I must put up with the discomforts of a changing world and a changing self, while also accepting the truths of the old world and the old self.

I'm stable and present while I do yoga and meditate. Taking a bath works to keep me present too, but as soon as I move too quickly, or unconsciously, the pounding starts up again and I feel like I'm tipping into the past. Driving is almost impossible, as I discover when I run out to get a few groceries.

My parents call, angry that I'm not visiting them today, the synchronicity of my dream visitation with them rather striking. I had briefly mentioned that I *might* visit while the kids were away and they obviously took it as a given. Now I feel guilty that I've disappointed them, but there's no way I can drive, nor can I be alone with them. I don't hate them; I just don't have a place for them in my world right now. In fact, as my dream pointed out, I'm totally reconciled to the truth of my parents. In addition, I refuse to be like them. They represent things staying the same, my father keeping the butter solid, my mother equally unbending in her ways, unable to access feelings, acting like nothing important has happened. My mother ignored the truth of the storm in my dream, which is that the entire world had been destroyed. That's what it's like inside me now, my old world too has been destroyed—and I can't ignore it—thus the daily experiences of disorientation and imbalance. As I try to navigate, I find the known world really isn't there anymore, and yet I haven't totally broken through to a new world yet either. The truth is, I feel like I'm caught in the whirlwind of a tornado most of the time. I barely get my balance before another one touches down and I'm whisked off my feet by powerful dizzying energy. For days now I've been living in two worlds, shifting back and forth at the whim of external and internal forces.

I stabilize myself with some very slow and deliberate sword movements, calmly and gracefully interrupting the head buzzing in my frontal lobe. The slow movements help greatly to hone my awareness. I know that I'm not walking solidly on the earth these days, and although I know it's leading to something good—that change is good—it's a little freaky!

As I come out of a very slow sword movement, my head suddenly clears and I realize that the newspapers in my recent dreams are not trying to tell me anything specific. They are my history, parts of which I haven't been willing to look at. They seem to indicate that there's still something I haven't recapitulated, and that it's being kept in cold storage for the time being. Jeanne, however, suggested that I not get caught wondering or worrying, pointing out that everything is just part of the journey. It's clear however, that there's something I'm still not quite getting. Is it another memory? Is that why I get the head buzzing? Am I just pushing something away in my attempts to stabilize?

April 14, 2003

I meet a charismatic wizard in a dream. Standing on a bare stage, dressed in a dark-blue velvet cloak and floppy wizard hat, he looks very much like the wizard in the dream with the prostitute. I stand with a group of other people as he tells us that he's going to teach us a game. We must learn how to execute this game if we are to advance to the next level, the wizard says. He slowly raises his outstretched arms. Shimmering light simultaneously rises up from

The Key

his feet and surrounds him. Crackling friction fills the air as a vast landscape materializes, brightly etched in iridescent blue light, as surreal as a hologram. In awe, I watch, as the wizard now stands amidst this shimmering blue creation, his long wizard cloak and hat replaced by glistening silver. Transformed into a knight in shining armor, he swings a gleaming silver sword over his head and tells us that we too will learn how to do this. He stands there for a few seconds, mighty and powerful, the sword glinting in the light. Then he slowly lowers the sword and the magical scene disappears. He stands on the bare wooden stage dressed in his velvet cloak and floppy hat, a kindly wizard once again. Looking out over the awestruck crowd, he tells us that we too will be able to do what he just did. It's the game we're about to learn: *how to create our own reality*. He tells us that all we have to do is *believe* in the possibility. We'll be learning wizardry of a *self-generating sort*, he tells us, the ability to make something happen simply because we are powerful enough to do so. "How do we get back?" I ask. "How do we get back to this reality?"

"Don't worry," he says, "you'll know how to get back when the time comes. That's the final test of your skills—getting back." He tells us to prepare for the water game, the first part of the lesson. It involves making a special game piece. He tells us that we all have a key in our pockets. We are to take it out and tie it into a purple scarf, knotting it into a neat little bundle. This is to be our game piece. Much to my surprise, there *is* a key in my pocket. I take it out and begin making my game piece, but I'm so inept that I fumble with the key long after everyone else has made their game piece. I just can't help it, but mine keeps falling apart. No matter how many times I tie it up into a knot, the key falls out.

While I struggle to make my piece, the game begins, like magic, conjured up all around us. The bare floor gives way to a gigantic circular in-ground swimming pool, the water deep and as iridescent blue as the holographic stage scene had been moments before. The pool is surrounded by an intricate maze of waterways, leading to and from it. I'm aware that there are deep underground channels as well. The large pool suddenly fills with all sorts of creatures, including manatees and dolphins, cats and dogs, and children on broomsticks. I'm aware that they live and breathe under the shimmering blue water, never breaking the surface, the pool a swirling vat of animals and people, swimming swiftly and gracefully in a clockwise direction.

There is one animal in the pool that you must avoid at all costs, a bad creature that is after your game piece, your key. If you are captured it will take you off into the underground tunnels where horrible things will happen to you in an attempt to steal your key. You won't know what those horrible things will be until you are there. How well you fare all depends on how hard you make it for the creature to get your key. The object of the game is to never give up your key, no matter what happens to you, because if you give up your key the creature has won and you will never get out of the pool. You will swim forever with the others, swirling endlessly in the same clockwise direction.

I watch closely. Even though the wizard says everyone will play the game sooner or later, I realize I don't want to play. Some of the others in the group discuss just getting it over with. I watch as one big fellow jumps into the pool and is immediately surrounded by all the creatures in the water. Darting quickly towards him, they swim around and around, swirling up the water, creating a screen of bubbles so he can't see, and so that no one else is clearly visible either. He's caught in a whirlwind, but from my vantage point on the side of the pool I clearly see all the creatures and the tactics being used to confuse the new player.

"How will we know who the bad creature is? How will we recognize it?" I ask the wizard, who's standing next to me. "You'll know it when you see it," he says, towering over me. And suddenly, I do see it, a huge bat-like creature darting quickly through the water, its head large and round, sinister black eyes and a lurid smile stuck on its pale white face. The rest of it, as black as ink, is draped in strands of seaweed. Its spiky wings and long tentacles stand out starkly against the bright blue of the pool. There is no mistaking it. This creature is archetypal, a demonic black entity, the embodiment of the evil predator heading straight for its prey.

The predatory creature easily snatches the big man, caught unaware and thoroughly confused by the foaming vortex. I get a good look at the evil creature as it passes right by me, swimming swiftly through the network of canals that lead to the underground tunnels. I see the big man, wrapped firmly in its black tentacles, looking quite stunned. In an instant they're gone. Now we all know what we're looking for. As I turn back to the pool, I see that the other creatures are once again moving in a steady clockwise direction, swimming swiftly and gracefully, as if they are riding a merry-go-round at an amusement park, as if nothing untoward has happened. In fact, I hear the lilting tones of a carousel organ, playing a happy song.

Some of the other students in the group jump into the water. I'm amazed that they don't get it, that they didn't learn anything from what just happened, that they don't see what I see! I'm aware that I must leave, that I don't want to play this game at all, but I'm frozen. Immobilized, I teeter on the edge of the pool, clutching my key in one hand and the scarf in the other. Gazing dizzily into the water, I try to figure out if the creatures and children swirling by are good or bad, safe or not. I'm in danger of falling in, but I can't move to save myself. Suddenly, I'm grabbed from behind and dragged from the pool's edge. Frozen stiff, I'm laid on a mattress. I'm frightened that the black creature has snatched me, certain that I'll be raped and tortured, but then the man who has just plucked me from the edge of the pool speaks in a calm voice and I recognize him immediately—it's Chuck. He speaks in such soothing tones I want to cry. I want to scream and let out all the pain inside me, but all I can do is lie there, stiff and tense, clutching my key.

All of a sudden, I realize that I've always kept my key safe, that the evil predator never got my key. And then it strikes me that I know everyone in the pool. They are the souls of people and animals I've known throughout my life, through many lifetimes in fact, as we have all been caught together in endless cycles of reincarnation. I'm aware that I've already played this game many times before and I really don't want to keep playing it—I'm done with it!

I see that there are enough other people like me, choosing not to play, still standing on the water's edge. I now understand that Chuck pulled me away from the edge of the pool because he saw I was in distress. He knew that I needed help. He saw that I didn't want to play, but that I was paralyzed by something. As he pulled me out of danger, far from the edge of the pool, he assured me that I was safe now. As I contemplate these facts, I suddenly realize that I've passed the final test—I do know how to get back! It's as simple as deciding not to play the game anymore, breaking the cycle of reincarnation. I gain the clear insight that the real "key" is to not play the game to begin with! And with that I leap up and run out of the poolroom.

I run outside, into a dark and dreary ancient city. It's nighttime and the streets are wet, as if it's just been raining. I hear the footsteps of someone following me. I'm immediately fearful and so I keep running. I run down narrow cobblestoned streets, lined with old stone buildings. I open many tiny doors to dark little cells as I run along. There are small children inside the damp, dungeon-like cells and I tell them that they are free now. They don't know how to react, they don't seem to know what I mean, but I push them along anyway, for I sense we must not tarry. "Hurry, hurry, run, run!" I say. "Get away from here; you are free! You don't have to stay here anymore. Go!"

They are as stiff and frozen, as stunned as I was when I stood on the edge of the pool. They've never been free before; they don't even know what that means, but that doesn't stop me—I push them! I make them run as fast as they can because I still hear someone running behind us. I'm aware that I'm breaking all the rules now, and that someone is angry. I push the children ahead of me and we run like hell out of that cold dark ancient city.

Feeling as if I've dreamed a thousand dreams, each a thousand years long, I run down the darkened street, the pounding of running feet reverberating behind me. As I round a curve, I'm suddenly stopped in my tracks by the word CRY suspended in giant watery blue letters, hanging like a curtain across the street, blocking my way. I cry out and the dark ancient street disappears as, strangely enough, I find myself sitting up in bed, staring at three giant watery letters, shimmering and vibrating before me. Slowly they dissipate, droplet by droplet, like gentle rain falling, until only silvery images remain, until only a mist of pale ghostly letters shimmers in the early morning light. I stare, striving for clearer vision and fuller consciousness.

What was that! Stunned, I lie down, then sit right back up again and stare at the spot where the letters had hung moments before. I see them still, ghostly pale images hanging in the air, letters comprised of water droplets, as real as the sheet that I pull up around me as a cold shiver courses through me. I must be going crazy! But I don't have time for that! The only thing that matters is the message! Of course I want to cry, but I can't!

The Key

I know I must confront the parts of myself that are like those children that I freed from the ancient cells, the parts of myself that have been locked away, my *feelings*. Accessing my feelings is still the biggest challenge I face, but a necessity, as I do not want to be like my staunchly emotionless mother. At the same time that I acknowledge this truth, I am struck by the fuller realization that I've been standing paralyzed on the edge of that shimmering pool of reincarnation for lifetimes, in a state of confusion, trying to figure out the deeper meaning of everything.

As if a switch has flipped, light floods my consciousness with unmitigated awareness that we have all lived previous lives. In an instant, everything about life and reincarnation is clearly revealed and fully understood. With brilliant clarity, I understand my personal attachment to my abuser's games, played repeatedly, because I had to play them, perhaps for many lifetimes. And yet, I fully realize the other truth, that I had the key to my release from him all along in my own spirit's desire to be free, as it pushed me to keep going, in spite of my trauma, to find the means to live life on my own terms. I *was* caught in the reincarnation game, just like the children and creatures in my dream. Indeed, I too had to play it until I no longer needed to—until now! Perhaps sexual abuse was the game I needed in order to discover the truth of my soul's journey, as it offered me the greatest challenges and the succinct means—recapitulation—by which to discover how to change my current circumstances, and my future circumstances as well. If this life is indeed preparation for what comes next, then I have learned the method of breaking the reincarnation cycle. It's as simple as refusing to play the games that life and circumstances have dealt.

The point of the Wizard's game was to learn how to create your own reality, and that's exactly what I'm doing as I take this recapitulation journey. As I break through the walls of the world as I've always known and perceived it, I am also tearing down the barriers that block access to even greater insights and experiences, like the ones that came out of this dream. The real answer to getting back is to recapitulate, to fully understand where I've been. I must go back if I am to go forward fully aware. I also understand that "getting back" means getting back to the true inner self, the only *true* reality.

As I take this recapitulation journey, I am discovering not only who I really am, but also that I hold the keys to all the deeper

213

questions that arise—and I always have! As I search among the debris of devastation now—my dismantled, recapitulated self—I look only for that which is personally relevant, for there is so much that was presented to me throughout life that does not belong to me or resonate with my personal beliefs. I am fully experiencing and partaking in the total dismantling of the foreign installation that the shamans describe, while simultaneously constructing a new self, a self built solely upon my own deepest truths. I am both dying and being reborn at the same time.

But who was I running from in the dream? I wonder if it's the old self, the frozen traumatized self who was just about to fall right into that pool and play the game yet again. Was I running from her? Or was I running from the predator, still afraid that he might get me? Or was Chuck running after me, wanting to help? Have I misperceived the intentions of the person following me?

When I stood on the edge of the pool, totally aware that I no longer wanted to play the game, I was my traumatized child-self once again, immobilized by the realization that she was caught anew. She did not want to play the abuser's games, but she was helpless as to how to get away. As I stood there teetering, I knew I had swum around in that pool like the children on the broomsticks for my entire life; I was one of them. This time, however, I was making a decision. I was no longer going to play the game. I was going to defy all the rules, go against authority. I was making a choice to save myself from what had always been a powerless situation. Still I could not budge. Something else still had power.

I was mesmerized by the ancient energy of the game, the swirling pool, and the utter clarity that blew through me as I stood there. It was a critical moment and I could have fallen into the pool had not my dreaming self done what my waking self often does: reaches out to Chuck for help, to anchor me and bring me back into present reality. And so I am not surprised that he appeared in my dream. Once the hypnotic spell was broken, I saw everything from a much clearer perspective. As I was lying on the mattress, safely removed from the edge of the pool, more new revelations blew through me. It was then that I gained the power to create my own reality.

It was only then that I could get up and run away without even a backward glance. In the blink of an eye, I shed everything that had once held me captive. However, my dream points out, I will not be totally free until I assimilate all my child selves and release all the pent up feelings of a lifetime. And so I was led down the dark and dreary streets of that ancient city to rescue the children locked in the dungeons, so reminiscent of the damp cave-like structure of the stone bridge on my abuser's property. I sensed they had been locked up for a very long time, like my sixteen little girl selves, their legs never used, freedom never experienced. I too am like them, stretching and using my legs to run for my own good now. For the first time in my life, I ran like hell from the predator's game. I am free at last!

My dreams expose and explore the truths of my life, and of greater life far beyond normal consciousness. They leave me deeply fulfilled and exhilarated, in a blissful state. I feel more whole today than I have ever felt in my entire life and I am completely satisfied with the progress I'm making. On another level, however, I'm so exhausted, so physically and mentally depleted that I decide I won't get out of bed today. I will lie here and let what happens happen. As if I am still lying on that mattress by the pool, I give in, because it feels like it's finally time to do so. It hurts so much to move, my body aching as if it had run a hundred miles down those cobblestoned streets of my dream. I discover that if I don't move at all, the pain lessens. And so, I decide to stay out-of-body most of the day. And that is what I do. I float.

I get up every now and then to walk around and stretch my legs—it feels important that I not end up like the children in the dungeons. The windows are open wide. It's a beautiful day and fresh breezes blow in on my face and body, but I still don't want to move from my spot on the bed. I want to lie still where I am and allow myself to just let go of everything for one day. I always say I'm fine. I pretend I'm fine, but I'm not. I'm faking it. I don't feel like faking it today, especially to myself.

April 15, 2003

Once again, I dream that I'm living in a stone house on top of a mountain. There's a small cottage on the property. I keep it locked up, but every day I take the key and go over to the cottage to check on it. Unlocking the door, I step inside. The cottage is dark and damp, unused. I always ask myself the same question: "Why am I here?" Although I have no answer, I know I must constantly return to the cottage, checking on it daily.

I feel more alert today and it's easier to get out of bed, especially as I have my appointment with Chuck. As we discuss my dreams, it becomes clear that the small cottage represents a stage of this recapitulation, a stage that's done. I know I don't have to keep going back, checking on the memories, just as I don't have to listen to my abuser's voice, or play his games. *I don't have to play the games*, as the pool of reincarnation dream so clearly points out. I've already swum in the churning vat of confusion, ignorance, and forgetfulness enough times. I've already gone over the memories so many times. Each day now, as I recapitulate, there is less and less that frightens me. As my dream points out, the past *is* like an empty lifeless cottage at this point, as the energy that had been caught there has been released, returned to me. There's nothing of importance left there. Now it's time to take my key and use it for myself. I've advanced to a new level, just as the wizard suggested would happen. I'm actually, finally, getting somewhere! It's really okay to walk away from the empty old cottage and the pool of reincarnation now. It's what this journey is about, fully taking back my energy and my spirit, so that I can move on into new life as a whole being, leaving behind what no longer serves me.

"Do you ever wish you had taken the blue pill?" Chuck asks.

"No! Never!" I say, enthusiastically. "I do still need to find a way to cry though, to let the tears flow," and once again the big blue letters shimmer in the air before me like ghostly reminders.

"Take a bath, be around water to start the process," Chuck says and this sounds so safe and doable, but then Chuck mentions that we won't be meeting on Friday and I panic.

"I'm not abandoning you," he says, looking at me with concern.

I can't say a word, but inside I'm crumbling and fearful, as if I'm standing on the edge of that vast pool again. I get up in a daze, stumble out to my car, and drive home where I tumble right back into bed and fall asleep. Later in the day, I admit that when Chuck said, *"I'm not abandoning you,"* that's exactly what I felt he was doing. I know I'm in a stronger place, but the old self is still scared and vulnerable. In spite of the incredible progress I'm making and all the mindblowing stuff I've experienced, I feel like I've just fallen right back into the pool of reincarnation.

April 16, 2003

I dream of being in my art studio, working on a project when a flood arrives. The studio is underwater in seconds. The flood washes through quickly and is gone as swiftly as it arrived. I am not harmed. Afterwards, I stand amid the total chaos caused by the sudden flood, feeling empty and sad, fully aware that this flood signifies the necessary devastation of everything.

I wanted to cry last night. I tried for a long time, but only dry croaking crow sounds emerged, painfully choked. No easy tears came to wash my sadness away, except in my dream. Just as Chuck suggested that I be around water, water came, but where is that well of tears that I know exists somewhere inside me? I long for a different kind of flood, a torrent of weeping, but I'm caught in a whirlwind of dry desert sadness, with no tears to wash the gritty sand away. I'm aware, however, that I've barely acknowledged the sadness and devastation that have lived inside me for so long, a huge blockage that must still be reckoned with. I must be patient.

As soon as I get out of bed, I am inundated with head numbing dizziness. A cold chill creeps across my scalp and down into the back of my neck and shoulders. If I touch my skin I expect it to be bumpy lizard skin. It's the Paxil. I don't like the way I feel anymore, as if side effects are starting after all this time. It's a freaky thing to feel my brain freeze like that, as if icy cold water were being poured over my head. "I'll be fine, relax. I can handle this," I tell myself. "It's just another bump in the road; just calm down and breathe." But there's another part of me that wonders what's really going on, because I notice how physically uncomfortable I am, as if there's something in my body that doesn't belong there.

As I step into the shower, I beg the water to loosen the blockage that I haven't found a way to remove on my own. "Wash it away! Wash it away and let me cry!" I beg. Afterwards I do some calming yoga and quiet breathing. And then I just sit still and wait for the chill to go away and the dizziness to subside. Eventually, I can move without interference and for the rest of the day I keep moving. I do things outside and inside—gardening, cleaning, laundry—bending and standing up quickly, daring the vertigo to return so I can gain control over it, but it doesn't.

The kids are still at their dad's. This alone time is proving to be very satisfying, very healing, as I am given the space to just be with what is. When night comes I go to bed feeling powerful.

April 17, 2003

I dream that I'm inside an ancient church filled with golden chalices, fine tapestries and many ornate objects. It's icy cold, dark and damp, and I'm bundled up in many layers of clothing. In spite of its richness there's a dreary, oppressive feeling about the place. As I walk up and down the aisles, I notice the quiet crowds glumly sitting in the pews, subdued, clearly depressed and sad. Outside, I hear singing. A man, sitting in one of the pews, knows the words and he softly sings along, but he's not happy. I know he wants to be outside, where singing is allowed, and not stuck in here. Suddenly, I realize that I've been living in this church for a long time. As I recall this, I think I've been happy and safe in this rich environment, but then I become aware that it's more like a dungeon or a prison than a church because the truth is we're all locked in. Now our leader commands that we leave. He tells us that the place is being invaded. The other people seem so resigned to their fates, but I approach the leader with the intention of convincing him that I should stay behind because I'm strong enough to fight now. He insists that it's time to leave; there's no need to fight any longer. "The place is being destroyed," he says. "Take only what you need, and prepare for a long journey."

There's so much to choose from, but I know I don't need much. I watch as others select ornate objects—vases and urns, statuary, and the tapestries from the walls—but in the end all I take is a simple walking stick. "You're only taking a stick!" someone comments, quite astonished, as I stand at the front of the church with my stick. Like an ornate shepherd's crook, it curls upward toward the sky, much like the golden crook carried by the Queen of Rhode Island in an earlier dream. I know that in every twist and turn it contains my past and I know it's all I'll need. I'm also aware that it will be helpful on my journey into the future, that it symbolizes a bridge between worlds. I stand excitedly before the huge doors of the church, stick in hand, full of anticipation, for I am certain that some great force is coming to storm the doors, freeing me at last. It's just a matter of time, but I'm ready.

I feel strong and certain as I awaken from this vivid, metaphorical dream, which certainly underscores the intent of this recapitulation journey. I'm more fully aware that I will not only fully recapitulate my past, but that I will indeed enter into new life. I also know that I'm heading into totally unknown territory and that little from my past will be useful as I go forward. Although the church is filled with riches, I'm not interested. Only the simple stick has meaning. I see it as a metaphor for this recapitulation and what made me the strong person I am. I'm aware that it bridges two worlds—the past with the future—weaving together the past, now known, with the future, totally unknown. Unlike the other people in the church, I'm not afraid. I feel strong and ready, full of exuberant energy, anticipating an exciting future that is full of goodness.

When I get out of bed, I immediately experience the same symptoms of dizziness that plagued me yesterday. I put in a call to my doctor, more sure now that I'm having a reaction to the Paxil, which I've been cutting back on lately. However, I also honestly note that many of these same symptoms have accompanied me throughout this recapitulation process. As I've transformed from being the depressed person I always was into the new me, it's as if changes have been occurring not only on a mental, emotional, and spiritual level, but also on a visceral and cellular level each day too. I've dealt with extreme fatigue, loss of energy and appetite, lack of concentration, headache, dizziness and trembling as I've gone through this transformational process, as well as excruciating body aches and pains. There have been changes in my brain too, as I've experienced head zaps, thumping pulses, and numbness, as if the old self is dying off, sloughing off dead brain cells, while my new self has been growing inside me and is now eager to be born. I take these symptoms not only as side effects of the Paxil, but also as signs of good progress. Real changes to my brain, my body, and my personality are occurring as memories are revealed, as depression lifts and new energy gains entry, as new channels that have never before been utilized or fully accessed open up and seek life.

My doctor suggests that I wean off the Paxil very slowly. He suggests that the vertigo and trembling are related to it, but the other stuff is probably trauma related.

April 18, 2003

It's Good Friday. Chuck had suggested that I pay attention to the energy of the holiday, not necessarily the religious aspects, but the cosmic events of the occasion. "There's a lot of energy attached to pain and suffering, leading to death and then release to enlightenment," he said the other day.

"*Release to light, to the light of the Aura*" is what comes to me as I awaken and set my intent to remain aware.

I'm convinced, more than ever, that Jeanne is somehow responsible for aligning me with this work of recapitulation and that she supports me wholeheartedly as I go through this process. But if I hadn't dared myself to take this recapitulation journey to begin with, I wouldn't be where I am now, doing what I'm doing. And so I am as much responsible for where I am now as she is. If I hadn't dared myself to go through the pain and suffering of remembering, I'd never fully understand who I am, why I'm here, or what I'm supposed to be doing with my life. And those things are important to me, as I look forward to one day knowing what this life is really all about. To take this journey is really my own choice, and so even as I thank Jeanne for her part in my process, I also thank myself for being daring enough and driven enough to continue this work of transformation.

I'm already changing. At every stage of this process I feel different, especially inside. I'm allowing myself to be real, the soft, sensitive person I really am and it's noticeable on the outside too. When I hear myself speak now I notice that I speak without a hard shell, a tough hide, or a shield of fear all around me. Now, it's the warm, soft, and open soul of me communicating from my heart. I've been noticing how people react to me now too, much more gently, as I've become much more gentle with myself.

April 19, 2003

I dream that my two children and I are living on a farm commune. The setting is beautiful, but what goes on behind the gates of the commune is anything but beautiful. During daily group sessions the leader humiliates and bullies people into accepting him as the one true leader. People join him on stage as they fall under his spell. Before each session, I take my children aside and whisper in their ears that I love them, telling them that the leader is a bad man and he only wants to control them, that his sole purpose is to gain power over others. I tell them that no matter what he says they are not to believe him, but if they can't resist and feel drawn to him, they are to remember that I love them and that I will save them. During one of the brainwashing sessions, as my children and I staunchly resist the commands of the leader, we are stripped naked and beaten in front of the entire congregation. I am in agony as I'm beaten to a bloody pulp and then forced to watch as my children are beaten, too weak to protect them.

We're separated afterwards. I am sent to the kitchen to wash dishes. I think I must be having a baby because there is so much blood pouring out between my legs. Even as I stand washing dishes I keep worrying about the baby, though I'm not pregnant. A woman comes into the kitchen. "Oh, My God!" she screams when she sees the condition I'm in. "I'm all right," I tell her. "I'll be fine." I ask her to find out if my kids are okay; I'm so worried about them. As we talk, she looks into a room adjacent to the kitchen, a small square room, and screams again. I see the room is covered in blood. As soon as the woman screams I have a vague memory of having been in that room for a long time, not given food, clothing, or blankets. I had screamed for my children and bled all over the room as I was attacked repeatedly by men with sticks, fighting them off until I was too weak to resist.

As I stand in the kitchen, washing the mounds of dishes, a large girl comes in to taunt me. She wrestles me to the ground and punches me so that I start to bleed again. She hates me for some reason. I don't know why, but I sense that I am the embodiment of everything she desires and can't have, so she is driven to destroy me. The leader urges her to physically attack me as often as she wants. He comes to watch and cheer her on. Whenever I see her coming, I know she intends to beat me again. I fight back for as long as I am able. The little room adjacent to the kitchen becomes even more blood-covered as the days go on.

Eventually, I see my children again. They are just about to march into the meeting room. I have time to whisper to them that I love them, and that I understand if they aren't able to resist. I tell them that I know it isn't their fault. But this time they don't go into the meeting room, they join me. Other children join us too. We sit quietly on the floor, leaning against a wall in a wide corridor. I notice the children trying to keep smiles on their faces while looking quite terrified. The big girl who regularly beats me glares as she walks past and goes into the meeting room. We hear the leader's voice, loud and commanding, bellowing through the doorway. My daughter goes over to look through the doorway into the meeting room, a low tunnel, as one must enter the meeting room by crawling submissively on all fours. I'm worried that she'll get drawn in. I send her messages of love, silently encouraging her to stay strong and connected to what's right. She sits in the tunnel, neither coming back to my side nor going through to the meeting room.

My nemesis, the big girl who regularly beats me, reappears with another girl, a much larger girl still. They stand over me ready to attack, but before they can make a move I leap up and wrestle them both to the ground. "I'll never give in," I whisper in their ears, holding them down with all my might. "I'll fight forever, even if you kill me." The children sitting against the wall watch in horror, because all of my wounds are once again spouting blood, but I tell them that I'm strong enough to resist and I know they are too. The two big girls pinned beneath me look very frightened now, especially when my blood starts flowing over them and as they sense my strength never relinquishing. We lie piled in a heap, and even though I'm much smaller I am clearly much stronger now too. Finally, I let the two big girls go. They slink down the corridor where they sit down and whisper together. The other children gather around me, looking relieved. They believe me now when I say that we're all stronger than the leader, who we can hear screaming commands in the other room. I see my daughter still sitting in the tunnel, but she is turned fully toward me now, and I know that sooner or later she'll join me, but it has to be her choice.

I am much lighter in spirit as I awaken, strong currents of my own power coursing out of the dream into my real body. I'm aware of my deep inner strength—utilized during my traumatic childhood by my child self—stirring and flowing once again. In the dream, the children turn toward me, bravely defying the leader, the prescribed protocol, and the old way of doing things. In spite of the pain and suffering that we must all endure, they join me, as we strive to maintain a sense of self and individuality.

At the end of the dream, my daughter sits between worlds, between the old and the new, where I know my inner child sits as well. Still drawn back to the known, demoralizing and destructive though it is, she is clearly turning to our new world as well. We both struggle. I, the adult, fight the demon energies of old that once overpowered me, taking back my energy. In fact, the big girl who comes to beat me every day in the dream is reminiscent of a big girl who beat me up every day in the girl's bathroom when I was in second grade. The beatings went on the entire school year and I often got into trouble, as I yelled at her to stop hitting me and as I attempted to dodge her blows. But the torture didn't stop there. She sat behind me in the classroom as well, where she constantly pulled my hair, poked sharp pencils into my neck, and pushed the front of her desk, which was higher than the back of my smaller chair, into my back. I knew she was angry about something or perhaps jealous of me for some reason, her meanness having arrived suddenly, but I could never figure out why or what to do about it. For some reason she felt empowered to bully me, one of the smallest in the class and I found her large size totally intimidating. My pleading with her simply intensified the bullying, and my constant whispers for her to stop got me into more trouble than it was worth, and so I endured the torture.

It seems I am at last facing what she once did to me in this dream, taking back my power. My child self, in the guise of my daughter sitting in the tunnel between worlds, is free to observe me in this new empowered state and decide for herself what's right, allowed to be fully done with the past on her own terms, but with a new impression of just who I am as well. I'm very optimistic. I have a sense we'll be joining up soon enough—in a new world. I have no doubt we'll get there.

April 20, 2003

In a dream, a naked man lies on a bed. A woman tells him to get up, but he can't because I'm lying on top of him. I'm a very small child and his penis is between my legs. He tells the woman that I crawled into his bed and fell asleep on top of him and he thinks I have a fever and should not be moved. The woman leaves me with the man because she thinks he's taking care of me. His penis grows bigger as he pulls me tightly against him, telling me he'll make me better. He tells me I want him to do this to me, that I came to him. I am full of shame and confusion as I feel my tiny girl body begin to float up like a cloud, a pink cloud. The woman comes back into the room to scold the man again for still being in bed, but he tells her to go away. "She's asleep now, I can't move her," he says. In truth, I'm suffocating, but I'm also aware that I can't do anything about it. I'm just a tiny little girl, held down by big hands.

I wake up in the dream, totally lucid. It's nighttime now. The ceiling is completely gone and the room is open to the night sky, which is pitch black and full of stars, more than I've ever seen in my life. I sit up in the bed where the man and woman are now sleeping together. I see that there are two other little girls sleeping with us. I'm an adult now and I'm worried about the two little girls, but when I see that even the man is sleeping heavily I decide they'll be okay for a little while. And so I step out of the bed and onto the floor, which is covered in a few inches of light fluffy snow, not cold at all. The floor slopes downward to a large picture window, the entire wall on that side of the room glass. At first, I think I'm outside because of the snow, but as I walk down the slope toward the window I realize that I'm still enclosed inside four walls. The night sky is the most beautiful sight I've ever seen, like being inside a planetarium. Stars begin to fall, one by one, turning into bright snowflakes that slowly fall into the room.

The two little girls wake up. I tell them to be very quiet, and invite them to join me. We stand together, quietly watching the falling snow. Soon the snow turns into shooting stars, a few here and there, and then suddenly we are watching fireworks. Shimmering lights shoot across the sky, a brilliant array, until it suddenly grows dark.

"Don't go back to the man's bed," I whisper to the girls, but they don't understand. "He's bad and he'll make you sick." Finally they get it. "We're safe here for a little while," I tell them, making sure the man is still sleeping. "Sleep now," I say, covering them with snow. I sit on the floor beside them, watching over them while they sleep undisturbed. In the morning, I wake the two girls before the man and his wife are up. I tell them that we're going to be very quiet and just stay in the house after the man and his wife leave for the day. Later, as we're sitting quietly looking out the big picture window, the man comes bursting into the room. We're frightened, and the little girls look at me with terror in their eyes. I tell them to hide under the snow on the floor again, that I'll take care of the man. I cover them over with snow just as I had in the night, and then I cover myself too, but it's too late; he's already seen me. I wake up, my heart pounding.

It's Easter Sunday. It's been a transformative weekend. All I had to do was acquiesce to my dream world to experience the "energy attached to pain and suffering, leading to death and then release to enlightenment," as Chuck spoke of the other day. Last night's lucid dream was a cosmic experience like none I've ever had. And once again, my dream supported what is simultaneously happening in my daily recapitulation process, as I constantly face my abuser. He is everywhere; I've lived with his energetic presence my entire life. However, as my dream illustrates, there are lucid moments of beauty and ecstasy, moments of sheer magic as well; perhaps a sign of what is to come. I'm not at all disheartened by the end of this dream, as it clearly shows progress in all aspects of this deep work that I'm doing; the past, the present, the future, the physical and the spiritual, all in total alignment.

April 21, 2003

I dream that I'm living in a dormitory. My wallet and shoes are stolen while I'm in the shower. I know that someone is jealous of me for some reason. Later, my wallet is returned, slipped under my door, but the money is gone and my shoes are still missing. I find another pair of shoes and join a tour group that is going to visit an art gallery. We travel on a bus, which stops near a cluster of ramshackle barns. No shoes are allowed on the tour, so I take mine off and leave them with everyone else's. I'm handed a flyer, the whole trip a big marketing proposal, aimed at enticing us into renting studio space. I've been talking on and off with Chuck, who is also on the tour. We talk about art projects we're working on. I feel so peaceful as we talk. We follow the tour group into a barn, set up as a cafeteria, and sit down on small rickety chairs, at a small rickety table, to eat. At the end of the tour I can't find my shoes again. Chuck tells me that shoes don't matter, that you can go anywhere and do anything without shoes.

Later, I return to the barn with the rickety furniture. It's nighttime now and dark. I'm helping to set up for another meal. Chuck and I fix the rickety table, hammering and adjusting the level. We fix the wobbly chairs too. I'm aware that we're doing something together that I am unable to do on my own. The table and chairs are like a sculpture that we're creating, intent upon getting everything exactly right. We work calmly and slowly, measuring and adjusting, knowing that in the end everything will fit and work perfectly.

I wake up in the energy of the dream, in a very calm state. The art gallery tour that turned into a sales job is related to an old world, a world of marketing that I am no longer willing or interested in participating in. Only being in Chuck's calm company, repairing the furniture—representing my recapitulation process, no doubt—feels right. I experienced a new sense of calmness, a wholeness within myself while I dreamed. When Chuck told me that shoes didn't matter, he was right. When I ended up back in the barn at night, working on the table with him, nothing else mattered then either, only the work at hand. I knew that when we were done the table would be beautiful, just as this process of recapitulation will lead to my own beautifully reconstructed self. What matters is the process, the impeccable work, as I make sure that each memory is thoroughly explored and put to rest. In the dream, we worked much as we do in our sessions, instinctively finding our way. As this dream implies, I have my own wholeness to look forward to.

As I rediscover and reconnect with my spiritual self, I better understand what I've been living with for so long, as well as what I've been living without. So much is being reawakened and rediscovered, but only because what happened to me as a child is real again, only because I have gone back and extricated my lost child self from the darkness of my inner world and reconnected with her. As I recapitulate, I'm simultaneously rediscovering my sensitive, empathic nature, my intuitive self. In learning to trust the voices I hear, those whisperers of truth, I'm more open to their guidance, learning how to acquiesce and let go of control, allowing myself to go where they take me. As I allow myself to fully trust this journey, I am becoming as innocent as a child.

As my dream points out, I have to stop worrying about the length of time this recapitulation is taking, because the work, if it is to be done impeccably, takes the time it needs. I have to focus instead on the quality of workmanship, how thoroughly and deeply into my inner world I can go. The direction of the rest of my life will become clear as I work on the inner spiritual structure; I am certain of this.

I notice that when memories arise now, I am no longer as stunned as I once was. Everything is more or less categorized now, neatly arranged, and so each time a memory emerges, I know where it fits, which cubbyhole to stash it away in.

I'm ready to move on to the next part of this healing journey. But even as I write these words the numbing goosebumps skitter along my scalp, reminding me that there's still work to do and progress to be made. "Don't stop," they tell me, "not until you've solved every riddle about the self!"

April 22, 2003

When I meet with Chuck we talk about how organic, how singularly alive, the recapitulation process has proven to be as it has naturally unfolded. In the beginning, the word recapitulation wasn't even in my vocabulary and I knew nothing about taking a shamanic journey. Even the idea of doing deep inner work was quite frightening! I couldn't imagine what venturing back into my past would involve or how the process would evolve.

"No one ever does," Chuck says.

I'm more open to this process every day as I wake up and discover something new about myself and the world I inhabit. Whether in dreams, in recapitulation, or in the signs and synchronicities in the world around me, I have become an explorer in a strange new land, discovering so much for the first time. I also understand how necessary this recapitulation is if I am to become whole, that calmly united and balanced person I have long wished to be; the person I was as I worked on the table and chairs with Chuck in the dream the other night. In learning how to do this recapitulation, I've learned how to let go of more than just fear and doubt. I've learned the importance of trust, of allowing myself to be vulnerable and innocent without fear, allowing Chuck to be an essential part of this very private inner process. I have finally let someone in.

I realize now that this journey could only begin because I was ready. I found my way to Chuck, albeit with a little help—the synchronicities of the universe in perfect alignment with my own spirit's intent. He is the conduit by which I am offered this grand evolutionary experience, whether he knows it or not, whether he would even accept that role. Humble though he is, it's only through his knowledge, expertise, and intuitive guidance that I am offered a means of reconnection with my own soul, which has been lying in wait within the deepest sphere of my own awareness. Where I go from here is anyone's guess, but go I will!

April 23, 2003

I wake up with good energy, enough to get myself over to the studio, where I haven't spent much time lately. I have several phone calls to make, as well as preparations for a studio sale we're planning for Saturday. In addition to getting some much needed cleaning and organization done, my studio partner and I have ample opportunity to talk about the future of our shared studio space. We've been tossing around the idea of moving to a new location on the ground floor of the building where we'd have greater access to foot traffic and a dedicated gallery space. The talk is good, releasing some of the recent tensions that had arisen between us after her sudden announcement that she would be going back to school fulltime, though nothing gets finalized. By four thirty I'm back at home with the kids, exhausted after spending so much time out in the world.

While preparing dinner, I note how anxious I am about Chuck's announcement that he would be away again for a few days. Why? Am I afraid he won't come back? Am I afraid I won't be able to handle things while he's away? Am I still angry with myself? Do I still blame myself? Whose fault was it? Was I bad? If my own daughter had fallen into contact with a man like my abuser, would I blame her? Of course I wouldn't!

Cooking and chopping veggies calms me, and before long my negative fears dissipate. I cook and stir, turning instead to considering the positive changes I've experienced lately. I note how differently I feel now, mentally and physically less tense. As the week has progressed, I've lowered the meds significantly and the wild dizziness and shaking are gone. I've experienced stomach pains and done a lot of yawning, but I definitely feel how much I've changed and how much I continue to change each day, both as I've reduced the meds and as I've let this journey carry me forward.

The old walls are definitely crumbling, walls made of old beliefs and old decisions, old misunderstandings, old feelings and old fears. As they begin to crumble and fall, as the dust rises from the rubble, I marvel at how much lighter I feel. Something else is beginning to rise too, a mix of joy and excitement stirring from deep inside me. Although such exuberance is a little challenging to embrace at the moment, the stirrings reveal something else: a greater sense of hope, and I'm okay with that!

April 24, 2003

I dream that I'm moving out of an old apartment. After cleaning it and leaving the keys, I walk into a beautiful summer setting, lush and green. Everything smells so sweet and I feel so alive, contented, and safe. Then I'm driving an old car with no power steering. I park on a familiar street in Philadelphia. I walk behind a building, go into a courtyard and close the gate, which immediately locks behind me. It's only then that I realize there's no way to get out of the courtyard. I run around, frantically trying doors and windows, but there are bars covering everything. There's a high metal fence at the back of the courtyard that I can probably climb over, and I'm just contemplating doing this when I look behind me and see that a child has opened one of the doors to the building. With the door open just a crack, she peeks out at me. As I walk towards her, I wake up.

I'm aware that I still have a lot of work ahead of me. I feel lost again, as the first part of the dream, with its hints of beauty and sweetness, dissolves into a familiar feeling of being trapped. Driving that old clunker of a car with no power steering was the first hint that I was going back into an old place, my unconscious telling me that there's still much to be confronted. I want to feel safe and happy like I did in the earlier part of the dream, but I have to admit that even though I've had glimpses of what that will be like, I know I'm not quite there yet. The truth is that I haven't faced everything yet. I'm certain that the little girl, in opening the door, is going to show me the way out—or at least that's what I hope—but I also know that she'll present me with where I must still go. She's actually leading me deeper into myself, often a sad place, but I have no choice; I must go there. It's where this journey is taking me, deeper still.

I walk into the studio and step on a pill, smashing it, a bright blue capsule lying right inside the doorway.

"Oh, I just stepped on a pill, is it yours?" I ask my studio partner.

"No," she says, "how did that get there?"

"Who knows? Very weird!" Then I think of *The Matrix* and the choice of taking the blue pill or the red pill. Well, I've already taken the red pill, and, as I told Chuck last week, I've never regretted my decision. Is the universe teasing me?

April 25, 2003

I dream that I'm living in a peasant village in the middle of the Dark Ages. All of the village adults are slovenly, incompetent, evil people. They don't care about their children so I take over. I keep the village running and raise all the children, who though innocent when young grow up to become evil too. Life changes all around me, but I never change; I am a teenager throughout the dream. Eventually, I am raped by a gang of men who take me captive, keeping me to themselves. This shuts down the entire village for several years because there is no one else to do all the jobs that I've been doing. Not only did I care for the children, but I grew the food, baked the bread, wove cloth, and did all the laundry. The village decays and most of the villagers leave. Green mold grows over everything, killing all life. I fall ill. Unable to move, the green mold grows over me too. I sleep in a coma beneath it for years. One day, I am awoken by a small child who comes to visit me, bringing a kitten. She misses me and wants me back again, she says, and so I return to take care of her. Though I never fully recover from my illness, I am able to care for myself and the little girl. Soon others return and the village gradually comes back to life. The bad men come back too.

I wake up out of this disturbing dream but soon fall asleep again, right back into the same dream. Now I'm back in the village, living next door to the same people who had raped me. I know who they are and what they've done in the past. I'm still afraid of them. I worry that everything I do will be criticized, that things will be taken from me, and that I'll be blamed for everything. I feel that I'm still their captive in some way. A neighbor invites all of the villagers to a potluck dinner. Even the men who had raped me are there, sitting at a long wooden table, but they won't look at me. It's as if nothing ever happened. When the man sitting next to me speaks, I turn to him and see that it's Chuck. "Everything has changed so much since then," he says. He hands me a notebook and says, "Write."

I put the notebook in my pocket and get up from the table. When I leave, I make sure I've shut the door firmly behind me. I run into the woods, hoping no one is following me because I just want to be alone. Under a fallen tree, I see several wild cats. They stare at me suspiciously. I speak calmly to them and they let me sit beside them, though one of them takes off running. The other cats tell me that she doesn't trust anyone, that she always runs away. The woods are lush with new spring growth and I'm happy and calm sitting there with the wild cats.

There's an overall feeling in this second dream that although things happened a long time ago, I'm still stuck, still a prisoner of the past. Even though new growth and healing are taking place all around me, even though I am behaving as a normal person, at least on the outside, I'm still suffering. I go looking for some kind of comfort, which I find in the wild cats; representing my untamed feelings, as of yet unassimilated, no doubt.

Chuck's dream statement, that *"everything has changed,"* is certainly true. Things *are* different now. The first dream points out how I've lived in the past, a slave to my fears, but also a hard worker, extremely capable and caring of others. It's only when the small girl comes with the kitten that new life becomes possible, my inner child urging me to take the recapitulation journey to a new level. Although I continue to be deeply attached to and responsible for others in reality, my dream points out that I also have another responsibility, to myself, to fully recapitulate.

All night I tossed and turned, soaked in sweat, my legs tight and burning while I tried to relax. I'm sure this sweating is partly due to withdrawing from the Paxil—as are the patches of itchy, dry red skin and the intermittent stomach cramps I've been experiencing—but that it's equally related to issues arising from this recapitulation process. I suspect, as well, that menopause has something to do with it, but I refuse to attach medical tags to symptoms I experience as related to my past and to unresolved psychological issues. Of course other things factor in, but for the most part I see all issues that plague me as originating in my past. I'm out of balance and my overall energy is greatly compromised, but I am certain that all of my mental, physical, and emotional issues will resolve as I continue this recapitulation. This is after all a healing process!

With a busy day ahead of me, I'm at the studio by seven thirty getting paperwork done before heading out to a gallery in a city a couple of hours away. I'm scheduled to pick up some artwork that's been on exhibit there for the past several months. The trip is uneventful, the traffic flowing and light, the weather beautiful. I arrive on time, load my artwork into the car, get paid for what I've sold, and set out to retrace the route back out of the city. Suddenly, I'm totally lost. I can't find my way to the highway I had come in on. I end up wandering around for twenty miles feeling like I'm probably going in the wrong direction, but something tells me to just keep going.

I stop to ask for directions at a florist's shop and then at a gas station, but no one can help me. It's as if I've landed on another planet, because the major interstate I'm looking for just does not exist in anyone's awareness. I get back into the car and continue driving. Then I notice the smells changing, a faint odor of New York City coming up from the briny river, but also the smell of old memories wafting in through the open car windows. I'm far from where I grew up, on the other side of the river, but I feel as lost as I once did as a child when the known world disappeared as soon as I entered my abuser's world. No compass in the world could have saved me.

One day, not long ago, when I was visiting my parents, the breeze held whiffs of my abuser. I sat in their yard and smelled him on the winds carried down from his place on the mountaintop. I caught glimpses of memories as they blew past. Now, as I drive, my shoulders hunch automatically at the thought of him. I notice that I still carry so much fear in me, my jaw exceedingly tight and painful. I try to shake off the past that so doggedly follows after me, even on this beautiful spring day, but it's persistent.

Following my nose and a car with out-of-state plates, I finally find the highway I'd been searching for all along; it just appears out of nowhere. I easily merge into the stream of traffic and speed up, intent upon airing out the stale air of old memories and leaving the briny smell of the past behind. Before closing the windows, I let out a strangled scream too. Then I relax, aware that I'm in the driver's seat now and I'm fully intent upon driving myself right into new life.

April 26, 2003

I awaken with my shoulders still hunched after my driving experience yesterday. Drenched in sweat again last night, I was somehow able to sleep, but today I awaken raw and ready to cry, wanting someone to love me, wanting someone to hold me, wanting someone to talk to, wanting someone real. We're having a warehouse sale at the studio, but it's cold and rainy right now, so it's anyone's guess if we'll have buyers. Later tonight, there's a gallery reception to attend, for which I have little enthusiasm. At this point, my focus is wholly on getting myself out of bed and seeing if I can make it through the day.

My studio partner and I make endless trips carrying our sale items down the stairs to the large porch outside the studio building. Although it's raining steadily, it's plenty dry under the large roof. We bundle up, make coffee and hunker down with our hot mugs to wait for customers. We've advertised and several other artists and businesses have joined us, so there's a bit of a jolly atmosphere to the whole thing, but it remains cold and rainy all day. With plenty of time to talk, my studio partner and I make the final decision to move our studio downstairs to the first floor because, we decide, change is good. This becomes the mantra of the day. *Change is good!* It echoes back and forth under the overhanging roof, taken up by the other artists, as it seems to fit where everyone else is as well. The decision to move becomes especially appealing when, at the end of the day, we have to lug all that we didn't sell back upstairs again.

I head home exhausted, having made only a few hundred dollars. I go to the gallery reception, but end up walking around in a tired daze. I talk to one or two people and leave as soon as I can. I don't even know why I go to these things. I guess I feel it's my duty, especially since I have some art in the show. I drive home, take a bath, watch TV, eat a little, and go to bed. To say the least, it's been a dreary day, but I have to remember that change is good!

April 27, 2003

My legs hurt after carrying things up and down the stairs yesterday and now I just want to stay in bed, writing in my journal, as instructed by Chuck in my dream last week. I don't feel very well either. My stomach is bothering me and I'm quite dizzy when I bump into a friend at the grocery store later in the day.

"You look white, very white, are you alright?" she asks. "You are so white!"

"Yes, I feel white and exhausted," I say because, really, I'm lightheaded and faint. It's a real first for me to admit that I'm not okay. I'm sure I'm dehydrated from all the sweating I've been doing every night. I just want my body back; I want to feel real. By evening I'm simply exhausted, lying stretched out on the couch, yawning heavily, when the kids come home from the week spent at their dad's. My daughter arrives a little cranky, headachy, sunburned and tired, though I know she's happy to be home. In contrast, my son is in a great mood. I urge him to go to sleep at a reasonable hour and, for the first time that I can remember, he doesn't disagree.

The night is warm and I have the windows open wide to the fresh night air. Before turning in, I stand outside for a while, gazing up at the starry, constellation-filled sky. "I'm holding on," I say to the universe, "I'm just holding on."

April 28, 2003

I stayed conscious of tension while I slept and was able to move into new positions and relax, though some painful memory still resides in my body, for I am tense and on-edge a great deal of the time, in waking and in sleeping. I know that the absence of fear will mean that I've gotten beyond the memories. I look forward to one day achieving an even greater lightness of being, a better balance within, having released the terrors that now reside inside me. In the meantime, I've noticed some positive changes. I'm definitely better, for I am unbothered by those old whispery voices. "Don't do it! Better not get too relaxed, it's a bad idea!" they used to say, urging me to be careful and alert. Instead, I'm experiencing a new sense of freedom, as I am released to seek relaxation all the time now, unrestricted. I just have to remind myself to do it and how essential it is to this healing process.

I'm also experiencing a greater openness. I find myself saying positive things, without even thinking, as if someone else is speaking. Everything suddenly appears open and energetically good. It's as if nothing negative will get in my way now, and that every positive word I speak is leading me towards something I can't even imagine at this point. A new insight strikes home as I soften and evolve: *the more open I am, the more I will receive.*

I still fight the fear, but it's not as daunting or as crippling as it once was. It lingers in the background now, while I'm up front creating a new world and a new self. I *am* creating my own reality, just as the wizard in my dream said I would!

April 29, 2003

I dream that war is imminent, annihilation almost certain. I prepare to leave everything behind, taking only what is necessary and important. I gather my children, my cats, and as many winter clothes as possible and pack the car. I don't want to frighten the kids, so I act as if I'm in total control, staying calm, giving them things to do, while also firmly telling them they must do exactly as I say. On the way out of town, I have to pick up some important documents from my abuser. As I drive to his house and prepare to encounter him, I consciously acquiesce to what may happen. I pull up in front of a city building. Telling the kids to sit quietly in the car and wait for me, I go upstairs. My abuser lies ill in bed, dying in fact. His messy room flows with rivulets of vomit. He lies in a wide bed, stinking of puke and death. I sit down next to him, even though I know he's evil and even though I'm afraid of him. He gives me some papers and says that I'll know what to do with them. He also says that once I've read them, I'll understand. I fear him, but at the same time I feel sorry for him. I'm upset about leaving him in the condition he's in, but he says he'll be fine and that it's supposed to be this way. I ask him if his daughter is taking care of him, and he repeats that he's okay and to stop worrying. "Just take what you need and go," he says. "I'm not worth the worry." I go downstairs to see that his daughter has gone into her own room with a man. She's having sex while her father is upstairs dying. "Just get out of here and forget about me; I'm a goner," he yells from his sick bed. As much as I hate and fear him, I also feel attached and worried about him. Back in the car with the kids, I explain that nuclear winter is coming and that it will be very cold, with no sun. I'm digging around in the trunk looking for warm mittens, hats and scarves when I wake up.

My dreamworld asks me to face my biggest fear. Am I prepared to actually let go of my abuser—my biggest and most real fear? And what are the important papers about, the truths of my abuse? I'm still attached to my abuser, though I am also fully aware that a major disaster is soon to happen. My psyche is preparing me for a big change!

April 30, 2003

I dream that people are visiting my studio, which is in an old barn. I begin telling a story about my sister-in-law, that she floated across the Atlantic Ocean to Paris in an inner tube with her baby on her lap. I notice that people are gathering around to listen, and so I continue telling the tale. "She could take only a few things with her. I told her to make sure she had lots of sunscreen and a hat," I say. "She floated to Portugal and then, by land, made her way to Paris."

While I tell the story I'm actually making the journey with the baby myself, who is perhaps eight months old. The ocean journey is arduous. At one point the baby falls overboard, but I'm able to grab her before she goes too far under water. There are sharks, dark waters and huge waves, but we make it, landing in a totally unexpected place, not Paris after all, but the sunny coast of Portugal. I don't speak the language, but we're able to make our way because communication happens quite easily, telepathically. People instinctively know what we need and where we're going. They line the roadways from Portugal to Paris, lovingly guiding and ushering us along, beautiful white light shining upon us all.

"The unexpected—the arrival in Portugal—and the journey are even more important than the final destination of Paris," I say, "which is simply a goal." I'm aware that a new goal must always be established because it's always the journey and the unexpected stops along the way that are important. I tell everyone that my sister-in-law and her infant daughter made the journey, but it's a lie because I made the journey. I don't want anyone to know, because that's not what's important. The important lesson is that it's possible to take a challenging, life-threatening journey and not only survive but continue growing and thriving. The truth is that the journey never ends!

I meet with Chuck for the first time in a week. We talk about the possibility of a new memory emerging, suggested by the constant pain that I've been experiencing. I tell him that the only way I've found to survive lately is to dissociate, to leave my body.

"That works," he says, and then I wait for him to tell me, "no, don't do that, go through the experience instead," but he doesn't. And so I tell him how the pressure to cry is torturing me.

"My feelings and emotions are being held captive inside me somewhere," I say. "Something just will not allow for release. Something is guarding or blocking, yet I must find a way to break through. I'm shown this in my dreams, but mostly I feel it in the tension in my body."

We do EMDR. I enter into my heart center. Calmly, I look around, but I find nothing! I know I have the ability to love and to be loved. I'm aware of my own deep well of emotion and feeling, lying hidden inside me somewhere, but where? I'm suddenly aware that this has to do with my most innocent self, who is fearful that any sign of tenderness will be misconstrued, seen as a weakness, a chink in the armor, sure to bring only pain and annihilation. My most innocent self is still fearful of being abused.

"I realize there's a battle going on between fear and trust," I say.

Chuck nods in agreement.

"This is happening at the deepest level. I know I have to get beyond the fear that guards the gate so that trust can come out into the air and breathe, so that my innocence, long held back by fear, may one day see the light of day and truly live."

Chapter 5

In Some Crazy Void

May 1, 2003

I dream that I'm at Chuck's house. I'm in a bedroom far removed from the rest of the household having sex with a former boyfriend. I know I'm caught in an old routine with this boyfriend. I'm also aware that Chuck is wondering where I am and, indeed, I would prefer to be working with him on my recapitulation. At this realization, I kick my old boyfriend away and tell him that I won't have sex with him anymore and that he can't treat me in the old way anymore either. I imagine that Chuck is angry with me for having sex with my old boyfriend, that he's gone away and doesn't want to work with me anymore. I want him to come back, to not desert me, even though I know I made a bad mistake by returning to an old place.

My daughter shows up. We go outside and follow a path leading into some woods. I don't want Chuck to see me because I'm so ashamed of my earlier behavior, certain he's aware of what I've done. I'm thinking about how angry he'll be with me when I notice that my daughter is naked and dirty. In a few seconds she has somehow gotten filthy. As I brush the debris off her, I think about how kids can get dirty so quickly and not even notice or care.

Suddenly a crowd gathers, pointing and making comments about kids and dirt, which I don't like. "It's not her fault, she's just a kid," I say, and then I kiss her and look her straight in the eyes so she knows that what they're saying isn't true, that as far as I'm concerned she can get as dirty as she likes and I'll never blame her. Meanwhile, I'm ashamed, feeling dirty myself. Then my daughter and I take off running into the woods. I make sure that we stay near the stone wall that surrounds the property, so that if Chuck should appear I can quickly jump behind it and hide.

The overall sense of this dream is that I still carry great shame and guilt. I'm ashamed of what I'm doing with my old boyfriend. I'm even ashamed to be found by Chuck, even though my dream is really presenting a therapeutic process, pointing out the issues and asking me to work through them, for only in doing so will I be able to trust at a deeper level. Deeper trust really means not only trusting what I've learned, and trusting another person enough to talk about it, but also trusting that I'm totally acceptable as I am, which I haven't gotten to yet. I must accept myself, just as I totally accept my daughter in the dream. Filthy though she is, I do not judge her or fault her; I see her only as innocent. And so, I must not find fault with my child self, or my adult self either for that matter, but take this dreaming insight even deeper, into waking life as well. I must be okay with who I am and where I've been; everything about me must be acceptable.

Fuller trust, however, feels impossible at this point, no matter how much I rationalize it, though I know that in reality Chuck is offering me a place to work all this out, and I do feel safe in his company. However, as the dream points out, shame, guilt, and fear overshadow everything. The truth is that I'm afraid Chuck will find me abhorrent, that he'll be disgusted by me, if he isn't already. At the same time, I need his help to get through this recapitulation. I must also trust the whole of my journey as meaningful, and the fact that Chuck isn't actually present anywhere in the dream seems significant. Has my unconscious removed him so I can face my feelings of shame and guilt totally alone? Even though he's not present I still feel his overall presence, which may be my unconscious letting me know that he doesn't judge me, that he *suspends judgment* in fact. Do I judge myself? When I clean my daughter off, looking her in the eye, I'm letting her know that it's wrong to judge others, but really I'm trying to convince myself that the abuse wasn't my fault.

The dream is about letting go of old beliefs and judgments about the self. It's about my new desire to be pure and innocent again, cleansed of my past. I question how I can possibly work with Chuck if I remain in an affair with my old boyfriend. How can I be doing this changing work while I'm constantly dragged back to old places and old feelings?

May 2, 2003

I dream that I'm back in the house I grew up in. I'm in charge, just as I often was as a child, even though there are other adults in the house. I'm carrying a crying baby around in my arms, a little girl whose mother can't soothe her. There are other little children too, whom I bathe and help to use the toilet. Each time the bathtub drains, I see that it's dirty. I keep cleaning it out so the kids can bathe in a clean tub. I do everything one-handed because I'm holding the crying baby. Eventually, I find the big old family Bible and put the baby down inside the pages, which receive her as if made of feathers. I close the giant book and pretty soon the baby stops crying and falls asleep. "Oh, that's what was wrong, she was just tired," everyone says, but I know they don't have it right. After a while, I think the baby might not be able to breathe so I take her out of the Bible and give her back to her mother, who is happy to take her back now that she's quiet. The mother talks about how she needed to do laundry and take a shower, how she wanted to be clean, and she didn't know what to do with the crying baby. "She just wants you," I tell her, "that's why she was crying." I leave my parent's house and go to the general store in a nearby hamlet. I don't want my parents to know I'm there. I have no intention of speaking with them; I simply want to buy what I need for the recapitulation process. I pick up bread, water, and canned goods. I pass by rows of wine but remind myself that I'm not drinking these days, that it isn't a good idea right now. I bump into a man who invites me on a date. "No," I say, refusing to let anything interfere in my process. "I have to go now; I have somewhere to be."

I note the references to the dirty kids, as well as the mother who wanted to get herself clean, as themes of recent dreams and this process of recapitulation, as I continue to face all the issues that are as of yet unresolved, shame being a big one. I am charged with caring for the crying baby, because in reality she's mine. The Bible is perhaps a reference to my own ancient history, confronting me with the deeper truth of the family I was born into, as well as the history of abuse. On the other hand, the baby calmed down inside the pages of the Bible, perhaps back where she belonged, fully recapitulated, both the abuse and my family confronted, resolved, fully detached from and put to rest. My intention to continue the recapitulation unabated was underscored when I went and stocked up on supplies. And I do have somewhere to be, just as I told the man in my dream. I have to get ready for my appointment with Chuck!

Chuck points out how my intent to change is working constantly through my dreams, as well as in my waking life, that I'm fully conscious and *intentionally aware* at all times now. If I'm to keep shifting out of old places and aid myself in the unfolding process, constant movement is necessary, he suggests. I'm very aware, I tell him, that I still get drawn back to the old fetal pose because it offers such comfort, more so than any of the other things that I've utilized as replacements. Yoga, breathing, meditation, shamanic magical passes, bathing—and even simply walking—have all become essential tools in support of this process, but none of them are as instantly comforting as that old pose. It's still the safest place I know, much like putting the baby into the Bible where she could curl up and experience comfort similar to being in the womb. While I constantly argue with myself about whether it's good or bad for me to go into the fetal pose, I go anyway, even though I'm simultaneously quite fiercely drawn to finding a totally new safe place, far from everything I know, far from what this world has so far offered.

As the session ends, I acknowledge to Chuck that every time I roll into the fetal pose I am tormented by feeling that I'm letting him down. I know it isn't really him I'm letting down but my own expectations of change. I should be doing something more to create a new place of comfort within myself, for I realize it's the only place that true comfort will ever be found. Perhaps that's what the Bible is really indicating in my dream, that in order to achieve real calmness I must go still deeper into myself, to my very soul. I must be patient; eventually peacefulness within will come.

"I'm in the middle of nowhere right now, between worlds, in a vast land of nothingness," I say, as I get up to leave. "Yikes!"

May 3, 2003

Once again, I dream that I'm at the house I grew up in when a car drives up the driveway. The driver looks like a good friend of mine from Sweden. I peer at her out an upstairs window, trying to figure out if it's really her. I wonder if she thinks this is the old art studio we once had together. "But that was a long time ago," I think, "things have changed." I'm also aware that change is really good. I go outside to talk with her and find her gone. My daughter has followed me outside and we get into my own car with the intention of finding my old friend. I drive down the road and turn up the steep mountain road that leads to my abuser's property. I pull up beside my friend's car, which is parked on the side of the road. I see her standing in my abuser's driveway, talking with a plain looking little girl. When I call her name and speak to her in Swedish she doesn't seem to hear me, nor does the plain looking girl either. Meanwhile, my daughter looks at me like I'm crazy. She thinks I'm talking gibberish to two complete strangers.

I wake up and know that two worlds have overlapped in dreaming, one foreign world with another. My friend from faraway Sweden was talking to my abuser's daughter—a little girl once again—standing at the entrance to the driveway of my abuser's property, another strange and faraway land. The meaning of the dream is unclear, yet I still see my daughter's surprised face looking up at me, wondering what the heck was going on. I could not penetrate the dream—I was neither seen nor heard—as if it were not my dream at all. In every scene I was only an observer, standing outside the dream, as if separated by a soundproof glass wall. However, the dream took what I had told Chuck yesterday— that I am in the middle of nowhere right now—and showed me something important, just as my dreaming self correctly stated: *the past is over, things have changed.* That is definitely underscored when I cannot be seen or heard. I can't go back to an old world that doesn't exist anymore, and thus, anything that occurs in those old worlds can't penetrate into this world either. That is certainly something to consider when I'm in the middle of recapitulating something that feels like it's happening now!

I seek equilibrium as I pull myself together for the day ahead. The kids are participating in the annual music festival where they will each perform a solo before a judge. We have plans to go out to lunch with some friends afterwards. It's a big day. I want to be fully present for them, yet I am so weighed down by this recapitulation. Last night I felt how bursting with anger I am, yelling at my daughter, lashing out when I knew I wasn't really angry with her. We just got started and couldn't stop, me full of old anger and she intensely nervous about today, though neither of us could articulate that those were our real feelings. We simply and conveniently became easy targets for each other's frustration. Then I stopped the whole thing and apologized; I felt so awful.

I plod through the day, diligently staying connected to my intent to fight the strong desire to withdraw. I sit up as straight as I can and constantly command myself to adjust my posture, aware that if I don't my shoulders will round down and I'll hunch with the weight of this past I'm attempting to free myself of. I shrug it off all morning and stay attentive to my brave children. Aware of their needs, I remain supportive and encouraging as they each prepare to face their own fears and play their best. I'm amazed, year after year, as I watch them go through this process, so confident and focused, so unruffled and serious as they take a deep breath and head into the room to face the judge. I stand at the door sending them love and confidence, knowing they will handle themselves with professional aplomb as they have been taught and as they do every year. And fifteen minutes later, I watch them emerge so relieved and happy, as all their hard work pays off yet again. This year is no different and they both finish the event with big smiles on their flushed faces.

We meet up with our friends and find our way to a diner for lunch. The kids, freed of their tensions and nervousness, relax and talk about the scary/nice judges and how nervous they were. The other parent and I, both exhausted from being single mothers, talk quietly, smiling at our strong, happy children. The morning's mature demands over, innocence reigns once again.

May 4, 2003

The desire to withdraw is great today, to stay under the covers, to cling to the old feelings and lose myself in their power. The thought crosses my mind that I could stop everything—call a halt to this recapitulation—just say, *STOP! I don't want to do this!* I could just curl up into a ball and stay here in bed for the rest of my life. It would be easy, so easy to get lost in the old comforts, but I can't do that. Although I feel the need for something familiar to hang onto, this is a weaning process as much as a recapitulation process. It's like getting rid of the last smelly shred of baby blanket or the worn old teddy bear, that last little bit of childhood comfort that isn't really appropriate anymore.

It feels like I'm at the midpoint of this recapitulation now, this rite of passage, this process of breaking through one world and into another. I reside in the tension between worlds, constantly tugged in both directions, one world so predictable, the other an exciting curiosity. I'm also aware that the idea of the old world as comfort is a myth, just as the new world is equally mythical. An indecipherable blank greets me when I look ahead, the future a total mystery. But even so, I have a sense of it already being laid out, just waiting for me. I have a sense that what will happen is meant to happen, and perhaps it will be good, and perhaps it will contain some modicum of comfort as well.

I'm getting so tired of myself now too—the old self so boring, the new self so undeveloped. A friend asked me the other day if I was considering dating. I told her I wasn't ready for a new relationship, it's too early. I'm still on shaky ground, not secure enough in knowing who I really am. I'm certain that, at this point, I'd repeat the same mistakes I've always made. I haven't come far enough yet. I must be very careful.

By day's end, I give myself permission to go back into the fetal pose every now and then, *if it feels necessary*, but I won't stay there—only a quick dip in and out. I couldn't stay there for long even if I wanted to, though there must be a reason that I'm still so strongly drawn to it. What's still there? What can possibly be left?

May 5, 2003

I notice that I'm constantly tense in the world, alert to danger and predators. I observe myself while out hiking and I can honestly admit that I still don't like anyone passing by or coming close. If I hear someone coming from behind, my reaction is to walk faster so they won't overtake me. And if I see someone coming toward me, I immediately clam up, trying to gauge whether they're safe or not. It's as if I'm a five-year-old child again, wondering if the person approaching me is going to harm me. And I do feel that age when I'm out in the world. I'm a frightened five-year-old and I'm sure I look that way too. I'm so much happier when I don't run into anyone else, no one to get my guard up about. In line at the grocery store, I'm hunched like a cat with its back up, hair raised, ready to flee. To be honest, I'm getting tired of it, my body aching from maintaining this heightened state.

I'm sweating every night now, waking up totally drenched, slippery with sweat, so much that I could wick it off in waves. My thought that this sweating is only partly due to menopause is being answered because lately it's been accompanied by the visceral sensation that I'm being held against my will and I don't have enough power to fight back. I called Chuck this morning. It was hard to do, to break through the hard shield I've constructed around myself and reach for the phone. "I'm stuck, full of fear," I said. "I don't want to go back, but I can't move forward. I'm teetering. I can't fight; I'm too exhausted."

May 6, 2003

I dream that I meet a young teenager with a baby and several other people at a teashop. We sit and eat baked goods and drink tea. Everyone is happy. I'm concerned about the young girl with the baby. I want her to feel good about herself, and about having a child so young. I want her to know that it isn't her fault, that I understand her predicament. It's important to me that she not carry bad feelings about herself into adulthood.

I wake up to weird buzzing in my head again, totally clenched, as if not yet back in my body after a night of dreaming. I was so tired that in spite of the usual pain I fell asleep quickly and slept deeply. Once again, however, I awaken damp with sweat, covered in a slick film. I'm not hot or cold, or even uncomfortable. I continue to see this sweating as a releasing process, naturally accompanying the recapitulation, as old stuff leeches out of me by every means available—now through my pores.

I meet with Chuck. We talk about residual negative energy still inside me, left over from past negative relationships. It pops up as soon as I dare to think about doing something for myself. This negative energy is especially protective of itself as I construct a new self, Chuck says, as I dare to step out into a totally new world and leave it behind. I realize it was my own teenage self whom I mentored in my dream, wanting to soothe away my own deep feelings of shame and guilt. My dream helps me to see how the issues we carry and the insecurities implanted in childhood repeatedly play out in our lives, in relationships with others and in how we act in the world. I understand how powerfully our fears control us, unconsciously for the most part.

My past relationships were based on who I was because of my past—because of my childhood experiences as well as the fears I'd assimilated from those closest to me—and not on who I really am or have the potential to become. I have been so limited; I see this clearly now, especially in my past relationships with men. Each relationship was built on such flimsy ground—on my fears and deepest insecurities—rather than on mature adult awareness and the desire for real intimacy on a deeper level. I've always been afraid. In the past, I'd run from anything that asked me to be honest with myself or to step outside my comfort zone, so why would I have chosen to be in a relationship that would have challenged me to grow? It was so much easier to remain the same: *safely unthreatened.*

"I will do one thing every day that empowers and helps me to grow," I promise myself as we end the session.

In the afternoon, a publisher stops in at the studio and my new intent speaks right up without censorship or forethought. I blurt out that I want to do more writing and illustrating and does he have any possibilities. I cringe as I hear the words slip out, but in the next second I'm met with graciousness, for he says he'd be thrilled and has been meaning to ask me anyway. I promise to send him some samples of my work.

I continue to feel that my brain is actually changing as I go through this process, that the release of long-buried memories has shifted the very makeup of my frontal lobe. Even as I write this I feel it shifting and changing, like the earth's platelets shifting during an earthquake, vibrating and trembling as the old gives way to the new. I'm demolishing everything that has defined me. A lot of the work is already done, but there are still so many structures to dismantle, so many architectural details to sort through, and so much demolishing still to do.

May 7, 2003

Dreaming, yet just on the rim of waking consciousness, I hear a loud crack and suddenly startle. In the next second, I'm floating, aware of neither dream world nor real world. I hang out in the air between my ceiling and my bed. I'm aware of where I am, and yet it doesn't seem at all strange, more curious than anything. I reach out to touch the ceiling and in the next second I land with a thud onto my futon. Dreams and sensations evaporate, whisked off into that great vastness where a moment ago I'd floated. I think I just went out-of-body!

"This is where I am now," I tell myself. "In the crazy void between worlds, out-of-body without a moment's notice." And so I decide I will not struggle against it; I will accept where I am. I will just be. And even though I just went out-of-body, I know I must more fully live *in-body*, in full-body awareness.

Remnants of dreams flash into consciousness on and off throughout the day, glimpses of my studio cleaned and organized, a place for everything and everything in its place. I sense that it's time to focus on my work now. Synchronously, my studio partner and I sign the lease on our new studio space. Now I must pack up and get everything moved by June 1st. It's time to take the emphasis away from the home, where everything is pretty settled and routines are running smoothly, and get back to work.

May 8, 2003

I wake out of dreams I can't fully recall. Maybe there's a reason, maybe I need to attend to other issues. I have a sense they were all business-related dreams, getting my priorities straight, though my kids were in the dreams too, happy and contented, underscoring my sense that it's time to concentrate on the outer world again. It's time to get out of bed and spend my days at work. Right now, however, I'm going to yoga class—I can't even think about anything else!

For the most part, I'm stable and balanced during the class. At one point, however, I feel myself about to pass out, but I won't allow it. I accept how I feel, but firm myself up and stay in the pose. We work on heart opening and hip opening, both of which leave me feeling vulnerable and cranky, but I laugh instead. My yoga teacher gives me such a kind and heartwarming hug at the end of the class. I feel his heart beating against mine and I know he senses what I don't say. I'll talk to him sometime...when I'm ready...when it feels right.

I have a meeting at the artist's gallery in the evening and so I hurry home at the end of the day, feed the kids, and leave them to do their homework before heading out. When I get home from the meeting, I take a bath and notice that a rash that started yesterday is continuing to spread. It started on my neck and went down my shoulders and back and now it's moved around my sides and chest. It's itchy and annoying, the withdrawal symptoms from the Paxil getting worse. The more I move in a new direction, the more I make empowering decisions about my new life, the worse the withdrawal symptoms seem to get. If I could just sit still all day until the drug is totally out of my body I might be fine. I can't help but wonder if there's a part of me that's reluctant to move into new life. Or is the drug like an entity that doesn't want me to leave it behind? I notice also that although I'm still physically exhausted most of the time, overall I have more energy than I've had in a long time. Emotionally, I still feel somewhat confused, but I'm definitely improving, and my work with Chuck is certainly evolving.

May 9, 2003

I meet with Chuck early in the morning. We talk about all the shifts and changes taking place, subtle and otherwise, as my two worlds overlap—the old and the new—in dreaming and waking life. Chuck reminds me that in order to connect the two worlds more fully, I must keep going back to retrieve the good; gathering the truths about myself, taking the glimpses of my true abilities and powers out of the past, bringing them forward into *now*. I must trust myself to take my life forward now, to go on where I once left off, fully funded by the difficult work I've been doing.

"Where before your state of mind didn't allow you to continue, now it will," Chuck says. "You can go on and live out what you ran away from in the past."

I drive to the studio and decide to look at a car that I've noticed in the parking lot for the past week, its *For Sale* sign staring at me each day, beckoning me to take a closer look, a Saab. I drive it around the block a few times and like how safe and solid it feels. It's well cared for and reasonably priced. I sense it was put there for me, as my old car is failing fast. I rationalize that if I buy it all the loose ends will be tied up, material needs attended to. Perhaps then I can concentrate on other things, like work!

Another artist approaches us about sharing our new space, and we're intrigued, provided there'd be enough room for all of us. The idea of less money going out every month is appealing. I'm struck by this coincidence at the same time that I find a car, which I badly need. Can things happen so fast and so well? Can things be this good without consequences? As I ask myself these questions, a familiar voice speaks up and I hear its advice so clearly.

"*Go forward with no fear,*" Jeanne says, her voice so gently encouraging. "*Leave the fear behind and believe. Just believe in yourself and your abilities.*"

I'm suddenly more cognizant of her presence in my life. As I replay her words it hits me that she never really left me, though I had sensed her absence. I think she had simply stepped aside to let me progress at my own pace for a while, for it was appropriate that I gain confidence in my own innate abilities. While I work, I feel her behind me, coming out of my dreams and into my reality. It feels good to have her here, and I wholeheartedly welcome her. I decide to take her advice as well.

"I will go forward with no fear," I whisper.

In the next second, I am filled with a strong sense of good fortune. Suddenly full of vibrant energy, I feel great!

May 10, 2003

For once, I didn't sweat so much during the night and I wake up feeling *real*. I like the feeling! I decide not to take a Paxil today—time to go cold turkey. The weaning process has gone on long enough! I'm tired of the way it makes me feel and I trust my body will be okay without it now. I will go forward with no fear!

We're doing another warehouse sale at the studio. At least the weather is nicer than the last time, beautiful in fact. By noon I feel fine, very clear-eyed and clear-headed, glad I'd made the decision to not take a pill. I am so done with that!

May 11, 2003

I dream that I'm driving a Saab. I go to the studio building and park next to my partner's car. We work in the studio all night long, cleaning and packing. We fall asleep for a while, but soon awaken to disturbances, noises and sirens, the smell of smoke in the air. I look out the window and see fire trucks in the parking lot. "Something has happened; we'd better leave," I say. In slow and heavy dream-walking, we make our way down the stairs to the parking lot. It's daylight by the time we get there. The sun shines brightly, but I barely recognize the place. It's as if we've slept for twenty years, like Rip van Winkle. Trees have grown very tall; there are new buildings in the complex and many new parking spaces. I look everywhere, but I can't find my car. My studio partner's car is still there, but mine is gone, apparently stolen. I can't believe it! I return to the studio with the intent of starting my search over again. I go through the same process all day long, leaving the studio, going downstairs, looking for my car, and then returning to the studio. The whole time, I am stumbling around in my heavy dreaming body, confused by how things seem to have changed over night. As day grows gradually into night again, my wanderings end. I have to accept that my car is gone.

I wake up drenched in sweat, dehydrated, exhausted from dragging my heavy physical body around in my dream all night. As opposed to my out-of-body dreaming self who floated lightly above my bed the other day, this dreaming self was half asleep. Even the loud fire sirens were not enough to fully rouse me from my dream sleep. My first impression is that this dream is instructing me in how change is happening all the time—twenty years seemed to have passed in the blink of an eye—and that it will continue unabated. Once set in motion, nothing can stop change. I am being carried always onward, everything in synch with my intent to change too, in both dreaming and waking life. And the lost Saab? I wonder if I'm *missing* a great deal if I don't buy it, that someone else will get the car before I do. Am I reading this dream right? I think so.

The kids and I go for a long hike and I return with an abundance of energy. Even though my head is weirdly woozy, as if I still haven't woken up from that dream, I ignore it and clean the whole house. My decision to go off the meds is proving to be the right choice, as my energy and mood have improved immeasurably over the past two days. I've gained weight and feel pretty bloated after nine months on Paxil, but I'll shed those pounds as I get back into a better and more active lifestyle. Nine months is a long enough gestation period for any kind of birthing process!

What is my final decision about the Saab? Buy it!

May 12, 2003

I dream that I'm driving a small white *Toyota!* My daughter is with me. We drive through a construction area where a new housing development is being built. Large dump trucks hog the street. They speed around, screeching their brakes as they come up fast behind us. It's a little scary being in the midst of all this construction, but at the same time I'm aware that the street leads into the heart of the city, our ultimate destination.

We soon drive out of the construction zone and enter an older section of the city. Here too there is renovation going on, as small row houses, derelict and in need of repair, are being torn down or completely gutted. The streets are deserted, no people or other cars are in sight, but I notice that some of the buildings are inhabited. There are signs of new life here. I'm aware that the plan is to revitalize these outlying areas and then move deeper into the center of the city, renovating everything from the outside in.

We soon enter a vibrant city center where all the buildings are fully inhabited and many people are out and about. I stop on the side of a busy street and turn to speak to my daughter, but she is no longer in the seat beside me. A grown woman is sitting there now. I feel a desire to get out and walk, so I ask this woman to take over driving my car.

During this conversation a young black girl hops into the backseat. I'm aware that she's a street kid, and street savvy. As I give the woman the keys to the car, the girl asks if she can get them copied. She'll bring them right back, she says. I'm immediately suspicious that she wants to steal the car. I tell her that no one can copy my keys; they can't be copied. I'm aware that she wants something from me, that she's needy in some way. I'm also aware that she *should* be here, that she's in exactly the right place, that she needs to be around me in order to learn things. I know that she's really a good girl and that she just needs guidance.

I make sure I have my purse with me before I get out of the car and then I watch as the car pulls away into traffic, the woman waving her hand out the window, talking to the girl still sitting in the backseat. I set off walking and soon come to a small outdoor flea market. There's a police car parked nearby. Several men are arguing. The argument escalates into a fight and pretty soon the men are tussling on the ground. I notice that a nearby vendor doesn't get involved. The police don't do anything either. I chat with the vendor who says that he used to be like that. "Drugs," he says. He was an addict and he didn't care about anything except getting his drugs, he tells me. His eyes soften as he watches the men. I see that the vendor cares about these men; he feels their struggle. He says it's time to pack up and move on; he doesn't want to be around those guys because it's too tempting. I set off again, once again checking that I have my purse with me.

I walk down the street and into a modern glass building. It belongs to some relatives who live and work there. They also rent out office space. All the walls are constructed of glass. Even the walls that separate all the rooms inside the building are glass. One of the businesses is a karate studio where my children are taking a class. I sit down in the waiting area outside the classroom and wait for the class to end. I have my back turned away from the karate room so I don't have to watch my children get punched and kicked, but through the open door I hear sounds of sparring, shouting, and punching. Agitated, I get up and walk across the waiting area to the windows overlooking the street. A chain gang, comprised of bedraggled and sad looking children, connected by heavy chains, walks by on the street below. One or two of the children suddenly break down, crying. They fall to the ground and have violent tantrums, causing the whole row of children to come to a standstill.

I'm aware that they're not bad children, just caught in a bad place. The supervisor of the chain gang comes into the building carrying a small boy, one of the children who had fallen to the ground in a fit. He asks me to take the boy to a doctor—a woman doctor who has an office in the building—because he can't leave the other children.

The woman doctor gently and carefully examines the boy, knowing that he's emotionally very fragile and could explode again at any second. The wrong touch or look could turn him violent. She sends him to see another doctor and, once again, I deliver him to the proper room before returning to the waiting area. When the chain gang walks by again, I'm aware that the small boy will be greatly upset if he catches sight of them moving on without him. I see him through the glass walls, standing forlornly at the window in the doctor's examining room. I will him to look in my direction, gesturing to him to turn his gaze away from the window, but I see that he's stuck, frozen in place. With his face pressed against the window, he stands immobile as the chain gang walks by. I'm aware that he's been abused, but now I'm aware that he'll be having an even harder time because he feels abandoned as well. Once again, I don't like the sounds of violence coming from the karate room, and so I turn my attention away from the boy and abruptly call my own two children to follow me. "We're leaving," I say.

We go outside to wait for our ride. My father is supposed to pick us up in front of the building. We wait and wait. I finally see him walking towards us on the sidewalk, looking confused and preoccupied. He's not very concerned that he's so late, nor does he seem aware that he was supposed to be picking us up. His only concern is where to park his car, but I don't see his car anywhere. He asks me to stand on the street and hold a parking spot for him. I know it isn't really necessary, as there are no other cars parked along the street, but I do it anyway. I wait, standing on the side of the busy street for a long time as cars whiz past me. My father never returns. I feel stranded, but at the same time I know the kids are safe and that we have a place we can stay, in the glass building with my relatives. I don't really want to deal with my father anyway. "Let him go; he'll do what he wants," my relatives say. "It's okay; you can stay here as long as you like."

This dream sequence is curious, but very insightful, full of messages. The concentric shape of the city in the first part of the dream is like an intricate mandala, the roads leading into the city center like the spokes of a wheel. I observe from two places simultaneously as I dream. From an aerial perspective I see my car driving along the network of streets. I'm aware of the entire circle and the bigger plan to reconstruct and totally revitalize the city, making it one cohesive unit. At the same time that I have this broader perspective, I'm in the car with my daughter—the known part of my child self—driving through the gritty details of a construction zone. These two dreaming perspectives, as well as the layout of the city, are reminiscent of this recapitulation process, as I too view my life now from a different, broader perspective, while also working minutely on a very deep inner level. I've also been recapitulating from the outside in, addressing what is already known and obvious, while moving closer to my center, to the key ingredients of who I really am. It's interesting to note that the closer I got to the central part of the city the more alive it appeared, and the center itself was vibrant and bustling, much like my own center, my spiritual self still vibrantly alive after all the years I've been away from it. No need to renovate there!

My daughter, my known child self, disappears from the dream and another child appears, a shadow child, in the guise of the black girl. I refuse to let this unknown child have the keys, though perhaps she's asking me to share the keys of my inner self with her, and to allow her to live as well. And so I know I must confront all the parts of myself, known and unknown, light and dark. The fact that I'm worried about my purse in the dream is perhaps my intent to take forward only what has value.

Although I'm startled by and somewhat fearful of the black girl, I'm aware of her innate goodness. It's the same thing with the small boy from the chain gang. I feel such compassion for them both, yet as regards the girl I experience a sense of paranoia and with the boy great tenderness. Since I let the woman drive off with the black girl, I wonder if that means I'm not yet ready to deal with this shadow self, though I'm keenly aware that we need each other. She needs me to teach her what I've learned and apparently I need her too, yet for some reason I don't feel the same tenderness for her that I feel for the children on the chain gang. Perhaps their dire predicament is so visibly touching and reminiscent of my own trauma, now known, while her wounds are hidden, representing the still unknown self. I am, however, aware of her being good at

255

her core, just as I'm aware that I've always been good in spite of the wounds that I too carry inside. It's clear this shadow girl and I have work to do!

Later on everything is transparent, nothing hidden, for all the walls in the office building are glass. I can see everything, and yet I can't communicate with the sad little boy, whom I know is suffering greatly. There is healing work going on and even fighting in this transparent building. Earlier there was fighting on the street and here there's fighting in the karate studio. I watch one fight and only hear the other. The fight on the street doesn't really bother me, though I intuit feelings through the vendor and experience tenderness and compassion for him. I understand that he's giving me the message to walk away from my own addictions, to avoid my old habits and behaviors—curling up in a ball the greatest! At the same time, I know I must face the turmoil inside myself and not turn away from the painful battles that I must wage on the deepest level as I fight to make sense of my deepest truths and as I heal.

As I deal with trying to protect the little boy, the sounds coming from the karate studio, where my kids are learning how to defend themselves, become increasingly disturbing. It gets to a point where I can no longer bear the tension. I react and put a stop to it in the only way I know how, by whisking the kids away. It's in an effort to keep them safe, but also reminiscent of what I've done my whole life. To keep myself safe from the truth, I've whisked it away, kept it safely hidden from fuller awareness. Throughout the dream my compassion is repeatedly stirred, by the black girl, the street vendor, and then by the children on the chain gang, for I wish only good things for everyone.

Once again, I dream of my father, and again I find I can't rely on him. In the first part of the dream, I'm driving my own car, which is a good sign, although it's a Toyota and not a Saab! In the latter part of the dream, my father doesn't have his car, perhaps because he already gave me the keys to it in a previous dream. Perhaps his failure to pick me up signifies the distance I've already established with my parents. This is just what I've worked for, independence from all that they represent. Realizing this in the dream, I'm able to embrace that I'm actually in a good place now, having arrived at a new place solely on my own. In returning to the glass building, I intend that the recapitulation work continue with total transparency, as I face all that is seen, heard, and felt. As I fully face who I am, freed of parental oversight and allegiance, I must bear both the tension and the responsibility of everything that I have experienced in my life. Everything about myself must be revealed and everything about myself must be acceptable if I am to fully heal.

It's a cool, wet morning, slightly drizzly. I go to yoga class feeling sort of sad, wondering if the dream is finally loosening my emotions. I'm tight in all the usual places of holding, but the depression lifts noticeably as the class progresses. However, by the end of the class I'm dizzy and my head throbs. Centered in the frontal lobe, in the place I peruse so deeply when searching for clues to my past, and where it feels like the memories are being processed, the dizziness pounds away. This area is highly alert as I do this recapitulation. Each time I enter a memory, this part of my brain activates. I feel it doing its work, cranking up and humming along, spitting out memory after memory. I go straight home and crawl into bed. I lie in some crazy void—nowhere really—waiting for some unknown thing to reveal itself.

May 13, 2003

I dream that I'm a child again, living with other children in a medieval castle perched high on a cliff, the same stone building that has appeared in many recent dreams. We're all unhappy, controlled, locked up in a cold, dark tower. There's weird sexual behavior with adults going on. We look down on the world from our high perch, able to see everything. The landscape directly below the tower is muddy and barren. We're permitted access to this desolate, lifeless area under strict supervision, though we're aware of prettier places because we can see lush green gardens just beyond the muddy marshland. We all have wings, but they've been either clipped or broken so we can't use them. Someone figures out how to fix their wings and dares to leave, sneaking out at night, flying out the window of the castle on the cliff and down into the lush lands. Some of the other children figure out how to fix their wings too. They too sneak out at night and go to the lush lands. It's a secretive and furtive operation as they prepare to leave each night, all of us shaking with fear, hopeful that they will return safely, unharmed and undetected by the masters of the house.

The ones who stay behind are anxious the entire time the daring ones are away, knowing that the masters—bad men and women—can come in at any time and find them gone. I am one of the anxious ones, waiting all night for the others to return. Each night there is great relief as they reappear, flying in to tell us thrilling stories of what it's like out there, reveling in the possibilities that await us all in that other world. "You don't get fucked every day," they say. "You get to go to a real school and have real parents." We're all aware of the deceptive tactics used to gain this information, that we have had to be disobedient and devious in order to learn this most amazing truth. We don't really want to be dishonest, but we can't help it. We're fully aware that the adults will punish us in some awful way if they find out, so the repaired wings are kept a secret, though the nighttime flying continues unabated. As we hear the truths of the lush lands, we all feel much bolder, full of wonder and daring, even those of us who don't act on it. It's enough to hold the secret alive inside. My own desire for love spurs me to want to fix my broken wings, so that I too can go out into the lush lands one day and discover love.

For most of the night I really was in that tower, living in a vivid dream world, fearful and yet exhilarated by the excursions of the daring ones. I simultaneously tossed and turned, unable to get comfortable. I'm wobbly as I head out to meet with Chuck, as if I'm still locked in that tower, my body unused to free movement. I can barely get out of my car and walk into his office. How I yearn for escape from the prison of this stiff body that I live in every day! I want to fly! And so I accept the insinuations of my dreaming self, pointing out the deeper longing to not only escape the prison tower but to release my feeling self to fuller life and love. At the moment, however, I suffer from intense pressure in my head and body, as if something else has taken over and is trying to break me down.

"It's the final push through the birth canal!" Chuck says, confirming that I'm not going crazy and that this is indeed the final push to full recapitulation and the emergence of a new self.

"And I'm fighting it, as usual!" I say, the energy of this birthing process vibrating just beneath my skin. "It's ready to crack through, trying every which way to get out of my body."

In a physical, visceral way I feel stretched to the edge of my being, as if a real pregnancy is growing inside me. I automatically clench down tightly, holding in this phantom baby. It responds, kicking at me as I tell it to wait. Knowing that it's the final push helps, giving me a visual anchor to grab onto.

I leave Chuck's office with no release accomplished; not birthing day after all. My only wish is to keep this baby inside me, for the time being under my control. I'm not quite ready to go into full labor. The baby, however, doesn't seem to hear me, for it kicks at me all day long, the labor pains intense. Luckily, I'm so busy at work that I have no time for it.

I work long into the evening. It isn't until ten forty-five at night that I finally take off my work boots and sit down, exhausted. Of course *it* lets me know it's still with me, POUNDING AWAY, pushing to get out. "Okay," I tell it, very firmly, "Wait until Friday, and then I won't hold back anymore! As soon as I get to Chuck's office I'll recapitulate as much as I can. This time I won't hold back," I promise myself. "Now breathe!"

Breathe, breathe, breathe, breathe, breathe, breathe, breathe, breathe, breathe, breathe, breathe, breathe, breathe, breathe, breathe, breathe, breathe, breathe, breathe, breathe!

Each time I write the word *breathe*, I breathe and relax a little bit more, promising myself that I won't be shy, I won't worry so much, and I won't hold back when I meet with Chuck. I'll finally give birth to whatever this creature is!

May 14, 2003

I finally fell asleep last night only to awaken an hour later drenched in sweat. In seeking relief, my body automatically reverts to its own mechanics—sweating—a natural form of release.

I was afraid to rest too deeply last night, just as I'm afraid to release this phantom baby. Each time I turned in the night I felt as if I really was heavily pregnant. It'll be good to finally birth these long overdue feelings and emotions! Until I meet with Chuck again, I strive with all my might to keep everything safely contained.

It will be okay! Everything will be okay! This is all I can give myself throughout the day, as I struggle to stay present at work and to keep the phantom baby in. As usual, being busy has its benefits and luckily my energy level is high, even a little frantic, though I fear I won't be able to turn it down, even if I want to. In the evening, I attend a concert at the middle school, both of my children performing. My daughter does a dance number with another girl, to African drumming, moving beautifully with such good rhythm. She receives special recognition for dedicating considerable time to working with the upper grade chorus. My son plays a stunning trombone solo in the jazz band concert. People come up to him afterwards, calling him "the famous kid trombonist," and his friends want their pictures taken with him.

"Am I famous?" he asks, somewhat mystified by all the attention.

"Yes, you're famous," I say, feeling such tenderness for him. "Right now, tonight, you are certainly famous!"

Good moods and energy are running high and I'm right in synch. As the evening finally ends and I retire to my bedroom, however, the pulsing vibration descends, pushing at me. I push right back, not ready yet. I go out to the garage a few times to gather myself, not with the intention of releasing anything, but only with the intention of shoring myself up to get through the night. I don't want to have a meltdown in front of the kids. I'm just not going to put them through any more crazy-mom stuff, nor get in the way of their exhilarating experiences. And so, maintaining my edgy, raw, and brittle stance, I resist the call to collapse.

May 15, 2003

In a dream, I'm helping to serve food at a wedding. I'm barefoot. There's something wrong with my feet, but I won't let anyone know that they're bothering me. When I get a chance, I sit down and carefully peel the tough outer layer of skin off each foot. I'm thrilled and amazed to discover soft, pink skin underneath. I put the rough outer layer back on and go back to work, telling myself that I'll deal with it later, because I still have work to do.

I glance at the clock. I clearly see that it says three forty-five, yet I'm still dreaming, still intent on the work at hand, still running around barefoot, serving food in a pretty lacy dress. I sense that this is a future self. "Yes, there are good things to come," this other self says, sidling up next to me, "but there's still more work to be done. We must stay focused."

Suddenly wide awake, I realize that this other self is alerting me to the real task at hand: *to finish this recapitulation*. It doesn't surprise me to feel clenching in my lower abdomen, in the second chakra, as soon as I think this thought, as if my uterus is contracting. This is immediately followed by a pulsing sensation in my brain. Placing my awareness on what's happening, I follow as one sensation triggers the other. It becomes utterly clear to me that there is a bonafide connection between body memory and mind processing. I am indeed storing things in my physical body and what my body knows must be connected to what my mind knows, and vice versa, for full recapitulation to take place. I more fully understand that between the two—my physical body and my mind—long dormant memories and emotions are being stirred to awaken and, yes, they must be connected, fully accepted, and finally released.

My dreams have been so vivid and atmospherically real lately. They float into my awareness during the day. Like the scent of roses wafting through the air they come, reminding me of the mysteries of other worlds. Sometimes this hint of atmosphere is all I can remember of my dreams and it seems enough. Last night's dream however was so real! I was not just dreaming when I pulled the thick calloused soles off my feet, I was totally lucid and present, as a part of myself showed me the new tender self waiting for me beneath the crusty outer shell I constantly maintain. I know I have to keep chipping away at that old crust and that, somehow, I will have to let the birthing take place. At some point, I'm going to have to relinquish my hold and acquiesce to this next inevitable stage of the recapitulation process. The old self must be fully shed so a new self can emerge.

Once again, I sense that I'm dreaming all the time, working on many different layers of awareness simultaneously. Worlds are overlapping and I live, for the most part, in a nebulous "between" world, in a crazy kind of void. As I head out into that void today, my intention is to have everything go much smoother, to merge my dreaming and waking selves into a cohesive unit because I have an extremely busy day ahead of me.

I arrive at the studio early with good energy and set about finishing a press release that's due. I get it into the mail and finish an illustration job and then deliver that too. In a moment of total frustration, I swear at my printer when I'm having trouble getting something to print properly and it actually speaks back. "It's not my fault!" it says in a loud voice. I can't believe what I hear, so I swear at it again. It speaks again and I fall on the floor laughing. *It's not my fault!* What could be more relevant than that!

The pulsing in my head and body stay in the background as I work, like gentle ocean waves rolling onto a sandy shore, as if I'm working alongside the coast rather than in my inland studio. The waves rise and fall depending on what I'm up to, for the most part a lulling sound in the background. I notice that when I'm fully distracted they stop completely, and luckily I'm so busy that I'm able to avoid any pestering intrusion. By nighttime, however, the waves come crashing. I lie stricken in bed, in no position to fight back, as they roar over me. The pulsing vibration in my brain accelerates and my body threatens to explode in raw emotion. I can't hold back! No welcome relief of cooling water washes over me though, no healing salty tears, for out of the waves bursts a speeding train. FLICK-FLICK! FLICK-FLICK! As the cars of the train roar over me, visions of what my abuser did rumble through me—FLICK-FLICK—pictures of torture—FLICK-FLICK.

I sense the speeding train seeking to connect the horror and the emotions with the visual images and the physical pain that sit inside me, all parts waiting to be rejoined in one long trainload of atrocities, everything finally linked. As the train speeds by, flashbacks flicker on the windows. As if I'm watching a movie, I see my abuser raping me, hitting me. I hear him yelling at me, threatening to kill me. He hates me.

I meet with Chuck in the morning and tomorrow can't get here soon enough!

May 16, 2003

I fell asleep quickly last night, only tossing and turning a few times, exhaustion and the flicking train eventually lulling me into deep and dreamless sleep. Today is Chuck day and the pulsing knows it, already revving up, going back and forth at a high rate of speed. As soon as I step through the door of Chuck's office the speeding train takes over completely. I can barely see a few inches in front of me. I stumble in, plunk down in "my chair," and stare at Chuck.

"I can't stop it," I say, holding my head. "I can't stop it!"

Barely batting an eye, he hands over the headphones and sets the EMDR machine to a very slow pulse, a lot slower than my own. We sit opposite each other in silence and the bilateral pulses coming through the headphones eventually override the speeding train in my head. They cancel out the flickering sounds and suddenly I'm floating in a white void. Try as I might, and as many times as Chuck asks how I'm doing, I am unable to speak. I just cannot get a word out.

"Better not push it," Chuck says after a while, turning off the EMDR machine.

Though lulled into dreamy quiet, and a lot calmer than when I'd arrived, I nonetheless grow physically tighter, my body staunchly resisting this gentle opportunity to release. For some reason that I can't fathom, there is a part of me that refuses to budge, and for the life of me I simply cannot think or speak. Not one word or thought comes to mind. I am empty. I remove the EMDR headphones and Chuck and I sit in strained silence. A few more uncomfortable minutes pass before he speaks.

"It seems we're at an impasse. It might be time to ask for guidance," he says, pulling out the *I Ching*.

He hands me a notepad and I ponder a moment before writing my question in shaky script: *Why can't I release this tension?* Then I throw the coins.

The *I Ching* responds with hexagram #44, *Coming to Meet*. An unfavorable and dangerous situation exists, the *I Ching* warns. The feminine, long eliminated and kept hidden below, seeks union with the creative above, but there is an underlying darkness embodied in that feminine and it must be promptly grappled with. Release at this time, the *I Ching* cautions, is a bad idea, perhaps suggesting that the release of my little girl shadow self might bring problems. I must not be enticed by her needs, because she spells trouble. Her emergence must be within the natural course of the process, thus it's really too soon, and if I attend to her now it could spell disaster. In order to come together we must meet each other halfway, but the meeting must be free of any ulterior motives, the *I*

Ching advises. In addition, I get a moving line at the beginning, which states that if an inferior element has already wormed its way in, it must be stopped at once.

I nod repeatedly as Chuck reads the guidance from the *I Ching*. Words seem so distant and inadequate, but when he asks me what I think, I'm finally able to move my lips and speak.

"What inferior element would that be? Is there something I'm not seeing yet?" I wonder. "Perhaps this inferior element relates to the young black girl, the shadow self, jumping into the car and demanding my keys."

"She's not necessarily inferior, but merely incomplete," Chuck suggests.

"Put a brake of bronze on it!" the *I Ching* says as well, and I take that to mean put a brake on the attempts to force a release of tension. Instead, I must continue to bear the tension because it seems it's trying to teach me something, just like the young black girl was trying to tell me something when she demanded the keys.

"Perseverance brings good fortune," the *I Ching* also says, letting me know I must continue working through this process of recapitulation and discover the meaning of the little black girl. It's perhaps too early to jump ahead to birth; perhaps what's inside me must cook a little longer. Perhaps my brain has been urging me only to stay busy so I can hold the unrecapitulated child self—the shadow girl—inside for a while longer. Perhaps there are still more memories to come. Perhaps I'm just not done yet, though I long to jump ahead and be done!

The *I Ching* advises that in consistently checking the tension, bad effects can be avoided. I must not underestimate the power of what resides inside me, but instead tame and transform it as I go, Chuck suggests. It's a slow and painful process, as I well know, this work of taming and transforming, but it's what this recapitulation is all about, taming the old stuff that has been eating away at me my whole life and transforming it into gold, my inner gold that will one day live.

I have to say that I agree with the *I Ching*. I've been afraid to let go because the letting go itself doesn't feel right—it almost feels destructive—but at the same time I wonder if I'm just afraid of the process, fearful of how it might change me. But this reading suggests that I'm not ready to release yet, that I'm overriding the natural flow of the process. When the pulsing was like the ocean waves it felt much more natural than the speeding train. So my intuition to hold on and to contain receives validation in this reading, though I still need to find appropriate expression for the energy so it doesn't overwhelm or destroy me.

I'll continue my yoga, meditation, and breathing practices, as well as the shamanic movements. Along with my creative outlets of expression I ought to be able to keep it under control. If I don't, it *will* devour me. Suddenly, I clearly see this energy as intense anger, extremely violent and destructive rage. I'm afraid of it. To release it in incremental creative expression seems a healthy way to deal with it.

By the time I leave Chuck's office I'm visibly shaking. Yet, I must concede that the *I Ching* reading makes so much sense. I do have an incredible amount of creative energy, a constant flow of it day and night. I must focus it all the time now, not only when I'm working, or making art, or writing, but by doing other things I might enjoy as well. I sense dark rage inside me again, rising, pushing like a volcano, its hot lava seething just below the surface, threatening to gush forth, raw and destructive. I am helpless before it. It could hurt me. Is this my abuser's energy, left boiling inside me? Is this the destructive inferior force the *I Ching* warns about? I know it has the power to push everything else away and drag me off to a dark place. In its presence I become a little abused child again, knowing I'm caught, as I get dragged off into the woods again. I'm teetering on the edge of the abyss and I sense that if I let go in the wrong way something bad could happen.

"Go into the garage to get hold of it, as you've been doing," Chuck suggested during the session. "When you're in the garage it's okay to throw some punches. Throw things around, smash some glass bottles. Let it out; it needs to find expression."

I'm a physical wreck trying to keep it under control. I'm aware that if I don't deal with it constructively and creatively then it will have me physically, with a stroke, a heart attack, or a car accident. I can barely drive as it is, the pounding filling my ears and pulling a veil over my head until I'm in a dream state, my vision compromised. I tried to explain this to Chuck today, how I often get caught in this dream state and that was exactly where I was in his office this morning—stuck. I got pulled into such frightening anger, volatile and fiery. I tightened up more and more as I sat opposite him, afraid of what might happen if I released even a spurt.

I get home safely from my session, crawl into bed and fall right into a deep sleep and dream the following dream: I drive into a village with my daughter. We park the car and go into a drug store, which is being renovated. She wants to buy something. I see old valentine candy hearts, a sad little pile sitting off to the side, but other than that everything is a blur, the intense pulsing in my head causing vision problems, as if there's a veil over my face. I tell my daughter I'll wait for her in the car. I stumble around blindly, repeatedly blinking my eyes and finally find the way out. I sit in my car, which is parked in front of the store.

I notice that a huge section of the mountain overlooking the town is being carved into some kind of monument. I can barely make out workers on scaffolding on top of the mountain, chiseling and sculpting a figure with a huge peace sign for a head and wings coming out of its shoulders. All of a sudden, I'm aware of children's voices coming from beneath my car. Jumping out, I notice a little boy scoot under the car and then I hear a little girl screaming. "Ow, it's hot, it's burning!" I take this to mean that the little girl's vagina is burning in pain. I jump back into the car, put it into gear, and pull away to see a little boy and girl lying huddled on the ground. There's snow on the ground and I roll them around in it to cool the burns they've received from the hot engine. Thoughts are swirling through my head. Who are they? Why are they here? What are they doing underneath the car? I also see that the little girl was not being sexually abused, but I suspect she had been in the past. At the same time, I remember that I'd seen them playing on the curb earlier when we'd arrived and I'd told them then that it wasn't safe to play so near the street.

Waking up, I wonder if I'm the inferior element the *I Ching* refers to. I wonder if the children inside me are not going to be safe if I let them out into the world because my adult self hasn't prepared them properly. I felt terrible when I found those two little kids underneath my car. I felt responsible for traumatizing them. I was just sitting there, but it felt like my fault that they got burned. Am I not taking good care of my inner children? Like the children under the car they too are traumatized by what happened to them. Also, I realize that the mountain I just dreamed about is the same mountaintop that has appeared in many recent dreams, the one I dreamed about earlier in the week where the broken-winged children were locked away in the tower. In that dream, my inner children knew nothing of the world until they dared to fix their wings and go discover it. In this dream they're out of the tower, on the street, and they don't know you aren't supposed to play under cars. They're innocently exploring, but they need me to explain how the world really works. In this dream the dark tower is being transformed into something beautiful, wings restored, spreading wide. This is what the *I Ching* suggests as well, that with perseverance good fortune and peaceful transformation naturally take place.

I get out of bed, feeling slightly better, and head to work at the studio, but for the rest of the day I'm particularly unfocused, still unable to see clearly. I don't get much work accomplished, but I buy the Saab. I feel good about the decision, ready to continue the journey in a new vehicle.

By the time I get home at the end of the day I'm intensely jumpy, my nerves on edge. Every little sound crushes me. Even a tiny drip of water out of the kitchen faucet is more than I can bear. I do some sword movements and take a long bath, but gain little relief. I go out and clean the garage, kick a few boxes and jump on some plastic bubble wrapping material, popping it loudly. The physical release feels good! I get more into it, jumping on some empty boxes, flattening them for recycling. My daughter joins me, but after a while I send her inside, telling her to work on homework and that I'll be in soon to make dinner. I just want to be alone for a little while longer.

In the kitchen, I make dinner slowly and carefully because even the sound of a spoon in a pot or the clink of a plate on the table makes me cringe. I put the food on the table and call the kids, but I'm unable to sit and eat with them. Feeling like a terrible mother—as bad as I felt in my dream when I realized I had burned those two little kids—I excuse myself and run to my room telling them I'm not feeling well, and the truth is I'm nauseous. I crawl quickly into bed; sure I'll splinter into a million shards if I don't get the covers over me in time. I lie there for a few minutes, wondering what will happen if I let go. What evil will invade me? Are loss of control and the inability to cope evils in themselves? If I let go, will

I be perceived as incapable of parenting my children? Am I afraid they'll be taken from me? Am I afraid for my own children, or is it for my inner child? Is she so badly damaged? Yes, I feel so terribly and utterly damaged. The little girl inside me is so needy. I'm afraid I won't be able to provide everything she needs, that I am not enough.

Returning to the kitchen, I nibble some food, clean up, and send the kids to do homework. Rather than return to bed, I find a website offering guidance related to withdrawal from Paxil. Even as I read the list of symptoms, I doubt that my own symptoms are related to the withdrawal process, even though they are clearly described. I'm convinced, at a deeper level, that I suffer from symptoms related to my traumatic experiences, part of the process of recapitulation and healing, part of the withdrawal from an old world and an old self. I know how necessary it is to go through this, to relive the past, to view it differently this time and resolve it in a new way. As I write these words, my body clenches in response to what I so strongly believe is true, signaling that I'm right. It also indicates that in time this trauma will work through me. Until then I'm just trying to hold on.

"Hang in there," Chuck said today, "try and hang in there."

May 17, 2003

I dream that I'm riding a motor scooter. I'm whizzing along a street in the same small village where I encountered the two young children in yesterday's dream. All of a sudden I come to a dead halt and the wheels fly off the scooter. People come rushing to my rescue, gathering bolts, washers, and the two wheels that flew far and wide. One man has a tool case and another man offers to help him repair the scooter for me. While I'm searching for the last nut, I find a child instead, sitting on the curb, a little girl. She's too young to be by herself, but there is no adult with her. The village people think she belongs to me, that she's my child. They ask where I live. Do you live on the hill? "No," I say, "I live on a flat street, but far away, not in this village." They seem disappointed when I say this. I realize they're wondering if I came down from the mountain, which I sense behind me, now topped by the statue with wings, protectively overlooking the village. While the men repair my scooter, the village women offer me clothing for the little girl.

I'm not sure what their reasoning is, but then I realize they're concerned about the child, that she lacks essential care. They sense that she's needy.

The child and I look for the last nut together. We giggle a little at the mistake the village people are making, but at the same time I know it's not a mistake; the child really does belong to me. I feel such deep love for her as I acknowledge this to myself. "Follow your stars," the child says, looking at me with such deep love in return. As soon as she says this I wake up to the quick hard patter of rain drumming on the windowsill. Sitting up in bed, I turn to look out the window and see that it's not raining at all. Then I notice that my bedroom ceiling no longer exists. I look straight out into the dark night sky, sparkling with brilliant constellations, the Milky Way, shooting stars and comets. In awe and wonder, I watch as celestial lights shower down upon me like fireworks bursting overhead on a summer night. I hear the voice of the child in my dream. "Follow your stars," she says again, but now when I look at the sky the magical display has completely disappeared and there's nothing but a swirling black hole. With heart thumping and head whirling dizzily, I bolt upright, but realize that I'm already sitting up and that I have, in one form or another, been dreaming.

It takes a few minutes to more fully awaken, for my eyes to adjust and my perception to return to normal. A little freaked out, I realize I just had another out-of-body experience. I look outside to see if it's raining, which it isn't, and then I stand up on my bed and give my ceiling a few good knocks. It appears to be structurally sound and so I feel confident that nothing untoward will happen as I fall back to sleep.

I dream again. I walk up and down the same country road three times through three different seasons, out of the darkness of winter, through spring and into summer. The first time I see and hear things that I don't quite understand. The next time I see more clearly, and by the third trip I seem to understand what's going on, everything beginning to make sense.

The first time I walk along the road, it's a dirt road; houses are few and far between, interspersed with woods, a remote area. It's nighttime, the middle of winter, and there's snow on the ground. There's a sinister feeling to the darkness, a sense that something bad could happen, but I'm aware that I'm an adult and that I'm dreaming. I hear children screaming and crying. "No, no, no!" they shout, and I'm concerned, wondering what it could mean. Then I hear the splash of water and a child screaming out again: "Don't make me do it!" I wonder what's up. The air is cold, damp and foggy, and although it sounds like swimming I know this is absurd since it's the dead of winter.

Suddenly, I find myself walking the same road again, starting from the same place, but this time it's spring and daylight. The dirt road is muddy. What I couldn't see in the darkness of winter is revealed now. I notice high walls lining the roadway. The houses I pass are poor and derelict, sad looking. I still hear children crying and shouting behind the walls and inside the derelict houses. The third time I travel the road it's summertime and once again the landscape has changed; where walls and houses once stood now there are empty fields. Eventually, I come upon a ramshackle old hotel. From the open windows I hear crying. This time I follow the sounds and enter the building. Wandering around, I notice how empty the place is, except for the guestrooms. At each room that I peek into I see little girls lying naked on mattresses. They are tied down and I know they're waiting for adults to come in and have sex with them. I try to convince myself that the hotel is their home and that the adults who run it are their parents, and that they really do care about them. I tell myself that they do the best they can and that when they throw the girls into the old hotel swimming pool—which is falling apart, the water green with algae—they're being nice, that they're just bathing them. At the same time, I'm keenly aware that my impressions are totally wrong, that in fact I'm lying to myself. I know full well that the girls are sex slaves and the adults are cruel captors. As this disturbing truth dawns on me, I turn away, aware that the only reason I can leave is because I'm an adult.

As I exit the old hotel and walk quickly toward the road, I notice how vividly etched in light the world is. As I look down at my feet walking along, every single stone, pebble, and blade of grass on the driveway turns crystal clear at each step I take. I'm aware that the truth is being revealed. At the same time, I still seek to veil the truth, telling myself that I'm mistaken, that the place is just a nice camp for girls. "They'll get used to it," I tell myself. "The water in the pool is cold, but they'll get used to it, and it's so hot now that they don't need clothing, and it's more like a spa than anything." Even so, I know that I'm lying, looking for an excuse so I don't have to confront the uncomfortable truth, the crystal clear truth that is being revealed.

I walk further along the road, away from the gritty and disturbing truth. On the opposite side of the road, not far from the hotel, I go into another old hotel, now turned into a tawdry ashram. Here I encounter grown women lying around on mattresses in a large and faded ballroom. I join them as they listen intently to their teacher, a guru who sits on a pile of pillows at the front of the room. Large and imposing, he talks about different yoga postures, how valuable they are for reaching enlightenment, and how it's better to be naked and give up all your possessions. He comes around the room and takes everything from us, demanding our clothing, all our belongings, even our jewelry. I refuse to take off my earrings, pulling my hair closer to my ears so he won't see that I'm wearing any. Luckily he doesn't notice. Then he videotapes all of us lying naked on our mattresses. He walks around the room, preaching, grilling us with questions, intent on making us fall for his rhetoric. Each time he comes near me I feel myself growing sleepier and sleepier. I constantly pull my hair over my ears so he won't see my earrings. Finally, the preaching over, we all lie down on our mattresses to sleep.

I awaken in the middle of the night, hearing whispering and crying. The little abused girls from the other hotel are coming into the room, naked and frightened. I get up and tell them to just lie down anywhere. I try to find something to cover them with. One little girl talks incessantly and I understand that it's a defense, a cover for her thinly veiled desperation. She tells me that she needs her jewelry fixed and that she had seen a sign outside advertising jewelry repair. Her boyfriend gave her the jewelry. "He loves me," she says, "but he can't keep me anymore, so I had to leave and go somewhere else." I realize that she's totally alone and abandoned, that her boyfriend is her abuser, for she is but a young child. "We'll fix it in the morning," I tell her, "We'll fix everyone's jewelry in the morning."

The other women help me find places for the little girls and then we all go back to bed, but I can't sleep. I lie on my mattress wide-awake now, worried that the sign outside about jewelry repair is misleading and that it needs to come down. I sneak out into the darkness and go to the front of the building where I see a huge red arrow pointing to the building. Beneath it a sign reads: *Jewelry repaired.* It's the size of a large billboard, but it's in disrepair, falling down. The guru comes out and tells me to put the sign back up, to fix it, but I tell him no. I have no intention of fixing his sign, and it's an absurd command because the sign is so huge that even if I tried I couldn't lift it. Angered by my refusal, he grabs me and drags me back inside. I know he intends to rape me. Talking incessantly, ignoring my protests, he lays his enormous body on top of mine, pinning me down. No matter how much I struggle, I can't get away. He's big enough that he can hold me down with one gigantic hand while he puts a pointy red plastic cap on the end of his penis. "To increase the pleasure," he says maliciously.

"Why me? Why did he pick me when there are so many other women in the room," I keep thinking. "Why me?" As if he hears my thoughts, he seamlessly weaves all the answers to my questions into his incessant patter. He says that I'm perfect for what he's going to do, that I'm pretty and he's been looking at me all day. He selected me above all the others because he sees that I'm perfect. I'm swimming in bizarre confusion, aware that he's manipulating me, yet savoring the attention, when he suddenly jabs his penis into me, the red pointy cap jarring me so sharply that I see red stars. He laughs grotesquely, greedily running his enormous hands up and down my body, until he sees my earrings, and then he totally flips out. Shouting now, he tells me that as punishment he is leaving the red pointy cap inside me for all eternity, to torture me for disobeying him. As he rips my earrings out of my earlobes, I sense that he's taking the last little bit of my old self from me, destroying me. With his enormous weight pushing me down into the hard mattress, I sink deeper and deeper, right through the mattress, the wooden floor beneath, and into the vast nothingness of the great beyond. With this crazy maniac raging on top of me, I feel nothing, only that I am disappearing.

I wake out of this dream, and out of my disappearing self, fully enlightened, having figured out the answer to the question left looming by the *I Ching* reading yesterday. What evil sits in wait, what is waiting to worm its way into me if I let go now? These are the questions I pondered before sleep last night and, as usual, my dreams came to the rescue. It's what's already inside me. It's the energy left in me by my abuser, like the pointy red cap, and the energy of denial, still so embedded as well. I too, like the little girl who came into the ashram to have her jewelry repaired, have carried the burden of my abuse and the energy of my abuser. Each of us carries broken jewelry. The little girl is caught in her childish illusion that her abuser was her boyfriend and really loved her. I myself have cultivated the illusion that I'm fine and everything is normal, but in reality I've been deeply wounded and I still bear the wounds. In order to fully heal, and so that I don't have to carry the trauma for all eternity, my broken jewelry must be repaired. What is of greatest value must be restored—my innocence and my spirit.

This dream points out my own process of recapitulation quite clearly, how in the beginning, before I remembered any of the abuse, I wandered confusedly in darkness. It took a lot of journeys into the woods to discover the truth of what really happened there, to gain clarity. Each time I went in more was revealed, another shocking tidbit of truth made known. It took quite a while to piece it all together, but I've made good progress. Now on each trip back into the past, just what did happen is more clearly viewed and experienced. I'm getting better at dealing with the physical and emotional traumas I've suffered too.

The final challenge seems to be, as this dream points out, *taking back the energy that is stored in the traumatic experiences.* My energy has always been compromised. To energetically take back my power will indeed result in a restoration of my jewels. In addition, as this dream points out, denial looms large. I won't be able to let go of anything unless I can get beyond denial. How can I truly heal, or even talk of healing, if I can't be honest with myself that there's something I must heal from? If I deny the abuse then why need healing? The truth is that my whole body tells me I need healing. My *whole* body—both awake and in dreaming—tells me this all the time. I say that I believe the abuse happened, and yet my dreams tell me I still struggle with accepting the truth of it. And this I know to be true, not consciously, for consciously I have no doubt. Denial, however, sneaks up on me very much like a worm, as the *I Ching* in *Coming to Meet* suggests—the old worm of denial.

Before sleeping last night I pondered the plight of my inner child, for I do fear her deep neediness and that I won't be able to adequately provide for her. In the first dream, when my child self tells me to follow my stars, she is showing me just how magical she really is and that I don't have to worry about her, but the second dream points out where I'm getting caught—in continued denial of the truth of the abuse. The women in the first dream, when they asked me if I came down from the mountain, were, in essence, asking me to tell the truth. "Yes," I should have said, because it's the truth, but I didn't, and their disappointment was noticeable, and they shook their heads, as if saying, "Oh, she's still in denial." In continued denial, I make no progress but just end up caught in the old dynamics, dominated by the negative energy of my abuser.

There's still a part of me that fears what lurks in the shadow self and that the full truth will devastate me, taking over all the light I've thus far achieved. I fear that the magical self, so newly discovered—like the brilliant constellations in my dream—will be consumed by the darkness and a big black hole *will* suck me in. I fear I will never return from the vast nothingness of such blackness. However, in the second dream, I was forced into that darkness—as I sank into the mattress, the floor and the earth, with the heavy guru on top of me—and I have returned from that vast nothingness enlightened!

Upon awakening, I am aware that this bodes well, that my dreams analogously relate to my process of recapitulation by pointing out the way to my eventual wholeness. For they show me that it is only in experiencing the total shattering of the ego self, as I disappear into the vast nothingness that I so vehemently fear, that I will emerge a fully new and enlightened self. In the darkness lies all that makes me whole. It is where my enlightened evolved self will spring from as I face everything there is to face, both the light and the dark of who I am, both my present self, my past self, and my ancient archetypal self. I have to believe that. There are sure signs of it, yet there is obviously still more work to do.

Ridding myself of my abuser's energy is key to this healing. I feel this truth as strongly as I feel that pointy red cap sticking inside me. Its presence keeps me stuck and blocked, feeling that I deserve to be punished, that those little girls and I are helpless against the abuser's energy and that he can still destroy us. This is the evil that underlies all that is good about me, the petty tyrant that still lurks inside, waiting for the chance to destroy my efforts at healing, keeping me permanently in check. I need to save all those exhausted, frightened, ragged little abused girls. They're holding onto whatever they can, even if it's just the edges of the mattresses they're tied to or the fabric under their thumbs, as my dream showed me so clearly. If nothing else, they have that. But I have to show them that there's so much more! Their inch of fabric is woven into a larger fabric, a magic carpet, energetically interwoven into all that surrounds them, even into the light of freedom. It's my job to give them back their jewels too, while I also take back my own. I am the only one who can save us. If I don't, then I am doomed.

I keep everything at bay for several hours by gardening. As long as I remain in a quiet, calm state I'm not bothered by even a tweak of the old stuff. However, as soon as I stop, it all returns full force with its usual pulsing and clenching. My happy daughter, coming outside to chat with me while I work in the garden, sets it off at one point. As if it senses her innocence, it flares up in retaliation and before I know it, everything comes rushing back: the anger, the frustration, and the volatile energy too.

"I'm so sorry, honey, I can't talk now," I say, very gently so as not to hurt her feelings. "I need quiet. I need total quiet."

Every sound grates on my emotions, scratching at the thin veneer that keeps me whole. In the evening, I work at the artist's gallery until nine. I stay present by pacing a lot, at each step tightening harder against the emotions, fearful that they'll explode out of me. I envision myself bursting and getting swept out of the gallery, down the street and into the river in a torrent of emotions, nothing more than broken shards. Oh God, I'm afraid I'll lose my sanity and everything I've been working so hard for!

I finally lock up the gallery and head home. Driving through the darkening night, I'm not sure how long I can tough it out, how long I can hold onto my sanity because it does feel like my sanity is at stake here, my ability to remain mentally present and in one piece. I feel like I could go crazy, that if I don't stay in control I will mentally lose it. I knew a long time ago that if I didn't keep myself mentally focused and strong I could very easily cross over into another world and never return. Arriving home, I flop onto my bed, grab my journal, and pour my fears and thoughts into it, fearful that I'm heading for a mental breakdown. Am I afraid that I'll tip too far the wrong direction and disappear, the vast bottomless abyss my only home? And why? It all comes back to him, to my abuser, and to the metaphorical pointy red cap he left behind, still piercing my soul, blocking access to my own true self.

As soon as I write those words, *pointy red cap*, my body spasms involuntarily. It suddenly dawns on me that I'm acting as if I don't want to give my abuser up, though it's not clear why. Perhaps I worry that if I release him, by accepting the full truth of the abuse, I will have nothing left, that I will abandon the one thing that has defined me my whole life. How can I continue to choose the trauma of abuse as my energy of existence when I know what it means? Is not the shattering and the vast nothingness that I fear better than this continued slavery? I know they are my healing challenges, but to be honest, I foresee only total aloneness and deep inner sadness if I get rid of my abuser's energy. I have to admit to a perverse sense of affection for him. He taught me to need him—he showed me that I was wanted—and, totally aberrant though this affection was, I feel a need to cling to it because when it's gone I will have nothing. For in my memory no other form of affection exists.

My body continues spasming as I accept that even though I feel incredibly sad and frightened, even though I'm teetering on the edge of the abyss, I am equally on the edge of new life, facing strong independence if I can release myself of my attachment to this fiendish energy. Rage boils inside me, flaring up in protest as I struggle between the known and the unknown. As the tussle ensues, I am once again utterly certain that I don't need anything from anybody, that I am enough. Just as my child self once so fiercely declared, I say it again: *I don't need anyone!* Yet, I know that such feelings are based on my background, distorted by the circumstances of my life, and that in my new reality I do need people. I also know I have to get to a place of utter acceptance about the truth of my past as it is being revealed to me, or I will not heal. I turn out the light and lie down as the spasms go on and on, my body involuntarily jerking. I don't even try to resist because I already know it's futile. Eventually, I fall asleep.

I dream that I'm visiting an old woman with a friend of mine. The old woman is a lawyer, a friend of my friend. I feel bad, but I don't trust the lawyer; she makes me feel ill. I get up abruptly, saying that I can't stay, that I don't feel well. No one stops me from leaving. As I leave the lawyer's house, I see that there are broken dishes and food spilled all over the kitchen, as if animals have gotten in. I rush out and see two large panthers strolling down the street, and I know that they caused the destruction. There are children on bikes and little girls all over the place, but I'm the only one who is aware of the panthers. I walk along the street and notice that the closer I get to them the smaller they become, until they are as small as kittens. As I walk past them lying docile on the sidewalk, I hear my friend calling to me, but I ignore her; I just keep walking. She catches up to me and hands me a huge doll. It's so big I can't even get my arm around it and so it falls onto the street. I look down at it lying there on the black pavement, a naked old doll. My friend laughs. "I know you want it," she says. "I can't carry it," I say. "I'm already carrying one." And it's true; for it's only then that I see I already have a large doll under my arm. "How will I carry both of them?" My friend picks up the fallen doll and pushes it under my free arm.

I walk down the road carrying these two life-sized dolls, aware that I don't want them, though I feel that I must take them anyway. "She wants you to have them," my friend calls after me. "The lawyer wants you to have the dolls!" Suddenly, I can't pretend anymore. I don't want to carry the dolls another foot, and so I throw them angrily to the ground where they instantly explode into a million pieces. I feel sick as the physical sensation of this bursting hits me, and I too begin to shatter. I am in pieces on the ground, being kicked around by the children playing on the street, and by myself as well. For I too am vehemently kicking the shattered parts of my own severed and bloody body as I jolt awake.

I'm scared; afraid to sleep again, for fear I'll blow apart upon dropping into unconsciousness, afraid of the intense physical pain and gut-wrenching nausea that coursed through me at the moment of explosion and disintegration. I wonder if that's what it feels like to die. At the same time, I can't escape the underlying meaning of the dream, which seems to indicate that my fear is far greater than reality, represented by the panthers, which are quite threateningly large and ferocious at first glance but diminish into nothing more than kittens, soft and cute. Even though I don't want to carry the burden of those dolls—the abuse—anymore, I'm still afraid. Once again I'm caught on the edge of the abyss, fearful of going over, but aware that I will only heal by doing so.

Lying in bed, I do a full body relaxation, starting at my feet. Tightly clenched, I jerk and twitch my way through the entire process, but I persist, slowly and deliberately, until I've broken through the brittle stiffness in each of my muscles, until I've gained, if not relaxation, at least a sense of equilibrium. No longer teetering on the edge, I have moved inland a little. I know I'm okay and that I'll sleep through the night now.

May 18, 2003

I dream that I'm in a hospital emergency room, having my bleeding wounds tended to. Someone sits beside me, holding me tightly, speaking kindly. "I'm glad you called; I don't know how you held out for so long." Blood surrounds me. A widening pool of dark red blood forms around the chair I'm sitting on, gushing out of my body. "I'm falling apart, I'm falling apart, I'm falling apart!" I say. "We'll be right with you," a nurse calls over to me, while I continue crying out: "I'm falling apart, I'm falling apart, I'm falling apart!"

Next, I dream that I'm traveling with two women. A kidnapping has occurred. We're speeding down a country road on the way to meet the kidnapper and pay the ransom. The landscape is vivid green with rolling hills. We can see the dirt road we're driving on, winding off into the distance ahead of us. The mansion we're headed toward lies in the distance too; we see its rooftops peeking over the edge of a hill up ahead. Although we're traveling at great speed, we never gain ground, and the mansion remains always in the distance. We discuss the demands of the ransomer, aware that we must get there on time and do whatever is required in order to get the kidnapped person back, a woman artist. I'm aware that this has happened in the past and that we've done this before, even been caught in this timeless space where no progress is made. But even so, we aren't sure of the procedure or if we're properly following the requests of the ransomer. At the same time, it feels like we're driving into an ambush. It's as if we know that getting there is a bad idea, as if we're energetically holding back in a protective manner. In the back of my mind, I'm also aware that we're rushing to help; that we're reacting instinctually and it may not, in fact, be the right thing to do.

I wake from these dreams full of anxiety and fear after only a few hours of sleep. The first dream seems to take up where the dream I'd had earlier last night left off, with my bloody body parts being kicked around on the street. As I bleed out onto the floor of the hospital, my psyche calls out for help and help is on the way.

However, in the kidnapper dream, things are not what they seem. The beautiful, calm green landscape belies the underlying feelings of terror and impending doom. This seems more in line with what the *I Ching* reading cautions about, and if so, it may indicate that I haven't fully understood the power of the underlying evil it warns of, that my instincts aren't getting it right. The dark predatory nature of this dream and the way things are not culminating as planned, suggest perhaps that I'm not in control either, which is my biggest fear.

The morning is sunny and cool. The birds chirping loudly awaken me more fully. I need to get up and move, even though I feel bruised and sore after clenching all through the night. I'm really getting to the point where I can't cope anymore. I'm going to have to break down because there will be no alternative. Leaving the kids asleep on this Sunday morning, I drive to a place where I like to hike. Few people are out so early and so I have the trails to myself for the most part. I try not to think too much as I walk, try to ignore the terror that keeps me company. Seeking distraction, I focus on the scenery, the spring scent of the woods, the wildflowers that line the pathway, the nesting birds. I spot an unusual stick in the shape of a capital letter N lying on the ground. As soon as I pick it up, calm energy flows into me, and suddenly my thoughts of terror erase. Then I realize it isn't a stick at all, but the leg of a deer, with dried skin and hoof attached.

I decide to keep the bone and walk on with it in my hand, lighter in spirit now, thankful for the deer for giving its life that I might have some peacefulness. Back home, I hang the bone in the garage and work outside in the yard for a while, cleaning up fallen branches and laying out planting beds. In the afternoon I take the kids to a movie, the energy of the deer granting more than just a few moments of freedom from the usual torment. I remain deeply thankful as the movie ends and calmness reigns still, though it's difficult to see through the cobwebby veils that hang in front of my eyes. Driving is hazardous, and I proceed very carefully.

As evening comes, I make the decision that I will not sleep tonight. Even though the calm energy of the deer has permeated the entire day, I'm so afraid to go through another night of terror. I don't want to have to call Chuck and bother him, so I set up a nighttime strategy to do whatever I can to stop the pulsing in my head. I find things to do in the house. I do the laundry and organize the books in the bookcases. I read the phonebook for an hour, for I've found that staring at the tiny font, running my finger down the long columns and saying the names out loud brings calmness. I stand outside in the dark of night and stare at the moon, wishing for a shooting star, wanting a sign that I'm going to be okay. I read a novel, saying words that are not my own, preferably out loud. I move constantly so I don't tighten up. Every now and then I try lying down, but find myself immediately clenching up in the old manner, instinctively preparing to fight the dreaded terror that is sure to occur, the shattering that feels so imminent. And then nausea overtakes me and I feel so sick that I get right back up again and look for some new distraction, for I see that if I stay awake and occupied I have control. If I let go to sleep I have none at all.

May 19, 2003

It's now four thirty in the morning and I've been awake all night. The birds are just beginning to chirp happily, though the moon still shines brightly. I'm so tired now. I think I may let myself sleep for an hour or two. As soon as I lie down I dream.

I'm a teenager again; driving home from work, although I'm not in control, for the car drives me, at great speed. I'm trying to get away from a gang of men who are following me in their own car. The roads are icy and I know that the car is going too fast for the road conditions, and for a second or two it feels like it's about to go airborne. The men push me to greater and greater speeds, screaming out their windows, "Get her! Get her!" I fear that I'll crash, but as soon as I outdistance them I gain control of the car and at the first opportunity pull off into an alley, skidding to a full stop. Immediately cutting the engine, I wait for them to pass. They speed right by, unaware that I'm hiding in plain sight. After that I drive very slowly and carefully to the large barn where I live. I'm late for bed; four teenage girls have been nervously waiting for me. "You'd better have a good excuse for being late," they say, as soon as I enter the barn. I try to explain that I've been working. Besides, I tell them, I don't want to sleep because the men who follow me everywhere are frightening me.

The girls think my excuse is pretty lame because the man who comes to us every night, to sleep with us and have sex with us—a friend of those men who followed me—is just a fact of everyday life. They are right. Every night I lie still and don't move a muscle, hoping he might not notice me. Every night I hold onto the hope that if he doesn't notice me, he won't touch me, hoping that one night it will prove true. The man comes in and sits in a rocking chair while we, all five girls, climb naked into a bed, our bodies pushed tightly together because there is so little room. The man tucks us in, adjusting us, pushing us against each other and fondling us all, one by one. I lie in the middle, petrified. He lays a sheet on top of us, drawing it up only to our chests, tucking it so that our small, girlish breasts show. We have to keep our hands down by our sides under the covers and not pull up the sheet, even if we're freezing cold. He sits in the rocker near the head of the bed and tells us stories. They are about his sexual escapades and as he talks he decides whom to choose for the night.

The two girls to the left of me have a small feather duster on a long handle and they're tickling us all under the covers with it. We're all aware that they're fondling each other and that they'll get us into trouble, but we're also aware of how desperately we all want affection. The two girls start giggling and the rest of us move our bodies, wriggling and squirming, to protect them. We know from experience that if we all move he'll be angry with all of us and not punish just one of us. The man, sensing that something is up, gets up and yanks the sheet off, screaming at us for being "filthy cunts!" He goes from being a sinister guy in a rocking chair, telling dirty bedtime stories, to a monster. The other girls scatter, but I'm so frozen with fear that I can't move from the bed. The man screams about how bad we are and that he intends to punish us severely, but first he'll take care of me. I deserve it the most, he says, because I was late. As the girls run out of the barn, I see a mix of relief and concern in their eyes, relief that they're getting away and concern for me, since I'm going to get it really badly and we all know it. I hear them talking outside the window, justifying my punishment, saying that I deserve it more than they do anyway, for being late. They're acting tough, but at the same time I hear real concern when someone whispers, "Do you think she'll be okay?"

I'm on my knees with my arms resting on a windowsill, listening to them talking, when the man comes at me from behind with a huge screwdriver. When he sticks the screwdriver inside me my face smashes against the windowpane and the startled girls look up in horror. "Oh God, she's getting it bad!" I hear someone say, and soon the glass is smeared with my blood. The man carves up the pillows on the bed with the screwdriver. Feathers explode all around me and I think it's snowing in the room. He bites and rips me to shreds too; like a mad dog, stabbing me with both his penis and the long screwdriver. I am covered with blood and I think that maybe I should have let the other men get me, the ones that followed me from work, because I would be dead by now if I had. Maybe I would have died an hour ago, I think, and I would be safe from this monster. I look out the window and see the horror on the faces of the girls standing in the yard outside. Another man arrives. "Save a piece for me!" he yells, sounding somewhat annoyed.

The other girls scatter away from the window now, looking for safe places to hide, leaving me alone with the two men. I hear the girls saying that it was my fault anyway, and I had better not be late again or they'll do it to me themselves, they'll punish me in the same way. I'm aware that if things were different and I was with them, I'd be saying the same things, acting as tough as possible, not letting the men know just how afraid I really am. I'm aware that to act as heartless and uncaring as possible is a means of getting through the horrors of this life. By appearing to not have any emotions, to let the men do what they want and act like it doesn't bother me in the least, is how to survive.

I work at a feather duster factory and I had brought home the feather duster that the two girls used to tickle each other with. I know it was wrong to take it, and I know it was a bad idea to let the others use it, but I was desperate for the feel of something nice touching my body, the feathers so gentle and soft against my skin. And even if it only lasted for a second's worth of pleasure, it was worth it, just to remind myself that I do have feelings!

I manage to sleep for one hour, most of which is spent in this nightmare, the horror of it startling me awake. I jump out of bed and get myself moving again, away from it and the possibility of more nightmares. I literally run into the kitchen to make coffee.

I note that the barn, which I first encountered months ago in the dream when I stood at the back of the hairdresser's shop, has finally been entered. I knew back then that it contained vital information and that one day I would have to go inside. And here I am, facing the horrors that I sensed it held. While I wait for the coffee to brew I do the sword form—anything to get away from the panic that follows me as I attempt to shake off the dream. I drink my coffee and then get the kids up, make their breakfasts and school lunches, and send them off to school.

During the night, as soon as I thought about going to bed I felt sick with nausea and cramping, and the only way to make it go away was to do something physical. Now I just feel exhausted. I want to sleep, but I'm afraid again, of the feelings, the dreams, and the state of my body, which is totally pinched with pain, signaling the continuation of this excruciating process. In spite of my firm decision to not bother Chuck, I need to talk. I call and leave him a message.

"Don't sleep now. Go as long as you can so you can sleep tonight," he says when he calls back. "It's a Catch-22. If you stay awake to avoid the nightmares, when you do fall asleep the nightmares may be worse."

"Yeah, as I just proved."

"You need REM sleep," he says.

"Okay," I tell him, "I'll go out and dig, do garden work, and get exhausted."

"Don't drive!" he says sternly.

It's noon; I call Chuck again, panicking. I've been crying on and off, the dreams pursuing me, the exhaustion probably fueling it all, causing great anxiety.

"Try a nap; as simplistic as it sounds, it might help at this point."

Dutifully, I give it a try, but as soon as I lie down the fear of nightmares comes riding over me like a stampede of horses, the truth hitting me, alerting me to the real need to finally let go. I'm aware that acquiescence is the key, but I'm too hyper to nap. I lie in bed and read, hoping for distraction and perhaps light sleep. It's impossible to concentrate on tiny meaningless words and before long I find myself nodding off, the words blurring in front of my eyes as they send me off, right into violent dreams full of fear that startle me awake.

I give up on rest and decide to remodel the pantry, cutting the doors short, adding a shelf and devising a recycling area in the bottom quarter. This keeps me busy; taking the doors down, measuring, taking them out to the garage for cutting with the jigsaw, fitting the new shelf in. At one point, while I'm in the garage, I see the deer leg and give it a rub for good luck, asking it to bring some calmness into the rest of the day, and it seems to work, for creative energy flows through me, bringing focus and stability. I also build a wall shelf and paint it. The concentration keeps me fairly sane, but allows no deeper release.

As night approaches, a slow buildup of panic rumbles deep inside my body. To calm it, I take a bath. I fall asleep in the tub, but wake up in a panic with Al Pacino running after me, yelling something. A man tries to grab me. "Al just wants to give you an award!" he says, but I don't believe him, and I don't want him or anyone else coming too close.

Aware that I must shift out of this craziness, I get out of the tub and lie on my yoga mat. I do quiet chakra breathing. I begin in the root, slowly breathing up through the second and third chakras. I spend a long time breathing into my heart before pulling the breath up to my throat, continuing into the third eye, and finally the crown where I release it. Right from the start I feel my energy stirring and by the time it gets to the heart chakra my breath is alive with good energy. For the first time, I feel that I really do have a heart. As it cracks and creaks in response to my breathing, I know that I have finally found it. It's as if I never really felt it before, not like this, because I'm feeling *with* it. I know where it is and now I know what it feels like to actually *feel with it*. I sense it just beginning to awaken from long slumber. Perhaps those sixteen girl selves are feeling it too.

Now it's eleven at night and I'm exhausted, but I'm still afraid of the dark and what lurks there. "Oh what the heck!" I finally say, acquiescing. "Maybe it won't be too bad, or if it is I'll just deal with it!" And so, after all that, I go to bed.

May 20, 2003

The shrill call of my alarm clock wakes me. Disoriented, in a heavy drugged-like sleep, I am jolted out of a dream. With shaking hand, I turn off the loud alarm and lie back down.

Breathing slowly, I calm my beating heart, as the dream begins piecing itself back together, like pieces of a jigsaw puzzle falling from the sky, landing perfectly right.

As the dream unfolds, I'm a young girl again, in a large room with several other girls. We're getting ready to learn some new fighting techniques. I'm standing in a small wooden box that is waist high. I can see the other girls standing in their boxes. The instructor is talking, but he stops repeatedly to yell at me, telling me to pay attention, but I can't. I'm too distracted by the hollow emptiness of the room, the vast open concrete grayness of it. It's not an environment that I find conducive to learning. There's nothing cozy or comforting about it and I feel exposed and vulnerable. I want to hunker down inside my box, to curl up, and hide on the floor so the instructor will stop picking on me. He's teaching us how to fight against the foreign installation, against what we're learning about elsewhere in our lives that may not be true or helpful. He's teaching us to break through our old stuff so we don't remain stuck in our little boxes. He's preparing us for a different kind of future, he says. But this place of learning is so cold and chilly, so depressing, that it turns me right off.

I meet with Chuck and the first thing out of his mouth is that it's war now and it's time to fight.

"That's exactly what I faced in the dream I was having this morning," I say, quite startled by his announcement. "But I don't want to fight!"

"All of your dreams are telling you that you're stuck," he says. "You're being pulled back to the old places and you have to fight out of them. Pick up your sword and fight!"

All I can do is nod tiredly.

"You can learn to control your dreams and work yourself out of the old places," he says, handing me a book to read, Patricia Garfield's *Creative Dreaming*.

He thinks the line from the *I Ching* that I got the other day, about evil lurking in the creative, was not about something else lurking beneath, but the creative energy itself lurking and working to destroy. And it does take over. Like a volcano erupting, I can go from a state of inertia to the fiery energy of mania in a matter of seconds. I notice how once the creative energy takes over it totally engages me. Everything else is kept at bay—I don't deal with anything—which I thought was a good thing, but perhaps it's just a cover, an excuse to *not* deal. I've also noticed that once I'm caught in the creative fire I can't get out of it until it's extinguished, and at that point I'm too burnt out to deal with what's happening in my life. This dynamic is similar to what happened when I picked up the deer leg. The intensity of everything dissipated, and I was thankful for the hiatus, but I also see how it just delayed the inevitable. After all, I'm still stuck in the same place I was before I found the deer leg. It all makes perfect sense, but this just sends me deeper into self-hatred. As much as I think I have control, I realize I have no control at all; it's a false sense of power.

"You are telling me to fight? Well you can go fuck yourself, because I am not fighting anymore," I mutter to myself, as I walk out of Chuck's office. "I have had it!"

I go home, get into bed and pull the covers over my head, hating Chuck for pushing me and telling me I need to fight, angry because he's just assuming that I agree and that I'll do it. I don't want to fight! I don't want to go to war! I just want to stay under the covers forever. Leave me alone! Shut up and go away!

I vent, and then I get angry at myself for hiding under the covers, even though I want to stay there forever. No one would notice, no one would care, so why should I care! "It's okay, just stay here," I whisper, acquiescing to the moment, "not all day, but just for an hour. Just lie under the covers and hide for a little while. It won't be forever because you'll get tired of it soon enough." As soon as I give myself permission to have the feelings I'm having, I'm able to relax. And then I realize the bigger truth is that I'm so exhausted that I have no energy. I simply can't fight.

"I can't go to war if I'm exhausted. So it's okay to rest; a warrior needs rest," I tell myself, and then I feel better. I feel better about wanting to hide out, and better about all the feelings that I constantly feel I must refuse and refute. After a while I get up and go to work, knowing that tonight I will sleep more soundly.

I'm starting a new journal this evening and I'm fully aware of its timeliness, for today was definitely a turning point. It became abundantly clear that I must stop fighting *myself*. If I can reconcile my feelings about myself then perhaps I'll be able to proceed, but until I do that I feel like I'm fighting *only* myself, getting stuck in this internal battle with my own stubbornness. In the past this stubbornness may have been a strength, but now it's only a block. This too is part of the message from the *I Ching*.

I came away from Chuck's today ready to quit. Boy, was I angry! The anger made me feel even more exhausted, but then I realized that the exhaustion was actually the key to shifting. How can I fight if I'm exhausted? How can I get anywhere, if I'm so exhausted that I don't even want to get out of bed? I realized that it's time to stop hating and fighting myself, and that it's really okay for me to admit that I am, in fact, utterly exhausted. Then I felt better, and I even felt better about hiding under the covers. Chuck said he never had a problem with me doing that, but I said *I* did. I couldn't let myself feel what I needed. It's time to stop being so hard on myself; it's the only way to move on. *I'm my biggest enemy*, as I think the *I Ching* was really pointing out!

The pulsing in my frontal lobe returns as darkness arrives. After being largely distracted throughout the workday it revs up again as soon as I'm alone in my bedroom. I've gotten good at getting rid of it, allowing busyness to quiet it, but it's still always there, waiting. It's now eleven at night and, yes, I'm tired, but I'm also afraid. What am I so afraid of? Everything! I'm afraid of everything, and it's about time I admit it. Admitting things and accepting my feelings need to be my new way of dealing with this recapitulation, and with life in general.

"I can be nice to myself," are my last thoughts as I fall asleep. I wake up thirty minutes later and write down this dream: I ride my bike to a shop where they are giving away items, *nice* things. I pick out a few things and thank the women who are running the store. They smile back at me. I get onto my bike, which becomes a car at this point, and ride home. The ride is not smooth at all, but very bumpy, along curvy mountain roads that descend abruptly into sharp hairpin turns. I'm having trouble driving because my knees keep hitting the dashboard, and I notice that I have the seat pulled too far forward. I round a corner and pull into my driveway and realize I never turned my lights on, even though it's a dark night. At this point the car turns back into a bike and I'm concerned about skidding on some gravel that's on top of the blacktopped driveway. In the end, however, all is well. I'm just so relieved that I've gotten home in one piece!

Okay, so maybe everything will work out okay in the end after all, after I get through this bumpy time, but now I just want to sleep!

May 21, 2003

I wake to a damp and drizzly morning—at least I won't have to water the plants! Thoughts about my garden excite me, but my inner mood matches the weather. I feel sad inside, the center of my being colored a deep midnight blue, a dark well into which silent tears drip, filling it one droplet at a time. I can dip my hands into this pool of tears, feel the wet yearnings like a strong sexual urge, a deep need for release that in spite of its intensity remains caught on old roots and debris sitting at the bottom of the well. If I catch hold of that yearning desire and pull it toward me, I know the water will muddy as sediment rises to the surface and as long buried memories scrape the edges of the perfectly formed well. Deep dark secrets will spill out into the light of day and what will I do with them? What will I do with the naked truths, lying limp and muddied on the edge of that open wet wound of a well? What will I do with the familiar shapes of my memories, lying in a tangle of umbilical cord roots, like wet and bloodied newborns? Breathe life into them? Do I dare? Do I dare give life to this mess? Do I dare admit that these memories are true? I don't remember what I was like before it all started, before this recapitulation started. I don't remember who I've been for the past fifty years.

At midnight, as soon as I get into bed, the pulsing buzz in the frontal lobe of my brain once again pushes me to remember or feel something. What is it, a memory? An urging to get to the bottom of the well of feelings and emotions? Or is it both? I know that I'm holding back buckets of tears, playing a game of tug-of-war with my body, which wants to let go, but I won't let it. I hold on fiercely, feeling the hot-in-the-face shame of my child self. Fiery redness creeps into my face. My abdomen automatically clenches to keep the tears and noise from erupting; it's too embarrassing!

I wonder if embarrassment is part of this reluctance to let myself feel and release even now. Why am I so embarrassed to cry? Because it's not allowed? Who wouldn't allow it? No one allowed it; I was not allowed to cry. But it's okay now. I'm an adult. I can cry if I want to, all I want, and as loud as I want. Who cares if anyone sees or hears? People cry. I'm allowed to cry. Yes, I too am allowed to cry. Why shouldn't I, damn it!

I read several quotes today from child psychologists and noted doctors who, over the past two hundred years, have been important influences in the field of child psychology. One psychologist, John Watson, a behaviorist, current through the nineteen-fifties, stated this regarding children: *Never touch them. Never hug or kiss them. Never let them sit in your lap or put your arms around them in any way. If you must touch them then a kiss on the forehead at night before bed is sufficient.*

I guess my mother read that.

May 22, 2003

I dream that I have a job selling tickets at an old bombed out movie theatre. No one notices me in the ticket booth; people just stream in without paying. A war has recently occurred and the movie theatre is located in the charred and crumbled remains of the war zone. The boss yells at me repeatedly because people aren't paying, and even though I arrange the bombed out entryway so they are forced to walk in my direction they still don't see me. The owners go off somewhere and leave me in charge. I'm immediately overwhelmed, especially as I am still not visible to anyone. People talk as if I'm not there. I hear one man speaking in a loud and obnoxious manner and I'm so fearful of his bullying energy that I abruptly exit the lobby. In a large cobblestoned courtyard outside, a fat policeman lies on the ground. He's flat on his back looking straight up into the night sky. My little orange wallet lies on the ground near him, a circle of white cloth carefully laid around it, like an orange square in the center of a painted white circle. I'm angry that I'd left it outside. I'd dropped it earlier and been too busy to pick it up. I'd hoped the policeman would deter any criminals, although he looks more like a friendly cartoon character than a lawman. Now it's raining and I'm sure the leather will get ruined.

Back inside the movie theater someone discovers several undetonated bombs and the building has to be evacuated. As I reenter the building to get the evacuation underway it becomes apparent that I am now visible, not only that, but I become an easy target for everything that's wrong. I accept the blame, especially as people are grumbling and complaining about how poorly organized and dirty the place is. They complain about the debris still lying around from the war as they clamber and stumble over it on their way out of the theater. They even remark about the lazy policeman still sleeping instead of aiding the evacuation. I automatically take the blame because I feel responsible; this is happening on my work shift. I realize that it's just the way things are unfolding, and yet I take the blame anyway. "Okay, okay, it's my fault. I admit, it's my fault," and everyone looks at me with disgust, making derogatory remarks about me as they file out of the theatre.

As the last of them exit the building, I go into the courtyard where the policeman is still lying on his back, but my body is suddenly leaden, my legs like dead weights. As if walking through sucking quicksand, I slowly and painfully drag myself along. Exhausted, I stand over the policeman and ask him to please look in my wallet and see if anyone has stolen my money. "No, it looks like it's all still there," he says, having looked inside without getting up off the ground. Although I know I should feel relief, I don't really care. I feel like I've been fighting forever. I'm so exhausted and it feels like I've just taken on the blame for everything that has recently gone wrong in the entire world; even the recent war is my fault. I seem to have absorbed everyone's anger and disgust. Heavy with exhaustion, I watch the last of the crowd walk away down the bombed out street, the pavement littered with bricks, the air thick with smoke. Looking for a place to put my own anger, I stand over the policeman, now snoozing away, angry that he didn't lift a finger to help me. Then I see my wallet lying next to him on the ground, surrounded by its white cloth circle, and I wake up.

The image of my small orange wallet inside the white circle stays with me as I get up and begin my day. Chuck has taught me that symbols in dreams are important, so I know this mandala shape is significant too, perhaps representing my wholeness, reminding me to value what I hold inside myself and to not be distracted by or feel responsible for what others want or perceive. I guess the policeman is suggesting that I relinquish the constant watch, showing me how to give up the fight by not doing the "neighborhood watch" anymore. My valuables are safe and protected and will be, even if I let down my guard. But I wake up frustrated that I can't control everything, with the old belief that I just let things happen. The need to blame myself still dominates; I am still convinced that I allowed things to happen because I never fought back. Not that it was my fault, but that I simply stood by and let it go on, without reacting. It's obviously unhelpful to stay caught here in this old belief; even if true, it does me no good. Besides, I'm too exhausted to fight now. I must acquiesce to my exhaustion and become more like the policeman if I am to get anywhere new.

All day I've been pondering where I am and how I got here. I feel so confused about where this recapitulation process is taking me and how I'm going about it, rather reluctantly at this point. Something isn't working for me. I think it has to do with having to find new positions in which to recapitulate memories. I'm trying like heck not to curl into a fetal ball, my favorite pose. I find that I can process memories just fine if I sit up or even if I'm lying down flat, like the policeman in my dream, but I'm not sure I'm experiencing them as deeply. So many feelings seem to be embedded in that old pose—the pose my child self took every night—and I struggle with finding a means of accessing the deeper stuff that's still wrapped up inside that curled up child self. I need something to stir it out of slumber. Perhaps my feelings need more compassion and kindness to tease them out of hiding. Fighting the need to roll up just doesn't work; it's antithetical to those very real human needs. I need to find a new way to comfort myself.

The mixed up feelings of a little girl have been emerging lately. Lost and sad, she shut the door to her heart a long time ago so she wouldn't get hurt. When I breathe into my lower chakras my abdominal muscles immediately clench. Fear lies there and the immediate "gut" reaction is to clench tightly, to hold it back. There's a closed door inside me. Although I can't see the door, I *feel* it starting to open but then get afraid to open it any further. My immediate reaction is to retreat and clench even more tightly, for I sense tremendous fear, sadness, and loneliness behind that closed door that I shut so many years ago. As I breathe, I trace its frame, finger the hinges and knob, but I'm not able—or I'm reluctant—to fully open it.

Breathing slowly and gently into my heart region, I draw up long buried feelings of pain, of fear of suffocation, feelings of worthlessness and hopelessness, but I can't release them. I'm so afraid to be alone when it happens. I'm afraid that I won't be able to comfort those sixteen little girl selves, that I'll do something mean instead, punish myself instead of care for myself. I'm not sure I feel that I'm really worth it. Am I truly worth going through this recapitulation for? My own children are important, but how do I allow myself to be as important, if not more so? How do I accept myself and allow myself to be kind and caring to me for a change, when there are others who need me more?

The little girl inside me, who closed up her heart so long ago because she didn't need anyone, needs comforting now. She needs to know it's okay to roll up and cry. She doesn't need to be so fiercely guarded anymore. It's safe now; *he* can't get her anymore, he's not here. She's safe with Chuck and she's safe with me; but when Chuck says, "*It's time to fight, get out the sword and fight to the death,*" it all feels so hopeless again and I just want to run and hide. I'm not ready to fight yet. I don't know what I'm fighting for. I'm confused. I think I'm supposed to fight myself. Maybe I am.

When I go to yoga class, I notice that the left side of my body is tightly clenched while the right side, interestingly enough, is loose and flowing. Perhaps something is releasing after all!

I get to bed at a reasonable hour, fall asleep for fifteen minutes and wake up after the following dream: I'm sitting in a café, stirring a bowl of soup that the café owner has served me. I'm not hungry, but I politely eat a few spoonfuls. She tells me that I once gave her advice about how people tend to go back to the same partner, back to the person they are familiar with, rather than try someone new. "Yes, I still believe that," I say. "You have to re-train them." I then find a razor blade in my soup and wonder how I'll tell her.

May 23, 2003

I meet with Chuck. I try to explain to him why I'm so afraid to let go and express the feelings and needs that are so deeply shut away inside me. I've finally gained access to the truth, I tell him, but I'm afraid of what will go in if I open up. It's not a one-way door, but a two-way door, and there is the possibility of something getting in to hurt me if I open up. We do EMDR to test what might happen if I open a hypothetical door. I begin by opening the door to my heart and I'm immediately confronted with BLAME, which leads directly back to the old response that I must accept blame for everything. I become aware that if I keep opening the door and face only negativity, then I'm going to hate myself for having opened the door at all. We decide I should practice reacting in a new way.

"What could you say that would be different?" Chuck asks.

"Fuck You! Fuck you!" I yell, but in the next second I meekly apologize. "Oops! Sorry."

"Cut it out! No apologies are allowed," says Chuck. "No more taking on the blame!"

The old me used to take the blame for all kinds of things simply to avoid conflict, but in so doing I refused to acknowledge whatever truth needed attention. I'd simply bury it until the next conflict. And then I'd rebury it. Conflict, I have to admit, stirs up all kinds of issues, fear being the greatest. Now I'm training myself to own the truth. My long habit of keeping things hidden is finally coming to an end. I must face the fact that I have basically been apologizing my entire life, for simply existing.

As insights flood in, I realize that it's okay to express myself without apology. It had never occurred to me before, and I notice how good the idea makes me feel. My dream from last night finally makes sense now. In the past, I would have meekly ignored the razor blade or felt bad about it, like it was somehow my fault that I got the soup with the razor blade. Now I know I must not feel guilty or take blame, but tell the chef that there's a razor blade in the soup! In addition, I must take the same advice I once gave the café owner because the razor blade is also symbolizing that I must cut out of my life what no longer works. I must get rid of the ingredients that just don't belong in the soup!

I follow through on that dream advice during the day and make some solid decisions about work. Squarely facing the truth of change, I accept new work without including my former business partner and, most importantly, without feeling guilty about it! It's a little tricky because even though we are no longer working together we are still committed to sharing a studio together, and we are still friends. However, I must not let the old guilt-ridden self dominate. I must do what I need to do to advance myself in the world and earn a living. I am not responsible for more than that. This is a hard fact for me to accept, as my natural tendency is to care for others over myself. "That's the old way," my changing self says, as she turns in a new direction and brushes the old guilt from her shoulders, more determined than ever to keep changing.

At the end of the day, I get into my new car and drive it home. I love it! At last I'm in a positive frame of mind. I decide that I can and should trust my intuition and ability to go with the flow of life as it unfolds. I have no idea where I'm going, but I decide it's going to be okay from here on out. I can't stop now!

The kids go off to their dad's for the weekend, giving me time alone with the decisions I've made, time also to rest.

May 24, 2003

I dream that I'm inside my house while a tremendous windstorm rages outside. I hear glass shattering and the sounds of things crashing and being blown about. A strange man is in the house. He tells me about all the mistakes he's made in the past regarding his own house, moaning on in a whiny, poor-me voice. I can't stand listening to him. I turn my back and stand staring out the window, focusing on the wild storm instead. The world is being destroyed; all the trees are falling, but nothing falls on my house.

I wake up at four in the morning with the wild storm of my dream coursing through me, on the verge of panic. Fearful of losing my sanity, I get right up, make coffee, and head over to the studio. I work non-stop, hoping to keep the storm at bay, the inner storm so like the storm in my dream. I get through the morning without incident, but by noon I don't want to fight anymore; I'm just too exhausted. I begin to detect some real loosening as I admit this. I even cry a little. More tears want to release, but I'm afraid I'll rage out of control, which I don't think I can handle. Although this turmoil only exists inside me, it's very real, but I must trust that nothing bad will happen if I let it loose, as my dream so clearly suggests.

"What is it?" I ask my deeper self, ready to finally confront what has me in such a grip. In a matter of seconds I am flooded by a wave of deep sadness. White-hot humiliation rides its crest, its power daunting, smelling of long forgotten days. I begin to release it in small tolerable waves of tears and choking cries that I can easily handle. My body protects me, offering incremental muscle releases that though controlled are quite riveting, especially for someone who never lets herself feel. Eventually, the flow ebbs. I realize I got a taste of what's inside me, but only a taste, for there's still so much more. I don't even know what it is. I haven't opened the door all the way yet, but I must trust that I'll be okay as I let the storm surge on. Just as my dream showed me last night, I will be okay; my house will not be affected. As the inner storm subsides, I clean up the studio and head home. It's eleven o'clock at night, and it's exhaustion alone that drives me to bed—and sleep, I hope.

I fall into a very light sleep and right into a frantic, paranoid dream. In the dream, I'm trying to wake my kids up, but they just won't get up. They lie asleep in bed, not hearing me. I'm aware that it's time to sleep, not time to wake up, but now that I'm awake I see that the house is in a shambles. There's garbage lying everywhere, as if someone has come in and trashed the place. I begin cleaning. I go into the bathroom and find that it too is wrecked. Suddenly, I'm aware that someone is listening to everything that goes on inside the house, and that someone has broken in while I was sleeping and made this mess. I pick up the phone and listen. I hear voices. "I know who you are!" I shout into the phone. "You are in big trouble now! I'm on to you!" And with that, I hold the phone up to the air vent in the ceiling and let the noise of the heat rushing through the ductwork flow into the phone, thinking it will sound threatening and scary. It wakes me right up!

I realize my dreams are showing me that I live in the tension between worlds, between now and the past, between my changing reality and dream reality, between the old self and the new self. With the predator always lurking, my dreams show me the true state of my damaged psyche. Traumatized by childhood sexual abuse, I continue to react to every situation in the same way, with fear and paranoia. Though I rarely allow this paranoia to escape and live in real life, I see how it lives inside me every day. I may have supreme control over my waking self and although I may have a certain amount of control to act and change myself in my dreams, I certainly don't have the same kind of control over my deeper truths and the direction they take in dreaming.

My dreams reveal what lies at my deepest self. At the same time they're full of the same kind of frantic energy that invades me during a recapitulation. There are even signs in my dreams of what's happening in real life, the fact that I'm taking control now, reacting, yelling and fighting back. My body responds to all of these insinuations with incredible pain! But I elect to ignore it! Off to sleep again!

May 25, 2003

I dream that I live on a big ranch. There's a cowboy in my bedroom, lying spread eagle on my bed. I scream at him to get out. He jumps up to shush me, closing the windows so my screaming can't be heard outside, but I don't care. I'm angry—fuming. I yell at him and tell him he must leave, but he takes his sweet time about it. I keep going back to check on him, to see if he's left. "Has he left yet?" I keep asking. "Has he left yet?" Then I'm outside with my daughter. She wants to go swimming in a nearby lake, but every time she attempts to jump in it turns muddy, the water recedes and she ends up flopping in the mud. She runs, chasing after the water, but it keeps disappearing until everything is dry and barren. I know that if I can just get the cowboy out then I can fix the house up and the water will return too. I'm good at fixing up places and I'm surprised that the ranch, once a beautiful sprawling place with fountains and gardens, is now almost totally derelict. I can't wait for the bad elements to leave so I can renovate. "Yeah," I say to myself as I wake up, "I can't wait!"

After taking a walk and doing a few errands I find I can't settle down, my energy at an all-time high. It's Sunday. I'm making myself take a day off from work, but I still have to keep busy. I do some work on the house. I don't realize I'm keeping something at bay until I stop to eat at around six in the evening and discover that I've spent the entire day running from the ever-present scent of my abuser. As soon as I admit this, I'm hit full force. *Wham!* As if I've been struck from behind, I fall to the kitchen floor, lost in sensory flashbacks. My face is not pressing against the hard vinyl flooring of my kitchen but into the soft ground of the woods, the strong stench of dirt and my abuser pungent in my nostrils. I retain awareness of where I am at all times and I'm able to pull out of the experience when it becomes too much to handle. I'm not so lost in the memory that I don't know what reality this is. I'm frustrated, however, by the need and desire to release more while also knowing that I can't handle too much. I eventually get up off the floor, aware that the predatory energy lurks not only inside the houses in my dreams, but inside me. I know I need to take my time with this process, let it unfold naturally, not push it as the *I Ching* so clearly states in *Coming to Meet*. Instinctively, I know I must proceed *very* slowly.

In need of comfort, I give myself permission to lie down for a little while, for just a few minutes. As soon as I crawl into bed, I receive immediate comfort. But then the kids call to tell me they'll be home from their weekend with their dad in a couple of hours and this gets me up again. I stay away from my bedroom, afraid to lie down again, and so in between work on the kitchen cabinets— which I unexpectedly began painting today in an earlier explosion of energy—I stretch out on the big chair in the living room. My bed calls to me so enticingly, with an almost magnetic pull, which I succeed in resisting. Before long the kids are home. Cheered by the brightly painted kitchen, and used to seeing me in paint-spattered overalls, they don't even blink an eye at how I've transformed the place in the few days they've been away. By now they're pretty used to my bursts of creative energy.

By midnight my stomach hurts, my shoulders hurt, my throat hurts and I'm dead tired, but I can't sleep and I'm afraid to try. I take a bath, hoping to soothe the ever-present anxiety. What am I so afraid of?

May 26, 2003

I'm running from something in a dream, wanting only to disappear and never be found, going on a long journey, going forever, never to return. Like a runaway slave traveling the Underground Railroad, or an escapee from Nazi Germany, I go from barn to barn, hiding out, escaping from evil. Many people and children help me along the way. I travel night and day through woods, over fields, and through a maze of towns and villages. Sometimes I'm hesitant to keep going, fearful and tired, but then I reassert my intent and press on, discussing the best route to take with helpful people I meet along the way.

I wake up in fear, my dream world reminding me of just why I'm so afraid to sleep. I can't wait for my appointment with Chuck tomorrow, but I'm afraid that I may not be able to talk about what's really happening as deeply as I'd like. On most occasions, when I finally get to his office—where I feel infinitely secure—I still hold back, even after all this time. As I drive to my appointment each week, I endure the pulsing anxiety that constantly courses through me, knowing that I will finally be able to talk. And then the shyness sets in, the hesitation takes over. As I step into his office I withdraw into silence, and I can't go where I so desperately need to go, where I want to go. Am I still afraid of him? Afraid that he'll judge me, hurt, blame, reject, or hate me? I feel like a little girl going to confession, facing Chuck the priest, preparing to tell the sins and secrets that I have vowed, with my life, to never tell.

It's raining today so there is no Memorial Day parade for the kids to march in with the school band, but I decide to get up early anyway and get the day rolling. For just a second or two, however, I curl up with the hurt inside me, the hurt of the little girl self. I find comfort with her, but only briefly. I begin to wonder why I'm so hard on myself, on my poor child self as well, for it's her that I push to get up out of bed every day and bear the tension and anxiety. I fight every need and desire. Why is it so hard to be nice to myself?

I go out shopping and get the last few household items I need for the upcoming week and bake a pie for a picnic we're going to. It's an annual event that I'm not looking forward to, fearful that I'll have nothing to say to anyone, or that I'll just want to leave as soon as I get there. Once there, however, I find myself talking—a lot. I just open my mouth and words come out. It isn't really that hard, but it's not too long before even that novelty wears off and I'm ready to leave. I round up the kids as soon as politely possible and we head back home where I continue painting the kitchen and part of the laundry room.

I've been up since eight in the morning, going non-stop, and now it's almost one in the morning and I still can't stop, but I force myself to call it quits. I take a quick bath to slow the energy down and then get ready for bed. As soon as my fanny hits the mattress the energy revs right back up again. Although exhausted, I turn to face it. I'd rather do that than fight it. I lie down and let myself feel. Intolerable fear creeps into bed with me, clenching my stomach, my throat. Something bad is going to happen to me, something really bad. I wonder how I'll ever be able to sleep through this, but I see the futility of trying to force sleep when sleep may not be where I'm headed next, and so I acquiesce. I decide I'll just do what comes next, letting the unfolding of this recapitulation decide if I'm to sleep or not. If sleep is what I'm going to do then I won't worry so much about the fear or anything else disturbing me. I'm in the throes of this recapitulation for better *and* worse, and I know it's taking me places I need to go. I just wish they weren't so horrific. "Just go to sleep, if that's what comes next," I tell myself. "Acquiesce to exhaustion."

SHIT! I must have dozed off because I am jolted awake by intense vaginal and anal pain. Even though I said I'd go with the flow of this recapitulation, I really don't want to. "Go away! Go away! Please go away! I don't want to do it now! Please go away! Go away! Ow! Ow! Ow!" I sit up and I'm immediately nauseous. Staggering, I run into the bathroom where I hang over the toilet bowl and retch. In drooling pain, I crouch, unable to think or focus, the fiery intensity excruciating. Eventually, I crawl back to bed. Pressing my hands against my crotch, I breathe into the pain. An hour goes by before the fire dies down. I'm aware that something big just happened. And there's that pulsing in my head again, which I just want to turn off! Forget what I said before about going with the flow. Please let me sleep!

May 27, 2003

I'm sound asleep when the alarm goes off at six. I get right up so I don't fall back to sleep, which is what I feel like doing. Instead, I head to the kitchen. Flipping the light switch, I am instantly cheered by my newly painted walls, the bright oranges, pinks and yellows greeting me with warmth and vitality. Taking it all in, I am flooded with the clearsightedness that I will succeed at whatever task I undertake and that my life will be good. "Thank you! Thank you! Thank you!" I shout to the morning, and to whomever else might be listening out there in the universe.

Emerging from my lonely weekend of recapitulation, I suddenly realize that I'm not alone anymore, even though this is a very lonely time and a lonely journey. I have Chuck, but I also have the divine guidance of Jeanne. Once again, I am keenly aware of her presence, of her input in this process, of her voice guiding me, and I'm so thankful for it. I feel safer and loved because of it. Optimism flows through me as I stand in my brightly painted kitchen and pour a cup of coffee. Awestruck by my luck—yes, I feel lucky—I sense only goodness and success ahead of me. Perhaps I've earned it. Perhaps I've earned some good karma in the trials of this lifetime. It certainly feels like it today, even though last night was incredibly painful. At this moment, however, I feel empty, cleansed almost; and even though I'm sad and exhausted, I also know that I will survive this process with flying colors.

In spite of this new spurt of optimism, I'm so tired when I meet with Chuck that I almost can't talk.

"You look very drained," he says.

"Yeah, well, I feel that way," I say, and I tell him about the pain that came in the night, sneaking into my body while I slept. "I'm recapitulating in my dreams. I can't tell if it's something I've already recapitulated or if it's something totally new. Could it be a new memory, and if so why, why now? I thought I was done with the memories."

"The emotions are waking up to the *fact* of the pain," Chuck suggests. "Even though you had dissociated at the actual time of the event, the pain remained stored in your body. It's not actually happening now, but the pain that was stored then is making itself known by triggering emotion."

"It may not be happening now in actuality, but it *is* happening now in my body! So don't tell me it's not now. It is now! And I feel it with what I assume is the same intensity and realness as back then, even though nearly fifty years have passed."

Chuck suggests that I channel the pain out of my body by focusing on a point in the distance and sending the pain away, along an imaginary line, to that point. I know exactly what he's talking about. I'd used that technique when I was a kid after reading about it, but the hard part is the intensity of the pain. It's extreme, so painful that I can't see, think, or talk when in the midst of it. It's drowning pain that totally engulfs me, dragging me back to some forgotten place. To get to a point of being able to grab it and send it anywhere at all will take a tremendous effort.

"I'm not sure I can do that," I say, "for the pain is deeply embedded. When it wakes up, it shoots to my very roots and anchors itself there. It doesn't feel like it will loosen anytime soon."

I'm exhausted by the end of the session. I go to work, but the exhaustion settles in even deeper and by nighttime I am its slave.

May 28, 2003

I sleep really hard, straight through until the alarm goes off. I know I was dreaming, but I have no dream recall and I'm thankful for that. My mind and body sure need the rest! I'm acquiescing to certain parts of this recapitulation more readily now, because of the exhaustion. Perhaps I'm getting a break for my diligence, and better sleep too!

With renewed energy, I go to the studio early, as soon as the kids are off to school. I have work to do on a newsletter, an estimate to prepare for a new client, and it's time to begin new work for an upcoming exhibit. By the end of the day, however, I'm feeling the strain, ready to explode like the dolls in my dream, simply disintegrate into a million tiny shards and fall into a heap of tears and bloody body parts. I know that if I push even the tiniest bit I will go over the edge and into the abyss. I find myself once again teetering on the crusty rim of that ever-present precipice, bearing the additional tension of knowing that I might slip and plunge over the edge at any moment. When I'm ready, I assume I will let go, that I will take the plunge because it will be the next thing to do, but until then I intend to hold back.

In the late afternoon, while gardening in the front yard, I talk to a neighbor and find out that the house next door, home to an old woman, is filled with dozens of cats. No one knows how many for sure, but if you look closely you can see them crammed on every windowsill, adults and kittens alike. The old woman fell over one of the cats during the winter and an ambulance was called. Since release from the hospital she's been living with a relative. During our conversation the neighbor tells me that the old woman's husband had been a child molester! Everyone in the neighborhood knew about him and children were duly warned to keep away. Now I recall that when we had moved in, my daughter's friend, who lives in the neighborhood, had said, "Oh my God, you're moving next door to the bad house." Luckily, the guy has been dead for years, but even so, his reputation lives on. I find it so ironic that here I am recapitulating my own abusive past and I've inadvertently moved right next door to a house that was once home to a pedophile!

I've monitored the sensations in my head all day, noting that when I'm busy they quiet down, but as soon as I sit down for a second of rest they immediately start up. As I brush my teeth at night they start up again, pulsing as I drag the toothbrush back and forth over my teeth, pushing me to remember something. Lucky me, just in time for sleeping! I send the intrusive energy away, projecting it outwardly, as Chuck recommended, though I'm concerned it may just prolong the agony. Sometimes it's better to just go through the pain, quicker and easier than numbing it or avoiding it. I hold a similar sentiment when going to the dentist. Sometimes I'd rather just have the pain than the shot of Novocain and the long agonizing wait for it to wear off. I also know that each episode of abuse will keep resurfacing until I've fully recapitulated every inch of it. I can't run and hide anymore. I have to go through the pain, retrieve my feelings, and gather what I can of value from the experience.

I'm starting to feel unsafe again, even in Chuck's office. I sense how important it is to protect myself, and so I am unwilling to be fully open and transparent. If I am to survive, I must be safe on my own terms, which means being highly protective. On top of that, I'm very emotionally needy, though I can't let that be fully known either—I have to keep quiet about that. I have to tell the neediness to go away with the bad stuff because it's connected to the bad stuff. I can't let Chuck know how afraid and needy I really am because letting people in, letting them know of the existence of this deeply needy self leaves me exposed and vulnerable. I must protect myself. Perhaps this is what's been pushing so hard to emerge lately.

"What must I protect myself from?" I ask my child self.

"From everything," she answers, "from being hurt, from being treated badly, from being rejected, from hating myself. I don't want to have to hate myself for talking to Chuck, or regret having spoken to him when I realize I shouldn't have. I have to be careful. I have to be so careful. I don't want to leave myself open for hurt and self-hatred, rejection and disgust. I don't want to be angry with myself for baring my soul, for letting someone know what I really think and feel, for revealing my raw self. I am crawling with fear. It pulses through me and directs my every move and thought, especially on bad days, on those curl-up-and-stay-in-bed days."

"It doesn't matter who I am or how I felt a day ago or even an hour ago," I imagine saying to Chuck on behalf of my frightened child self, "underneath I'm still an open wound, raw and torn apart, and fear is like acid dripping into the open wound. I'm afraid that if I show you my wound you might pour acid on it too. And although I've been able to come to see you week after week, I still feel extremely vulnerable and so I'm reluctant to let you into that deepest place where it really hurts."

May 29, 2003

In a dream, I'm standing naked in a barn looking out over fields and trees. I see a woman walking toward me. I wonder who she is and why she's on my property. I run out of the barn to confront her. When she sees me, she takes off running in the opposite direction, away from me. "Nudity has its advantages," I

303

think. I'm back in the barn when the phone rings. It's a friend calling to say that she had been on her way over to visit me when she saw me "inappropriately dressed for company," and so had gone home again. The truth is, I'm searching for something in the barn and I don't want to be disturbed. I don't want contact with anyone or have to explain myself. I just want to be left alone so I can search in peace.

Lying in the bathtub at the end of the day, I realize—and this is not a new realization by far—that I *do* need to relive the memories, and that I'm not actually "stuck," as both Chuck and I sometimes imply. In fact, I realize I'm reliving some part of some memory at any given time—all the time—as each memory takes the time it must to fully blossom. The memories *are* leading the unfolding of this recapitulation, and since I don't completely capture the whole of them the first time around, they come back again and again, until I pass the test, until everything is fully recapitulated.

Some memories are of short duration because, I believe, the traumatic encounter with my abuser was of short duration. If a traumatic event was forty-five minutes long, then I need to relive all forty-five minutes of it. If it was three hours long, then I need three hours to get through it. If I happen to dissociate while I'm recapitulating a memory, the total memory is not retrieved and only partial recall will result. This means I have to return to the same memory at another time for a fuller, more productive recapitulation. I need to experience every detail of every memory, otherwise they will continue to haunt me, teasing me to come back and finish them once and for all. My dream points this out, as I am once again in the same barn that I'd spied across the field from the back of the hairdresser's salon. I must keep returning to search and fully recapitulate all that still remains there.

I'm wary of meeting with Chuck tomorrow. I've felt unsafe all week, lost in the past, teetering on that very scary precipice where the memories take me. As soon as they come, I'm thrust back in time where no safe place exists and I know I could fall into oblivion at any moment. Don't I trust Chuck? Or is it myself I don't trust? Right now, I'm fearful that my neediness will get me into trouble, that I'll gravitate to a bad relationship because I feel so damned emotionally needy. I don't mean loneliness, because I can deal with that. I'm talking about basic needs of emotional support. I fear that I will attach myself to some inappropriate person just to have an inkling of comfort and support. So the situation I'm in leaves me not feeling very self-trusting right now. I'm unsafe, in both my memories and my present emotional condition.

In the dream I had last night, I didn't want anyone to come near me. I needed isolation so I could find something in the barn. I was angry when I saw the woman coming, and running after her was both an effort to see who she was and to shoo her away. The nudity didn't bother me. I didn't really notice I was naked, until she mentioned it. "Well, who cares!" I thought when she remarked on my 'inappropriate dress.' Why the morals? It's just a body!

May 30, 2003

Why am I still so guarded and tentative, still on heightened alert? Why still so unsafe? There may be more stuff coming. I know I have to experience everything, without fear and resentment. I must stop judging myself so harshly as well. I'm also aware that it will be impossible to hold anything back. It's good to state this because I sense that a shattering is about to happen. The truth is, I don't want to hold anything back, nor do I really have the strength anymore. I ponder these things as I drive to my session with Chuck. Facing my fear of him, I tell him that I'm not stuck.

"I'm recapitulating all the time," I say. "I need to allow the recapitulation to lead me, to proceed along its own course, to show me where to go next."

He doesn't dispute me, in fact he's always encouraged me to stop pushing it and let the recapitulation lead, but I've come to a deeper understanding of just what that means. He has deep respect for my intuition as I go through this process, he says, and so we agree that the recapitulation must be in control. I must let it show me where to go and what to do next.

"You just need to be ready for it," he suggests, "to meet it in full awareness."

"Yes, I feel that's what I've been working toward," I say. "I haven't consistently been able to do that yet, but now I can. Now I'm ready."

And so, I humbly bow to the recapitulation as I put on the EMDR headphones and open up to it as fully as possible. It leads me through a wandering mess of emotions and sensations as I physically experience myself opening and unblocking. My chakras open in ever-widening bursts, my muscles release their holdings, and my brain expands as I follow the recapitulation trail. Like a dog on the scent, I let myself be led through the dark tunnel of self until I emerge quite exhausted, but much calmer as well.

"Once you've gone through a memory," Chuck says, "once you've taken it in and gotten what you need, once you come out of it, the trick becomes to merge it with what you already know. To, in effect, be in both places at once, assimilating the missing pieces so that you can eventually be in a new place."

"A new me."

"Yes, a new you."

I've been walking the tightrope between old fears and new fears for a long time now. I've gotten to the point of exhaustion, where I can't fight the old any longer nor keep the inevitable new away. I'm worn out with fighting, drained from constantly battling, so worn down that I no longer have the energy to block out the memories or resist when they call to me. To go into them now, without resistance, is really handling them in a different manner. This is where the recapitulation has led me and this is how I will let it lead me in the future. I will no longer resist.

I go for a quiet walk after the session. I have so little energy, but I need to be outside. I have the great expanse of fields and views of the river to myself along the river bluff as so few people are out in the early morning. Later I work at the studio. I finish artwork for an upcoming show and pack up for our move downstairs to the new studio tomorrow. As I work, I realize that people have been so nice to me lately, genuinely happy and excited for me, and this has allowed me to be nice to myself in return.

As I take the next step on this journey, I sense I'll be fine. In allowing myself to go deeper into the recapitulation without resistance, I must remember to go without resistance into all areas of my life. I must acquiesce to the flow of my life on the deepest of levels and accept that everything will be just fine, that I can't go wrong. This is such a path of heart. How can it be wrong?

As I go to sleep, I set an intention: I will dream about healing, how to heal and how to release, for that is where this path of heart is leading me. This is a healing journey.

May 31, 2003

I'm in a dream that takes place in two locations, both of which are under construction, my studio and my house. I'm moving my art supplies to a new studio, starting over, doing a lot of planning and organizing. The weather is stormy and I'm cold and wet from being in the rain. People arrive to help. I hang up their jackets to dry, both in the studio and in the house. My daughter is a small child again—as she usually is in my dreams—wanting lots of love and affection, to be held, protected and cared for. I take time to give her what she needs. At the same time, I struggle to get everything packed and moved into the new studio space. I'm tired, but unwilling to give up, because I know it's what I'm meant to do and also because I've experienced enough success now that I know everything's going to work out just fine. In spite of the construction going on, both places have a unique look and quality, with an overall feeling of progress and prosperity.

If I am to heal, I need to give myself the things that I so readily and easily gave my daughter in the dream. I need to take care of the wounded inner child, so hurt and needy. It's also time to focus on my work, to take back the time and attention I give so easily to others. I feel a new excitement that I haven't felt before, a new urgency embracing this deepening solo journey. Each day, I feel myself growing more independent, getting more strongly anchored in my new life, as I continue caring for my children and, most importantly, myself. My feelings and needs are more present now, making themselves known, waiting for me to give them my full, undivided attention.

I've recently noticed that the pulsing in my head stops when I pay attention to it, when I pause and say, "Okay, let's go someplace quiet and figure this out." And then the precipice doesn't feel so uncomfortable; it actually becomes quite necessary and acceptable. And even though I must go into painful places within my psyche, I am better prepared now to listen and learn, which is what this recapitulation is all about, listening to and learning about myself at the deepest level.

Just as in my dream, we have help moving the studio downstairs to our new space, which really saves the day, otherwise we wouldn't have gotten much accomplished. We work in tandem so none of us has to make too many full trips up and down the stairs. By the afternoon things are looking pretty good. I leave to take the cats to the vet and the kids to a movie, and then go back to do more packing.

It's now eleven at night and I'm too tired to worry about anything. As if my dream last night was predicting this very moment when I lie in bed needing to cry, my daughter comes in to my bedroom. She's cranky. She strives to be independent, but at the same time she's clingy and demanding, wanting to be coddled and soothed, just as in my dream. Oh the struggle to individuate!

Taking her into bed with me, I commiserate completely, for I know exactly how she's feeling as I'm in the same boat. She's tired and bemoans her challenges as too much for anyone to handle. I know how frustrating everything can seem. I also know that sleep is a great cure-all and that she'll wake up feeling better tomorrow. It's late now and we all need our sleep. Soothed, she goes back to her own bed after a while. The example of her ability to release and vent her emotions, however, has me in a vise grip, feeling pressure from all sides. I sense a breaking point coming, as the pressure to release and the pressure to hold on converge on my precipice. I too bemoan that I don't know if I can handle it, but of course I will, I always do, and life will go on, but this time I intend to go along with it! The pressure in my head pushes me to curl up into a ball and let stuff release. Okay, I will. The time hasn't been right all day, the place hasn't been right either, but I'll go there now and see what happens.

I roll into a little ball under the covers, just as I always did as a child. I am exhausted, lonely, and unhappy. Something feels different though, perhaps because I'm going to let it in. I'm going to let in the intense pressure that I pushed away throughout the day. Now, at night, it's finally the right time, but I'm scared as hell as I crawl deeper under the covers.

Chapter 6

Long Live the Queen!

June 1, 2003

I dream that I'm with a group of children, wandering through empty warehouses in desolate cities. I try to keep everyone focused on the journey. "We're almost there, we're almost there," I tell them. "Just keep going; we're almost there." After a while, we come to a newly renovated area where signs of life are plentiful. The warehouses we pass now are fully stocked; one has been turned into a library, another a bookstore.

I awaken from this dream more certain than ever that this journey into my past will eventually be worth it, that it will lead to new life. For the time being, however, I'm aware of still being in a city of desolation and that I have more to recapitulate before I reach the renovated districts teeming with new life. The child self that I'd pushed so hard to keep going in the dream refuses to get up on this rainy Sunday morning. She asks me to hide in bed all day, to cry like a baby and tell everyone to go away. She wants to be left alone in her misery.

I let her have her way for a while, but then drag myself out of bed when I hear the kids getting up, though my child self whines all day with no sign of let up. I bear the pressure of her insistence, but I'm edgy, the slightest sounds making me jump. I intend on holding her back because I'm afraid. It's the emptying process I fear the most, that I'll have nothing inside me as I let go of everything that has been my reality up until now. I admit, I'm consciously choosing the torment of this place of uncomfortable comfort over the emptiness of the vast nothingness; for the time being I will cling to the old stuff. It represents a known and predictable path and there's a sense that I am still wanted and needed here. If I let go of the old stuff, I'm certain that I'll plunge into the depths of the abyss that I've perched on the edge of for so long, right into the annihilating terror of nothingness, abandoned by even myself. As I hold myself back from the edge, I admit that the bad memories carry comfort. How absurd, but how true!

I spend the day angry, in a rotten mood, constantly berating myself for my stubborn failure to let go of the painful enigma inside me. The child inside stubbornly pesters me to give in. My own children notice and feel it. Their energy bristles back at mine, yet I refuse to feel their frustration. I don't care. Growing cold, I go more deeply emotionally dead as the day goes on, effectively rejecting everything I've been working toward. Stuck in the desolate city of my dream, I am unable to see what I already know is ahead. So lost am I that I no longer feel a thing.

I give everyone a respite from my biting mood in the afternoon and spend a few hours moving things from the old studio to the new one, a slow process, and still so much to be done. Tired of all the stairs, my grumpiness grows heavier each trip I make, the loads I carry weighing me down in more ways than one. When night finally comes I fall exhausted into bed, right into a dream. I'm in a new house where everything is empty, clean, and very white. The house is unfurnished. I'm aware that I'll only be here for a short time. I've driven down narrow, crowded streets to get here. Children ran up to me as I drove, their faces alive with excitement, but as soon as they caught sight of my face they stopped just short of stepping off the curb. Their exuberance quelled into silence as they somberly watched me drive past. I'm inside the house for a short while when I realize I'm not alone. I see that a sliding glass door has been left open and someone has tracked snow onto the carpet, the big footprints of a man. When I look out the door I see footprints in the snow outside as well, circling the house. Suddenly fearful, certain that someone else is in the house, I no longer feel safe. I search all over for the man I am sure is hiding. I can't find him, but I also see that there's really no place for him to hide. The house is empty; there are no possessions and no furniture to hide behind. I'm aware that this is only a temporary house of fear, intense and real though it appears.

Jolted awake, I see by the clock that I've only been asleep a few minutes. I'm immediately aware that this dream is telling me that as long I insist on keeping in what my psyche is pushing me to release then, yes, I must suffer. The children in the dream seem to be eagerly awaiting me—my inner children waiting all day for me to turn to them—for they rush up expectantly, calling out, "Here she comes! Here she comes!" They are stunned that I won't receive them. They are perhaps expecting me to be different in dreamland, but I coldly drive by. Standing silently, with serious faces, they watch me drive past, my dour expression revealing that I'm not ready yet, that I'm on a different mission, still entangled in the trappings of fear. But it's as if I've conjured up the fears, for although I see the footsteps of a man, there is really no man in the house and thus nothing to really fear. I understand that if I fail to release my old fears, they will continue to haunt me. My dream makes it pretty clear that this is a transitional stage. And I get it— choosing to conjure up fear is of my own doing!

June 2, 2003

The alarm wakes me. For a few seconds I don't know where I am or even who I am. All I want to do is go back to sleep, back into the unfocused and scattered dreams I've been having, but I can't. I have to get up, though my stiff and achy body refuses to move. Mustering all my energy, I roll over and sit up, shifting myself into alertness, setting the intent to stay present in each moment of the day. It's the least I can do to break this stranglehold. I'm going to apologize to the kids for last night's grumpiness, get them to school, get the car inspected, and go to the studio. I have a tremendous amount to do today, so I'll be busy. Is that good? I think it is. And so I push myself out of bed, hoping to be open to what this new day may bring. In truth, however, I'm still stuck in that empty house of my dream, stalking the fearful enigma inside.

The day is as stressful and busy as anticipated. I rush around doing errands and spend a great deal of time coordinating things for the upcoming art show that I'm curating at the artist's gallery. I end up taking a lot of phone calls from artists who don't have their work ready. Still others haven't submitted their work properly framed and ready for hanging. I get more frustrated by the hour and finally conclude that my duties at the gallery are taking up way too much time and energy. I'm tired of it. I decide to back down after fulfilling my commitments for the year. I put the resentment and anger to good use though, and paint the floor in the small office area of the new studio. In spite of constant interruptions from the outside world, I keep everything in my inner world under control.

I drink way too much coffee, using it to literally drive myself to distraction, staying always one nervous step ahead of the pressure from my psyche to take the leap into the abyss. I hear the tension in my voice, which is rushed and chatty, unlike me. Over the weekend, I started to stress out about money, not maintaining my usual calmness about everything working out just fine, feeling overwhelmed by all the tasks before me. Not just little things like making healthy dinners every night and taking the cats to the vet, but big things like setting up the new studio, my commitments to the artist's gallery, restarting my business alone now and making enough money to support it along with my two kids, my house, and myself. I'm trying not to get overwhelmed and I know that eventually I'll calm down. I hear Jeanne's voice underscoring that truth, reminding me: *"You'll be fine; everything will be fine."*

I pick up the kids after school. As soon as we get home I lug out the mower and mow the entire yard. It takes me over an hour, but I'm a different person by the time I'm done. Pushing the heavy mower is hard, sweaty work, but afterwards I feel as if I've run three miles on a hot day. Purged, and enormously lighter in mood, I take a shower and make dinner. The kids are both in better moods too. Aware that I'm just barely staying in control, I realize that I don't really want to be the old self anymore. I don't want to "hold on" or "hang in there" anymore. I'm exhausted and fairly sure I won't be able to keep up this charade much longer. I'm wearing down. One of these days I will have to let go.

"Try for stillness. Go for stillness," I hear Jeanne saying.

I barely remember concluding last week that I do indeed need stillness—unhurried, unstressed, quiet living—and a break from this torture. I hoard my feelings, afraid that when they're gone I won't have anything left inside me and yet this is my torture as well. At this point it still feels far better, and safer, to retain my stoic stand, though the children in my dream clearly expected me to be a feeling being. Their disappointment and sense of rejection were palpable as I coldly passed them by, heading straight for the house of fear rather than turn to them with equal joy.

If I let go, I fear that all that keeps me connected to life will go too, that all my desperate attempts to align myself somewhere in this world will disappear. Maybe I don't need to try so hard, as Chuck constantly tells me, but there's a part of me that cannot abide the idea of not being in control, the thought alone sending me into a place of deep shame and anxiety. I know that such deep shame stems from my upbringing, for it was expected that I handle everything so expertly, without a show of emotion, coolly and without expressing needs or desires of any kind. Rather than be laughed at or scolded for showing emotional neediness, it was far easier to become cold and unemotional. I deduced that to want affection and love were shameful weaknesses, to be avoided at all costs, though I harbored a secret desire for them. I was deeply ashamed of my desire for simple human touch and affection, and yet I do not blame my child self for such basic human needs, nor do I wish to reject her. She needs to know that it's perfectly acceptable to want and need simple affection, to know that it's allowed and necessary. Love is allowed. It is, isn't it? An epiphany: Love *is* allowed! *Wanting to be loved* is allowed too!

The whole idea of needing or expressing love and affection was presented as something shameful: don't even go there; don't touch or be touched, it's disgusting! This is what I was taught at home. Emotions were disgusting; expressing them was disgusting, letting anyone know you had emotions or feelings was strictly forbidden. No touching, no gentleness, no love was exchanged between parent and child, perhaps very rarely a pat on the head, maybe, if I was sick. No hugs, no kisses, no emotional support. Such an unemotional upbringing is wrong. To make a person feel so ashamed and so emotionally isolated is wrong. To deprive another of the most basic of human needs is wrong.

On top if it, I had to deal with my abuser, but I see where his abusive affections, as perverted as they were, tapped into that void created by my upbringing. Even though his type of attention was totally aberrant, I wouldn't have known that as a child. I had nothing to compare it to. Perhaps I was drawn to him as much as he was drawn to me. I was trapped coming and going. I had no choice. I was a child living in a family completely devoid of human touch and emotions, the most basic of which were squelched at an early age. And then I walked into a family where they took their clothes off and touched each other all over the place, where feelings

I never knew existed inside me were drawn out. And then I had to go back to my own family, which with its cold, distant, and strict Victorian morals was as insidiously bizarre and abusive as my abuser's family. And all I ever wanted was for someone to simply love me, just for who I was. I see how easily a young child, starved for affection, could be confused and tricked by the attentions of a pedophile.

June 3, 2003

I dream that I'm walking amongst a group of men. They carry guns, stopping every now and then to shoot at ducks in the sky. Bored, I watch and wonder what would happen if they turned and shot each other instead. I wonder at the folly of it all, for I see no purpose in what they're doing, simply shooting for sport. The landscape is muddy and flat, a cold winter morning. We're circling around a desolate stone tower, everything colorless and dark. As I follow them, I know, deep down, that there must be something else to life, that this can't be all there is. I go inside the stone tower and down into a basement boiler room. I figure out how the hot water heater and furnace work. Then I get stuck in a repetitive behavior. I climb a ladder up to the top of the tall hot water tank, wait for the coils to ignite, and then slide down when I hear them click on, landing in a plop on the ground. I climb the ladder over and over again—making a ritual of it—until it becomes clear that something is missing. I understand how the hot water heater works and everything seems okay, but then I notice that there's no hot water coming out of the faucets. All of a sudden, I realize that the furnace generates the hot water and that the water tank is not a heater, but simply a storage tank.

I go over to the huge furnace and pull a big red switch to ON. Immediately the furnace roars to life. I jump back, startled, and hear that scared little voice inside, so full of shame and fear, warning me: "You're in trouble now!" My mother arrives at just that moment and scolds me for touching the switch. "I had to," I say, staring at her blankly. "It wasn't on. There wouldn't be hot water if I hadn't flipped the switch." I watch the two machines humming away. I feel good knowing that I've corrected something that wasn't working properly; but there are still all those men outside, walking around in the mud with their guns. I see their muddy boots as they tramp past the basement windows, circling the tower, shooting and killing, with little regard for life. "Just don't shoot anyone," I hear one of them say.

Thank you, Dream World! My own body is just a storage tank for all that is unexpressed inside me and there will be no release if I don't turn my emotional self on. Once again, a mandala appears in the guise of the circular tower with the men—my fears—circling around it, and my recapitulating self at the center doing deep inner work. The red switch is like a pilot light at the very center of the mandala, the flame of the spirit inside me, patiently waiting to be ignited, the very thing that I sense is missing. Synchronously, as I prepare to meet with Chuck this morning, I struggle with finding a way to express myself—as usual! My adult self is like the self in my dream, still controlled by the inner voice of a frightened child, afraid of doing something wrong, expecting to be blamed. But it isn't my own inner voice I most often hear, it's my mother's voice, and indeed she shows up right at a crucial moment in the dream, when I take action.

Although I determined a long time ago that I would not be like my mother, I see how her voice still infiltrates and controls my inner world, for it is her voice that constantly scolds and tells me that I'm doing things wrong, that I'm not allowed to feel or talk or receive, that I must remain solidly encased and unemotional. This is the voice I must excise from my subconscious, giving my own true voice access to the pulpit. This is the same challenge I face each time I meet with Chuck. I must override the scolding voice of my mother—telling me that I must not talk or reveal anything personal—and allow my true self to be open and fully present in the sessions with him. I must help my true self to feel safe enough to speak and express what she's feeling. It's a slow process of learning that my feelings and needs are legitimate, that my deepest inner thoughts and my spiritually seeking self have value—that I have value. I'm discovering that a fully emotional self is a healed self.

It's ridiculous how I still hold back in sessions after all this time, but it's the same way I hold back inside myself, constantly reprimanded by the voice of the unemotional mother inside me. She's as big a petty tyrant as my abuser. My dream shows me that I'm still so afraid of her, and for what reason really? I feel good in the dream when I finally get both machines up and humming, satisfied that I've corrected a big mistake. As I face meeting Chuck,

I must remember this self. Although I was still fearful of what was happening outside in the dream, at least I resolved something at a deeper level inside. I'm hopeful Chuck will understand what I'm getting at with all of this, but I know that if he doesn't at first, he'll keep trying until he does. As these thoughts go through me, I hear Jeanne's voice:

"*It's time; it's time to let him know,*" she says, speaking very clearly and tenderly. "*He's the only one. No one else will even allow this; no one else will really care. There is no one else in the whole world to relate this to; he's the one. Don't be afraid. Don't be afraid to tell him what you have discovered. He'll understand. He's there.*"

Jeanne is giving me permission to be gut-wrenchingly honest, to not hold back, to indeed turn on the furnace and let everything flow, but that's always easier said than done. By the time I'm in the car driving up to Chuck's office I have a little mantra going—*Don't freeze up; you have to talk. Don't freeze up; it will be okay. Don't freeze up*—and when I get there, I am indeed able to talk. Though I'm never sure if what I'm thinking is coming out as articulately as I want it to, I'm able to communicate to Chuck what has been happening lately in my inner world, my dream world, and my struggles around new revelations as regards the lack of emotion and affection in my family.

"I see how I became the perfect prey for my abuser," I say.

"You were a predator's perfect target, yes, but although you were ripe for affection, it wasn't as simple as that. A predator targets his victims, and you were targeted," Chuck says.

He mentions research conducted after World War II that studied the role of affection on the mental stability of infants and young children. Referring to the work of John Bowlby and maternal deprivation theory, he tells me that infants who received little or no human contact eventually succumbed to significant developmental arrests and mental health problems, including failure to thrive.

"Well, I certainly survived. At least I had a home, food, and brothers to play with, as well as a modicum of attention from my mother, negative though it mostly was," I say. "And as the big sister in a large family I became a caregiver. I found a place for my affections and I accepted the affections of my siblings in return.

And I had my best friend. She was a most important person in my childhood. I saw her goodness, her gentleness, and her sensitivity and knew that I too had such innocent qualities inside me somewhere. I've spent my life being compassionate toward others but hard as nails on myself. I almost panicked over the weekend about all the stuff I have going on—most of it for others!"

"If you did for yourself one-quarter of what you do for others you'd do amazingly well," Chuck says. "Don't worry, you're going to be fine! You became a giver. Now you have to learn to give to yourself and take in what people give to you. Can you take in the compliments you receive?"

"Yes, I'm learning to," I say, "but do I really? I don't know. Sometimes I feel good about myself, other times not at all."

I mention the fear that I am mostly in the grips of, the fear of letting go, and the vast nothingness that I anticipate awaits me. I envision that letting go and leaping off the edge of the precipice into the abyss means entering an even darker underworld, filled with more fear, more shame, more guilt. Disgust lies down there at the bottom of the abyss too, disgust that I have needs and desires.

"I need other people, I know this, but when I see my mother turn away in disgust at shows of affection—as I've observed her doing my entire life—I know I must go elsewhere," I say. "And so I go inward. I tell myself to be sad for what I didn't get, that it's okay to be angry, and that it's okay to have needs and to want to be loved. Along with my mother's scolding voice, I must learn to push aside the shame and disgust that I always thought were proper responses to shows of affection, and teach myself how to accept what I need. I must learn to be as open and as receptive as the little girls in my dream, who rushed to greet me, expecting to be met with equally open arms."

"Yes, that's a place to start, learning to receive."

"It's actually pretty amazing," I say, struck by the wonder of it all, "this life I've lived and this recapitulation I'm doing."

"It is! It's an amazing life, and it will be even more so when you get through this process," Chuck says. "Let it in, acknowledge it, and move on. That's the stage of the process you're in now. Let the pain in and allow yourself to say, yes, I have had a very devastating life and I am in pain because of it, but if I let the feelings go through me I will get better and better. All right?"

By nine thirty at night, pain—kept at bay throughout the busy day—creeps back into my body. Blinding anal pain inches through me, and before long I'm shaky and raw with it. I practice letting go. I practice turning on the furnace of my dream, pulling the big red switch to ON, letting my inner fire produce some steam. I whisper to it as it goes through me, letting it escape, a little at a time. "I acknowledge you, pain. I know what you are and why you're here. I feel you! What will you do to me if I fully let go to you? What else is there to show me?" The pain lessens and the fires quell as I write, as I acknowledge and receive them into my body.

"*Let it be felt and then move on*," I hear, such kind and gentle words from Jeanne. I receive her words along with the pain, for there is no more fight in me; I am worn down and worn out.

June 4, 2003

I'm with two friends in a dream, helping them move their belongings out of several warehouses they own. The warehouses, scattered over several blocks of an old city, are huge metal-beamed structures, ancient and rusting, filled with all kinds of things. Stacks of boxes and tall filing cabinets burst through the roofs of the warehouses, towering high into the sky. My friends take what they want and destroy the rest. Afterwards, I wander through the debris that spews out onto the streets, destroyed as if by bombs, left in ruins. I conclude that it's the right thing to do, to take only what you need and leave the rest behind. "Look at all the shit you don't need!" I say, as I wander among the remains.

An animal rescuer approaches me with a scruffy little black dog. I try to pick him up, but he repeatedly falls from my grasp. We laugh about this, making a comment about his ability to always land on his feet. I get down on the ground and look right into his eyes. He seems so sad and lonely, about to give up on love. I pat him very gently and he gradually warms up to me. Soon I have him asleep in my arms and I know I will keep him. I know that he needs me and I decide that I need him too. "We are two beings in need of love," I say, looking at him lying in my arms. As soon as I say this, he turns into a tiny girl, and I know that she needs me. I know it's her I have to rescue from a desolate life of wandering among the warehouses of ancient times.

The first message in this dream seems to be, take only what you need, only what is of value or necessity, and leave the rest behind. Chuck mentioned World War II yesterday and I dreamed a war-like dream of destruction, but out of the devastation comes new life. The second message is that I must learn how to love myself, the little girl inside me who needs me. I must receive her, accept her and everything she brings to me. I must give her the love and affection my own mother could never give. My dream plays a little trick on me too, getting me to fall for the cute little dog, so that by the time I see the child in my arms I am melted and soft, in a loving place, my heart warmed. As soon as I say that we are two beings in need of love, the simple truth of that statement appears in the form of the child. She is the needy one, the one who has clung to the idea of someday experiencing true love herself. I can't disappoint her now; I must love her. My dream is showing me that everything I need, including that love, is inside me.

I continue to get through the days by staying busy, but even if I decide not to think about the recapitulation process, or attach to it in any way, I can't escape it completely. It's with me no matter how much I might want to curtail it. I also notice that the pain is different each day, and that each encounter brings new insights. I've noticed that sometimes when the pain takes over, the adult self is nowhere to be found. I become the frightened child, alone again, blinded by the intensity of the pain. I often don't know why it's happening or what's triggering it, and I don't always know who I am or where I am either. All I know is the pain.

I can ignore the pain and the recapitulation, but it's also important that I let them come, as they will. Staying in balance is crucial and so I'm constantly juggling the need to feel with the need to function, keeping the anxiety and the pressing recapitulation at bay until I have more time to attend to them. I try to act normal, though I have such devastation going on inside me, for in truth, I'm crying inside, weeping such buckets of sadness, shushing it, pushing it down during the day, trying to keep it from leaking out. But I know I am no better than my mother upholding her non-emotional world. In reality, I'm in the same place I've been for decades, my body—the hot water tank in my dream—the holding container for all that boils inside me. I'm constantly bothered by the impending release of the floodgates. I know I must turn on the heat more often, move the red switch to the ON position and let some of the pressure out—even if I don't want to.

All day I'm aware that I'm guarding the switch, asking my body to hold out just a little longer. The strain is apparent. By nine at night, I'm exhausted. When I brush my teeth, I see how tired I look. I know I need sleep, but I stave it off, aware that something could unleash as soon as my head hits the pillow. But so what if the floodgates open and everything pours out? I'll find a way to deal with it. I just have to remain anchored and aware of where I am and who I am, of what's happening and why it's happening.

I sit quietly breathing. I meditate for a few minutes, aware that it can only help, that the tension I feel now is present for a reason, part of this process. As I go through this period of the recapitulation, I have a feeling that I'm not dealing with specific memories anymore, but a lifetime of stored emotional energy. I'm being confronted with recognizing that the feelings I hold inside me are real and necessary, and although I see them as some sort of enigma—some ghostly concept—I am in fact facing what my body is storing, what belongs to me and my experiences. Each time I *feel* something, I'm being asked to accept the truth of my emotional devastation, to accept that I am, in fact, still devastated. On top of that, I must allow myself to be okay with the pain, knowing that it's been waiting for this time of release. I must give myself permission to feel it.

I'm challenged now to feel the fuller impact of everything that happened to me. I'm not blocking, not running, not denying anymore. I'm just trying to deal with it in increments so I don't go crazy, though I sense I'm about to go over the edge of the abyss, back into the vast nothingness, not in a dream this time, but in reality. I'm trying to be normal on the outside, maintaining my sanity in the world, while constantly trying to accept the truth of what's inside. This is where I've gotten to now, letting it in and accepting it, which is good, but it requires feeling and, frankly, I am so sick of FEELING!

June 5, 2003

I sleep deeply, the essence of a dream fading away as I awaken. But even so, part of me stays dreaming, walking in a river, up to my knees in the blue and green of it, long grasses swirling around my legs as I buoyantly wade through its watery coolness. The part of me that's waking up discovers that my legs are so leaden that I can barely move them. In contrast to my light dreaming legs, they are as heavy as plaster casts and they do not budge as I slowly push myself up to a sitting position. Hoisting them one at a time over the edge of the bed, I hear my feet hit the floor with two loud thunks, but I don't feel a thing. It's as if my legs don't even belong to me. And so the day begins.

Eager and willing though I am to complete this journey of recapitulation, I must acknowledge the pain of the process. But I also know that the pain is healing pain, pain that resolves and clarifies all other pain, makes it real, makes it factual, and then releases it. Yes, I admit, I've lived this incredible life story, and I'm still living it as I seek the truth of who I am and why I am the way I am. I know there's no stopping the process, nor will there be any stopping me. Once the intent to recapitulate was set, I was off and running and everything that has accompanied me on this journey is in alignment with that same intent. I also realize that I get to this point of hesitancy often enough, the pain bringing out my old avoidant self, but I fully intend to keep going, right over the edge of that ever-present abyss. It's the only way to achieve my highest potential—there is no other direction and no other goal. Once taken, this path of heart is undeniable, and so it becomes impossible to veer from. It has led me to the edge of this abyss where I have perched for a long time now, but I will not be staying here for much longer.

My legs, those heavy foreign objects that no longer seem to belong to me, take me to a morning yoga class. I'm the only student. My teacher introduces me to what he calls "restorative," gentle yoga, though to me it seems more like "destroy-a-tive" yoga. It involves a lot of opening up and releasing, draping over bolsters and folded blankets in—for me—very vulnerable poses. My leaden legs resist, but the poses slowly eat away at any semblance of control as I incrementally let go. "Allow for release, allow for release," my teacher says softly, encouragingly, as I drape, as I encounter the inner reluctance of my muscles, as I try to relax into each pose. The poses themselves are simple and indeed gentle resting poses, requiring little more than simply lying still, but I do not find them either gentle or restful. Even just lying in bed is painful for me. As I dare myself to acquiesce more fully, the poses respond, reaching deeper into pockets of resistance, slowly destroying my familiar body self. My lifelong issues come shrieking to the fore, protesting wildly: "How dare you ask me to do that!" And so I'm in agony as my hips and legs retaliate with their usual clenching, long ago trained to resist even the subtlest of changes. In addition, I experience a slight trigger as I lie on my back, my head pulsing with pain. I'm brought right back to my abuser, my frontal lobe pulsing a mile a minute trying to recall some memory. I'm aware of pain, of being tied up spread eagle on the ground, but I don't let it go any further; I shut it down.

"I feel like it was too much," I say, at the end of the class. "I was just begging for it to be over, almost ready to burst out of the poses, barely able to keep it together. I feel like I'm going to burst open and a putrid mess will pour out."

"Don't worry, it will come," my yoga teacher says, "it will. Give it time."

"Ha-ha, very funny," I say, but I know he's right—all in good time.

By the end of the day I'm *very* tired, physically worn out, exhausted by all the work at the gallery, the show going up, the meetings, the talking on the phone, and the worries that plagued me today. I have never felt so worn out in my life. I'm sure the deep-reaching yoga poses are part of this tiredness. I know how the suggestions fed to the subconscious mind and body during a class can make their way, slowing slipping in and taking affect without notice and then suddenly they are doing their work. There's a part of me that just wants to go to bed and sleep and cry, sleep and cry, sleep and cry—for days—just like a big baby.

June 6, 2003

I awaken abruptly, one of the cats meowing loudly in my face. Her furry snout bumps against my lips and I sit up with a jolt, wondering if I was shouting or crying out, too loud and assaultive for her skittish nerves. She jumps onto the floor. I get up and let her out of my room. Another day begins.

During the day, the owner of the yoga studio I've been attending for several years stops by to tell me she'll be closing at the end of the month. I'm sad that one of my safe places will be gone. In the meantime, I'll practice on my own, as I've done for most of my life, though I'll miss the regular practice that I've anchored so deeply in and I'll miss my fine teacher. I have to take care of myself and learn to give to myself, not only learn how to do it, but learn that it's allowed. Giving and wanting love are so basic. I'm also slowly learning that I'm allowed to have feelings, that they offer access to other human qualities and needs. I must accept that I'm human, though my experiences of being human have been far from delightful. That's why it's so important to keep going deeply into the devastation inside and acknowledge it, not only accept the truth of it, but really allow myself to understand that I have indeed been devastated by it, by the lack of affection in my upbringing and by the sexual abuse, and every other abusive situation I've landed in. The choices I'd made in order to survive as a child, and all the choices since, have gotten me to the point I'm at today, and excavating and understanding the dynamic behind them is the solution to changing how I react to and live my continuing journey.

Though I understand now that I was desperately needy as a child, I mostly recall the bubble of numbness where most of my childhood was spent, my needs dulled and untapped. I realize that I needed love and affection then and I need it now; and although those needs were rarely acknowledged, I'm learning that in order to become a full-fledged human being I must wake them up. I must learn to give to myself, but I also need to learn to accept from others. I deserve, just as every human being deserves, the experiences of being human.

We all deserve access to our authentic selves, to the expression of our highest potential, and to the release of our deepest emotions. I deserve the praise, the thanks, and the well-meaning gestures of recognition from others, so that I might discover who I truly am and access the untapped potential inside myself. I deserve the opportunity to achieve wholeness and to fully experience the greater meaning of my own life. I must accept that it's okay to be happy with my accomplishments and that it's okay to feel. All of these things make me real. So yes, it's okay to *feel*.

Feelings! I have them crammed inside me, stuffed into the corners of my being, jammed into airless passageways, clogging

325

arteries of love and acceptance. It's time to split open and RELEASE! I yearn to hold and caress all the little girls inside me—all sixteen of them—to comfort and tell them I love them. I love that little girl so full of fear. I love that little girl so full of sadness. I love that little girl so full of blame. I love that little girl so tightly bound with pain, and the shy one, the embarrassed one, the one who is so ashamed and resigned to her fate. I love the ones who are lost, rejected, broken, abandoned, in denial, stubborn, wise, angry, full of hatred and goodness too. I love them all.

"It's okay to accept love," I tell them. "In spite of what we were taught, it's okay to love ourselves, every part of us, physical, emotional, mental, and spiritual. It's equally okay to feel the pain and sadness, the devastation inside, to acknowledge it and comfort our wounded selves. It's okay to give to ourselves what we give so easily to others, to give what we clearly know everyone else needs."

I pick up my daughter after school and we drive to the nearest animal shelter to look for a kitten for her twelfth birthday. We've been feeling the need for something soft and cuddly to love, a new place to pour our feelings, or simply a new distraction perhaps. When one of the shelter volunteers tells the touching story of a pair of kittens, how their pregnant mother got locked inside the basement of an abandoned building and had her babies—most of whom died—I get all choked up. Two survived by nursing off their dead mother until they were discovered, near death themselves. Now nursed back to health, I hold these two fragile lives in my hands and begin to break down, for I identify with their story. I want to rescue both of them, but my daughter sees the bigger picture.

"Mom, we are only taking one!" she says, very firmly, and so we settle on one very fluffy gray kitten and take her home. However, I just cannot forget the other kitten, but the possibility of having two more cats in the house doesn't make sense. It's not really fair to our two old cats. And probably not fair to me either. "As much as I want to rescue that second kitten," I say, "it would be too many cats!" And I leave it at that.

It's eleven at night now. I finally give myself permission to sit and think about my FEELINGS. I've been hiding them all day, and hiding from them too, except when I reacted at the animal shelter to the plight of the kittens. Tears spontaneously filled my eyes and I wanted to weep, but I sucked them back in and held myself in tight control, though everyone could see I was affected. I notice how droplets of emotion are beginning to come through now. For so many years I've been hard, taut as steel, but now I'm softening and I want to keep going. I know I shouldn't be rescuing any kittens at this point. I should be rescuing myself; *my orphan self needs rescuing.* But it might also be good for me to have something to help mitigate the hard walls of control. A kitten might be just the thing—*one* kitten!

Each day, I wake up to a new day of inner devastation, but behind that is the energy of new growth, pushing me to hurry up and do the things I need to do, pushing me to get on with my life. Okay, I *am* getting on with it! It's like the dream of the warehouses of destruction, out of which only what has value and is absolutely necessary is taken. Every day, I sort through my own devastated warehouse, searching for what should go forward into my new life. I think it's going to be easier now; life is going to be easier. I have a new desire to look better and feel better because I have really been looking like hell! I need my beauty sleep!

June 7, 2003

I dream that I live in two places. I'm moving to a new place and yet I'm still living in an old place. The new place is in the country, beautifully calm and peaceful, green and happy. The old place is an apartment in a desolate city, recently destroyed by war. I keep going back to the old apartment to get things, clearing out, checking the mail and packing things up during each trip. On one trip to the old place, I rescue a tiny kitten-sized baby girl. She's covered with scabs and crusty dirt. I try to give her a bath, but the sink is filthy and only dirty water comes out of the faucet. Carrying the tiny baby, I make my way back down the broken and cluttered stairs. I go outside to where my son sits waiting for me in my car. I leave the baby with him and tell him that I'm not finished yet, that I have to go back upstairs and finish the work there. I notice that an attempt is being made to renovate the building. Young people are beginning to move in and fix it up and there's a new café downstairs. I pass a pregnant woman on the stairs. Upstairs, in my old apartment, I am suddenly overcome by feelings of deep sadness. I decide it's best to come back another time, when I can handle it better. I rush for the door, intent upon leaving before the sadness overwhelms me. I cannot get out of the building fast enough. All I want to do is get back to the baby; she needs me.

It's a gray and rainy Saturday morning. I sleep late, until around eight thirty. As usual, I'd rather lie in and let the day go by, but I have things to do. I commend my daughter for the good job she's doing with her kitten. She understands that it will take some work and attention to keep the kitty both safe and happy. As I do the weekend chores I notice that I don't feel so dead anymore. I'm still sad, but definitely not dead. I ran from my emotions in my dream—I couldn't get away from them fast enough—but now that I'm awake they slowly actualize, seeping into the light of day. I don't resist them this time. Even when I'm out in the world running errands, I let them come. I'm in the midst of releasing to them when I run into my yoga teacher. He asks if I ever came down from the effects of the "destroy-a-tive" yoga the other day.

"Yes, I did," I say. "I had so much to do that I had to land."

"Lots in there," he says.

"Yes, I know," I say, but I can't tell him about it, not yet, but sometime—maybe.

Right now there is only Chuck. It's taken such a long time but I've finally found the right guide. I realize, however, that it was impossible before this; I just haven't been ready until now. I also realize my ex-husband's greatest deed as my partner, besides giving me the most amazing children in the world, was to bring me to Chuck Ketchel. He didn't know that when he made an appointment for us to do marriage counseling with Chuck that he was really giving me another child, my inner child, delivering me to my own birthing process. I thank him for that. Since then, Chuck has guided me to this place where I am now: no longer dead. I AM NOT DEAD!

This recapitulation journey is clearly spelled out in last night's dream. The past is desolate and uninviting, though there are signs of change, just as there are inside myself as I do this recapitulation. And my dream is clearly telling me that I'm halfway to new life, still between worlds, but moving fluidly back and forth, collecting what has value, preparing to bring it forward with me into that new life. This shows good progress. Eventually, I won't have to go back at all, because this recapitulation will be done and my inner world will be at peace.

I am like that old building, both devastated and being cleared out while also being repaired and made ready for new life. The new work being done in my psyche and body is changing everything about me, creating a whole new organism. All of this has been represented in my dreams, especially over the past few months. The tidal waves have come and washed away the old. New parameters are being set, new perspectives are forming, and new strong structures are being established, all in intricate alignment, claimed as the inner foundations of a new evolving self. As this dream points out, the beauty and calmness of a peaceful green countryside are now present, supplanting the old land of turmoil. A woman in the dream is pregnant, but at the same time a child has already been born: I am both pregnant and nursing, preparing for new life while deeply involved in nurturing that which already is. And that's pretty much what my life feels like right now!

My main intent, as in the dream, remains the rescuing of the innocent self from the traumatic past—just as I've rescued my daughter's little kitten. I must take that innocence forward with me into the new greener environment of my future. As I dreamed, it became clear that, eventually, remnants of the abuse would no longer greet me when I went back into my inner world. At some point, the recapitulation will be complete and my inner world will be a different place altogether. Then I'll experience only the newly constructed self. I won't be triggered by memories of what used to be, for none of the trauma will remain, all will have been resolved. This is what a shamanic recapitulation is all about! My dream is showing me the process, exactly what Chuck has been hinting at for years. I just haven't quite been able to fathom what it would mean to be done with the past, for it has always felt so present. Inside me it's still alive and kicking, and I can't imagine not being affected by it. Now, however, I understand that one day it will have a different quality.

I also understand now what Chuck means when he tells me that one day I'll "perceive differently," that I'll see and experience life from a different perspective. I've had glimpses of what that new perspective might be like, but even so, I have no idea just how that shift in perception will happen or indeed what the world will look like. How it unfolds and just what greater perspective I'll gain is a mystery. I see, however, the eventuality of it in this dream, which is not just a dream but my unconscious alerting me more fully to this most amazing process. I feel the changes in my body now too. I have skin that I can feel. I have real feelings and emotions. I have desires. I am no longer dead and unfeeling. I can feel! I can feel! I can feel! I feel a melting, an unclenching, a loosening, a softening taking place. All those terms mean that I'm slowly but surely unfreezing. I'm coming alive, indeed changing. The recapitulation process is working!

In the evening, I go to the gallery opening of the show I've worked so hard on. It's nicely attended. I feel looser and more present than normal. I'm able to move around and talk. It seems the recapitulation and yoga are both working well, doing their destroy-a-tive work. The show looks good. In spite of all the problems with reticent artists I've done a good curating job. I receive a lot of nice comments on my own artwork too. I've used photos of my naked body in collages, incorporating ink and paint.

I'm introduced to an older man in poor health, spiffed up for the occasion, eager to meet me. He stands with his arm around the woman who invited him, hugging her to him, being protectively embraced by her and simultaneously possessive of her it seems. It's clear that he's uncomfortable; not his usual scene, I gather. He stares at my boobs the entire time he's talking to me. As if he's speaking directly to them, he makes a comment about how he still has the postcard from an earlier show tacked to his fridge, the one where I'd painted a self-portrait of my naked upper body. He's so intent on looking at my boobs that if no one else were there, I'm sure he would ask if he could see and touch them.

"I am so glad to meet *you*," he says, very earnestly, pointedly staring at my small perky breasts one last time before he leaves. And I just can't help myself, but I burst out laughing. I find it strange what men will say to women, that they feel they have a right to comment about our bodies, that it's okay. I'm not angry— not at all. In fact, I continue laughing because everything I hear after that strikes my funny bone. "You are one crazy lady!" a woman says to me, as I stand there laughing even harder, unable to stop myself.

"Great body!" another woman says, while looking at my artwork, and I find this comment, coming from a woman, as hilarious as the one I'd gotten from the man.

"She has a great body. Why not use it in her artwork?" someone else says. Touched and humored by all of this interest in my body, I am indeed grinning like a crazy lady, because even though I'm standing right next to these people, listening to them talk about me, it's as if I'm not even present. Now my body is a piece of artwork and I, the real thing, am invisible.

I turn to pondering just why I'm using my own body. The only thing that comes to me is that I'm in the process of reclaiming it, making a bold statement: I have this body; it's mine to use in my own way. It's not sinful or disgusting or dirty; it's beautiful! There's only 102 pounds worth of me and by working with my image in a small hand-sized format I'm making a statement to myself as much as anyone. I can finally take in the whole of me. I can literally hold myself in the palm of my hand, step back, and say: *That* is who I am," because for the longest time I had no idea who I was. But now I see, in this world, I am *that*.

June 8, 2003

I dream that I'm with Chuck, sitting in his office. "I'll be right back," he says, and he gets up and walks away. I sit and wait for him to return to the little cottage where we meet. At first, I assume he just stepped out to use the bathroom, but after a while I become anxious. I start searching for him. I wander all through his house, which is adjacent to the cottage, but I can't find him anywhere. In a room in the attic, I find huge pastel drawings and photos of bridges laid out on an architect's table. I wonder if he's designing bridges, or writing about them, or putting together an exhibit, because there are so many pictures. I soon realize that he's just not coming back. Feeling totally abandoned, I go back to his office where I discover another man sitting in his chair. He invites me to sit down and have a talk. He seems to know who I am, but I can't talk to him. Instead, I run out of the office and down a path into the woods. The only thing I can think to do is find a place to hide. Going back in time, I pass an old barn. Then I take another path that runs alongside a stream. I go so far back in time that I reach the old days, the days of my abuser, until I am a four-year-old child again, back in his woods. I crawl under a bush and curl up into a fetal position, lost in the old sadness and loneliness. No one can see me. I decide to stay under this bush and die.

Whenever I think of Chuck getting up and walking away like he did in that dream, I am overcome with frustration, pain, and anger. I fear that if I lose contact with him I *will* regress, that I will curl up and die under a bush back in the dark past and never complete my recapitulation. But I realize it's a dream and not to be taken literally. I have to figure out what it's trying to tell me. Am I too dependent on Chuck? Will he not always be available? Will I have to go on without his support? During most of the dream I was looking for him and that was okay because I assumed he was around somewhere, but the longer I searched the more anxious I became until I realized he wasn't coming back at all. Am I going to be disappointed by Chuck in some way?

I think the dream is anticipating change, and that although we are busy building a bridge, connecting my past self with my future self, life does go on. There is, however, still a lot of work to do. The drawings on his desk are unfinished, only partially colored in, but they don't seem to be abandoned. My bridge, a beautiful suspension bridge lies on top of the heap, painted all the colors of the rainbow. I recognize it immediately as the structure that my own recapitulation process has taken. As I ponder the dream, I fear that the greater trust I place in Chuck won't last, that he *is* going to disappoint me in some way, and then I'll have to face the rest of this bridge building process alone.

Full trust is still hard for me to come by, as there is so much disappointment in trust. That's what the girls in my dream where asking me to work on when they ran up to me with open arms, but to embrace a belief that someone truly cares about me is still quite foreign. However, do I really think, at this point, that I'd once again feel those old feelings so intensely, or that I'd actually choose death? I don't think so, but I do feel that I'm teetering on a narrow precipice again, and that, yes, there is always the possibility that I could fall either way. But if I fell back into the dark past I don't think I would stay there. I'd eventually re-emerge and keep going on my own, but would I ever trust another person again?

I also realize that I have a transference with Chuck, and I think that's really what this dream is asking me to face. I have asked him to be the adult my child self never had in her life, to always be there, to unconditionally love me, to receive me without judgment, and to never disappoint. And he has not failed me in these respects. So why did I have this dream? It still feels like a premonition and as I go deeper and deeper into the feelings of my child self, she warns me that she *expects* to be disappointed; it's par for the course. She still fears rejection, she tells me. So okay, I can acknowledge that even my adult self fears rejection. At the deepest level, I'm still afraid to reach deeply toward another human being—Chuck in this case—and fully trust that his intentions are pure, that his words and actions are truthful. Learning to fully trust and being able to confide my deepest feelings to this man I meet with each week, continue to be the most difficult steps in this recapitulation process—still fear inducing. I realize this may mean that I'm approaching a difficult part of the recapitulation process, as I arrive at the point where I must let my child self spill out her sorrow and allow the adult self to fully feel it, to not only take it in and be okay with it, but to unconditionally love that child self as well. I must be my own Chuck now.

He has shown me how a compassionate adult thinks and acts, how a loving person responds to deep pain, and how a feeling person responds to the needs of another. I know I have these same qualities inside myself, for they have been active for others my entire life but disconnected from my own needs. And so I must take back the transference. I must learn how to nurture and love myself, both my child self and my adult self. As I become the parent for my inner child self, I must become as trustworthy as I expect Chuck to be. It's the only way that my injured soul will be granted the freedom to fully grieve, for that's what this is really about, freeing myself from the old scolding voice so that I can accept my past and mourn its truths. I also understand that this transference is an essential part of the therapeutic process, and that it's to be expected. Until the loving adult that I have projected onto Chuck is brought home, I must not judge myself, but continue to offer my inner child safe and sacred space to experience all that she needs. If I am to fully heal, the child's needs must not be judged or dismissed, or the adult's either for that matter. That would really be disappointing!

I can flippantly enjoy the evenings at the gallery openings now, actually have fun because they don't have any meaning for me. It's the stuff that has meaning and significance that's hard to handle. The untangling of all the mysteries, dealing with the deeply embedded fears, and becoming a real person—now that's hard! Deep inside me the fears rage like hurricanes, fiercely whipping up storm after storm that knock me down as often as they pick me up and carry me along. Those fears are so deeply ingrained and, as of yet, unresolved. Although I still don't feel that I'm totally safe anywhere in the world, I'm certainly working on it!

June 9, 2003

I dream that I'm living in a barn with another woman and two men. I've been kept in this barn against my will for a long time. The other woman and I had recently asked for help in getting out. We had put in an application to "file for freedom" with Social Services. Our request has been granted and I'm aware that I can leave at anytime; I am no longer a prisoner. I'm ready to take advantage of the opportunity to free myself, to leave my life of bondage and go out into the world. The other woman doesn't understand the meaning of the papers we filed with Social Services. "It means we're free," I say, "and it also means we get assistance to help us get away." I tell her I'm going out by myself, that after all these years of being a prisoner I can finally go outside. "The door is right there, where it's always been, but I just had to see it," I say. "Don't you see it too?" I'm half-dressed and pregnant, full term pregnant, and I'm barefoot, but I'm going out for a run, a freedom run. I go outside. There's a cold drizzle and snow on the ground, but I run through the complex of dreary barn structures anyway. Sad people look at me from the windows, yelling that I'm crazy, that I'll get caught, that I'll be killed. "No," I say to them, "no, I'm protected. It's okay now." I know that I do have protection, and besides, it doesn't matter if I'm killed, what matters is being free.

I see a pair of small diamond earrings on a windowsill. I recognize them as my own and remember having left them there a very long time ago. I hear the two men back in the barn talking about raping me when I get back, to show me where I belong; then they'll kill me, they say. Now I don't feel particularly free. Paranoia sets in and I sense that I'm being followed, every move watched. I'm worried about the other woman back in the barn, the baby I'm carrying inside me, and the threats made by the men. I lose my energy; I can't run anymore. I decide I must go back into the barn, but I stop to pick up the earrings on the way. A man from Social Services comes up to me and tells me that I don't have to go back. "I know you understand what I'm telling you," he says. "You're an intelligent woman. You know you don't have to stay here. I can help you find a new place."

As much as he begs me to leave, I ignore his pleas and go back into the barn, but I've seen enough of the outside world to know that I will eventually leave for good. Upon my return, the two men attack me. Afterwards, worn down, beaten and injured, I know I'll have to wait until they're asleep before I can leave again. The other woman is upset about Social Services being involved, about my having spilled the beans to them about everything that's been going on in the barn all these years. She's embarrassed and ashamed. She now feels not only trapped but also mortified. I tell her again that we're free now. Although I'm shaking with fear and still feeling a little paranoid, I know that I can and will, in time, escape. And it will be good.

"See? I went out and I was okay. They only got me because I came back, but it's possible to get out," I tell her, "and next time I'm taking you with me. We'll never return, and it *will* be okay."

I'm holding on until I meet with Chuck tomorrow. This physical letting go is as painful and frightening as facing the memories for the first time and I feel unraveled and unsafe. I think that's why I went back into the barn in my dream. Freedom feels like too much to handle. With no boundaries or limitations, and no defined rules, anything could happen. My dream is also suggesting that there's still unfinished business back in the barn too. The other woman, an obvious reference to another side of myself, presents some of the deeper issues of shame and self-loathing that I still struggle with. At the same time that I move forward, I must still go back to resolve all issues. I note also the earrings, the jewels I picked up. My foray into freedom may have been short-lived, but I took back something of personal value long ago left behind, some of my own energy. I wonder if feeling safe is really the big issue here. No, I don't think it is. Fear of rejection is, but rejection by whom? Chuck?

June 10, 2003

I wake up with a start, popping right out of a dream as the alarm goes off. The little kitten is up and perky, little bird voice, little body hop-hop-hopping, cute and sparrow-like. She explores my bedroom while the big cats, looking bigger than ever, roam the hallway and guard the door. I watch how innocently and fearlessly the kitten investigates her surroundings, and how the big cats move out of her way to let her pass. I'm aware that my own process of exploration and letting go is tainted, that it has a bitter and angry feel to it. I am not innocent or fearless enough yet. I lie in bed and notice how tightly I clench, as physically uncomfortable as if I'm about to give birth, the pain of labor intense as old feelings and beliefs wait to push through. My body shows me that first I must purge myself of all the old misconceptions, the old scolding voices and the dangerous beliefs perpetrated upon me before the new innocent and fearless self will emerge. In this laboring, in painful release, I must physically let them go.

When I meet with Chuck we talk about my dreams. He remarks that I have incredible defenses, that my ability to hold on is amazing, making this sound like a fine asset, which I understand it really is, but at the same time I know he's pointing out where the problem lies. Still exceedingly uncomfortable, I try to explain what I *think* I'm feeling. I understand that fear of rejection lies at my core, but I'm so drawn to protect myself that even the experience of freedom isn't quite enough to draw me out, not yet anyway. The known, as bad as it is, is still so predictable and thus safe. It's the unknown that opens the door to fears of rejection, as I face the total unpredictability of new life. And even though I know that freedom means the possibility of positive experiences, I'm too scared to make the leap. When the session is over, I leave slightly frustrated. For the time being I'm still in the metaphorical barn, for that's how it feels, both my past and present worlds strangely real and strangely unreal at the same time.

I spend the day clearing out and packing up the last of my belongings at the old studio. As if to underscore where I am in my recapitulation, I find the work draining and unproductive, the old world letting me know that it's no longer energetically invigorating.

I leave the boxes and piles of art related stuff stacked by the door, ready to be taken downstairs, then pick up the kids from school. My intention is to take a short break, have dinner, and go back to the studio while the kids do homework because something inside me is intent on movement, even though I can barely move my heavy-with-depression body. Instead of returning to the studio, however, I put it to work. I mow the lawn, weed the garden, and sweep the garage out. By ten at night I finally slow down and call it quits. Stopping before this was not an option, for I was driven to keep moving, though exhaustion dogged me all day, at my heels like a faithful pet.

Before bed, I do some yoga. A memory stirs, tugging at my emotions, stirring them too. I sense that a breakdown is imminent. A slow wearing down has been taking place. At some point there will be no resistance left and then I anticipate falling apart, shattering deep into my core. When? I don't even want to think about it. Only thoughts of sleep allowed now. And so, quite exhausted, I head to bed.

June 11, 2003

All day I teeter on the edge of the abyss, feeling the urge to just fall into it. I give myself permission to let go—if I really have to—to just release to the oblivion that I know will take away my misery. I just have to want it badly enough. Fear enters the struggle and freedom does too. I know that if I don't volitionally take the leap, I'll be cast into it unawares, and then what? My head aches with the stress of the tussle and my allergies bother me, affecting my face and eyes so that I can't see clearly, compounding an already stressful stage. I'm so tired, so distraught. I *want* to let go...

June 12, 2003

I need some kind of new security, but I can't find any. Don't I need something to hold onto? As I envision letting go, giving up control of that so-dependable old self, only visions of nothingness loom before me, no security and no self whatsoever. Chuck says that I've built up a reputation as being always available for everyone else and that's how people see me, as able to handle everything, and so they automatically turn to me, but I need to change that perception now. Okay! I set the intent to begin that change, because I really am on the verge of mental and emotional breakdown.

As I head to the studio, I decide I won't take on any more tasks at the artist's gallery for at least the rest of the year and I immediately act on this solemn promise. Before fear can set back in, I call up the members of the steering committee and tell them that I'm overwhelmed and will be backing down from my many posts over the next few months. My decision is totally understood and accepted, and I immediately experience the sheer relief of burdens released. I feel like my daughter's little kitten, fearlessly strolling right past the big cats, my big fluffy tail just out of their reach as I skitter happily away.

I get some things accomplished at the studio and even delegate some work to my studio partner, asking her to be responsible for certain things that need doing, and she gets right on it. I almost have to laugh because it's actually easier than I thought. Normally I would have just buckled down and done everything myself, not even thinking to ask for help, feeling like I had to do it all, but I would have been fuming with resentment as well. If only I had known how easy it was to ask, if only I had dared to face rejection before! Now I realize that if I could just let go of all the stuff I'm holding *inside* me as well—all the needless tasks I give myself, all the old rules I uphold, all the old voices I replay—my inner world would be so much better off too!

It's apparent that I'm being guided to resolution, shown what it might feel like to have inner peace as well, for I am squarely met with compassion and gentleness as I "let go" of things in this world. As I prepare to take the leap and let go in that inner world, I realize I must make the process easier—I must stop fighting it. In my fear of falling, I've decided that I need something to grab onto, a lifeline, but in actuality I just need to experience the fall.

June 13, 2003

"I'm fine!" I say when I sit down in front of Chuck, but then I say, "No, I'm not fine!"

I put the EMDR headphones on and go back into the past. Curling into a ball, I retreat into emotions and feelings, going deep into a recapitulation experience. I have a tremendous headache. I can only breathe as much as it allows, until my breath bumps into the pain in my head, blocked from going any further. I can't feel my legs, or anything below my diaphragm for that matter, but I make myself go down there, into what hides there, though the experience is extremely intense. Part of me wants to dissociate, but I force myself to stay present.

"I don't really want to be here," I tell Chuck, suddenly sitting up and jolting out of the memory.

"When you're ready, go back," he suggests, "see if you can get clarity."

Like a good pupil, I do as my teacher requests and plunge back in. Whatever the experience is, it sits in my body taking up space. Though it was recorded long ago, it's still largely unknown. Accessing it is nearly impossible, as all my defenses immediately rush in to protect me. I'm fully aware that if I don't get to the truth of the experience it will stay inside me, forever blocking, forever keeping all the parts of myself in this fragmented, disconnected state. The emotional must be connected with the physical, and although they've never been anywhere near each other inside this body of mine, I'm aware that they're supposed to be. It's a slow process of connecting circuits that have never been used, never evolved from their infantile states, never been nurtured, and so getting them open and in good working order offers a new challenge, as well as the solution to finishing this recapitulation. I leave the session with this insight, though no deeper resolution.

I spend most of the day on writing assignments and straightening the new studio, occasionally dipping back into the morning's recapitulation experience. Though I remain in a slightly dissociated state, I notice that the intensity of sadness and the pressure of my defenses lessen as the day goes on. Something is opening; *I'm opening*. I realize how utterly tired I am of people wanting things from me, how tired I am of giving away so much of myself. I'm tired of my abuser's old energy still sucking the life out of me too. I begin to feel a new kind of withdrawal taking place, an energetic withdrawal, a new kind of protection slowly wrapping around the self who'd been abused, the self who felt she was only there for others to use. I want my energy to be there for me now, and so I consciously set the intent to refuse pressure from the outside. I will not be pressured to give away my energy. The test comes immediately. I am called upon to give.

"Call someone else," I say, letting myself react in support of this new protective energy. I get to say it many times throughout the day, as the phone keeps ringing. "Call someone else."

My daughter has friends over for a birthday celebration and with the sounds of happy young girls echoing throughout the house, I realize that I'm okay. Two years after this journey began I can say, with a modicum of amazed delight, that I survived the past and I'll continue to survive. I will even get beyond mere survival, but first I will fully discover and accept just what it is that I have indeed survived.

June 14, 2003

I stare at a wall of photographs in a dream, photos of myself as a teenager with my family. When I look closely, I realize the pictures don't portray the truth. I know I'm looking at the past as it was portrayed, but it's utterly clear to me that things weren't at all as I thought they were, nor were they ever truthfully presented. The deception was insidious.

I wake in great pain, my legs caught in a tight cramp, a headache sweeping in. I'm aware that the pain might go away if I move, but the weight of it keeps me still for a while longer. I lie in bed wondering how I got here again, back in the midst of what feels like an old place. It's like that dream where I was set free from my life of bondage by Social Services and yet for some reason felt like I had to go back. Why am I still here when I know I can be free? It all got started again yesterday when I tried to figure out what was still bothering me and of course I found pain. It's just the stage I have to go through now, recovering the physical pain. Oh God, how will I get through the day!

Well, I did get through the day, a quiet lonely day, but I think I needed it to be that way. I cried tonight. I couldn't help it.

June 15, 2003

The kids are with their dad for Father's Day and I head out for a quick visit to see my own father. I start crying on the long drive for no reason that I can come up with, but I let myself. Just a release of emotions, I decide. I arrive at my parent's house feeling the depths of my sadness, the truth of my past coming to greet me in this place not far from where it all happened. I'm aware that I must be mindful to take care of myself today so that negative energy does not slip in.

I greet my parents and immediately feel bitterness slipping in alongside the fake self who automatically appears to play the happy and entertaining daughter my father expects. Suddenly I feel exhausted. I just cannot play the old meaningless game today. Making an excuse to go outside and into the sunlight, I ask for some plantings from their overgrown gardens. I dig up some flowering shrubs and then make small talk for about an hour before heading back home.

I plant the bushes as soon as I get home and then do little else for the rest of the day. Even so, by the end of the evening I'm emotionally exhausted, the beginnings of panic rolling up out of the pit of my stomach as soon as I think about having to hold on until I meet with Chuck again on Tuesday.

What is wrong with me?

June 16, 2003

I crack open a new journal. I can't help but wonder who I will be when this one is filled. Each new journal seems to invite new energy and change, as I've discovered an old self I barely knew existed and experienced the unfolding of a new self, equally mysterious. It's five in the morning and already I feel low. So the first question I pose to myself in this new journal is: *Why do I hate myself so much?*

Even though my abuser preyed upon me, injuring me deeply, it doesn't mean that I have to hurt myself as well. I don't have to punish myself. In fact, I don't have to be punished at all! Truthfully, I'm really bored with always being so pathetically sad, tired of holding everything inside. It's making me sick, poisoning me, but the other truth is that I *do* hate myself for what I did and I feel that I *must* be punished. None of this will simply go away, no matter how many times I tell myself that it wasn't my fault. I was there too; I did it too. I was made to feel stupid, to feel that I wanted it, made to feel that it *was* my fault. There's a part of me that still doesn't want to acknowledge and deal with this truth. I think it's the little girl self.

We're fighting. The little girl self reacts so fiercely to the truths my adult self brings to her attention. Anxiety and fear arise each time I ask her to listen to me and her usual response is to dissociate. I feel her rejection of the new ideas I present. Each time I ask her to confront the pain, to just go through it, she automatically blocks it out and leaves me to deal with it. That's what it feels like, as if we're caught in this ancient dynamic where she dissociates and I'm left to bear the pain. I know I told her I could handle this, but it also feels like this child self doesn't want to let go, that she's actually choosing to return to the dissociative state rather than gain clarity and resolution. But *I* want to know what really happened. I want to get it over with so I can move on, but I can't while this child self is so resistant. And I don't know if I, the adult, can fully access the experiences and go through them if she's going to fight me and flat out reject all that I bring to light. Her old misconceptions about what really happened and that she is to blame are proving harder to dismantle than I thought. And so, I sense that a conversation is in order. It's my assumption that she's not wholeheartedly accepting of this journey of healing.

"Aren't you tired of fighting? Why won't you let go?" I ask. "All you have to do is let go and it will be over. The pain can pass through me, the adult. I can stand it. You've already fought for so long. Let me take over now, little girl; let me feel the pain of the experiences. Let me be the one to get us through this last difficult birth. You can trust me. I'm not going to let anything bad happen to us ever again. I promise that all the good stuff that has been happening lately will keep happening because we're ready for it now, but first we have to keep releasing the old stuff, making room for more good stuff. I'm ready. You know I am."

"Your final job," I tell her, "after keeping us safe all these years, is to let me take over. This adult that I've grown into is as strong as you are. You taught me to be strong. I can get us through the rest of this so we don't have to suffer anymore. We don't have to live like this. We *can* let go. I know we're both afraid there won't be anything to grab onto, but we don't really need anything because everything is waiting to *receive* us. Life is waiting for us."

June 17, 2003

I dream of being in an old worn out city, wading through waist-high, murky floodwaters. The city is overrun with ocelots, many spotted panther-like creatures. They're everywhere, climbing in and out of houses and apartment windows, swimming past me in the water. As I look for things to float on, I wonder how I'll ever get out of the flood. Except for the small ocelots, I'm alone; the city appears deserted. Even though I'm caught in the floodwaters, I'm aware that I have a place to go. I envision an apartment, on a high floor in a tall building. I know I just have to get there and then I'll be safe. I don't really care anymore what others think about me, or my past. "It wasn't my fault, it wasn't my fault, it wasn't my fault," I tell myself, as I trudge through the rising muddy waters.

Suddenly it starts to snow and I hear a voice announcing that the weather is shifting, that it's going to get increasingly worse. Now a blizzard is expected. "If you don't have anything important to do, please stay at home!" the announcer says. All of a sudden the city is overrun with people frantically trying to get out before the snow gets worse. The rising floodwaters hamper the evacuation; the situation is dire. I finally get to my own apartment, the one I had envisioned, high in a building. It's overrun with ocelots, also seeking higher ground, but that doesn't bother me in the least. In spite of the ocelots, I'm going to stay put. I think about my kids and although I miss them a lot, I know they're safe. I call them and tell them to stay where they are, and then I calmly settle in with the ocelots to wait for the storms to pass.

As I go through this time of imminent rebirth, I know I must also go through the final stages of a real birthing process, everything from painful labor contractions to the flush of fetal waters as I birth not only my child self into new life, but my adult self as well. My insights are keen in this dream; I have the clear sense that I do have a place to wait out the storms, high above the turmoil of it all. The ocelots are a little puzzling, but I see them as kitten-like animals and I have no fear of them. In fact, I feel quite good in their company. Perhaps they represent my child self, letting me know that my conversation with her yesterday had an affect and that she's really with me on this journey, no longer fighting but letting me know she's right by my side. In spite of the storms and the sense of impending disaster, I remain very calm throughout the entire dream. It's as if the adult self that spoke to the child really is that insightful. I'm interested in getting to know her better, but first this stormy turmoil must pass!

When I meet with Chuck, he says that in the old days, in a dream like that, I would have been focused on the kids, which is true. I would have gone on an epic journey until I'd rescued them, but now I want to be safe myself. The focus has shifted away from others and this shows significant progress. As Chuck sees it, the dream is mythological in scope, a Noah's ark dream bringing cleansing waters, with the animals seeking refuge in my apartment, knowing they will be safe with me, the adult.

As soon as Chuck mentions the word mythological, I recall the Dionysian question that arose at the very beginning of my recapitulation, as we tried to figure out what had happened to me as a child. My earliest memories with my strange little friend, my abuser's daughter, contained more than a hint of the unleashing of Dionysian archetypal energy. In researching the myth of Dionysus, we discover that he had to endure many years of great suffering at the hands of others before taking his place among the gods. In one myth he was ordered, by his father Zeus's jealous wife Hera, to be torn limb from limb as a child, then boiled and also eaten. His blood spilled to the ground in another myth, where it grew and flowered, bearing fruit—the pomegranate—a profusion of seeds offering possibilities of regeneration and rebirth. In another version, it's said that he descended into the underworld to search for his true mother, a hint at the necessity of a deep inner journey like recapitulation to achieve wholeness. As in all heroic journeys, his trials and lessons, though numerous and deeply challenging, offered him the transformative material to attain his divinity. This is what I seek as I take my own heroic journey through this recapitulation, perhaps not divinity per se, but a transformation of my fragmented fearful self into a woman of the world, wholly united and fully present.

I know I have suffered no more or less than others, but I do acknowledge that I have been greatly compromised. As I come out of the fog of my past, as I break through old feelings of inadequacy and self-loathing, I feel myself coming alive. As I shed the old self, I discover that I do wish to live fully and actively in this life. For the first time in my life I can really breathe with a sense of ease, and I sense that one day I will be at peace. Now I understand more completely what it means to take my life into my own hands, to take full responsibility for myself and for this life, the past as well as the future. It's what I do with my suffering that matters. Do I let it overpower me right to the grave, or do I tackle it head on and give myself the opportunity to really live? There's always time to live!

As Chuck and I talk of myths and heroic journeys, I feel certain that I will indeed successfully complete my own heroic journey. I will ride this recapitulation to its very end. I will reclaim my own energy, in the shamanic sense that Chuck has hinted at so many times. I will take back my own power from the darkness within myself, from my own underworld.

I'm not really surprised to learn that Dionysus is often portrayed driving a chariot powered by panthers. This reminds me that I dreamed of panthers last month as well, wreaking havoc, destroying the contents of a house, appearing as frightening wild animals before turning into docile kittens. I see this now as another indication that my dreaming self is fully and actively involved in this recapitulation. The panthers in that dream represent Dionysus entering the underworld, as they tear apart the untruths stored inside a body no longer capable of housing an old self. The job done, the panthers walk away in calmness, their true natures revealed as both fierce warriors and gentle beings, mere innocent kittens at their cores. I too hope to walk away from this recapitulation in calmness one day, brought into new life by this deeply transformative journey, my warrior self fully acknowledged and my innocence fully accepted, polar opposites finally reconciled and instilled in my being as the deepest truths of who I am.

I finalize my session with Chuck by setting the intent to take this recapitulation to the next level, into *conscious relaxation*, for that is what feels necessary. In order to release whatever still hides in my body, I must initiate a process of softening from warrior to kitten. I begin immediately, consciously unclenching in increments throughout the day, reminding myself to relax each time I feel tension creeping into my body. My focus is now on taking this mythic recapitulation journey to the ultimate end, to total transformation—in full awareness!

June 18, 2003

I had some success yesterday with relaxing and releasing. Last night, however, I was so tired that I went to bed at nine. As I lay there exhausted, I clearly understood that I've been feeling the rising tide of many emotions for a long time. Those emotions have become almost too much to bear. Like my poor child self I've resorted to what I've always done; I've clamped down and held them back. Now, however, I'm interested in a different approach. I *want* to change. So for today, I set the intent to do as many chest opening yoga poses as possible, to keep opening and releasing. And I intend to use my breath to help me change more fully now. I've already experienced the transformative power of the breath, both in the recapitulation sweeping breath as well as in all the yoga breathing I do. I actually *feel* change happening inside my body each time I breathe now.

As always, life continues on schedule; and so I have to get up and get the kids to school and then get to work. Even if I have critical issues to deal with, life is not about to stop. If I am to be fully present and involved, I must remain responsible, attentive, and disciplined, even while I must also flow with what comes. I resolve to be aware and to release throughout the day; to be conscious of how my body chooses to react to what comes from without and to what comes from within. It's pretty clear that I'll never be able to function or work at full capacity if I don't get beyond these physical and emotional blockages. One of these days I'd really like to be a happy, functioning individual, totally relaxed and at ease in my body. Wouldn't that be nice!

The day is busy and for the most part I remain conscious of how I hold myself, how I'm naturally tense and tight. It's habitual; just me being the old me. Chuck constantly alerts me to this when I'm in sessions with him, telling me over and over again to relax my shoulders. I guess I never thought it was noticeable before, but now I'm struck at how obvious my adopted shoulder position is, tightly raised and alert, always ready to take off running at a moment's notice. As soon as I consciously relax, I'm aware of tension seeping out, but then immediately creeping back in as I feel my shoulders rise back up to my ears, hunching protectively all over again. It's always been difficult for me to stand upright, as my usual stance is one of cowering fear. Now I have to be alert to my body every minute of the day if I am to break through that damned habit! It seems nearly impossible, but—as with all habits—I know that if I keep challenging myself, I should eventually succeed in breaking through. All day long I hear Chuck saying: "Relax your shoulders. Relax your shoulders. Relax your shoulders."

It's night now as I lie on my back in bed. Breathing into my third chakra, I wait to feel the first real breaking up of tension. I feel my solar plexus incrementally grow soft and expansive, gently releasing. Moving my breathing attention up into my heart chakra, I experience my chest opening wider. My shoulders, like two wings, begin to unfurl. I make a mental note to just keep breathing into the painful areas of my body as I go through this difficult stage, no matter how tiresome or torturous it becomes. As soon as I stop the focused breathing, the old curling mechanism tries to reassert itself, inviting me into its cozy circle of warmth and safety. I reject its tug, countering with a full body stretch, pushing my chest outward, throwing my shoulders back, releasing myself from the grip of the old pull as much as I can. I must be watchful of the old self's attempts to sneak back in, even as I drift off to sleep. It's tugging at me to stay the same, to revert to the old habits, constantly returning to tempt me back, because that's how it operates. Its tactics are pretty predictable at this point and so I know I must stay alert, be trickier than it is, adept at stepping aside—for as much as a part of me would still like to curl up and fall asleep like a child, I know it won't help. What once was a means of survival now feels like death closing in on me, but I'm not interested in death—I resist it wholeheartedly!

I intend to stay on my back through the night. It's time to attack this thing directly, even when unconscious.

June 19, 2003

I'm inside a derelict old house in a dream, the milieu as dark as the shadowy hues of a Rembrandt painting. A friendly man accompanies me as I walk through the house. He reminds me of the man from Social Services in a previous dream and, like that man, he too insists that I leave at once. I know I should leave the derelict old house, and that I can, that I'm free to go at any time. There really is nothing here for me; my kids and cats are already gone. What am I waiting for; why do I need to stay?

Another man comes in and pursues me with a movie camera. He's intent on reviving old tortures that I had once been involved in; he wants all of my memories on film. His intent is predatory, for he wants to steal my memories for his own use. I throw him out, but I'm afraid he'll come back and take all the food from the house and lock me out. And so I go into the kitchen and begin gathering food, so that when he comes back and locks me out I'll be able to survive.

The friendly man follows me around the house. "You don't need to be here; no one needs you anymore," he says. But I have a reason for staying; there's something I must attend to. There was a baby girl once, so small and weak, but she died. As soon as I remember this, the dead infant appears in my arms. "The situation here is bad, just move on. You can't do anything for the baby now; just get out," the friendly man says. I know that death has come, but I can't just walk away. I need to make peace with my own conscience and bury the infant's corpse, put it someplace safe where it won't be disturbed. I go into the basement. I am certain that if I can just find a safe place to put the corpse then I'll be able to go in peace. I'll be able to walk right past the man with the camera, who I know is hanging around outside, and I'll be free. I search in the basement until I find a protected area to leave the dead baby. Carefully laying her down, I let her go. Now I'm free. I go upstairs and leave in the company of the friendly man. Carrying a big jug of celebratory wine between us, we dance away, heading down the street toward a bright light on the horizon.

I take the message of this dream to heart. It's time to let go now, to give up the attachment to the old stuff and leave. "You don't need to be here, no one needs you," the friendly man in my dream said, and I think he's right. There's nothing left in the past. Perhaps I really am done with it. Perhaps now it's just a matter of mastering this process of release, keeping only what's necessary. The baby has been such an important part of this recapitulation, but according to this dream she's dead. I don't need to keep carrying her corpse around with me. It's almost as if I wasn't even aware that she was dead. I was just so used to carrying her that I never checked if she was alive, much like the carrying of my fears. Do I still need to carry them too?

Can I really resolve everything about the baby by burying her corpse in the foundation of the old house? Can I really resolve the tension in my body by constantly releasing it? I need to find out what else keeps me attached to that old world because something does. And then I fully intend to follow that guy with the jug of wine right out of the desolate past and into new life!

In spite of the conclusions of the dream, I suffer through all kinds of emotions and feelings as the day unfolds, ranging from complete hopelessness and not being able to see any future whatsoever, to desiring death in order to get away from the pain and mental anguish that constantly plague me. Intense self-hatred and inadequacy arise as the old scolding voice of my mother pops up repeatedly, tormenting me, filling me with shame for even trying to change.

"I'm not good for anyone. My kids would be better off with their dad. I will never be successful. I can't change. I'll always be stuck in this terrible, depressing place," says the Old Queen of Negative Thoughts, raging on. But then I fight her; I fight like a banshee. By the time night rolls around I don't even know who I am anymore. I lie in bed, as desolate and lifeless as the old house in my dream, something dead inside me. I am unable to foresee any future whatsoever. Wallowing in darkness, I hear a familiar voice.

"*Just let go,*" Jeanne says. "*It's safe. You are safe. You are in a safe place. It will all be okay; everything will be okay,*" and I feel her energy body crawling into bed next to me and I fall asleep in her loving arms.

June 20, 2003

I meet with Chuck first thing in the morning, but I'm steeped in bad feelings, royally depressed. I didn't sleep well either. I'd feel Jeanne's arms around me and wonder why she was with me, but thankful for her presence as well, restless though I was. The kitten was active all night too, mewing and running around my room, acting kind of crazy, literally climbing the walls. You'd think she'd seen a ghost! She'd shoot over my head, her tiny sharp claws grazing my hair, her bushy tail swiping across my face. The old cats didn't like it either and none of us got much sleep.

"I feel like two totally different people, and neither of them is me," I say to Chuck. "I'm a lost little girl, sorry and sad and lonely, but I'm also a deeply frustrated adult trying to make sense of everything."

And so we work on getting these two disparate selves to communicate, but neither is willing to acknowledge the other; they just want to stay in their separate worlds. Every attempt to initiate a conversation is thwarted and so there is no reconciliation. When I get up to leave, I take both the sad little girl and the frustrated woman with me. As if I'm split down the middle, I carry these two beings inside me all day. Shifting back and forth between these two discordant selves, one minute sad and lonely and the next angry and stern, *I* am nowhere to be found.

Sparked by my dream, I drink two glasses of wine in the evening in an effort to force a shift. The only shift I feel is the shift toward sleep, but that's enough!

June 21, 2003

I dream that I'm at a recycling center. It's early in the day. An elderly woman comes in with a lot of stuff to recycle. She begins sorting while I drag my stuff in and do the same. I notice how well-organized and neat the venue is and how cooperative everyone is. There's another sorting room next door, but that room, I notice, is a complete mess. I peek my head in and tell the women in the messy room that I'll come back later in the day and help them. When I return later, I see that the same elderly woman is still there. I'm aware that she's worked all day without a break. The next time I look at her she's sprawled on the floor, apparently passed out. I try to revive her, yelling to the others to call 911, that there's an emergency! The woman on the floor wakes up. She tries to get up. I tell her to stay down, that she just passed out, that she's overdone it, that she's exhausted. As I talk, I realize that I'm headed for the same thing, that for all my organizing and sorting,

I'm just going to exhaust myself in the end. I know I'm being cautioned.

I realize that the shift I so wanted has been granted! I've gained important insight into how I've been handling things. I must take better care of myself or I will indeed collapse like the woman in my dream. It's only six-thirty in the morning, but I have so much to do at the studio that I want to get an early start. This totally overrides my dream advice, but the kids are at their dad's for the next two weeks—the first weeks of summer vacation—and so I'm free. I'll spend the day setting up the gallery at the new studio. I also decide to call Chuck because I feel so much better after this dream and I want to let him know that I'm on the mend after yesterday's strange personality split.

I realize it wasn't me at all sitting in his office yesterday, but two vestiges of the old self, unreconciled entities from the past, my old child self and my old adult self, the two parts that I've been working so hard to change and release from my body and psyche. I guess they were putting up a last stand.

"So, things have shifted," Chuck says, and I tell him I bought a bottle of wine and drank two glasses.

"Now you're going to become a damned alcoholic!"

"No, I'm not, but I *was* able to sleep!"

"Well, that's good," he says, but then he tells me to remain aware that the old stuff can jerk me back again at any time, as it has my whole life.

"I'm aware of that!"

"Be patient," Chuck says. "You need to slow down, take your time, and don't exhaust yourself. Just take life slowly, one step at a time."

I feel better about everything today, as if I've stepped out of one dream, a dark one, and into another lighter one. During the week I was overwhelmed, feeling there was no end in sight and that I would never get out of the heavy morass of feelings. They snuck up and settled in upon me in such a quiet way when I had expected a flood, an outburst, or something much more striking. But my way of doing things is quiet, and so perhaps the expectation of a violent flood is out of character, except in my dreams.

I'm aware that when the Old Queen of Negative Thoughts takes over, I just don't know where I am or what world I'm in. As my mother's scolding voice of old grows louder and more insistent, the adult self immediately recedes. I become a lost little girl again, shamed and under the thumb of another's rule, and then I literally can't find myself or get my bearings. Hopelessness, all-consuming and deeply disturbing, accompanies the negative thoughts until nothing else exists, until I don't exist. The feeling is so reminiscent of when my abuser left me after he was done, left me to die if I so chose, though I never did choose death. Somehow, I always got up and walked away, tried to become myself again, to be normal, but *inside* I remained curled up and dead. Really though, negative thoughts swirled through my child's mind in an endless chorus of hopeless dread. All I was doing was numbing myself, doing away with all my feelings and emotions in order to escape the pain, the physical and mental pain. My soul curled up with death every night, but now I feel incredibly lucky to have escaped its cloying desire, though the stench of it still resides inside me.

Perhaps that's the meaning of the baby's corpse in the dream the other night, for sleep in childhood was like going into the arms of death each night, as I rolled into a fetus and begged sleep to take me into the forgetfulness of darkest oblivion. If I've conquered that demon, then perhaps the final one is the Old Queen of Negative Thoughts, the scolding voice of my unemotional mother that dominates still. Long present, that voice has grown increasingly distorted. Though its tone is that of my mother's voice, scolding her child for her imperfections, it has gone far beyond that. Embedded in my psyche all these many years, it now reigns with a far more destructive quality.

I got to the point last week where I convinced myself that I didn't matter to anyone, that no one would ever love me as much as I would love another, that it was impossible—I was not worthy of love. The Old Queen of Negative Thoughts has quite an imagination! But the real truth is that I want to believe that real love is possible, that I will one day be open to it and experience it.

June 22, 2003

In a dream, I'm at an auto supply store, needing to pick up a part for my car. I follow a salesman around, telling him exactly what I'm looking for, stressing that I know it's a difficult part to find, but I'm sure they'll have it. He commits to helping me find the part. We search throughout the store and eventually go outside too. We come to a cliff. The salesman leaps right off the cliff. I watch as he falls through the air to the ground far below and lands firmly on his feet. Leaping looks too risky to me. I choose to take the stairs instead, which are huge stone slabs jutting out of the rocky hillside. Rough and uneven, they present a treacherous descent. I'm a tiny woman compared to the enormous steps, but I take them carefully, one at a time, hopping and scrambling along. It's physically very challenging, but I'm in good shape. Midway down, I realize that taking the steps is probably as nerve-wracking as leaping off the cliff. As I near the bottom, I see that I'll have to leap over giant mud puddles, the size of small ponds, to finish my descent. A crowd has gathered to watch. I intuit that they don't think I'll make it, but I successfully leap over the puddles one at a time. As I come to the last puddle, I hear whispers of uncertainty, but as soon as I clear it a cheer goes up. "She did it! She made it!" They receive me with joy, extending their hands in congratulations, so happy I've made it. "I did it!" I say, as if I've accomplished something for all women. "I did it!"

I experience a lot of physical energy in this dream. I'm aware that the "part" I'm looking for is hard to find, but the man who offers to help knows that I know what I'm talking about. He doesn't doubt me for a second. He's aware that I will not be daunted by anything that might get in my way. The dream ends with such exuberance, with strong *self-confidence*, the "part" that's been missing for so long. He led me to this part by presenting me with the obvious next step in this recapitulation, taking the leap over the edge of the ever-present abyss. Not only do I feel happy and satisfied, but also fully in my body in this dream, as I experience keen physical strength and prowess. By the end of the dream I've accomplished a major feat, perhaps not as daring as leaping off a cliff, but each giant step I climbed was, for me, just as challenging, perhaps even more so.

I lie in bed, half-awake, thinking about my abuser. I feel infected by him, like he gave me a virus. I don't have a full-blown case of it anymore, but I still bear some of the devastating side effects and I believe they'll always be with me, that I'll always be fighting them. I feel the depths of the woundings, the deep recesses where his toxic energy is embedded. Can I flush it out? Can I purge my body and get healthy again? Did I ever feel healthy? Suddenly a voice speaks to me.

"*Don't let someone else's sickness destroy you. Don't let someone else's illness poison your whole life,*" and I know that Jeanne is with me every step of this journey.

Every time I conquer more of the legacy left by my abuser, I open up more space for my true self. This dream is pointing out just how much energy I have inside me, as of yet untapped. Even if I fear that my abuser's negative energy will never leave me, I must continue learning how to release it. It probably will pop up every now and then, as Chuck suggested the other day, and so it's incumbent upon me to remain alert as to its tactics, how it sneaks up, grabs me, and digs its torturous claws into my shoulders. I'm aware of what it is now, and how and why I've carried it; and I know my other demons as well. I am lucky to know my demons.

I'm feeling very quiet today, innerly quiet, after a week of swirling in a vortex of conflicting inside/outside forces. One vortex has been swirling clockwise and the other counterclockwise, like the swirling vortex in the pool of reincarnation that I dreamed about, creating such confusion. But I'm finally sorting it out; I'm finally gaining clarity. I understand that I'm on a spiritual path that's leading me to discover myself, my authentic real self, a separate spirit on my own unique journey. Everything that's happening is helping me to understand why I've had to deal with all the fears and sufferings of a traumatized being. I didn't even know that I was traumatized when I began this journey, and now here I am in the midst of an unbelievable process. I accept and follow the guidance offered, no matter where or who it comes from. An eager seeker now, I want only to see where it's taking me.

As I make my way through the most difficult of terrains, and as I find my balance in the whirlwinds of the vortexes that seek to confuse me still, I know that one day the terrain will even out.

The confusion will stop and I will have clarity then, just as I did when I stood on the edge of that pool and realized I was done with playing that game. My energy will be my own; my strengths—so hard fought for—will be my own as well. In the meantime, I'm happy to invite Jeanne more fully into my process, her advice always so gratefully accepted. And perhaps I'm only able to hear her so clearly because I'm taking this deepening journey into myself. As I siphon out the poisons of my abuser and make room for my own spiritual energy, and as I release the negative scolding voice of my mother, I gradually open up. I'm accessing my lost innocence at last, more able to trust all that the universe offers. I'm coming alive now!

I go to the studio. It's rainy and dark and my good mood gradually diminishes, growing sadder and more depressed as the hours go on and the vortexes swirl. I can barely keep my head clear. What am I doing here? Why didn't I just stay home and rest? What is wrong with me?

As I ponder how to handle the challenges of this new world that I find myself in, panic shows up and sidles in next to the old worries, and before I know it the Old Queen of Negative Thoughts has slipped into the dreariness of the studio. I have to get my confidence back! I yearn for the missing "part" that I found and so handily claimed in my dream. There's no reason to be so negative; that's the old way. I'm more fully aware now of the Old Queen each time she swoops in, though I haven't figured out how to resist her, how not to fall right into her arms. I must struggle with all my might to get out of her grasp!

My studio partner comes in for a little while and my inner tension gradually subsides. My demon does not like company, I see. We work quietly, the rain pounding outside, but as soon as I leave the studio and head home my demon reappears. Alone once again, the tension returns with the night and before I know it I'm swirling in its darkness, my demon right beside me, for I am nothing but a poor unworthy sinner. Mea Culpa, mea culpa, mea maxima culpa! My fault, my fault, my most grievous fault!

I am drawn down into the depths of the old world, returned to the pool of reincarnation by the Old Queen, to the swirling vortex where the demon tentacles grab my throat. I am taken down into my own darkness where the old conclusions swirl: Everything is my fault. I let it happen; I let everything happen.

I bathe, seeking release from my shame, seeking to wash away my sins, to gain release from the tentacles that hold me so tightly.

"Mea culpa! Mea culpa! Mea maxima culpa!" I scream out, pounding the water, splashing the walls and floor. I am to blame! I am to blame! Everything is my fault. And if I fail now as a mother and a provider that is my fault too! My fault! I don't know how to convince myself otherwise. That damned religion! That damned Catholic religion!

I want to be dead. I want to be dead. I want to be dead. While I live everything is my fault, the Old Queen reminds me. The pain can only leave this body if I am dead. I believe that. I believe that nothing will change until I am dead, for I am in too much pain, fully encased in it for as long as I am encased in this physical body. The only way to be rid of it is to physically die. If I am dead then there will be no pain for me or anyone else, for I carry it within me like a deadly disease, infecting all in my nearness. I want to be dead in order to end this torture, to relieve the world of my nightmarish existence. I want to be dead in order to end the worry and the certainty that everything will be my fault again and again and again, my most grievous fault forever! The Old Queen taunts me. I stand up in a rush, tearing myself away from her tentacles. Do I really believe this? Do I really believe death is the answer?

"ABSURD!" I say, my own voice growing stronger as I step out of the bathtub onto the wet floor. "And it's not my fault, damn it! It's not my fault at all! None of it is my fault. I was a victim. There's a huge difference between being a victim and being at fault. I am a victim. I am a victim. I am a victim. I am a victim. It's not my fault! As a victim I did what a victim does—it was all I knew. I didn't know any other way. All I knew was how to survive. So why do I suddenly want to be dead, when all that time I just wanted to live? Why would I welcome death now?"

"Because the pain is too intense, the agonizing pain and the knowledge of it all," the Old Queen implies. "The rush of truth and emotion is so great that the only release you can think of is death, blessed death, bringing painless nothingness."

"I don't want to be dead, you old demon," I say, drying off and getting into bed. "I don't want to be away from my children, but I want to be rid of this pain. I want the death of this torture."

I want the demons with their clutching tentacles gone, the Old Queen of Negative Thoughts and my abuser. I want to get out of the pool of reincarnation once and for all. As if they hear my thoughts, my two demons transform into two vultures. With their tremendous claws digging into my tender flesh they fly me to the precipice and drop me over the edge of the abyss. I swirl down, down, down into the vast nothingness where they attack me. Tearing into me with their enormous beaks, they peck away, bit by bit. Such deep, deep pain emerges, howling out of me. I don't think another person could understand when I say that death would be easier than this.

Killing myself would be easier; driving into a tree, a quick turn of the wheel and it would all be over. Blessed oblivion! So easy! Every day I drive the razor's edge, the instrument of death in my hands, that simple steering wheel that so easily flips to one side or the other, a vehicle to pain removal. PAIN REMOVAL! And the vultures would be gone in an instant! I know what a tortured soul is. I know what that really means, for I am a tortured soul. But who isn't? I know plenty of them; I know a lot of sad and tortured people. We survive. We end up sticking with it and surviving. I guess I'll survive too.

I hate myself. I am pathetic, a sad pathetic, tortured soul. I don't even deserve to die—just keep her around to be pathetic and sad, a lonely sad soul for the vultures to pick over. Give her just enough rope, not enough to hang herself, but enough to let her feel like she's in control. Pathetic, sad bundle of shit! I am an exhausted bundle of shit. Mea culpa, mea culpa, mea maxima culpa!

Eventually, the vultures drop me back in the present and then they leave me. Croaking out their last reminders of the old world, they flap their heavy wings and ascend into the darkness of the night. Beaten down, my shoulders pecked raw, I can't see. It's as if the very sight has been plucked from my eyes. I am returned to this world, but I am blind! I feel the heavy sadness and the desperate loneliness of that old place and the need to blame myself, to punish myself, but at the same time I know those voices don't belong in my head anymore. They're from the old times, the old voices that came before I started to learn, before I knew anything had happened, before I was aware.

It takes a long time before I'm fully back. I realize how deeply lost I've been, taken down to the bottom of the abyss, taken on my own mythological journey into my own deepest underworld, like Dionysus, by my two vulture companions. I went for a long spell—just what Chuck warned me about—yet I have successfully returned from the dark and dreary depths of that vast nothingness within me that I have feared for so long. I fell right into the gloom and despair of my darkest fear and stayed there for an hour and a half. The vultures, their shadows falling like dark hoods over my eyes, pecked away, pulling horror after horror out of this body, showing me the truth of everything.

As they tore the truths out of me, I saw and felt my bloody flesh being ripped out of me. And just like in the dream of going into the vast nothingness beneath the weight of the guru at the ashram, I am still alive! I knew at that time that I would one day have to *consciously* enter the darkness of the vast nothingness, for I knew that all that would make me whole lay there waiting. I've finally done it. And I've returned enlightened! I am even present in a new way, for the old has somehow broken through to the new! Perhaps that was the final battle I will have with those old demons.

A certain sadness still lingers, a dark shroud still hangs over my eyes. I can't see clearly yet, but I'm not so lost that I can't imagine life and love and forgiveness and beauty. I know those things exist. Perhaps I *will* experience them some day.

"*Unclench and let life flow. Unclench and be a part of the world,*" Jeanne says, her voice lighting the darkness.

"*There was no future there, ever, but that is not now,*" she reminds me. "*Now is different, a different time, with different people, and different surroundings.*"

June 23, 2003

How do I feel today? I don't know yet. The old feelings and the vultures perch nearby, but I'm not going near them. I'm waiting to see how I feel beyond them, in the other parts of my body and soul, in the healed and still healing parts. I stretch and my body is tight and holding, resistant as ever. My mind, however, works on things to accomplish today. Floating down its river of thought, it leaves the Old Queen sitting on shore, ignoring the fact that pain and sadness still dwell in every stiff muscle and limb. But I must admit to the sadness nonetheless, because that's how I feel today, sad—perhaps that the old self is gone.

Determined to make it through the day without incident, I begin counting down the hours to tomorrow's meeting with Chuck. I accept that today may be a day of sadness but busy as well, and that will help. I got through the weekend and, in spite of such anger at myself last night, I survived the fall into the abyss. I have to refuse the pull of the underworld and focus instead on what I need to accomplish. Like a mountaineer throwing out a line, climbing toward it and then throwing it out again, I must keep climbing upward now, out of the abyss, following that line into the future, into *life*.

It's now ten thirty at night and I must say I had a pretty good day. I kept very busy. A lot of things are happening at work, new jobs are coming in, and things look like they'll work out just fine. Sadness crept in, but I successfully kept it at bay, long enough to get my head together and involved in a project, and I had plenty of projects to keep me occupied. Over the next two weeks I intend to concentrate on caring for and about myself. With the kids away it's just me in the house. I should be able to handle just me.

June 24, 2003

"I set my intent to be fully present and not off in some torture zone, but I get jerked back without warning," I say, as soon as I sit down opposite Chuck. "Zap! And I'm back there in the old world, so easily lost in its grip. It isn't until afterwards that I realize where I've been and the process of getting out isn't so easy. Once there, I tend to stay until I'm done—sometimes a few minutes, sometimes a few hours—but no matter how long or short, it's torture. And when I'm trapped in that old world of shameful feelings and deep emotions, full of self-hatred, the incessant mantra that it's *my fault, my fault, my fault*, plays loudly, chanting its endless tale of blame."

Chuck nods as I tell him about the Old Queen of Negative Thoughts, the demon energy, and the vultures. I tell him how they took me into the abyss and that somehow I came out of it alive, still in one piece. Horrific though it was, the experience did not annihilate me. And so, I do not fear the abyss anymore; I realize its usefulness. I have to go there, my adventures in the darkness as enlightening as my ecstatic experiences in the light.

Chuck looks uncomfortable as the session nears an end. He tells me that the work we're doing has a level of intimacy and none of that has changed or will ever change. I think he's going to tell me that it's all over, that he's moving, or that we have to quit working together for some reason.

"I got married," he says.

I am stunned, in shock. My dream of the unfinished bridge pops immediately to mind, how I couldn't find Chuck, how I felt abandoned by him, perhaps foreshadowing this moment, because yes, the Chuck I know is gone. All of a sudden he's different. My child self immediately pops up too, declaring, "See, I told you, you can't trust anybody." And just as in that dream with the maps I feel her skitter away, down the path and into the woods where she crawls right under that bush.

I feel hurt too—my adult self—though I'm not sure why, because of unadmitted feelings perhaps? But it isn't a secret how I feel about Chuck. I've told him numerous times that I feel such deep love for him, and though the child self shyly declared it, the adult self meant it in the most grateful of ways. I certainly cannot bear intimacy or any part of intimacy, even touching or physical closeness, and I don't know if I ever will. But even so, our work has made me feel as close to another human as it's possible for me to feel. Sitting across from Chuck twice a week—in his role as my teacher and guide through this recapitulation—is as close as I can come to intimacy.

It's not that you got married, I think, but I fear something will be gone now, but maybe you're so good at what you do that it won't matter. I remain stunned as I get up and walk out, politely congratulating him. I don't even know his wife's name. As I drive away, I sense that my child self is lying under that bush back in the woods of my abuser where she knows no one can see her and no one cares about her. She intends on staying there until she dies.

She forgets that I know where she is though; she forgets that she's not alone anymore.

I understand the significance of the transference that I've been having with Chuck, how deep it is, and how appropriate it is for my healing that I confront this moment and move beyond the transference. It's important that I can love him and that I grow and leave him too, but maybe my adult self never really admitted that she did love him in deeper ways.

"*One thing at a time,*" I hear Jeanne say. "*You still have work to do. I told you this recapitulation would take three years. Don't let anything interfere with that. Stay focused on the work. Love will happen some other way. Don't worry about that now. You have other work to do.*"

I accept her guidance, and yet I must delve deeper into understanding my relationship with Chuck right now. For the most part, I feel like a child in my clinical relationship with him, like one of his own children. It's the child in me who meets with him twice a week, who sits before him so shyly seeking help, needing someone to talk to. It's the abandoned and unprotected child who reacts to the traumas, the tensions, and the memories, and it's the child who runs away and hides under the bush as soon as her expectations are not met. She doesn't wait around; she reacts quickly, seeking a kind of known protection, and that's what she did today when he told us the news.

It's night now. I sit in bed waiting for sleep to overtake me. I can't help but think that I will never have a close partner, a deep relationship. I know Jeanne told me not to think about it, but I can't help myself. I have to if I am to remove my transference from Chuck, but I just don't think I'll ever meet anyone compatible. I have met Chuck on a deeply intimate working level, but even when I thought about him in other ways, it never felt right. In fact, it's a relief to me that I don't have to think about him in that way. But why do I feel such devastation, such sadness? Do I feel abandoned by him, the way my child self so clearly does? Do I feel unsafe, unloved? He has always been there for me, my only partner during this entire recapitulation journey. I haven't shared it with another human being. Every week for the past two years I have walked straight into the little cottage on his property, sat in my chair, and done my recapitulation work, my gaze always turned inward. Although I was aware of new domestic life, that he was with someone—there were obvious signs—I just never really looked or fully took it in.

I have to search my own soul for the partner I desire, for someday in the future I would like to be at a place where I will be able to fully love another human being. I'm not there yet; I know that. I still have my own journey to take, another road to travel right now—the inner road—and that's a solitary road. My fuller journey may just be one that I take totally alone, and I have to be okay with that too. I know I must look to myself for the strengths I desire in another. I must find them inside. I must fulfill myself. I must somehow find my way out of the dark underworld, out from under that bush that I seem to have been under ever since that dream, and possibly my whole life, and learn to love myself.

It's apparent that I'm still fighting the inner demons, long after the outer demons have ceased being factors, and so I must stay focused on my recapitulation, on my search for wholeness in this life I'm in. I must attain peace within myself, demon-free. Jeanne's right, the only thing that matters is doing this inner work. At the same time, I feel like I've lost something else now, another support, as if part of Chuck is gone, just as the yoga studio is gone, my business partner gone, my marriage long gone. Things are rapidly changing. I can't stop any of it, just as I can't stop the changes going on in my inner world.

This current journey of change will continue until I've resurrected and resolved every square inch of my past, until I've finished building every square inch of that new bridge. I must continue to face whatever arises as I take this journey to completion, now more determined than ever. I must continue to enter the dark torturous zones and go to battle against my abuser's poisonous energy. I must accept the truth of my own complacency and accept that when presented with the truth at other times in my life I did not wake up, for I was helpless in the face of mind-numbing fear for so long. But now I'm not, and so I must fight that old habit of complacency whenever it reappears. I must fight the demon energies that seek attachment, and as my own energy returns I must use it to act on my own behalf. I must also tackle the issue of my self-abhorrence, for the truth is that, yes—in my numbing fear and resulting inertia—I do and did let things happen to me, repeatedly. The Old Queen got that right. Far more often than not I shrank out of sight, overtaken by dissociation and forgetfulness, choosing to follow the same habitually self-defeating patterns rather than defend myself or create a scene. Now, however, I must change. I must break the old habits and disengage from the old voices that have kept me unenlightened as to my true self and my true journey. I vow that I will work this thing to the end, by going inside, until I find *myself*, until I find out who I really am and why I'm here in this life. My entire life focus now is this inner work and this healing path to wholeness.

June 25, 2003

I dream that I'm driving a car at great speed through a jungle, careening down a narrow winding road. The trees are so close they scrape against the sides of the car. It's night, pitch black, and I can't see a thing, as if I'm barreling down a dark tunnel. I'm only aware of speed and distance being covered, the trees a blur as they flash by. *"Go ahead, keep going. You'll get there,"* Jeanne says as I wake up. *"You're on the right track, keep going."*

The speeding energy of the dream and the encouraging words spoken by Jeanne carry me through the morning, but they soon peter out and my demons swoop in. My fears return, nestling deeper into the pit of my stomach. I fear that I'm out of my league, that I won't be able to handle this recapitulation process. As I sense the vultures looking for more sustenance, I lose my own appetite. I can't eat. I am drained of energy, my dream car out of gas—I have no enthusiasm for life. I just want to sleep. *I need another shift!*

June 26, 2003

I'm sulking in a pool of self-pity, feeling that everything is hopeless and that, as usual, I'm a total screw-up, when the phone rings—a client accepting my bid on a big job—and suddenly I shift. Now I'm *much* happier!

As soon as I contemplated being childfree as the summer began, I immediately envisioned how much work I could get done. I planned to overwork, to work until all hours in order to forget, to run away and lose myself in a sense, hiding under the bush just like my child self. But another part of me said, quite sternly, that I didn't want to do it that way anymore. I'm listening to that part. I'm taking it seriously. The truth is, I'd rather take some time to care for myself, take things slowly. It can be my vacation too.

I see no end in sight to the pain. Almost every day I fight the urge to give up and crawl under that bush and wait for death. I am not, at my core, a negative or pessimistic person, but right now I see no end to the struggles. It's hard to imagine that I could ever be totally happy and contented, for as I do this recapitulation more misery is always being dredged up. I do achieve a certain plateau of calmness and even some happiness, and I can stay there for a certain amount of time, but I still feel the heavy load of the past riding over me. An ever-present burden, it weighs down my body, my emotions, and my mental state, smothering my spirit.

Perhaps writing will be the key to getting through this recapitulation, along with doing my art. They both provide an outlet for the troubles inside, a means of expression, however direct or indirect. Being an artist has enabled me to survive. As an outlet of expression and as a career choice—as a freelance artist—I have been able to both make use of my talent to make a living and to simultaneously remain safe within my shell, solidly in a world of my own choosing. When I turn to my art as a means of deep inner expression and release, I know the resulting artwork can make people uncomfortable. In visual expression I don't really have to explain anything. I can be mysterious and leave the viewer to get what they will out of the work. That is the beauty of art. I've always expected my viewers to come away from my work with their own interpretations, untainted by mine, but really I do my artwork for myself alone, and in the doing express all that troubles me and all that delights me too. Once it's done I can barely remember having created it, nor am I much interested in it then. It's the act of doing, the creative outpouring, that's so empowering and important.

I find that words are different from art. They require directness, precision, and total honesty. They require a tell-it-like-it-is raw truthfulness that I hint at in so many ways in my artwork, but never feel that I have to fully reveal, as if I'm stringing myself along with the viewer, dropping hints of deeper stuff but never really going there. I feel differently about writing. Words require that I be totally honest with my own deeper self, for a vaguely implied almost-telling will not suffice. Only gut-wrenching honesty will do the trick, and for that I must know the full truth myself.

Drifting in and out of sleep and dreams, I catch sight of my teenage self, strong and powerful now, standing high on a cliff, her wings unclipped and in full working order. On the ridge below her lie dark caves filled with lost, abandoned children. Forces of good gather, and my teenage self flies into action. Fierce fighting ensues and she succeeds in liberating those trapped children. Salvation is followed by a healing journey to a calm idyllic place.

June 27, 2003

"As much as I want this recapitulation to be over," I tell Chuck when I meet with him, "I know I'm not done."

"Your dream world is such a creative place," he says, nodding sagely. "Plan to work it out in your dreams as much as you can."

So, I plan to drive that speeding car right out of the jungle tonight, out of the tunnel of darkness and into a place of light, for I know that's where I'm heading. There is energy in my dreams—magic, lucidity, and awareness of something grand to come. I must work harder at the process. I'm the driver. It's all in my hands. Like my teenage self I now have the power to bring myself to salvation.

Most of the day I'm unhappy, feeling lonely, hurt, and bruised. I even cry a little while working at the studio. Gradually, I push aside my feelings and reaffirm my commitment to this recapitulation process, determined that my work will carry me forward: my inner work, my dream work, my artwork, and my writing. I anticipate that loneliness will continue to accompany me as I continue this journey and I can't help but wonder if I will ever be happy again.

Tonight, I dream with intent to shift.

June 28, 2003

I dream that I'm standing outside a large barn, three stories high, painted the gloomy earth tones of an old master painting. It's nighttime and I'm aware that the barn is ancient. People are standing on line to enter the barn, which is purported to be haunted. I talk to a man who says that if you go in, you don't come out alive. "I don't advise anyone go in there," he says, each word he speaks appearing like subtitles on the outside of the barn. I'm greatly disturbed by noisy activity in the barn, children running around, screaming, looking for ghosts. They shouldn't be there. "No one should have to go in there," I think, though I also know that sometimes you have to. I'm aware that it's haunted in a sense, but I also know that I have to go there myself because I've left some things inside. I try to communicate this to the man, but every word comes out as gibberish. No matter how hard I try to articulate what I'm feeling nothing comes out right, and then I realize I'm talking to the wrong person. The man in the dream is not the right man to be talking to. I'm aware that I must tell my story and that I will be able to do so one day, but not to everyone. I'm aware that in order to heal I must use words, that I must speak, write, and present my experiences in words—but only when the time, the place, and the people are right.

I wake up more fully certain that I am indeed on the right path, the one that will lead me out of the darkness: on the path of true self-discovery. I believe that dreaming with intent really does work, for I do it all the time, and I learn what I must in my dreams. How do I get out of the darkness and into the light? The answer comes from my dream. It seems to be telling me to use words, but it's also clear that I'm not done with my recapitulation yet, and just the thought of that makes me sad. Once again, I'm overcome by a strong desire to run away and hide, to let everything just go on without me, the old inertia as dominant as fear. As I teeter once again on the edge of the abyss, snared by old urges, I am grabbed at the last second. Not taken by the vultures this time, I am thankfully pulled back into the present by the scent of new life wafting on the horizon.

I spend the morning running errands, mow the lawn, and then drive to a family get-together, but I'm distant and leave as soon as I can. I cry again too. It doesn't feel too good, but it's necessary and much easier to do this time.

June 29, 2003

It's a nice morning and I decide to take a walk. As I walk, I make the firm decision to put the darkness of the underworld behind me. I commit to getting some kind of control over the recapitulation so I can function, stop the wild ride, tame it. I have the skills to do that; I'm not just on a runaway rollercoaster, though it feels like that at times. I do have control. I don't want to partake in a tempestuous process anymore, with its violently spinning energy that simply exhausts me. As much as I've enjoyed the ride—and I admit that a few weeks ago I opted to let this process lead—it's my turn to take over now. I think my speeding car dream is letting me know that unless I'm in control, things can get out of hand. To be in alignment is to be partners: the recapitulation and I must share the driving.

I think about the idea of writing, my dream suggesting that I capture my experiences in words. I like the idea of taking a naturalist's approach to my inner world, a deeply soul searching exploration of my own psyche and how it works—I'll be the Annie Dillard of the inner world. As I walk, I force myself to slow down to a stroll, to just let the walking happen naturally, as opposed to my usual style, which is pretty close to speed walking. As I walk calmly in this new manner, with no pressure to do otherwise, I still detect an old urgency to hurry away from the phantom energy that I sense is constantly in pursuit. I acknowledge that whatever I have run from only exists inside me and I refuse to run away from it any longer. I will face it without fear now. As I make this commitment, I must also find a way to quell my need to rush this process. To rush is to be out of alignment, not in the right partnership to allow this journey to naturally unfold.

Although I've reached a breaking point—a good thing in one sense—I realize it may not be good in the long run, for I am only weakened by it. In addition, it's decidedly too lonely a state to be in for long, dangerous as well, with the underworld and its thoughts of death lurking so near. However, I also understand that

I must go as deeply into my inner darkness as possible in order to find my way to wholeness, and so the breaking point must become an acceptable part of the process. The rescue of the spirit self from death, and the body self as well, is the ultimate intent of this recapitulation. I must not leave one stone unturned as I continue on this mission of self-rescue, even though it means I must constantly return to the death trap. If I am to survive repeat trips into the darkness, I must be in control or I will indeed die. I must remain aware at all times now. I must be ready to capture myself like an injured animal stuck in a bog. I must avoid sinking even more deeply into the mud, so far down that I can't get out. I must take better care of myself, so that I am fully prepared to make this most daring rescue at a moment's notice.

"Did you eat a lot of lemons as a child?" the bright young dentist asks. "Something has eaten away all the enamel on your teeth." Semen, I want to say, but how can I say that? How can I say that my mouth was full of gagging, choking, mouth-aching semen from a very young age? Decay set in early. He poured it out of his spout, forcing it between my tightly set lips, suffocating me with his putrid pus, gagging me with his sewer spew. I kept my mouth shut about it, as he so frequently admonished, while it ate away at my teeth, slipped down my throat and into my soul. It pushed me deeper into myself than anyone should ever have to go. His ugly, heavy meanness crushed me, as if I were but an ant beneath his blackened thumb. "If you tell, I'll kill you!" I saw the gun on the seat of the truck often enough to know he meant it. He showed me the bees who would sting me to death, the row of hives that would swarm at his command, a gunshot fired at the neat row of white boxes and my final torture would begin. So I kept my mouth shut and rotted from within. Where are your guns and bees now when I don't want to live your torture anymore? Where is the swarm that will numb me and leave me lying like a log rotting on the ground?

I don't like where my thoughts are headed, too close to the edge of the abyss, the darkness of the underworld just a tumble away. Shifting away, I go outside into the humid darkness of the night. I walk quickly, gaining clarity on how I've been pushing this recapitulation way too much and way too fast for the past month. I see just how destructive this can be and so I retaliate by slowing my walking pace, letting my spirit know that I am listening. Paying attention to the yearnings of my own soul helps to slow the wild swirl of thoughts in my head too, until they are no more. Letting the warm night air bathe my skin, letting the mind and its busyness wick away, I sense my own energy's desire for alignment and partnership more fully.

I contemplate how I've been on this path to my true self for a long time now, steadily looking for how to best connect with my spirit, to finally utilize it for my own good. To conserve my energy, I've lately begun questioning everything I might consider doing. "Is this something I absolutely need to do?" I ask. Then I wait. I look at the pros and cons, weigh the consequences, but ultimately I wait for my spirit to respond. If I don't absolutely need to do something, or if my spirit reacts negatively, then I don't do it.

After a forty-five minute walk through the neighborhood, I am refreshed in mind, calm in body. It turns to midnight as I step back into my house and I'm immediately aware that the shift I so desired happened quite naturally, as I slowed my pace. I feel the difference in my mood, for I am innerly quieter, and the quiet is good, allowing me to ease out of the pain a little, as if taking off tightfitting clothes. It's a new kind of quiet, deeply satisfying. In the old quiet, death was my silent companion, lying always beside me, its dark shroud heavy. Now I only want light loving arms around me, and so I hope to dream tonight of where to go next and how to get there.

June 30, 2003

I clearly realize how necessary it was for me to hit rock bottom, to imagine I wanted death more than I wanted new life, for I must face the death of the old in order to embrace new life. The Old Queen returned with her negative tone and thoughts of death became my eager companion once again. I admit it's all I've thought about for the past month. She whispered in my ears, distorting reality, until I even thought about severing all ties, convincing myself that I had nothing to keep me here, that I was not worthy of life. Today, however, I awaken clearheaded, totally aware of where I've been and that it's not at all where I want to be.

I do realize, though, that as a most valuable part of this recapitulation process I had to go into the underworld where death lurked, to grasp what my child self experienced: a deep-seated relationship with metaphorical death, in the guise of forgetfulness, offering such welcoming release. Left alone, curled up on the ground, raped, sodomized, rolling into the comfort of her own darkness, my child self blindly wrapped her arms around the stillness of death's dark warmth. She was safe there; her sadness and confusion embraced in return, the Old Queen waiting always to receive her, offering a sanctum of escape from the brutal truth. At one time, the decision to embrace that Old Queen with her thoughts of death meant that I was embracing life, a half-life to be sure, but life nonetheless. It meant burying everything that had happened in childhood inside the heavy sarcophagus I carried always inside me, the place I turned to in order to resolve the pain and conflict of being an abused child. It was the right decision once, for it meant survival, but the decision I made yesterday to sever all ties with death is right for *this* time, because of course I don't want to die; *I want to live.*

My recapitulation whirs at top speed now, such energy accompanying it. Unwilling to sit with death for long, I am fueled by powerful creativity, tamed now by the promise of new life. A sarcophagus is no place for the birth of new life! I must, however, also acknowledge an old truth: *sometimes living the truth is harder than dying even a metaphorical death.* At one time that statement kept me alive, but times have changed, and so have I. And so I must return to the darkness one last time, to displace the Old Queen inside me who has lain in her sarcophagus all these many years.

I sneak into her tomb under cover of her own darkness and overthrow her! I have the upper hand now, as I topple her from her heavy hideout, spilling her onto the floor, fully revealed as the inner predator she truly is, her dominance once so necessary but now so useless. Of course she doesn't wish to relinquish her power, though she knows her time is up. I cannot even thank her, for that would be blasphemous. In truth, we are two queens fighting over the same throne. I will not insult her, but I will not let her reseat herself either.

"I'm in charge now!" I say. "Never show your ugly face here again!"

And then I pull away from her, known for what she truly is now—*the total denial of my humanness.*

I watch as she sinks into the swallowing darkness, then I turn and lift my arms outwardly, toward the light. I am strong and steady now.

Unwaveringly committed to my journey, I gaze out over the landscape before me, confident and secure in my own abilities to navigate what lies ahead. The New Queen has taken over the throne, and the future never looked so beautiful!

Long live the Queen!

About the Author

J. E. Ketchel is an artist, writer, and certified hypnotist, as well as a gifted channel. In 2001 she began a life-changing journey into the lost self, a soul retrieval that she thoroughly documented over a three-year period and now shares in *The Recapitulation Diaries*. In addition, she regularly writes on the mystical and the ordinary in her weekly blog, *A Day in a Life*. Her writings, as well as hundreds of channeled messages from her spirit guide, are posted and archived on her website, www.riverwalkerpress.com.

Other books by J. E. Ketchel and published by Riverwalker Press are available through www.amazon.com.

The Man in the Woods
The Recapitulation Diaries: Volume 1

The Edge of the Abyss
The Recapitulation Diaries: Volume 2

The Book of Us
with Chuck Ketchel

***

Coming next:

The Recapitulation Diaries: Volume 4

www.ingramcontent.com/pod-product-compliance
Lightning Source LLC
Chambersburg PA
CBHW051938090426
42741CB00008B/1191

* 9 7 8 0 9 8 0 0 5 0 6 6 0 *